Joyce's *Finneg*
The Curse of Kabbalah

John P. Anderson

Universal Publishers
Boca Raton

Joyce's Finnegans Wake: The Curse of Kabbalah

Copyright © 2008 John P. Anderson
All rights reserved.
No part of this book may be reproduced or transmitted in any form
or by any means, electronic or mechanical, including photocopying,
recording, or by any information storage and retrieval system, without written permission from the publisher

Universal Publishers
Boca Raton, Florida • USA
2008

ISBN-10: 1-59942-963-2
ISBN-13: 978-1-59942-963-2

www.universal-publishers.com

Also by the same author and published by Universal Publishers:

Finding Joy in Joyce: A Reader's Guide to Joyce's Ulysses
The Sound and the Fury in the Garden of Eden
The Poltergeist in William Faulkner's Light in August
Faulkner's Absalom Absalom: Uncertainty in Dixie
Flaubert's Madame Bovary: The Zen Novel
Conrad's Victory: Resurrection Lost
Conrad's Lord Jim: Psychology of the Self
Conrad's Heart of Darkness: Rebirth of Tragedy
Mann's Doctor Faustus: Gestapo Music

From Joyce's *A Portrait of the Artist as a Young Man*:

> [Teacher/Priest speaking of Stephen's essay]:
> __This fellow has heresy in his essay. . . .
> Here. It's about the Creator and the soul. Rrm. .
> .rrm. . .rrm. . . Ah! *Without of possibility of ever*
> *approaching nearer.* That's heresy.

> Stephen murmured:
> --I meant *without a possibility of ever reaching.*

> It was submission and Mr. Tate, appeased . . .
> --O . . . Ah! Ever reaching. That's another story.

As Joyce said in a Trieste lecture about Ireland:

> The economic and intellectual conditions that prevail
> [in Ireland because of the British] . . . do not permit the
> development of *individuality.* [emphasis added]

In considering this book, remember what Samuel Beckett said in an article about Joyce's *Finnegans Wake*:

> Literary criticism is not book-keeping.

Table of Contents

Thanks

**to Bernie and Harriet Lipnick,
righteous people who didn't waste their lives**

Section I: Introduction

Protocol and Debts

I am not an academic and do not scour all of the literature to see if someone else has already said the same thing I am saying.

For the Finnegans Wake text, I used the 1960 printing by The Viking Press and took the text off line from trentu.ca/jjoyce/fw-3.htm. Joyce's *A Portrait of the Artist as a Young Man* is referred to as Portrait. Ulysses is referred to as such without the bold and italics.

For the sleep analysis of the FW text, I am inexorably indebted to John Bishop's *Joyce's Book of the Dark Finnegans Wake*.

Many of the factual and foreign language interpretations in my text come from McHugh's *Annotations to Finnegans Wake*. Glasheen, *Third Census of Finnegans Wake* was useful for names and places. Their citations were too numerous to indicate in this text without a mess. Where I used interpretations from Campbell and Robinson's *A Skeleton Guide to Finnegans Wake* or Tindall's *A Reader's Guide to Finnegans Wake* or *A Reader's Guide to James Joyce*, or Atherton's *The Books at the Wake*, or Hart's *Structure and Motif in Finnegans Wake*, they are cited by author. McHugh was also helpful on Joyce's sigla, as was McCarthy's **The Riddles of Finnegans Wake**. The material on Schopenhauer, particularly on homosexuality, is from Bryon Magee *The Philosophy of Schopenhauer*. Humpriad is an on line analysis of certain portions of FW.

For Kabbalah, I used Drob's *Symbols of the Kabbalah* and *Kabbalistic Metaphors*, Waite's *The Holy Kabbalah*, and Scholem's *Kabbalah*. For Rashi, I used the English translation of the Genesis volume of *Pentateuch with Rashi's Commentary* as translated by Rosenbaum and Silbermann and published in 1929 by Shapiro, Vallentine & Co. For the Jewish Legends, Ginzburg's *The Legends of the Jews*. The Pirke is from **Pirkê de Rabbi Eliezer** translated from Hebrew by M. Friedlander 2004 • Jewish Publication Society electronic version. For the Zohar, Tishby's *The Wisdom of the Zohar*. The reference to Brivic is to *The Mind Factory: Kabbalah in Finnegans Wake* in the James Joyce Quarterly.

The reference to Joyce's first drafts are taken from Hayman's *A First-Draft Version of Finnegans Wake*, University of Texas Press. I used them only when the general sense seemed to remain the same.

Vico is from *The New Science of Giambattista Vico* Unabridged Translation of the Third Edition by Bergin and Fisch, Cornell University Press. Vico was well worn after Ulysses.

For the life of Jonathan Swift, I used Hardy's *The Conjured Spirit*. For Mohammed's, Holland's *Mohammed*. For St. Patrick, his autobiography, Confessions and Oliver St. John Gogarty's *I Follow St. Patrick*. For Joyce's aesthetics, Aubert's *The Aesthetics of James Joyce*. For aesthetics in general, Bosanquet's *History of Aesthetics*. Danielou is from his *The Myths and Gods of India*. For the primal horde, Paul's *Moses and Civilization*.

Some of the interpretation of the Garden of Eden myth appeared in my earlier book *The Sound and the Fury in the Garden of Eden* with a Faulkner twist. For the text of the myth, I started with van Wolde's in *A Semiotic Analysis of Genesis 2-3*. I also used many other versions of the text of the myth and shifted between them without regard to consistency.

EB means the Encyclopedia Britannica current edition unless other noted. Wikipedia is the on-line encyclopedia.

Capitalization and gender of god are intended to be random. Materials within [square brackets], including those inside of quoted material, are my own editorial comments. Material taken from the novel is reproduced in **bold**. The Hebrew Scriptures are the genuine articles; the Old Testament is different in terms of the books included in the official canon. The Roman Catholic Church is often abbreviated RCC.

My intent is to explore this novel as an art object, to examine how it works as art. I call it a novel, but it fits in no known category other than wisdom literature.

My first task is to try to explain the conceptual material that I found in FW. In an effort to show the curse of Kabbalah at ground zero of this most mysterious and difficult novel, this book decodes on a word by word basis all of the first and second chapters and part of the last chapter. I hope my decoding will help you share some of the riches of Joyce's last blessing on all mankind, a blessing 17 years in the making.

You will find that I don't understand everything in FW. Perhaps you will fill in.

Is the Book Worth a Thousand Candles?

You have to work to read Finnegans Wake. It takes a long time and plenty of dedication. If you wonder whether the value of deciphering your version of the novel will be worth the work, that will very much depend on you.

Only a few readers, a select few, find Finnegans Wake worth the work. In general, I believe that the more of an independent individual you are, the greater is the chance you will cherish this work. In most cases you will find it as unique in literature as you are in the human kingdom. And the great wonder is that this is no accident but the product of deep order only Joyce could muster.

Some testimony: Finnegans Wake inspired a symphony named "riverrun" [the first word of the novel] by Stephen Alberts. John Cage wrote several musical creations based on Joyce's work. Nobel-winner Murray Gell-Mann's reading experience confirmed his decision to name a fundamental subatomic particle after the word "quark" in Finnegans Wake.

Our renown mythographer Joseph Campbell, rest in peace, who took several years off to devote to this book, described reading Finnegans Wake as a Zen experience; it gave him a hallucinatory conceptual reorientation, and:

> But when you are reading Joyce, what you get is radiance. You become harmonized, and that is what it's about. It is not teaching you a lesson. It is feeding you, giving you spiritual balance and spiritual harmony.

So for a dose of spiritual balance and harmony from Joyce's last work, let's give it a try. Let us join the privileged few.

Difficulties of Finnegans Wake

Finnegans Wake is James Joyce's last and most sophisticated work of art. To the consternation of many would-be readers, Joyce deliberately made it difficult. There is no E-ZPass access to this literary paradise.

Much of what makes this novel difficult makes it good. In the final analysis it seems that the difficulties came as part of Joyce's ultimate objective to expand the possibilities of literature as art, to make it do more than it ever had before. As part of this process he bequeathed to us magical new combinations of message and medium, content and form, and a new language medium that is pregNNNant [for example] with meaning.

This new language is designed to communicate the nature of the human mental experience during sleep in this "Book of the Night." This is novel and daunting subject matter which adds to the difficulty of understanding and the level of achievement. For the Book of the Night, only obscured and distorted language would do.

These distortions are the primary language of the novel. This "distorted" language is playful, juvenile, sex-oriented. Among other methods, these distortions use the techniques of dreams such as unification of several subjects and displacement or separation of a single subject.

It is a mistake to try to read this Book of the Night in terms of just an interpretation into linear, daytime logic language. You need to find that daytime meaning as an intermediate step to determine what direction the distortion takes and what that distortion direction suggests. This is where the ultimate meaning of the novel is.

Joyce comments on the difficulty of his text at several points in Finnegans Wake, including the following address to the reader:

> You is feeling like you was lost in the bush, boy? . . . you most shouts out: Bethicket me for a stump of a beech if I have the poultriest notion what the farest he all means. (112.3-6)

"Lost in the bush" is Joyce's shorthand for the human experience in this world ruled by the lord of the abyss as understood in Kabbalah. Lost in Finnegans Wake and lost in the bush of the abyss—that is an example of Joyce order—lost in reading Finnegans Wake and lost in human experience in terms of the ultimate meaning of life. The identity of this lord and the location of the bush referred to may surprise you. To give you an example of reading Joyce's distortion: Paltry [means trivial and derived from words meaning trash] is distorted to poultry and triest in **poultriest** to suggest that only a chicken won't try to find out and will be sorry he or she didn't.

Finally, this novel is also difficult because its foundation is in Kabbalah and Kabbalah features an unusual view of the relationship of humans to the gods, the subject of theosophy. Kabbalah is a Jewish gnostic and mystical tradition that presents a strange but compelling view of the human experience. So compelling that even someone like Madonna has been reported seeking meaning through Kabbalah. Kabbalah also worked for Joyce to create meaning. It worked for both of them, different though they may be.

Madonna's T shirt said, "Kabbalists do it better." Joyce's T shirt would have read, "Kabbalists do it independently." And therein lies the tail—I mean the tale.

Achievements of Finnegans Wake

Joyce's final work achieves a revolutionary expansion in the possibilities of art. In both content and form.

FW is a new kind of presentation, not a novel, not a myth, not a legend. It is something of all of these in its presentation of a truth about the human condition in the form of a story. The story is blurred and blurred for a purpose. Its distorted language takes us into the Night, where we find primitive, mythical soul space, Joyce's take on the cumulative history of the human experience. It is a form of wisdom literature. Let us call it a novel for convenience.

With its focus on independence and dependence, FW is something like Kafka's **The Metamorphosis** [1916]. In that short story a change—a metamorphosis—to partial independence by a young man is visualized based on his dependent parent's perspective as a large bug living in their apartment. The son had a picture of a young woman with a fur boa, a furry Eve. If you read the young man as Adam or mankind, and the parents as the gods in our limited and finite experience, you will be on the trail. FW also features independence, a remarkable bug and many versions of furry Eve.

Content enjoys a remarkable synergy generated by a merger of human spirituality, theosophy and aesthetics—that is in life, in relation to the celestial powers that be and in art. The result of the synergy is expansion of human possibilities in these three areas.

The common synergy is the condition of being complete in oneself and independent of external factors. Joyce found this condition in the lives of independent individuals, in theosophy in the ultimate god of Kabbalah and in art based in objectivity [he called arrest] and organic unity. The enemies of this complete and independent condition are human efforts to achieve external approval, the curse issuing lord of the abyss registered in Genesis, and their analogs "non-arrested" art based in desire or loathing.

Kabbalah's ultimate god contains unlimited possibilities and as viewed by Joyce sponsors independent human individuality as the path to god. Independent human individuality produces more life possibilities than approval-seeking and dependent repetition. Art produced in arrest, as opposed to desire or loathing based art, can access more possibilities in terms of form and content.

More possibilities in art gave birth in FW to a revolutionary new subject matter and language, a language invented by Joyce just for this book to complement the new subject matter, the Book of the Night. This language approaches being complete in itself, complete in itself without regard to traditional English. More possibilities also forged new connections between form and content, even new types of connection.

Additional human possibilities are Joyce's ultimate objective. Indeed, it would not be too much to say that additional human possibilities are Joyce's god, or put another way that additional human possibilities are the path to or the manifestation of the real god. Composed with new possibilities in art, Joyce's book itself is an example of what it sponsors. It is a demonstration of the amazing things independent individual humans can do when the circumstances are right. But they have to be awake, and in FW sleep is the condition of less possibilities.

As with anything this "elevated" and difficult, Joyce certainly didn't spend 17 years of his post-Ulysses life writing this book for the approval of others, but for himself. It is a product of his fiercely defended independence. If you don't like it, that's ok. If you do, you can create your own version of the possibilities inherent in this text, your own individual text.

From now on Finnegans Wake is abbreviated sometimes as "FW."

Kabbalah

First, what in god's name is Kabbalah? Or Cabala or Cabbalah or Kabala? And what is Madonna doing studying Kabbalah? Should you be? A connoisseur of ideas himself, Joyce bought into Kabbalah for use in FW because it supports his emphasis on independence as the ultimate human value.

Kabbalah [sometimes abbreviated as "K"] is first of all a theosophy, that is an attempt at knowledge of ultimate matters, knowledge of the celestial powers that be in relation to mankind and what that means for mankind's future.

At the present time K is gaining traction among a broad range of spiritual seekers and showing up in the "New Age" sections of bookstores. Its popularity is based on its intuitively satisfying explanation of the unsatisfactory human experience in this world and because in this age the mystical approach means "me."

And don't lose interest just because this is new age and about "god." Everyone believes in a god as a first cause. The only question is what god or the gods are like. A benevolent shepherd or energy without purpose or an impersonal will force igniting the big bang for fun? And what does that mean for me? This has always been and remains the ultimate issue, divining the future for the good and bad produced by god. For eons mankind has sacrificed to gods in an effort to secure a better future. Living in a world apparently filled with accident and coincidences, mankind has yearned for knowledge of or better yet control of the future. In the Hebrew Scriptures, one premium version of this control was filling the future with manifold offspring just like daddy, chips off the old block.

K has been nurtured over centuries in Jewish mystical circles. Mystical means that individuals independently intuit this truth themselves and do not receive it in dependent instruction at the feet of others. It is attained by independent personal intuition often during isolated meditation. While it is a "received" tradition, it is flexible enough to allow for subjectivity and individual differences. Doctrine has shifted significantly over time. There has been no K Inquisition. And it has been free of the responsibility of consistency. True to this tradition, Joyce uses his own customized version of K. He cherry picked.

Kabbalah was known to followers as the Hidden Church of Israel, the inward spiritual and mystic church. It claimed to hold access to the "light of a secret traditional knowledge preserved among the chosen people" [Waite]. It was derived from the Hebrew Scriptures, but was the secret oral doctrine behind the written law.   Mystics are notorious for claiming to see into the heart of the matter but not being able to communicate the cardiology to the rest of us. The Kabbalists are no different; they have made do with metaphors instead of photographs.

Because Joyce designed Finnegans Wake as the psychospiritual history of mankind, he gave an important part to Kabbalah. New Age Kabbalah is actually quite old. As stated in the 11th Encyclopedia Britannica [Joyce's edition]:

> [Kabbalah] is the technical name for the system of Jewish theosophy which played an important part in the Christian Church in the middle ages. The term primarily denotes 'reception' and then 'doctrines received by tradition.' * * * It is only since the 11th or 13th century that K has become the exclusive appellation for the renowned system of theosophy which claims to have been transmit-

ted uninterruptedly by the mouths of the patriarchs and prophets ever since the creation of the first man.

With venerable source claims reaching back to first man, Joyce was attracted to K doctrine as foundation stone for his history of mankind and his focus on first man in the Garden of Eden. Kabbalah reads the human experience as the product of a curse deliberately imposed on mankind by god. The curse is heavy, a curse of death and limits designed to restrict the potential of mankind. This is what I mean by the curse of Kabbalah.

Major Points

With that as K background, let me give you a rough summary of major points I would like to make about some of the conceptual structures of FW:

- The foundation of FW is the curse of Kabbalah, namely the deliberate restriction on the possibility potential of humans by the secondary and limited god of this world [TZTZ god]. This curse serves to create fear and dependency.

- This curse on human potential restricts individuality and produces uniformly limited and secondary persons described in FW as "here comes everybody." Lacking individuality, they are incomplete. This restricted condition is experienced most forcefully in sleep during which voluntary free will and consciousness are off line. Joyce uses the human night experience in order to capture the essence of this limited condition, a condition that plagues most of mankind during daytime as well as night. Joyce called FW the "Book of the Night."

- Like dreams, FW has its own language delivering a manifest content derived from conscious experience and a latent or hidden content derived from the unconscious. The manifest content consists of Joyce selections from the entire collective human conscious experience. The latent content hidden in the repressed unconscious of the race is the curse, the knowledge that the god of this world is death. As latent content distorts the dream, the curse operates as a black hole to distort the presentation in FW.

18

- The curse is hidden, repressed and latent, because it causes fear, particularly the fear of death. We try to forget about our inevitable death. We joke about it but don't make friends with it. If we had to consciously recognize that TZTZ god wants us to die, then the fear of death would be increased exponentially, perhaps to an unmanageable anxiety.

- The Garden of Eden myth as interpreted by RCC tries to convince us that humans are responsible for their own mortality and death is "natural." As interpreted by Joyce, the Garden of Eden, Babel and other Genesis dream-like myths featured in FW teach us that TZTZ god wants humans to be small and especially wants our early death. That god reduced maximum human longevity from a thousand to 120 years. Coming first in Hebrew Scriptures, Joyce treats these myths as illustrative of the most elemental aspects of the man-god relationship.

- Despite the curse, every person every new day can "wake" up to additional human possibilities. With sufficient courage to overcome the fear of death, each can wake up at their own wake. These continuing possibilities point to the primary and unlimited god in Kabbalah [Ein Sof or ES]. To this god, independent and courageous human individuality is the ticket.

So with these major points at least in mind if not in the convinced zone of your consideration, let us start.

Section II: Conceptual Material

Foundation of Finnegans Wake

In my reading, the foundation of FW is the curse of mankind by god as understood in the Kabbalah tradition. Joyce found this curse at the heart of the Garden of Eden and Babel myths.

In order to read FW you need to understand the curse of Kabbalah and the implications of Kabbalah doctrine because Joyce starts his novel with the implications of that curse already in place. As usual, Joyce gives no Kabbalah primer.

In Kabbalah doctrine the curse is described as an excremental function of the ultimate god known as "Ein Sof" or "Ain sof," pronounced something like **Enne** Sof. The independent and unified god Ein Sof ["ES"] contracted to produce our world but remained concealed—ES pulled what Joyce calls a "French leave," which means an unnoticed departure. Our world came with a secondary, dependent god interested in separation. This god issues blessings and curses, good and evil. For reasons set forth below, I call this god TZTZ god. As we shall see, it is Joyce's position that the path to the secondary TZTZ god is dependence and fear [humility] whereas the path to the primary god ES is independence.

For an example of the curse in its foundation role, consider the structure of the interconnected end and beginning of this circular novel. This mimics dream structure in which separate parts are always connected by the same latent content.

The novel ends mid-sentence and connects right back to the beginning which starts in mid-sentence. The ending—**A way a lone a last a loved a long the**—features many "a's" that are loose or standing alone while the opening features the many bent over "r's" loaded in the first word **riverrun**. The "a" serves in English to deny individuality, to depict a general type not a specific example—as in "a person." The bent over and humpbacked "r" reflects the effect of the curse. Separated by the ending and beginning, the loose and individuality denying "a's" and humpbacked "r's" combine in *Arar*, the Hebrew word for curse. For Joyce, the biggest curse is the loss of individuality.

That is an example of Joyce's combination of method and message. If you don't get a charge out of that, stop reading. This book is not for you.

As we shall see, this curse foundation supports the materials that are repeated in revised form throughout the novel—for example materials about the Wake for Finnegan, the Fall of just about everyone including the Fall of Napoleon at Waterloo, opposition of brothers Shem the independent Penman and Shaun the dependent postman [who delivers the views of others], incest dynamics in the Earwicker family, the humpbacked Norwegian Captain, the shooting of a Russian general, the first riddle of the universe and the culminating debate about the nature of colors.

Curse as Latent Content of a Dream

In Freudian terms, the curse of Kabbalah is the latent or hidden content of the dream-like structure that is FW, the meaning that has been repressed in the collective unconscious of the human race because it creates fear. Because it is the latent or hidden content, the curse is hidden in FW behind the detail that is the surface.

In Freudian analysis, the latent content is protected by a censor that is vigilant during the day but somewhat relaxed at night. The censor allows the latent content to appear in disguised fashion, so it will not cause too much fear.

In Jungian and Vician [more on this later] terms, the Garden and other stories in Genesis are an important part of the collective conscious of the human race. The curse of Kabbalah is also their latent content. The Jewish Legends help us to find the more censored parts of the latent content, such as the serpent buggering Adam. This content is hidden because it is too frightening, that god "has it in" for mankind and wants a limited, dependent and short-lived humanity.

These transhistorical factors in psychospiritual human life are the basis for the curse of commonality and limited possibilities presented by the ruling entity of FW—which is HCE, Here Comes Everybody. Sleep and the dream, lacking voluntary free will and new possibilities of action, are the cable service for the restrictions of the curse.

FW, the Garden of Eden and Curse of Kabbalah

FW is, among many other things, a riff on the Garden of Eden myth, a myth about the relationship of god and first mankind, about the "Fall."

A powerful piece of writing, the Eden myth still speaks to believers and non-believers alike after thousands of years. It speaks about the relationship of the powers that be and humankind and the effect of the perceived relationship on the human spirit. Like FW, the myth speaks through a particularly potent kind of art. Harold Bloom our literary arbiter described the author as the direct ancestor of Kafka and "uncanny, tricky, sublime, ironic, a visionary of incommensurate . . ."

K helped Joyce find a radically new meaning for Eden's message to mankind, a meaning that makes the most of the text of the myth itself, particularly the deliberate denial by god of human access to the Tree of Life.

With K help, Joyce reads the myth as a clear expression of the curse of mankind by god in order to restrict human possibilities. God clearly wanted humans to be mortal. Later, just before Noah's adventure, TZTZ god limits the maximum human lifetime to 120 years. TZTZ god is impatient in the desire for death. TZTZ god can't wait.

Institutional Christian religion used the Eden myth to point the finger of blame at a seducible Eve. She was the source of "Original Sin," and in the "Fall" she and Adam shrunk spiritually to something less than they could be. Thanks to St. Augustine, Catholicism taught millions of dependent faithful that Eve's Original Sin and reduction in the "Fall" were inevitably passed on to every subsequent generation through sexual intercourse, apparently on the corruption gene. This made sex the connection to the past, the bad past.

The basic point of the traditional interpretation, the manifest content, is that mankind is to blame for its own troubles in life and to blame because of disobedience, breaking god's rule about eating from the Tree of Knowledge. For this disobedience mankind was hit with a big timeout, time out of paradise. This punishment made mankind's life less than it could have been. Compared to gigantic pre-fall mankind, fallen mankind out of the garden was like a bug.

This was the "Fall," the fall to lesser possibilities and a lesser life in a time-ruled world full of trouble and death that Joyce calls the "weedworld." In the traditional interpretation mankind is to blame for its own problems and can come to god only through a sense of sin and dependency. Independence and striving for more in life only feed the primal sin of pride.

In a radical reinterpretation, Joyce reverses the traditional judgment. Rather than mankind, God is to blame for the trouble in the world and inevitable human death. Inspired by Kabbalah doctrine, Joyce uses the same Eden myth as evidence to point the finger of blame at god. God is to blame for mankind's problems. This is the first "Fall," the fall of god [Atherton], not of man.

As Joyce reads it, the Eden myth registers a curse in the god/man relationship, a curse of mankind initiated by god for god's own purposes and not because of disobedience. The purpose of the curse is to produce a fearful and dependent mankind limited in potential, a fallen mankind. God generated dependency with the blessings of paradise and fear with the sufferings of curses. God wanted the Fall of mankind; god wanted small humans, dependent and fearful humans. God wanted fewer human possibilities. God wanted humans to die, and soon.

And Joyce's reading, as we are to see, makes much more sense of the actual words of the myth than the traditional interpretation. This reading turns on identifying the god in the Garden according to K.

TZTZ Creation

Joyce's reading of the Eden myth is inspired by the creation doctrines of Kabbalah. These creation doctrines are known as the *Tzimtzum* theory of creation ["TZTZ"].

In the TZTZ theory the original creation of our universe occurred within a formless ur-unity in which god was all and all potential was merged in god. Nothing could or did exist separately. The ur-unity god merged everything everywhere at all times. The essential characteristics of this god are unlimitedness and unity.

This god [ES that literally means "nothing without end"] made a hole or void in the ur-unity especially for this creation. In this hole cleared out of the boundless unity, ES contracted and deposited its own opposite, namely a bounded experience, a limited and separate experience, a universe separate from ES. That experience is our universe. In other words, ES god defecated.

In this separated creation everything is finite, so it **inevitably** features death and limitation. As we shall see, this creation also **inevitably** came with its own god, a limited, secondary and finite kind of god who has human death for breakfast. This limited god is

24

TZTZ god, the Jehovah of the Hebrew Scriptures, the bearer of curses as well as blessings. Meanwhile ES—the infinite, unified and now purified of the finite—remained concealed behind its creation and unknowable and unreachable.

This **inevitable** presence of death and limitation is the curse of Kabbalah. Since it brought death and limitation, Joyce treats the TZTZ creation itself as the first fall, the original fall of ES god brought on by ES god's apparent desire to manifest the limited and finite part of his unity [Atherton]. For Joyce, this TZTZ creation is a fall because of all the possible creations god could certainly have done better than this one. And to manifest in a creation that is totally limited and finite was an indecent exposure of ES, the ultimate celestial pornography.

Joyce built FW on the principle that the actions of humans in general throughout the ages follow a hardcore version of this original desire of ES god to be manifest in finite and limited terms. In the finite and limited TZTZ creation humans live finite and limited lives—lives born of survival instincts and characterized by limitation and separation. The purest expression of the TZTZ spirit is competitive activity for survival resources. This competition has ripped apart the human unity starting with Cain and Abel. Per Joyce, humans could certainly have done better than they have—just as god could certainly have done a better job of creating than it did.

TZTZ God and ES God and FW

The product of a manifestation by ES, this TZTZ creation came with its own god, a secondary and inferior TZTZ god. That secondary god and not ES is the co-star with Eve in Genesis. As we are to see in a detailed analysis, the Garden of Eden screenplay makes more sense if TZTZ god is the god on the garden set.

This TZTZ god, this forger of a god, falsely claims to be the creator god whereas, as the Kabbalah close reading of the initial lines of Genesis shows, all he really does is separate and discriminate what is already here. Unlike the independent, unity-based and concealed ES, the TZTZ god reflected in Genesis is manifest not concealed, operates in this world to separate and discriminate rather than unify and relates to humans and is interdependent with them.

The primary mode of expression by TZTZ god is to create opposites, a primary source of friction. The Tree of Knowledge of Good and Bad will come to mind in this connection. TZTZ god is all too human.

By contrast, ES is simple, of one piece, complete in itself, reconciled even in opposites, unified without multiplication, without sex or form, unknowable and symbolized by the letter Aleph. ES is also symbolized as the Vast Countenance with hair like fine wool, eyes always open, and a baldhead. TZTZ god gets the Lesser Countenance referred to as "I am"; this secondary god comes with black locks and eye lids [eyes closed sometimes]. TZTZ god blinks and may even sleep.

Unlike ES, this TZTZ god is not independent; it depends on humans, on others. It is not complete in itself. Humans make this god with human behavior. This all too human god gets mad, issues curses and urges the Israelites to commit genocide against those tribes standing in their way of their territorial ambitions.

With the TZTZ god, what is above must be below and what is below must be above. This is the celestial closed feedback loop. A close parallel, and a striking parallel, is the concept made famous by the philosopher Immanuel Kant—that what we experience in this phenomenal world is subject-dependent. The experience received is conditioned by the limitation of the humans experiencing it—through human developed concepts of time, space and causality that do not necessarily exist independently. The TZTZ god is also subject-dependent in the same sense.

The TZTZ god isn't all a god can be so it doesn't want humans to be all they can be. Misery loves company. TZTZ god delivers the curse of Kabbalah; it serves as postman for the curses—delivering curses that limit and make humanity suffer. With humankind, TZTZ god wants separation, limits and dependency. TZTZ god wants little bent over humans, humans that look like the letter "r" not upright like the letter "l". The fire bringing Prometheus is exactly the kind of hero TZTZ god doesn't want. TZTZ god would personally eat his liver for breakfast. TZTZ god has made this world of violence and injustice ending irrevocably in death of "living" creatures.

Theoretically at least, TZTZ god is not permanently stuck in its curse-bearing mode. Interdependent with humans, the TZTZ god can be brought by way of sanctified human behavior to a higher level. Humans can make TZTZ god better by living better lives. But TZTZ god cannot get better on its own. When humans through their own activities create a TZTZ god that is like ES, then there will be celestial reunion. This process is known in K as Tikkun. When Tikkun is achieved, TZTZ god along with our universe will merge back into ES. Disappear into the merged unity.

Tikkun Olam is the Jewish concept of "mending the world," a concept that threads together tailor references in FW—such as the recurring story of the humpbacked Norwegian Sea captain, the tailor and the tailor's daughter.

All we know about ES is that it represents the infinite and unlimited and despite this nature it started the finite and limited TZTZ creation. ES represents all possibilities merged in unity and remains independent and concealed. Tikkun is the way back to all that.

Independent Individuality

For Joyce, the way back to a better life, a life closer to the real ES god, is to overcome the fear of death and expand human possibilities through unfettered independence and individuality. Independent individuality alone can access the new and unlimited possibilities in life. This is the only possible resurrection from the fall into dependence and fear in this limited world.

Unlike TZTZ god, ES doesn't need humans so ES-like humans would not need god. I believe this is where Joyce came out. To be like ES is rely on yourself, be all that you can be within respect for the individuality of others and by extension the total pool of human possibilities. In this process you will find the path to ES, the real god. Acting on your own you find god.

As Joyce reads the Eden myth, this is what Eve tried to do, to come closer to the real god ES by living the individual life of greater possibilities. Like Joyce did. Joyce would not sacrifice what he considered the important aspects of his individual being to religion, culture, book sales or even [as Ulysses records] the dying wishes of his mother for him to kneel and pray to her god. His independence was expensive; his mother died with a heavy heart and he and his wife Nora paid with many years of abject poverty for his refusal to write for sales.

The difficulty of this independent approach of unfettered individuality is no surprise. It goes against the fundamental grain of the limited and finite nature of the TZTZ creation. That grain pulls humans in the direction of dependency, to limited and finite possibilities. That is the easy life—beer and the telly and follow the crowd. The crowd at Earwicker's pub in FW will be a familiar group, the dumb-down target of advertisers. Independent individuality is the difficult reach back past all that toward the infinite and unified ES, the spirit of unity and greater possibilities, a very decent exposure.

27

For Joyce independent individuality versus dependent submission was always the issue. The Dubliners stories chronicle dependency-producing corruption in Dublin lives. Portrait is a testament to developments in Joyce's youthful personal struggle to live freely [matched by changes in literary style]. The opponents of individuality were featured in the first chapter of Ulysses, the usurper chapter. Bloom teaches Stephen the Buddha-message that compassion expands his freedom.

In the Kabbalah tradition, Joyce happily found an organized theosophy whose highest god was distinguished by independence and unlimited possibilities, Joyce's primary values. Too independent to be a "true believer" in any system, Joyce was not a true believer in K. But he used it just like certain other systems that appealed to him for "all it was worth" and then some. K gave him the tools, the conceptual grid and metaphor set, to express individuality and independence as the true religion.

Independent individuality requires some basic tools—consciousness, voluntary control and free will. Note that these are absent in dreams, where the Here Comes Everybody TZTZ troll waits to pull us under into the lair of dependent fear. To make us dead to the world when we are awake.

Tikkun—Why Finnegan Doesn't Wake Up

For Joyce, Tikkun can be achieved only by the expansion of human possibilities through individual realization based on independence within respect for the human unity. Only with this approach can humans maximize their own possibilities and thus the race as a whole approach the infinite possibilities of ES. This is the Joyce spin on Tikkun—individuality increasing human possibilities. He builds this spin on the nature of ES to contain all possibilities. Classic K puts more emphasis on ES's unity and thus on charity and sympathy.

The Joyce way of individuality requires courage, making decisions to satisfy only yourself and struggling for what you think is important. TZTZ god can easily corrupt this approach with the snares of narcissism and selfishness. The individual "I" can easily become "me me me." I think the border between individuality and selfishness is drawn at the individuality of others. If you are restricting the individuality of others in what you think is the pursuit of your own individuality, then selfishness has corrupted your own individuality. Pursuing your aims at the expense of others is the zero-sum survival game in weedworld.

In summary then with the Joyce twist, ES is the unifier and represents more possibilities while TZTZ god is the separator that restricts possibilities. These binary oppositions are the power poles in the novel; they carry the current. FW presents the view that female humans are more like the unifier and male humans more like the separator. Males instinctively separate with violence and females instinctively put the pieces back together to build new possibilities. The main female character in FW overcomes the fear of TZTZ god and death at the end of the novel.

While Tikkun may sound good, FW registers Joyce's view that the TZTZ god must be getting worse, going the other way, and may even want it that way. In Joyce's presentation, it seems like the TZTZ god doesn't want to merge into ES. Like its interdependent humans, it doesn't want to go out of existence. It wants to continue to manifest and survive separately. It wants to survive just like humans. So TZTZ god denies increased human possibilities by denying individuality. That way it won't have to merge into ES. Humans must die in limitation so TZTZ god can survive to deliver more curses.

This aspect of TZTZ god is the answer to the question raised by the title of the novel—why at Finnegans Wake the mourners don't want Finnegan to wake up and Finnegan doesn't wake up. As an avatar of all mankind, Finnegan tries to wake up to the smell of spirits and new possibilities but the mourners convince him otherwise. Speaking more of their own values than of Finnegan's, these mourners, these representatives of TZTZ-based institutional religions, think the changes that have occurred since his death would only disorient him and waste his energy. New possibilities are not worth the effort. They convince him to stay dead in the coffin of restricted possibilities, receive ablutions to that effect and continue to rest while the limited life game is presided over by the lord of the abyss.

No one at the funeral is surprised that Finnegan wakes up, if only momentarily, because FW is a dream and Finnegan wakes up within the dream.

Resurrection—Tikkun in Christian Terms—Trinity

Expressed in Christian terms, Joyce's approach to resurrection is individual realization. For Joyce [and earlier expressed by Oscar Wilde] Jesus was the ultimate individual. He was the radically independent man preaching the unity of humanity without compromise to the claims of his family or Jewish authority figures and most importantly without fear of death. In this role, Jesus would be the son of ES, not of TZTZ god. And this is the kind of radical idea that would appeal to Joyce.

The interpretation of Jesus as the son of ES has one undeniable advantage. It brings some critical scripture into a clearer focus. For example, it gives real meaning to those otherwise troubling words of Jesus on the cross—Father why have you forsaken me? The son god sounds sad and frustrated, the son god without woman like the junior male in the primal horde. If the Father god is death, then the consubstantial son god must die. Apparently Jesus didn't totally appreciate his role. The flip side of Jesus as interpreted by institutional religion is that you need the Savior for resurrection. He was crucified so you have a chance. You need Him and you may or may not make it. In any event, you are dependent on Him, he the ultimate independent individual. This makes a mockery of Jesus' example as an individual.

Critical to an understanding of FW is the traditional Roman Catholic concept of the Trinity: that the Holy Spirit issues only when the relationship between the Father god and the Son god is proper. If that father-son relationship is one of charity, then the Holy Spirit issues as love in this world. The trinity is not idle idol speculation but an attempt to understand the relation of the gods to human kind.

As Joyce draws the script, curses rather than love have issued in this world, and thus charity must be lacking in that father-son relationship. In Joyce's view, the relationship of father and son has been continuously warped by the nature of TZTZ creation and reinforced by the curse, and thus the Holy Spirit has not, does not and cannot issue in this world experience. Put another way, there is nothing for the HSS to do since its nature is love and unity, supposedly the love of god in the world after the son has gone.

In K, a similar Trinity is deemed to have been created by TZTZ god as part of its efforts at separation. This Trinity is said to be broken. As a result the Shekhinah [pronounced something like sha **keeen** ah], a force very much like the Holy Ghost, has not been with humanity. Her light is missing. In K the Shekhinah is considered female.

In addition, and this is very important in Book I of FW, the trinity as conceived by the RCC is of three different persons but of the same substance—a condition known as hypostasis. This means that the Holy Spirit cannot be different in substance from the Father god, that the Holy Spirit cannot be an individual and must be a dependent member of the group. It must be a separate person with common substance—Here Comes Everybody in the Trinity. If the Father god is death and limitation, the Holy Spirit cannot be love and unlimited possibilities. The best she can do under these circumstances is to try to put the pieces back together.

As we are to see, in Joyce's view the only role played by the Holy Spirit under these circumstances is the sexual impulse, putting the pieces together through procreation, combining the love-unity interest of the female with the possession interest of the male. Put another way, the sexual interest is the only outlet for love that is consistent with desire and frustration—the current status of the father and son god relationship. In K, this would be expressed as sex is the only human experience that is consistent with ES as well as TZTZ god, the only aspect of ES that survived in TZTZ god. Putting the same point in a darker way, the sexual interest is the view of love through death. Sex is a temporary connection made necessary by death.

This common substance limitation also means that the Holy Spirit cannot influence the future independent of the father god. That, in turn, means that contrary to some predictions there will be no third phase of the independent rule of the Holy Spirit on earth after the rule of the Son in the second. Guess who came first.

In the interdependent man-god-man relationship in K, lack of individuality in the gods means you know what in humans. Here Comes Everybody in humankind.

Basic Formula for FW—The Power of L

In Joyce's view, the counterpart of TZTZ dependency is the report card life, living for the approval of others and denying your own individuality. This is generalized in FW as hesitancy and linked to forgery, the falsified human condition leading to the wrong god, the TZTZ god who falsely claims to be the creator god.

The hesitancy and forgery links stem from the trial of Parnell, the Irish freedom leader, who was falsely accused by one Pigott of participating in the Phoenix Park murders in 1882 of two high Irish functionaries appointed by the British. In this effort to implicate Parnell, Pigott forged a letter allegedly from Parnell. But in it Pigott misspelled hesitancy as "hesitency" and repeated the same spelling error at trial. His forgery was unmasked and Parnell went free, only to be brought down later by the priests for sexual indiscretion.

The parallels between TZTZ god's attempts to bring down Adam using Eve and TZTZ religion's attempts to bring down individuals of independence are clear enough. The independent individual threatens to bring down TZTZ god through the god/human Tikkun interaction. In Joyce's view, the TZTZ religions include the institutional Christian religions and Islam.

By contrast, the ES life is to live life for what you love regardless of what others think, regardless of the amount of prestige or compensation or pain involved. Joseph Campbell called it "following your bliss." Those who live for self-respect are not hesitant and dare to be great. They are genuine articles, not forgeries. They create with new possibilities. They respect the human unity. An ES writer writes for art not for sales.

So here is the **basic formula for FW,** which is built on the waste aspect of TZTZ creation: The independent individual life is like ES because the dependent waste element is flushed away and the unity is respected. The possibilities are unlimited. The dependent report card life is like TZTZ experience. Your possibilities are limited, and you waste your life.

In summary then: ES—independence, individuality, more possibilities, and unity. TZTZ god—dependency, repetition, less possibilities, and separation.

The independent life is also like ES in that both have unified bases. The infinite possibilities of ES exist in unified solution, in a unity complete in itself. Against this unity TZTZ god separates, differentiates and discriminates. The independent individual has a "simple" soul, that is all of one piece, whereas the fearful dependent individual has a divided soul, one part for himself and other parts for the opinion of others. This is the subject of the Eumaeus episode of Ulysses, the "ambush at home."

Likewise, the Trinity in Catholic doctrine functions in much the same way. When the base is unified, when the Father and Son are in charity, then the Holy Spirit issues. When the base is separated, when the Father and Son are not in charity but in opposition, then the Holy Spirit does not issue.

Just to show you that Joyce uses many means to deliver his message, note that he repeatedly uses a "L/R" split or substitution—a substitution in a word of a letter "r" for an "l" or vice versa. While this is apparently justified by peculiarities in the Celtic language, Joyce uses these letters as pictures of dependence and independence. The bent over letter "r" [*resh* in Hebrew] pictures dependency as opposed to the capability suggesting upright "l". For example, "flyday" is Joyce's name for the day of the independent spirit, rather than

"Friday" the Sabbath for the Muslim faithful to dependent submission and predestination.

As noted, in the last line of the novel—**A way a lone a last a loved a long the**—the "a's" are separated to float independently so they can easily hook up in the opening with the many "r's" in the first word **riverrun.** With the "a's" stripped away, we have four words at the ending that start with the letter "L," the upright symbol of potential. These L's grace Anna Livia Plurabelle's novel-ending emancipation from the fear of death.

This technique of using letters for important meanings has the blessing of K. Hebrew letters are thought to have sacred power. May the power of "L" be with you.

Dream

Joyce constructed most of FW to reflect a kind of sleep or dream consciousness. He spoke about this directly and consistently throughout his life, particularly to Jacques Mercanton, whom Joyce apparently selected to be the spokesperson for FW as Gilbert was for Ulysses. This allowed Joyce to take FW into dimensions beyond any human experience, into unexplored regions.

Mercanton reported [in *The Hours of James Joyce* contained in *Portrait of the Artist in Exile*] that Joyce said to him:

> Work in Progress? A nocturnal state, lunar. That is what I want to convey; what goes on in a dream, during a dream. Not what is left over afterward, in the memory. Afterward, nothing is left.

> The hallucinations in Ulysses are made up out of the elements from the past . . . Here [FW] is the unknown. There is no past, no future; everything flows in an eternal present. All the languages are present, for they have not yet been separated. It's a tower of Babel. Besides, in a dream, if someone speaks Norwegian to you, you are not surprised to understand it. The history of people is the history of language.

> He conjured up the two characters Shem and Shaun: the one who acts and the one who watches others act, and who between them make up the complete figure of the artist.

> I reconstruct the nocturnal life . . . as the Demiurge goes about the business of creation, starting from a mental outline that never varies. The only difference is that I obey laws I have not chosen. While He?

It is I who could draw up the best indictment against my work. Isn't it arbitrary to pretend to express the nocturnal life by means of conscious work. Or through children's games?

And Joyce's Night Book reads in K. In K, sleep is considered as 1/60th of death and a return of the soul to the Tree of Death while waking is to return to the Tree of Life. You will sense inherent in this notion Joyce's construct of sleep as restriction and waking as possibility liberating. And remember that we "fall asleep," fall suggesting restriction of possibilities.

This does not mean that FW is presented as one or several dreams. It is too long and contains too much for that. Rather, it is more like a composite made up of dream-like materials. These composites hang together by association around several themes, most related to the curse. The composites read like allegories or myths, primitive myths.

FW represents a development from the waking dream of Molly that ended Ulysses. The best I can do is to describe the construction of FW as existing in the border region between dream and caricature. It is of the theater and opera, where the essence of the true is presented in non-realistic materials. The direction of the departure from reality in FW is in the direction of abstraction. As the Master said[to Adolf Hoffmeister],

> Work in Progress has a significance completely above reality; transcending humans, things, sense, and entering the realm of complete abstraction. Anna and Humprhey are at the same time the city and its founder, the river and the mountain, as well as both sexual organs; there is not even a chronological ordering of the action. It is a simultaneous action, represented by the novel's circular construction, as Elliot Paul has pointed out very accurately. Where the book begins it also ends.

FW cannot be totally dream-like because it is composed of words whereas dreams are composed of images. The reader must try to invent images to go along with Joyce's words. The language of FW does produce overall distortion just as dream images, while "real" to the dreamer, are distorted in terms of their ultimate meaning. As dreams distort the images relative to meaning, Joyce distorts the words relative to regular English. Joyce's distortions attempt to use analogs of techniques of dream distortion. The meaning is found in the direction of distortion, the latent content.

Here are some of the factors at work in sleep and dreams, factors that will visit the FW text:

Physically, only the body [including the brain] is involved. Very little outside stimulus is felt. The body is independent of external factors, very much unlike the waking experience. The body is immobilized, the eyes are blind, the ears and nose largely off duty. The overall experience is like a vegetative state or that of a wax museum figure. The body is "dead to the world."

Mentally, the body experiences only its own thoughts, its own independent mental activity. Dreams are real mental activity and the dreamer believes in them. With the liberation from the external world, contradictions and impossibilities are accepted. Dreams appear in visual images, not conceptually. Dream sequences are governed by a loose law of association. Symbols are used. The dream is completely egotistical, about only the dreamer.

Psychologically, dreams hallucinate by constructing situations and experience. The self, the voluntary free will self, is not in charge of this process. It is more of a passive experience. Dreams are composite psychical formations and the images have various psychic values attached. These energy values can shift. The dreamer floats in psychical space like clouds. The subjects involved, the real subjects, are those the dreamer cares most passionately about. These are the hidden or latent content of dreams that arise in the form of wish fulfillment from repressed subjects in the unconscious, subjects that cannot be accessed by the waking mind. The wish fulfillment aspect of the dream has the highest intensity as does the starting point for most of the trains of association. The censor that prevents repressed thoughts from entering consciousness is relaxed enough during sleep to allow disguised versions of repressed subjects through during dreams.

In terms of dream techniques, we find that attached energy is the principal guide to meaning. Dreams use various techniques, primarily condensation of several subjects in one image or displacement which separates the ideas from the affect attaching to them and even separates the ideas into several images. Simultaneous replaces logical connections. Temporal is changed to spatial. Contradiction cannot be expressed so reversal is used. The more subtle relations of thought like conjunctions, prepositions, changes in declension and conjugation are dropped. The same latent content informs different dreams during the same night as well as the form of the dream.

Note that ES god is the analog of condensation and TZTZ god of displacement.

The flexibility of dreams allows FW to transcend the built-in and conditioned limitations of the phenomenal world daytime experience, which is subject-dependent. To this end Joyce used unusual sequences proceeding on a basis other than logic and highly unusual invented words or word combinations, particularly contradictory combinations. In dreamscape opposites can coexist and characters and situations easily blend into each other. In this night world, legend, fantasy and myth stand equally "real" with history.

In FW language is the message, at least one of the messages. Pregnant with multiple meanings, Joyce words are the procreative vehicle. They are preg**naaan**t with meaning. The reader literally gives birth to this novel through his or her own interpretation of these pregnant messengers, a kind of mystical-subjective K kind of reading experience.

Ellman reported:

> That Finnegans Wake should be a night book as Ulysses was a day book was also already decided. The night required and justified a specific language. 'I am done with English,' Joyce said to August Suter: and he remarked to another friend, 'I have put the language to sleep,' As he explained to Max Eastman in a later effort, valiant but unsuccessful, to win a convert to his method, 'In writing of the night, I really could not, I felt I could not, use words in their ordinary connection'. Used that way they do not express how things are in the night, in the different stages—conscious, then semiconscious, then unconscious. I found that it could not be done with words in their ordinary relations and connections. When morning comes of course everything will be clear again. . . . I'll give them back their English language. I'm not destroying it for good.'. Joyce set out upon this radical technique, of making many of the words in his book multilingual puns, with his usual conviction. He called it 'working in layers.' After all, he said to Frank Budgen, 'The Holy Roman Catholic Apostolic Church was built on a pun [rock of Peter Petrus]. It ought to be good enough for me.'! To the objection of triviality, he replied, 'Yes. Some of the means I use are trivial-and some are quadrivial.'!

During the flow of the night book as a dream, there are dreamers dreaming within the overall dream. This suggests the view of ultimate reality as pictured by Hindu speculation. As Joseph Campbell put it:

THE notion of this universe, its heavens, hells, and everything within it, as a great dream dreamed by a single being in which all the dream characters are dreaming too, has in India enchanted and shaped the entire civilization. The picture opposite [not included] is a classic Hindu representation of the ultimate dreamer as Vishnu floating on the cosmic Milky Ocean, couched upon the coils of the abyssal serpent Ananta, the meaning of whose name is "Unending." In the foreground stand the five Pandava brothers, heroes of the epic Mahabharata, with Draupadi, their wife: allegorically, she is the mind and they are the five senses. They are those whom the dream is dreaming. Eyes open, ready and willing to fight, the youths address themselves to this world of light in which we stand regarding them, where objects appear to be distinct from each other, an Aristotelian logic prevails, and A is not not-A. Behind them a dream-door has opened, however, to an inward, backward dimension where a vision emerges against darkness. Are these youths, we might ask, a dream of that luminous god, or is the god a dream of these youths?

The Vishnu dreamer in FW, according to Joyce per Ellman, is Finn himself, the:

> . . . Irish prototype, the legendary hero and wise man Finn Mac-Cumhal. As Joyce informed friends later, he conceived of his book as the dream of old Finn, lying in death beside the river Liffey and watching the history of Ireland and the world—past and future—flow through his mind like flotsam on the river of life. But this was perhaps only to indicate that it was not the dream of any of the more obvious characters in the book.

As the dream is in all parts an expression of the dreamer, this novel is Finn. The night reveals his the collective human experience. C. G. Jung wrote:

> . . . [there] is a little hidden door in the innermost and most secret recesses of the soul, opening into that cosmic night which was psyche long before there was any ego-consciousness, and which will remain psyche no matter how far our ego-consciousness may extend. For all ego-consciousness is isolated: it separates and discriminates, knows only particulars, and sees only what can be related to the ego. Its essence is limitation, though it reach to the farthest nebulae among the stars. All consciousness separates; but in dreams we put on the likeness of that more universal, truer, more eternal man dwelling in the darkness of primordial night. There he is still the whole, and the whole is in him, indistinguishable from

nature and bare of all ego hood. It is from these all-uniting depths that the dream arises, be it never so childish, grotesque, and immoral. So flowerlike is it in its candor and veracity that it makes us blush for the deceitfulness of our lives.'"

In K terms, consciousness that separates reflects TZTZ creation. The collective unified experience of mankind mired in TZTZ excrement is what FW tries to record. It is Here Comes Everybody.

What all of this says, according to Campbell, is:

> For in dreams things are not as single, simple, and separate as they seem, the logic of Aristotle fails, and what is not-A may indeed be A. The goddess and the lotus are equivalent representations of this one life-enclosing sphere of space-time, wherein all things are brought to manifestation, multiplied, and in the end return to the universal womb that is night.

FW is like that—not single, simple or separate. It proceeds on the basis of its own kind of logic. You could call it dream logic or unifying logic or even ES logic. For a description of the collective subject matter of FW, I can do no better than to quote Jung on the unconscious:

> If it were possible to personify the unconscious, we might think of it as a collective human being combining the characteristics of both sexes, transcending youth and age, birth and death, and, from having at its command a human experience of one or two million years, practically immortal. If such a being existed, it would be exalted above all temporal change; the present would mean neither more nor less to it than any year in the hundredth millennium before Christ; it would be a dreamer of age-old dreams and, owing to its immeasurable experience, an incomparable prognosticator. It would have lived countless times over again the life of the individual, the family, the tribe, and the nation, and it would possess a living sense of the rhythm of growth, flowering, and decay.

So the big dreamer in FW is all of humanity, or if you prefer, the ground of being in humanity. That is what is meant by the legendary Finn as the dreamer. Finn's dream is the only immortality registered in our mind experience, a kind of retrospective immortality.

Joyce tried to capture the ultimate ground of humanity through avatars—the likes of Adam, Noah, Finn and H.C. Earwicker. That is why for Joyce everything today has the press of old times, times that started in that magic Garden of Eden, a word that derives from delight, pre-curse delight.

Dream Language

First a little primer on Joyce's language, the language of infinite possibilities. I cannot do this subject full justice now so just a few examples.

First the obvious. Joyce created his own language so that it could cover greater possibilities, in its own realm reach for more. Compared to Joyce's language, our regular English, which is given to us by others, is like TZTZ limited dependency.

As Louis Gillet reported,

> He spoke of the language he had used in order to give to vocabulary the elasticity of sleep, multiplying the meaning of words, playing with glistering and iridescences, making of the sentence a rainbow where each drop is a prism assuming a thousand colors. This language cost him infinite pains.

For some easy ones, where the word itself is distorted and the nature of the distortion indicates its meaning:

- Lonnnnng for really long
- LLarge for large
- Smal for small
- Ptee for petite
- Graab—a grab with a long reach
- Mness for mess
- hull of a wherry for hell of a hurry with the u and e exchanged because in a hurry
- Inher for a picture of the prime act
- Saack for extension in pregnancy
- Childher for pregnant
- Manifest becomes mamifest in the feminine version.

Many words are the product of merged meanings. For example, **Zmorde** combines TZTZ, merde and mort, excrement and death. Some words acquire meaning by comparison with nearby similar words, such as **alltitude and malltitude.** The implied comparison here is between attitude and altitude. "All titude" would be the "all" or dependent group attitude and "at titude" would be the "at" or independent individual attitude. The all titude is changed to malltitude, or bad for all from on high, high altitude.

For a different type of distortion, Gillet again:

> The same process is used in the description of a meal where some spoonerisms, some reversed syllables, *naboc* (bacon), *kingclud* (duckling), *eaps* (peas), represent the act of chewing, while the onomatopoeia *XXOXOXXOXXX* is a funny portrayal of a mouth occupied by a gruel of potatoes. . . This kind of verbal humbug gave him exceeding pleasure.

So chew on that for a while. The overall dream aspect justifies distortion in general and, as we will see, the curse plays a major role in the particular direction of much of the distortion.

Aesthetics: Terror and Proper Art

In Joyce's aesthetics, an artwork must be complete in itself in order to be proper art, art that reaches the greatest number of possibilities, has the longest reach. In this respect, it shares fundamentals with ES god in Kabbalah and Joyce's ultimate values for human life as lived.

In terms of Joyce's objectives, his theory of proper and improper art is instructive for understanding what is at stake in FW:

> The tragic emotion [result of proper art], in fact, is a face looking two ways, towards terror and towards pity, both of which are phases of it. You see I use the word arrest. I mean that the tragic emotion is static. . . . The feelings excited by improper art are kinetic, desire or loathing. Desire urges us to possess, to go to something; loathing urges us to abandon, to go from something. The arts which excite them, pornographical or didactic, are therefore improper arts. The esthetic emotion (I used the general term) is therefore static. The mind is [by proper art] arrested and raised above desire and loathing. [material added]

This treatment is an expansion of Aristotle's theory of tragedy. Aristotle thought the experience by the audience of pity and terror would bring the audience through an excited state back to more of a repose. Joyce takes the concept of arrest one step further.

Kinetic art, for or against something, connects with TZTZ god. This is art with a separate agenda. It is not complete in itself in that it refers to something outside the work and generates desire for or against it. That outside something has a history and properties that are not included in the artwork, and to this extent the work is not self-sufficient. Note that the intent of ES in creating TZTZ creation in order to manifest Itself would be pornographic in this definition.

Contrast that with arrested art, art like ES that is complete in itself. Note the emphasis on aesthetic arrest, which raises the mind "above desire and loathing." Consider preliminarily the common aspects shared by aesthetic arrest and general Buddha-like compassion-driven detachment, in whose gentle arms the ego-induced emotions of aggression and desire are arrested.

Since pity and terror are proper effects of art but their near relatives desire and loathing are not, Joyce's definitions of pity and terror are key:

> Tragedy aims at exciting in us feelings of pity and terror. Now terror is the feeling which arrests us before whatever is grave in human fortunes and unites us with its secret cause and pity is the feeling which arrests us before whatever is grave in human fortunes and unites us with the human sufferer. Now loathing, which is an improper art aims at exciting in the way of tragedy, differs, it will be seen, from the feeling which are proper to tragic art, namely terror and pity. For loathing urges us from rest because it urges us to go from something, but terror and pity hold us in rest, as it were, by fascination. When tragic art makes my body to shrink terror is not my feeling because I am urged from rest, and moreover this art does not show me what is grave, I mean what is constant and irremediable, in human fortunes nor does it unite me with any secret cause for it shows me only what is unusual and remediable and it unites me with a cause only too manifest. Nor is art properly tragic which would move me to prevent human suffering any more than an art is properly tragic which would move me in anger against some manifest cause of human suffering. Terror and pity, finally, are aspects of sorrow comprehended in sorrow—the feeling which the privation of some good excites in us.

The phrase "grave and constant" means what is "irremediable" or inherent in the human condition; and the "secret cause" refers to ultimate and unknown factors that produce human suffering. Factors that nothing can be done about. As Aubert interpreted secret cause,

. . . what is grave in human fortunes, in tuches, or encounters, is ultimately discovered to be 'the privaton of some good,' as exile from the Good as the Secret Cause of Creation and of the individual creature.

There it is folks. The Curse of Kabbalah right there at the bottom of Joyce's aesthetics. The secret cause is the nature of creation—creation as exile from the Good, exile from ES. The secret cause is the hidden content of the FW dream.

These grave and constant aspects of the human condition are the mortar in Joyce's art. This is the material with which he intends to connect with the reader. This is the principal Joyce subject matter, the eternal aspects of the human condition that transcend time, culture and locale.

And these basic concepts of proper art translate into important lessons as to the proper method of literary composition. They suggest how to do it to get the right result. Here are the lessons as to proper composition method issued by Stephen for Joyce in Portrait:

> Even in literature, the highest and most spiritual art, the forms are often confused. The lyrical form is in fact the simplest verbal vesture of an instant of emotion. . . . He who utters it is more conscious of the instant of emotion than of himself as feeling emotion. The simplest epical form is seen emerging out of lyrical literature when the artist prolongs and broods upon himself as the centre of an epical event and this form progresses till the centre of emotional gravity is equidistant from the artist himself and from others. The narrative is no longer purely personal. The personality of the artist passes into the narration itself, flowing round and round the persons and the action like a vital sea. . . .The dramatic form is reached when the vitality which has flowed and eddied round each person fills every person with such vital force that he or she assumes a proper and intangible esthetic life. The personality of the artist, at first a cry or a cadence or a mood and then a fluid and lambent narrative, finally refines itself out of existence, impersonalises itself, so to speak. The esthetic image in the dramatic form is life purified in and reprojected from the human imagination. The mystery of esthetic like that of material creation is accomplished. The artist, like the God of the creation, remains within or behind or beyond or above his handiwork, invisible, refined out of existence, indifferent, paring his fingernails.

This is the position of Joyce in FW. He is like ES, the independent god of creation, who remains beyond his work pairing his fingernails and concealed from the reader. His work is self-sufficient and does not excite desire or loathing, except desire for more Joyce. It creates joy in the reader, the kind of joy that is the particular attribute of the Holy Spirit when the Father Son relationship is proper. As Campbell said, it harmonizes you, reduces your fragmentation.

The interdependent TZTZ god would be the analog of a writer in the lyrical mode. In this inferior mode, the artistic end product is slave to the author's emotional subjectivism and agenda. For this reason, the end product does not have access to the unlimited possibilities that flourish only in artistic independence. This is the artistic version of the curse of limits by the TZTZ god. It is also, as we shall see, the end product in another sense.

TZTZ in FW—Excrement and Flatulence

The K literature literally refers to the TZTZ creation as an excretion by ES—the elimination of the finite and limited from the infinite and unlimited. With Joyce's impish nature and relish for matters of the body, it is no surprise that FW treats the experience in this world, in this hole, as if it were god's water closet. We are in god's rest room. Joyce refers to the "hole affair" as the whole god made a hole.

As Joyce uses it, the curse of Kabbalah is akin to celestial excrement issuing from the backside of TZTZ god, the secondary lord of the abyss. This backside features the bush that humans get lost in. That's right—the rectal bush of the lord is where we get lost. That dingle berry tangle is the existential nightmare. The FW dream will show it to you in its darkest corners. FW is a colonoscope.

Joyce treats human experience under TZTZ god as if it were a shower of god waste, and treats thunder as TZTZ god's fart, a warning of more waste to come. This gives new meaning to TZTZ god's boast in the Hebrew Scriptures that mankind only experiences god's backside not his face. FW features several prodigiously long thunder and excrement-laced words, big brown thunder. That thunder causes fear by threatening more excrement. As we are to see, fear was in the Vico system the first organizational motivation for primitive humanity post-flood. Joyce also finds it in the Garden of Eden and other Genesis myths. Fear of god.

This excrement metaphor produces a comparison that is important in FW. And the comparison may provide a tool for some understanding of ES. It is a comparison, a part to whole comparison. The finite and limited TZTZ creation is to ES as human excrement is to humans. The nature of the relationship is part to whole, but a special part to whole—that part not absorbed by and eliminated from the whole. This special kind of part to whole understanding gives us at least some limited understanding of ES. And this special kind of part to whole relationship helps us understand the relationship of the Babel-like and fragmented surface text of FW to its hidden unities.

The emphasis on the backside also appears in FW in the nature of soldier sex, same sex back to belly without any attachment or unity or new possibilities. In Joyce's view, heterosexual behavior face to face can lead to love, unity and new possibilities. Soldier sex is directed at the non-individuated backside. One backside is pretty much the same as any other. And you wouldn't want a a child pro-created and delivered through the anus.

Soldier sex is "behind" the story of the cad who approaches the modern iteration of Finnegan in the park with the traditional homosexual proposition "Have you got the time." Mortality introduced time which began as Adam and Eve were expelled from the Garden to the TZTZ life. At the time FW was written, homosexual encounters, especially those in the park, were "quick hitters" and could not become genuine unifying relationships given society's values. Homosexuals were separated from society.

Park sex, including that in the Garden of Eden, is TZTZ sex, sex that separates. In one version of what happened, FW's principal male character Mr. Earwicker is to be "done in" by three soldiers in Phoenix Park in Dublin. Just as, according to the Jewish Legends, Adam was done in by the serpent.

In this excremental context, keep in mind that in Joyce's view all literary creation is digested personal experience. With an emphasis on excretion as creation in the TZTZ world, certain types of literary creation would be "excreation." This would be the exposed types of literary creation, those in which the author is visible in an indecent exposure. Unlike human procreation, this type of creation issues from the anus, where non-procreative sex takes place. Hosty's Ballad in Chapter 1.2 is an example of excreation.

The Family of Curses

So here is "how it comes down." Gods fall. Humans repeat the Falls of the gods. Artists face the same forces; they fall when they produce non-arrested dependent art.

In summary:

ES god

Independent
Unified
Infinite
and thus neutral or arrested

Created TZTZ creation and TZTZ god in
a fall and an indecent exposure

Remains concealed behind creation

TZTZ god

Dependent
Separate
Finite
Emotional and not-arrested

Separates and discriminates in TZTZ creation.
Produces friction producing opposites including blessings and
curses of mankind

Wants humans dependent and fearful not ES god-like independent, unlimited and unified.

Created Adam and Eve and ruled events in Garden of Eden.
Fathers Cain and Able through serpent.
Causes fall and makes humans dependent and fearful.

As part of separation-created view of Trinity, prevents charity
between Father and Son gods so Holy Ghost does not issue.

Reflects same pattern in primal horde and oedipal relationships—failure of charity between father and sons and incestuous possession of daughters.

With his conception of FW founded in the curse aspect of
TZTZ creation, Joyce planted in the mythical background haze of
FW a particular take on the Babel, Flood, Noah and other legends in

Genesis. They are the offspring of the Garden of Eden myth. Joyce reads these Genesis legends as dream-like, containing as latent content the god curses, efforts by TZTZ god to enforce human limitations, to reduce human possibilities.

FW registers the offspring of the curses from these legends in the human arena in the primal horde, Oedipal family dynamics and nation-state warfare. God/man conflict sponsors man/man conflict, conflict even in the family that tears apart the most basic human unity. The angry father before his trembling young son repeats the thunder of Jove that caused primitive man to fear and stutter. In FW, brothers Shem and Shaun, brothers that reflect the opposite characteristics, compete against each other within the background haze of the Cain-Able legend.

In the primal horde, thought to be the first social organizational format for humanity, the senior male restricts the realization of the dependent junior males in the interest of exclusive sexual privileges for the senior male with the wife, his own daughters and female captives. Repeated ritual humping reminds the male juniors of their reduced position. This father-son abuse delivers the curse of limitation to the next generation in which the abused will become abusers. The second paragraph of FW features examples of this inheritance. This abusive relationship continues the patterns set forth in the Genesis myths, particularly the "angels" coming down to procreate with human females and producing giants.

Continuing these curse-based power relations to the present day, the Oedipal complex relations in the modern human family famously feature potential robbing and incest powered conflicts and guilt revolving around parent/child possessive love and eventually sexual attraction. Love and acceptance are necessary for these issues to be resolved successfully. The Earwicker family foregrounded in FW features father/son conflicts, son/son conflicts and father/daughter attraction. They are not resolved successfully.

Moving beyond the primal horde and the family, Joyce finds the curse active on the modern battlefield for the nation-state organized slaughter of thousands. For Joyce, this is the inheritance of the Tower of Babel catastrophe. The early pages of FW contain an extended scene at the muddy Battle of Waterloo complete with competition for female cheerleaders. Joyce uses the name Waterloo to remind us of god's water closet [the "loo"] as well as Napoleon's fall.

Joyce presents these conflicts as the same old repetitive story of humanity—human-to-human conflict. The conflicts are cycled and recycled on cyclical looms of history [more on this later], each cycle being powered by ES god's original and continuing fall [Hart and Atherton]. The human experience—whether personal, family or nation-state—has been and continues in god's water closet with only husks for wipes. Noah's killer flood was the first big flush.

This is the path of the TZTZ god-human interaction. The abused becomes the abuser next time around. Or in the terms of the Upanishads, this is how the Brahman becomes the atman, how the god of the universe becomes a spark in each of us. How each of us becomes "that." Thou are that. Thou art god excrement.

I get the impression that Joyce believes that as long as we consider god to be the TZTZ god and we fear death, strife will always be with us. Or put in terms of the novel, Father H.C. Earwicker will necessarily be "Here Comes Everybody" as long as he is connected with TZTZ god instead of ES. His wife Anna, the Anna Livia Plurabelle or the principle of unity and more possibilities, overcomes the fear of death and TZTZ god on the last page of FW.

Joyce and FW

The Oedipally conflicted archetypical family experience featured in FW must have been close to home for Joyce. Ellman's biography suggests that Joyce's daughter Lucia was jealous of Joyce's wife and played up to him or tried to make him jealous in order to grab more of his attention. This on her way to institutionalization for serious psychic disturbance. He told Jacques Mercanton: "Sometimes I tell myself that when I leave this dark night, she too will be cured."

The aspects of the excremental-like TZTZ creation make human sexuality critical. Procreative sex overcomes death and love sex temporarily bridges separation. This connection of death and sex is, in my opinion, what was behind Joyce's notorious experiment with Nora. According to what should have remained his most private letter, he had her defecate on him while they were having sex, his own personal mini-sequel to TZTZ creation.

Having taken on the subject of fear of death, Joyce died in 1941, not long after completing FW, during an operation for an ulcer, an ulcer he did not take care of. I gather from Ellman that Joyce was not afraid to die—even though he had one more book planned—but he was afraid of losing consciousness. The night before his ulcer perforated he was afraid of remaining in a friend's house on a hill because of lightning. Afraid of thunder and lightning in this hole of creation, a hole in his stomach took him away.   During the writing of FW Joyce was threatened with blindness. His eye disease caused him to see not at all or the wrong colors, a subject featured in the last chapter of FW.

Joyce's last work was written from 1922 or 1923 to 1939—after the human carnage of World War I, during the Great Depression and leading up to World War II and the Nazis. These experiences flooded god's water closet with evil and death and made the TZTZ theory of creation all the more credible. These times, including collaboration with the Nazis, raised the ante considerably on the issue of independence versus dependence.

As Hart said, this work was "developed in a period of time that was conscious of a powerful tension between. . . the forces of fragmentation and. . . those arising from attempts to reimpose order on the fragments by arranging them into artificial patterns [e.g. alliances]. . ."

The lack of effective patterns of unity signals the absence of ES.

FW in General

For a summary of the overall concept for FW, I give you Richard Ellman, Joyce's major biographer [all quotes in this section from Ellman's biography of Joyce].

FW was to be a universal history of mankind:

> This was the 'universal history' of which Joyce had spoken to Miss Weaver; it would mix history and fable in a comic leveling. The characters would be the dreamlike shapes of the eternal, unlikely family, Everyman, his wife, their children, and their followers, bobbing up and down on the river. In the twentieth century Everyman's avatar was to be Humphrey Chimpden Earwicker, keeper of a public house in Chapelizod, whose wife was Anna Livia, whose children were the twins Shem and Shaun and their sister with the split personality, Isabel. Behind and within Earwicker, that compound of bounce and bluster, were all men of enterprise, strong or weak; his twin sons were every possible pair of brothers or opponents, his wife was all homekeepers, his daughter every heart's desire from Iseult of Ireland to Swift's Vanessa. Beyond these manifestations, Earwicker was a primordial giant, a mountain, a god, with a double aspect suggested by the sons, and Anna a river, a principle of nature, her daughter a cloud. It was a wholly new book based the premise that there is nothing new under the sun.

You will sense a serious threat to individuality in this generalized approach. The ability to write a convincing universal history of mankind suggests that individual realization has been severely limited throughout history. The precious few heroes recognized in FW try to rise above the limitation. Joyce's heroes are those who struggled against the grain of the power in their societies—for example Moses, Buddha, Jesus, Mohammed, Parnell and other Irish patriots who fought English injustice.

In FW, Humphrey Chimpden Earwicker tries to be more than most; he is an independent business owner and he runs for political office. The local crowd tries to bring him down, to make him "Here Comes Everybody," as a result of his transgression in the park, an event with mysterious outlines that is the successor to the events in the Garden of Eden.

In FW, you don't have distinct characters in the normal sense but characters blend and blur into other characters and situations into other situations because [Ellman]:

> The accumulation of identities is intended. For Joyce no individual is so unusual and no situation so distinct as not to echo other individuals and situations. Stephen Dedalus goes out to encounter reality for the millionth time. Ulysses, as Victor Berard confirmed for Joyce, followed established trade routes in his legendary wanderings. Joyce not only binds fable to fact, but also fact to fable. He was forever trying to charm his life; his superstitions were attempts to impose sacramental importance upon naturalistic details. So too, his books were not to be taken as mere books, but as acts of prophecy. Joyce was capable of his own claims of prophetic power-he does so in one section Finnegans Wake-but he still made the claims. For Joyce life was charmed; nature was both stolid and magical, its ordinary details suffused with wonder, its wonderful manifestations permeated by the ordinary.

You can feel this charm magic when a word, phrase, line or section comes alive for you, when the epiphany springs forth.

Joyce's method is based on repetition, repetition of basic patterns. This method feeds on the assumption that in our TZTZ universe coincidence the condition of repetitious happening at the same time or place or the condition of being identical without purpose—is the ruling reality [Ellman]:

> Joyce's fictional method does not presume that the artist has any supernatural power, but that he has an insight into the meth-

ods and motivations of the universe. Samuel Beckett has remarked that to Joyce reality was a paradigm [a typical example of something], an illustration of a possibly unstatable rule. Yet perhaps the rule can be surmised. It is not a perception of order or of love; more humble than either of these, it is the perception of coincidence. According to this rule, reality, no matter how much we try to manipulate it can only assume certain forms; the roulette wheel brings up the same numbers again and again; everyone and everything shift about in continual movement, yet movement limited in its possibilities. . . . The characters pass through sequences of situations and thoughts bound by coincidence with the situations and thoughts of other living and dead men and of fictional, mythical men.

The Wheel of Repetition plays an important part in FW, from the opening sentence to the cyclical nature of the whole. Indeed, many of the unifying structures used for FW are cyclical and repetitive. Joyce calls them the **Herewereagain Gaieties** and the **Royal Revolver**. This suggests little hope for progress in the Tikkun restoration toward the unlimited possibilities in ES unity.

Details of the Curse of Kabbalah

The venerable doctrine of K is presented here as if there is only one view within Kabbalah on all major subjects, certainly not the case but good enough for this purpose. As usual, Joyce cherry picked what he wanted out of the doctrine. He started with the tree of Lurianic Kabbalah.

K is a system of mystical theosophy. Theosophy means god knowledge, knowledge of god. Mystical means the god knowledge results from personal experience, not from catechism instruction. It is knowledge usually gained by contemplation while in withdrawal from the world. But it can also be a sudden epiphany that erupts while walking the streets of Dublin.

The main book of K is the *Zohar*, a work from the 13th century. Its doctrines derive in part from the Book of Enoch and other ancient apocryphal writings but not directly from the canonical Hebrew Scriptures or Old Testament. It uses some of the ideas of Marcion, an early Christian but for the Catholics a heretical theologian. K's concept of creation involving an inferior god is common among earlier religions that preceded Christianity.

The Zohar reads creation in Genesis in a way that is totally different from the interpretation of traditional Christianity. For most of

Christianity, YHWH the god of Genesis is the creator of the universe and not a secondary Demiurge kind of god. In K, YHWH took over from the real creator ES and controls the material world. In K, the TZTZ god came with creation and is the lord of the abyss. There is no need for an independent Satan. TZTZ god does both good and evil. The serpent in the Garden of Eden is one of TZTZ god's bench players.

Before TZTZ creation, ES contained all possibilities, limited and unlimited. After TZTZ creation, ES contained only infinite and unlimited possibilities and TZTZ creation contained only finite and limited possibilities. ES remains concealed behind its creation that is fundamentally different from, could not and thus does not reveal anything about ES. ES and TZTZ creation are as different as a human and his or her excrement. It does tell us by metaphor some of what ES god eats but eliminates rather than absorbs—the finite and limited. What ES god eats and absorbs is the infinite and unlimited, all of the rest. For the ultimate god, this distinction is the fundamental issue in all of, for lack of a better word, being. Joyce follows suit in his grand slam.

The effort of creation necessarily implies limitation because it involves intention, desire and work. Creation necessarily involved a wish to become manifest. These are properties that involve limitation and a finite being. So the infinite ES had to work through intermediaries established for the purpose, the Sefirot or intelligences that emanated from him like rays. With these, the unlimited ES could do limited.

In Kabbalah, one of the ten power sources or Sefirots is called "Din." [Sefirots is not the plural of sefirot in Hebrew but it is easier to understand.] Din is a harsh judgment power source operating without its companion aspects mercy and compassion. Din caused the creation limitation. Joyce orchestrates Din as thunder. For Joyce thunder that produces god fear is the divine fart that accompanies the divine excrement in our world. There is much brown thunder in FW, described in long flatulence-suggestive words.

The TZTZ creation is in Joyce's view the original fall and the original indecent exposure. ES showed his limited side in order to become known and manifest. Notice the parallel with inferior art as defined by Joyce. ES, who presumably could have created anything, created a finite world full of limitation and death. ES could, for example, have created a world in which a real kind of permanent eternity could be reached through art. For Joyce, this indecent creation was self-abuse by ES—producing a creation that was less than it could be.

The curse of death—the fall—in the Garden of Eden legend echoes the prior and parallel fall in the godhead in the very act of creation. This curse passed to the spiritual dna of Adam Kadmon, the primordial first man and then to Adam in the Garden of Eden. Joyce passed it in this novel to Finnegan and then to his modern iteration H.C. Earwicker and thus to all of us. It migrates in the archetypical soul that we all share as humans, our biological heritage. You will note that this migration treatment is similar to the Catholic idea that Eve's original sin in the Garden of Eden is passed to all successors through sexual intercourse. After the curse, the condition of inevitable mortality is also passed through sexual intercourse.

According to K, the world described in Genesis is what takes place after the original TZTZ creation by ES is over. The evil already in the Garden reflects the curse built into creation. The TZTZ god described in the Hebrew Scriptures develops in a relation of mutual interdependence with humans. Satan is a manifestation of TZTZ god and humans.

This TZTZ god wants to be recognized as the only god and the creator of the universe. TZTZ god is needy and high maintenance. This all too human and kinetic TZTZ god is the god in the Garden of Eden, the Tower of Babel and the other myths in Genesis and generally in the Hebrew Scriptures, which with some changes are the Old Testament. Like humans, this TZTZ god makes rules and punishes and is jealous and possessive. This is the god that instructs the victorious Hebrews to act out the primal horde: to kill the defeated tribe's men and children and keep the women in the Hebrew harems. This god issues blessings and curses, the instruments of dependency and fear.

The main limitation that derives from TZTZ god is dependence on others. As TZTZ god is made by others, most humans live their lives for the approval of others. Most writers write for sales. Most humans make ethical decisions on the basis of pleasing their bosses and fear of displeasing them. For Joyce this lack of independence, the report card life, is the ultimate curse, the ultimate limitation that reduces human possibilities.

First a summary of the principal ideas of K from Drob [source of quote unless otherwise noted], with the strange words being Hebrew [readers not interested in details of Kabbalah can skip to the next section]:

Ein-Sof (The infinite Godhead), of which nothing can be said. . . is the Union of being and nothingness, of "everything and its opposite."

Ein-Sof performs a Tzimtzum (Divine Concealment, Contraction, Withdrawal) which leads to a . . . Metaphysical Void (Tehiru), a circle surrounded by Ein-Sof on all sides. . . containing a residue (Reshimu) of divine light, and into which is emanated. . . the light of the infinite (Or Ein-Sof), a thin line (kav) through which. . .

Adam Kadmon (Primordial Man) spontaneously emerges. Lights, also conceived as holy "letters," flashing and recoiling from Adam Kadmon's eyes, nose, mouth, and ears form. . .

Vessels (Kelim) for containing further lights, thus forming the "World of Points" comprised of . . .

the Sefirah (Archetypes of Value and Being; constituents of the body of Adam Kadmon): Kerer (Crown, Will, Delight, the highest Sefirah) Chochmah (Intellect, Wisdom, Paternal) Binah (Understanding, Maternal) Chesed (Loving-Kindness) Tiferer/Rachamim (Beauty, Compassion) Din/Gevurah (Judgment, Strength) Netzach (Glory) Hod (Splendor) Yesod (Foundation) Malchurl/Shekhinah (Kingship/Feminine principle). . . .

The vessels are also composed of the Otiyot Yesod, the twenty-two letters of divine speech, and are organized into. . . Worlds (Olamor): Adam Kadmon (AK, identified with Ein-Sof and Kerer) Atzilurh (Nearness) Beriah (Creation) Yetzirah (Formation) Assiyah (Making, the lowest world, includes our material earth). The weakness and disunity of the Sefirot leads to their shattering and displacement, known as . . .

The Breaking of the Vessels (Shepirar Hakelim), which produces. . . a rupture in the conjugal flow between Masculine and Feminine aspects . of God, and. . . Netzotzim (Sparks), which fall and become entrapped in . . . Kellipor (Husks), which comprise the. . . Sirra Achra (the "Other Side," a realm of darkness and evil).

Lights from the forehead of Adam Kadmon, also conceptualized as mystical names, reconstitute the broken Sefirot/vessels as: Partzufim (Faces or Personalities of God): Artika Kaddisha (The Holy Ancient One)! Kerer Abba (The Father)! Chochmah Imma (The Mother)! Binah Zeir Anpin (The Impatient One) Chesed-Yesod NukPah (The Female) MalchurlShekhinah. . . .

This begins. . . . Tikkun ha-Olam (The Restoration of the World), which is completed by man, who via the "raising of the sparks" brings about the Reunification of the Partzufim, the masculine and feminine principles of God.

In this view creation was and continues to be a contraction and concealment by ES:

> The doctrine of Tzimtzum, in its simplest form, holds that creation is a limitation upon the utter fullness of God, who, if not for a constriction or concealment, would fill the entire cosmos with his own unitary Being. It is only because God, as it were, removes or conceals himself from a "point" or "region" within his own Being, that a seemingly independent cosmos, which includes individual finite souls, can arise. An "illusion" of independent, finite entities is created by this Tzimtzum or concealment. . . In doing so Ein-Sof actually conceals one aspect of Himself (God) from another aspect of himself (man). In this manner he furthers and deepens the act of **divine repression**. Several startling propositions follow from the doctrine of Tzimtzum: evil is necessary for creation, creation is evil, evil is necessary for good, and evil is good. The meaning of these seemingly paradoxical propositions should become quite clear as we proceed. That evil is necessary for creation follows from the notion that creation is a limitation upon God, a limitation upon the ultimate Good. [emphasis added]

Now to concentrate on god's fall—creation as Ein-Sof's elimination or excretion of the finite and evil:

> According to kabbalistic tradition, evil originates in a cathartic act within the Godhead, one in which Ein-Sof seeks to purge itself of the very roots of Din or Judgment that exist at its core. **For example, in the Zohar, the origin of evil is understood as a process of excretion through which the divine organism maintains its pure essence as the good.** The Zohar speaks of a fire within the Godhead that melts and refines the roots of evil, or din. The "dross" from this "smelting" process is externalized into the Kelippor ("Husks") that constitute the substance of the "Other Side." In this way God's severe judgment is externalized and gives rise to a counterworld, which parallels the world of holiness and is ruled by Satan. ***We shall see that evil, for the Kabbalists, is the very essence, definition, or equivalent of creation, inasmuch as both evil and creation are the restriction, delimitation, differentiation, and negation of the fullness of the Absolute God. [emphasis added]

54

The etymology of the word "elimination" echoes these ideas: it is derived from Latin stems meaning to thrust out of doors, out of the house. While human waste would naturally have been removed from the residence, this idea easily extends to lack of hospitality. This was a big sin in the old world. Abram was tested by the degree of his hospitality to the three strangers who appeared at his tent. Adam's first and too independent wife Lillith, who was denied hospitality in the Garden of Eden [more on her later], creates havoc in FW as the "prankquean." The wordsmith Joyce would also note that elimination contains the word "limit."

Back to K. The world must be imperfect in order to be different from ES god. Its creation is a process of various degrees of negation and contraction or emanation away from the nature of ES:

> The Kabbalists held that the act of Tzimtzum occurs by gradations and degrees, in such a manner that a system of worlds is created, each world being characterized by its relative admixture of divine light and darkness. Our world is among the lowest of such gradations, and is characterized by individuation, separation, darkness, and only a small spark of holiness (which even the most evil of things must retain in order to subsist). It is because our world is near the end of the series of contractions that all mundane affairs are severe and evil and wicked men prevail. It is for this reason, and from this point of view, that creation is evil. We have in this doctrine some elements of a Neoplatonic theodicy: Evil is the result of an estrangement, concealment, and diminution of divinity. Further, the very condition of human existence and desire, the material world, is the most illusory and the most wicked of all things.

Ten in number, the Sefirots were pictured in a pattern—three vertically on the left, three vertically on the right and four vertically down the middle. These Sefirots are forces that were contained in Admon Kadmon and to a lesser degree in humankind. These combine in various ways not relevant for our purposes. See, however, chapter 10 of FW for an extended *tour de force* use of these ideas. One concept plays a role in the last chapter of FW [from Sholem]:

> When this point is represented as a source welling up from the depths of nothingness, the third *Sefirah* [Binah or intelligence] becomes the river that flows out from the source and divides into different streams following the structure of emanation until all its tributaries into "the great sea" of the last *Sefirah*.

The last Sefirot is the closest to TZTZ creation where death reigns. Joyce images this as the river of life repetitively flowing into the salt sea of death.

This process of creation necessarily brought evil into the world:

> Evil is written into the very idea of creation and is woven into the fabric of the human soul. The "Other Side" exists within our own hearts and, indeed, it could not be otherwise, for without evil we could have no hearts, no freedom, and indeed no individual existence whatsoever. Evil, according to the Kabbalists, cannot simply be dismissed as an illusion; neither can it be transcended or ignored.

Evil is separation from ES. The characteristics of that separation by its very nature include freedom and mortality. TZTZ god increases that separation.

Evil is viewed through the metaphor of breaking the vessels:

> The third symbol, Shevirat ha-Kelim, the Breaking of the Vessels, gives a group of symbols and ideas that constitute the most unique and original kabbalistic contribution to the theory of evil. Evil, according to Luria and his disciples, results from a necessary and inevitable shattering of the Sefirot, the value archetypes through which God structured the world. This shattering, or "Shevirah," results in the many contradictions and failings of worldly life that are embodied in the symbol of the Kelipot or "Husks." These Husks result from the intermingling of divine sparks with the dead shards of the once pristine but now shattered Sefirot. The Husks constitute the Sirra Achra, the dark realm of unholiness and evil. It is mankind's task to gather the sparks (nerzorzim) of divine light, extract (birur) them from the kelippot, and restore them to their place in a newly perfected God and world. This process, known as Tikkun ha-Olam (the Restoration of the World) reveals that the full purpose and significance of evil in God's plan is to provide the context for man's and the world's redemption.

In the restoration of the world, Adam Kadmon starts with lighthouse-like light beam shining from his forehead:

> However, immediately after the Breaking of the Vessels, a process of healing or reconstruction begins. Restorative lights shine forth from the forehead of Adam Kadmon. Thus begins the process of Tikkun ha-Olam, the repair and restoration of the world, a process that is to be carried out in full by mankind. According to the Luri-

anic Kabbalah, it is the purpose of each individual man and woman to discover his or her own personal Tikkun, his or her own role in the restoration and reconstruction of the self and world. Tikkun is conceived of as a liberation of the divine sparks of light entrapped by the Kelippot and the return of this light to its source in God.

Individual Tikkun, Tikkun by each individual, not by the church. Joyce's individuality-based approach.

In FW the sound "tic" is repeated frequently. It is the sound of the necessity for Tikkun, for restoration, for resurrection. In the terms used in the Garden of Eden myth, it is the sound of the scratching by the tips of the branches of the Tree of Life.

Time, space, matter and separate existence—the products of the Garden of Eden experience—are some of the finite products of TZTZ:

> Space, time, and matter as well as individual personal existence can now be understood as the logical consequence of Tzimtzum as concealment or epistemic limitation, for each of these "categories" serve as a vehicle through which conceptual knowledge is limited. That which is remote in space or time, that which is concealed in or by material objects, and that which belongs to another person or self, is in principle unknown or only partially known. As philosophers since Kant have understood so well, the concept of a world requires the existence of the categories or principles of space, time, matter, and personal identity to provide the means for differentiating finite experienced things.

Now for some more metaphors [K is pregnant with them]—the Garments and the mystical number 231. Joyce uses this number in his current version of the Eden park experience—two girls, three soldiers and one HCE. This number is also used by Joyce in reversed Hebrew order [Hebrew read from right to left] as 132 and 1132. Here is the source of these magic numbers:

> . . . Sarug held that God's pleasure in his own self-sufficiency produced a "shaking" of Ein-Sof within itself. This shaking aroused the roots of Judgment, Din, and caused "points" to be engraved in Din, such engravings forming the contours of the metaphysical void. The light of Ein-Sof acted upon these engravings in such a manner as to create a Primordial Torah, which serves as a garment (malbush) for Ein-Sof, woven out of the very fabric of his being and barely distinguishable from him. The structure of this garment

is composed of the 231 two-letter combinations of the twenty-two Hebrew letters (the so-called 231 "Gates" of *Sefer Yetzirah*). Tzimtzum, according to Sarug, is a folding of this garment that leads it to occupy only half its original space, creating a rectangular void within which emerges the finite world.

Here you have Garments on the void, garments covering over what is missing. This is another idea echoed in the Garden of Eden when post "Fall" Adam and Eve cover their privates. The 231 two-letter combinations fundamentally built into the nature of reality result in Joyce's obsession in FW with the years 1132 and 566 [folding the garment in half] as time garments of TZTZ.

These garment metaphors also sponsor the recurring story in FW of the roving and humpbacked Norwegian Sea Captain who mates with the land-based tailor's daughter. You can anticipate how Joyce will use *malbush*, the bad bush. It becomes TZTZ god's rectal hair.

Here is a description of the healing process of Tikkun, of returning the parts or separates to the whole:

> We can now see that there are two related but distinct aspects of the Tikkun process. The first is the repair and restoration of the Shevirah through human acts that bring divine/human values into our world. The second is the meditational or mystical/rational act that enables the kabbalistic devotee to transcend the Shevirah, as it were, and intuit a divine reality, i.e., become a witness to "higher worlds." At times those two aspects of Tikkun are combined and the Kabbalist is deemed, by virtue of his proper intention . . to be capable of healing separations within the upper worlds as well. It is in the concept of Tikkun that the confluence of inner (spiritual) and outer (worldly) acts that is the hallmark of the Jewish religion, finds its fullest kabbalistic expression. The reason for this is that just as the higher worlds resolve the antinomies that exist in our own, our world was created to resolve the antinomies of the higher, more Godly realms. This is because it is only in our material world that the values that are abstractions in the higher worlds become instantiated and real.

Here is the fundamental reciprocal relation of god and man, man and god. Only man can heal god and only after understanding the higher worlds.

The reciprocal relation of god and man is:

As we have repeatedly seen, for the Kabbalists there is a reciprocal relationship between God and man. God is the ultimate source of the human attributes of thought and emotion, but the psyche of man is the realization of what is only potentiality within God. As with Carl Jung who was to expound a similar view two centuries later, for the Maggid the Godhead has a hidden life within the mind of man.

The god in this world is a finite god, the only kind of god that could exist in this finite-based creation. It is not ES unless and until humans make it so. This TZTZ god can get angry whereas the real god is impassive. This god creates opposites from unity in order to create friction whereas ES reconciles opposites in order to create arrest. TZTZ god can make covenants and deals whereas the real ES god is beyond all that. TZTZ god can be elevated back into ES only with the work of humans. TZTZ god becomes the product of all humanity.

In the ultimate reality of ES, opposites are reconciled:

> For the Chabad Hasidim, it is precisely the unity of opposites that provides for the she/emut or completeness of Ein-Sof itself: "For the principal point of divine completeness is that. . . in every thing is its opposite, and. . . that all its power truly comes from the opposing power, and, according to the strength of the opposing power, thus the power of its opposite will be found truly." Within the godhead, the contradictory nature of earthly oppositions are [sic] nullified.

In this material world, TZTZ god separates unity in stasis into opposites, a process that like fission produces energy, the energy of opposition and strife. ES is echoed in Joyce's created words that combine opposites.

Since what is above in TZTZ is below in humanity and vice versa, TZTZ has a sexual aspect:

> A fascinating series of symbols, related in certain respects to the symbolism of Adam Kadmon, express the idea that the Sefirot represent the process by which divine procreative energy flows and is received in the world of emanation. On this view the creation of the world is the consummation of a divine sexual act. ***The relations between man and woman are represented in each of the Sefirot. Each Sefirot is conceived bisexually, as male to the Sefirot below and female to the Sefirot above it. The entire sefi-

rotic scheme announces the idea that sexual and romantic union in man is a reflection of basic cosmological dynamics.

Even an Oedipal aspect:

> Therefore, the supernal world [mother] says to her [to the daughter]: "Is it a small matter that you have taken away my husband? [Gen. 30:15] for all his love is centered on you. "Conversely the "mother" is said to favor the son over her husband, thus completing a sort of cosmic Oedipal triangle: a vision of the cosmos in which "the world" is conditioned by archetypal interest and desire, the very desire that contemporary psychoanalysts have found reflected in the psyche of man, and at the foundation of human society.

The Shekhinah is the restorative female principle:

> For example, the Zohar speaks of evil resulting from the "banishment of the queen"; here speaking of the exile of the Shekhinah as a theosophical event in which the masculine and feminine principles within God have been separated as the result of human sin. The concept of evil as exile is reflected in the Kabbalist's interpretation of Genesis. Adam's sin is said to have exiled the Shekhinah and caused a cleavage between the masculine and the feminine, between the trees of life and knowledge, and thereby between life and death. . . The Zohar understands the "splitting," resulting from the exile of the Shekhinah, as a blockage of cosmic libidinous energy. Accordingly, redemption will see the masculine and the feminine "carried back to their original unity, and in this uninterrupted union of the two, powers of generation will once again flow unimpeded through all the worlds. "

In FW the Shekhinah or its Christian counterpart the Holy Spirit is grounded. It appears as a bird picking up fragments on the battlefield.

Freedom and death are mutually interdependent, as the Garden of Eden experience would suggest:

> Goodness, it seems, can exist in and of itself but evil requires the free choice and responsibility that can only be attributed to an individual. . . Man, on the other hand [compared to angels], more distant from God, in possession of free will, and hence partly immersed in evil, is an individual. Indeed, human individuality is another expression of the potential for both freedom and evil within the soul. As we have seen, the Tzimtzum, God's contraction and

concealment, is the process by which both evil and individuality come into being. According to the Kabbalist Azrid, Adam's fall, which further alienated man from the divine, is responsible for his individualized condition. Paradise would be a completely nonindividuated state. Cast out from Eden, man lives his life in an estranged condition in which he is knowledgeable and free, and yet burdened by guilt, responsibility, and isolation. Individuation, freedom, and evil are stations on the train to death. They are partial deaths, partial alienations from the All that is the source of life. We are free, quite simply, because we die, or more precisely because we already know death in the midst of our lives.

Death and Chaos from Berg and *The Essential Zohar.*

> One of Kabbalah's most important teachings states that negative thoughts are the origin of chaos in our lives. And of all negative thoughts, doubt may be the deadliest. Kabbalah teaches that chaos—and death, which is the supreme manifestation of chaos—are illusions fostered by doubt, which creates an opening for negative energy. More specifically, doubt is a questioning of the efficiency—or the existence—of the spiritual system. It is doubt of oneself, and of one's own ability to reveal Light. While we still existed under the influence of Tree-of-Life consciousness—before the serpent instigated the tasting of the fruit from the Tree of Knowledge of Good and Evil—death did not exist. Humanity had no connection with "mortality consciousness." But once the fruit was eaten, uncertainty entered the picture. That is, we now doubted that we would live forever, and consequently, we do not live forever. It is the doubt itself that brought us the seeming "reality" of death. When humanity is at last transformed, all chaos, including death, will cease to exist. These burdens will evanesce like the Cheshire cat, vanishing into thin air. To new students of Kabbalah, this must surely seem a radical assertion, and perhaps even an incredible one.

This is a radical idea, that we die because humanity as a whole doubts that we are immortal and if we dared to be great we could be immortal. Let's watch for this idea in Joyce. And remember that like Woody Allen, Joyce wants to live forever not just in his works but also in his Paris apartment.

The Dark Side

In some versions of K, there is a parallel bad universe consisting of the adverse or "averse" elements. The Tree of Knowledge is averse to the Tree of Life, and there are shadow Sefirots and averse angels or demons. Lillith, Samuel and Adam Belial are numbered among the demons. Tohu was a world full of demons, Bohu one free of demons.

Joyce once stated that the first Book of FW suffers from an increasing sense of darkness or shadow, that the first eight episodes bring on a kind of immense shadow as the sleeper goes from conscious, to semi-conscious to unconscious. The Dark Side as the Dream world.

Kabbalah Celestial Family

As in Christian doctrine, K constructed a holy trinity from the consonants in the Holy Name JHVH. H is the letter He and is considered feminine. J and V are masculine. The name produces two pairs: JH and VH.

J and H, Jehovah and Elohim, Abba and Aima, are the celestial union of divine male and female principles. When in union, they are said to complete and perfect the Holy Name. They function as father and mother in the celestial realm and produce a son V. V or Vau is the son which sponsors the son below and H again is his betrothed or twin sister. Together they sponsor the Shekhinah in the world below.

As with the Christian Trinity not in charity, this union is considered broken so that the Shekhinah like the Holy Ghost does not issue below. Union is broken in both places—between J and H and V and H.

Mystery of Sex

According to Waite, the inner most secret doctrine in K is the Mystery of Sex. This Mystery revealed explains why proper versus improper sex is such a big deal in the Garden of Eden myth and why mankind was created in the image of god male and female.

According to Waite, a child conceived in a marriage of love, from seed issued by a circumcised penis preferably on the Sabbath, will receive a specially sanctified soul from the celestial sources. This special soul is the result of the divine union above produced by the sanctified union below. The humans in union produce the body and the gods in union produce the special soul. These are the Children of Grace and they add to JH above.

62

Bad unions on earth cause bad unions above. If couples don't have children or if the husband neglects his wife, the Shekhinah cannot reside with them. For example, one-parent households would produce children lacking in Grace from above. The worst activity is that of Onan, spilling his seed to avoid procreation.

Use of Kabbalah in FW

First, let me assure skeptical readers that there are scholarly proofs of Joyce's knowledge of Kabbalah. For the doubters who have to see for themselves, see Brivac in the James Joyce Quarterly. The following are a few examples of Joyce's use of K in FW in the first two and last chapters. Ainsof is mentioned by name in FW.

The doctrines of Kabbalah, particularly the TZTZ doctrine of creation as necessarily finite and limited, fund Joyce's notion of the curse—making humans incomplete and less than they could be, first and foremost making them dependent on and made by others. These limitations are at the center of FW. You can see how Joyce would have jumped from the TZTZ creation ideas to a water closet [a hole in the ground], to the Battle of Waterloo and human elimination in general.

In FW, TZTZ creation of our universe in a hole made by ES becomes the "hole affair," because the hole is the whole and the whole has a hole, an absence, an absence of god. The human hole affairs are sex and togetherness in the womb, the last taste of ES. The last hole is the grave.

The folded garment of TZTZ creation becomes the polarities, the binaries, the strife producing combinations.

The TZTZ view of creation is also the rebar in the recurring motives and stories in FW, which serve as the running walls of the foundation:

- As noted in detail below, it makes much more sense of the Garden of Eden myth, the prototype for the fall.
- The story of the Prankquean stealing children of a stand-in for TZTZ god answers to this foundation. She is the residue of the independent Lillith, who was eliminated from the Garden of Eden by TZTZ god. She steals TZTZ's Trinity children and makes them evil.
- It provides contrasts for the long Battle of Waterloo scene in the first chapter.

- It powers the conflict between the brothers, Shem the "penman" aligned with the independent ES and approval oriented Shaun the "postman" aligned with the TZTZ god. Shaun delivers the views of others. Sacrificing his own individuality, he "dies" for others.

- The Russian general who was shot by an Irish soldier Buckley when the general, like ES, used sod [the earth] to wipe his behind, to eliminate the finite.

- The K garment metaphors power the recurring story of the Norwegian Sea Captain and the land based tailor. The captain [ES] claimed the tailor [TZTZ] could not sew [unify] and the tailor claimed the humpbacked captain could not be fitted [discriminate]. The captain is humpbacked [like the letter "r"] because of his fall. The ship's "husband," its chandler and friend of the tailor, plays the role of the Church.

- The dependent fearful human is the answer to the "first riddle of the universe": "when is a man not a man—yours till the rending of the rocks—Sham." TZTZ man is a sham man, not an individual. He accepts substitutes. He sacrifices his real self, *asham* in Hebrew meaning sacrificial offering. Sham also gives us the shamrock and sham sex between the rocks of the buttocks.

- The K cosmology explains Joyce's emphasis on the Trinity and the failure of the Holy Spirit to issue in the world as well as the primal horde form of social organization and Oedipal Complex.

Near the end, FW features a culminating debate between an Irish ArchDruid [a disguise for Bishop Berkeley] aligned with ES and St. Patrick aligned with TZTZ god. On the surface about the perception of color as absorption versus reflection, color absorbed versus color eliminated by reflection. This debate revisits the relationship of part to whole, of mankind to god. The fundamentals of this debate turn on the differences between the two conceptions of god, less possibilities versus more possibilities. This in turn governs the ultimate reality of the relationship between humans and god and the way humans can move closer to god—by getting smaller or bigger. The differing natures of ES and TZTZ gods call for different kinds of human life.

But the concept that apparently excited Joyce the most was the idea that events in the macrocosm are necessarily mirrored by those in the microcosm and vice-versa. That is why in FW the Fall of God came first and was mirrored by a Fall of Man. The Fall of mankind was to be what we call human, to be subject to temptation and death.

To be less than we could be. The Fall is the subject of the first chapter of FW. There Adam falls, Finn falls, Napoleon falls, Babel falls, Humpty Dumpty falls, the market falls. Everybody falls.

Joyce emphasizes the curse aspect of the Eden, Lillith, Cain, Flood and Babel legends. And to the story of Abraham, what is normally considered the start of a process to reverse the disintegration of the god/man relationship, Joyce counters with his version of the story of Lillith, Adam's first wife who was eliminated from Eden because she was too independent.

Tikkun or rebirth is the subject of the last chapter, when ALP as the representative of life goes down the tidewater black whirlpool. But she goes down independent and not afraid of the male saltwater death awaiting her. She goes down her own person.

The concealment aspect of TZTZ creation and the confusion of the TZTZ god with the creator ES god sponsor the many deception and mistaken identity aspects in FW.

Joyce uses the Sefirot concepts selectively. Since the highest is the Keter or crown, the Waterloo episode in the first chapter features hats and human emotional control limitations. The highest faculty of man is will so the Wellington character is named willingdone, not well done. The lowest Sefirot is the Malchut, which governs this world. Chute is cascading water and malchut would be bad cascading water, in FW the repetitive river. The language of god in this finite Malchut world includes time, and in FW the special K numbers 1132 and 566 play important roles.

One way the process of Tikkun is symbolized in FW is by the "Ford of the hurdles," the ancient name for Dublin and a prominent feature of the old township. This hurdle was a wicker web laid across the Liffey river that allowed one to cross the river that otherwise separated the township. The hurdle bridged separation in favor of unity of the two parts of the town.

As with the Shekhinah in K, the heart of the female function in FW is to put things back together, beginning with sperm and egg. The Shekhinah is the Middle Pillar in the Sefirot system where opposites are reconciled and unified. Joyce's Shekhinah is a hen on the midden heap.

Salmon are used often in FW since they carry the K image of the salmon of knowledge and are born in fresh water, migrate to salt to mature and then put things back together by returning to fresh water to die and spawn. Fish also provide a symbol of fecundity.

As latent content often shapes the form of dreams, the curse of Kabbalah is the pattern for not only content but also form in this novel. First and foremost, the relation of the hidden unity and totality of ES *vis a vis* the separated and differentiated TZTZ world is reflected in FW. The hidden unifying techniques and structures of the novel reflect ES while its fragmented and busy surface reflects TZTZ creation.   Given this unity-fragment kind of connection, Joyce can use any kind of unifying technique because any kind of unification is capable of suggesting the original unity of ES. The hidden structures include cycles of time, cycles of space, geometric forms, inverse relationships, correspondences, seasons, leitmotifs and nested dreams, just to name some. Vico patterns play a big role. Patterns are piled on patterns. FW works like a constantly varied repetition gathering energy as it proceeds [Atherton]. Since later chapters are more organized [Hart & Atherton], Tikkun appears to be progressive.

Joyce tried to make FW boundless, not subject to the death and limitation curse. FW has no end; it just goes round again. FW feels like endless becoming. Unlike the channeled River Liffey, it seems to flood endlessly in all directions. Its language knows no limitation in customary usage or one language.   In Garden of Eden terms, it is the fruit of both trees, of Knowledge and of Life.

Sacred Ground

Let us for now explore briefly just one new Joycean combination of content and form, one that works within the unity-fragment formula and on the macro level of the reader and the meaning of the novel. This will give you an insight into the level of art promised by reading FW.

With a wave of his magical wand, Joyce produced a new kind of reader-author relationship. The text is so full of meanings and layers of difficulties that the reader can and must create a personal meaning of the text for him or herself, an individual reading. Unlike most works of literature and even Joyce's Ulysses, there is no single "objective" meaning in the totality of the Finnegans Wake text. You can dig and dig only to realize that the subjective you are alone in the hole.

This personal, individual and subjective creation of the reader requires active participation. There is no manna for the lazy reader with a dependent "feed it to me" attitude. The children of television will not make it. With Finnegans Wake, you have to feed yourself. You have to feed independently.

But even an independent and active reader will have a limited take compared to the full store of goodies in the text. Even with anthologies at hand, the take will leave plenty behind. The take is limited by all the factors that reduce human possibilities—reduced energy, attention, knowledge and time.

As Joyce created before the reader, the reader creates in the act of reading after Joyce. Just as with the Kabbalah tradition of received and independently explored doctrine, the reader receives and creates independently with his own but shorter wand from virtually unlimited possibilities in this genie bottle of a novel.

And now for the rub Joyce gave the bottle. This author-reader-author relationship itself produces meaning. As we have seen, this kind of relationship is part of the Kabbalah way of the interdependence of god and humans.

The author-reader relationship and other creative innovations Joyce developed for Finnegans Wake have important analogs. They share important common characteristics with god activity as understood in Kabbalah. By creating these common characteristics, Joyce mimicked the Kabbalah gods. The relationship between surface detail and underlying foundation in Finnegans Wake is analogous to the relationship of everyday reality and ultimate reality in the Kabbalah world.

Joyce the artist is Kabbalah god. This sharing is one example of the common ground of Joyce's art and ultimate reality. On this common ground metaphysics meets art. And that is the sacred ground in Joyce's Kabbalah-inspired Torah. When this sacred ground comes alive, when you feel the vibrations from the common structure of ultimate reality as depicted by Kabbalah and of the structural elements of this artwork, you will be in manna land.

Opposites

The nature of TZTZ creation is to separate and generate opposites, to break up unities. In this respect, it is embodied in the fruit of the Tree of Knowledge of Good and Bad, a tree whose fruit is constructed in the fundamental opposites of good and bad [as discussed below, not good and evil]. Compared to a unification of opposites producing arrest or stasis, opposites naturally produce tension and flux, even strife, competition and warfare. Nuclear fission is the biggest example.

The first generation of opposites was the TZTZ creation itself. ES created a universe separated from the remainder of his undivided nature. This creation made ES and the TZTZ universe direct opposites—infinite versus finite and concealed versus exposed and unified versus separate. The Garden of Eden myth records the second creation of opposites—the blessings of TZTZ god versus the curses from TZTZ god. This pair of opposites produced another set of opposites—fear and dependency in mankind.

The opposition of unity and separation is the bitumen [bytwomen] in the foundation of FW. On the level of the gods, it is the difference between ES and TZTZ god, the independent god versus the dependent god, the unifier god versus the god of separation and discrimination.

At the level of the Earwicker family, the unification of HCE's and ALP's spirit in marriage is separated into sons Shem and Shaun and daughter Issy. The separation itself produces tension and strife as these characters share only some common characteristics but mostly differences.

The main opposition polarity in FW is between the sons Shem and Shaun. Shem is the penman, the artist, and Shaun is the postman, the man of the world. Here is a list of their differences and related oppositions:

Shem	Shaun
Penman	Postman
Genuine	Sham
Create	Copy
Independent of others	Dependent on approval
ES	TZTZ god
Same inside and out	Different inside and out
Tree and growth	Rock
St. Paul	St. Peter
Mystic	Acolyte
Druid	St. Patrick
Goat	Sheep
Satan—independent	Christ—dies for others
Esau	Jacob
King Mark	Tristan
Bad eye good ear	Good eye bad ear
Time	Space
Stephen Dedalus	Buck Mulligan

The forces for unity in FW derive from Tikkun and the Shekhinah-Holy Ghost. They include womanhood in general and ALP in particular. Joyce's art, grounded in the human unity, is there to lend a hand, a mending hand.

Ultimate Issues

The subject matter of the god/man relationship fills the mosaic of FW with potshards from many of the world's religions. They are collected as attempts to understand the relationship. For a few examples among many, we are treated to Balam's ass as well as Mohammed's camel "cropeared" along with the Norse Eddas and the Egyptian Book of the Dead. The Four Old Men in FW stand in for the four Gospels of the New Testament based on personal experience with Christ, the Christian connection of mankind to god.

Joyce visits these shards in an attempt to find ultimate meaning, to find what the full genie vase looked like. Joyce's answer is that so far at least, Balam's ass and cropeared could do as good a job as humans have done in figuring it out.

Finn

Since Joyce said Finn is the big dreamer in FW, we need to know more about him. Finn led the Fianna, legendary early inhabitants of Ireland. From Wikipedia:

Birth

Most of Fionn's early adventures are recounted in the narrative *The Boyhood Deeds of Fionn*. He was the son of Cumhal, leader of the fianna, and Muirne, daughter of the druid Tadg mac Nuadat who lived on the hill of Almu in County Kildare. Cumhal abducted Muirne after her father refused him her hand, so Tadg appealed to the High King, Conn of the Hundred Battles, who outlawed him. The Battle of Cnucha was fought between Conn and Cumhal, and Cumhal [Finn's father] was killed by Goll mac Morna, who took over leadership of the fianna. [Finn orphaned]

Muirne [Finn's mother] was already pregnant, so her father [the druid] rejected her and ordered his people to burn her, but Conn [the King] would not allow it and put her under the protection of Fiacal mac Conchinn, whose wife, Bodhmall the druidess, was Cumhal's sister. In Fiacal's house she gave birth to a son, who she called Deimne. (Note that *cumal* is Old Irish for a female slave; Fionn may once have been "the slave-girl's son" before a more noble origin was invented for him.)

Boyhood

Muirne [Finn's mother] left the boy in the care of Bodhmall and a warrior woman, Liath Luachra, who brought him up in secret in the forest of Sliabh Bladma, teaching him the arts of war and hunting. As he grew older he entered the service, incognito, of a number of local kings, but when they recognised him as Cumhal's son they told him to leave, fearing they would be unable to protect him from his enemies.

The young Fionn met the leprechaun-like druid and poet Finn Eces, or Finnegas, near the river Boyne and studied under him. Finnegas had spent seven years trying to catch the salmon of knowledge, which lived in a pool on the Boyne: whoever ate the salmon would gain all the knowledge in the world. Eventually he caught it, and told the boy to cook it for him. While cooking it Fionn burned his thumb, and instinctively put his thumb in his mouth, swallowing a piece of the salmon's skin. This imbued him with the salmon's wisdom. He then knew how to gain revenge against Goll [who killed Finn's father], and in subsequent stories was able to call on the knowledge of the salmon by sucking his thumb.

The salmon's place in this tale displays the esteem in which this particular family of fish is held in many different mythologies. The particular species thought to be referenced in this tale, is the *Salmonidae midlandus* variant. This species held a special place of esteem in traditional Irish stories due to its strength, its appearance, (significantly more scales than other species, and therefore a more striking range of colours), and its relative scarcity. The story of Fionn and the salmon of knowledge bear a strong resemblance to the Welsh tale of Gwion Bach, indicating a possible common source for both stories.

Adulthood

Every year for twenty-three years at Samhain, the fire-breathing fairy Aillen would lull the men of Tara to sleep with his music before burning the palace to the ground, and the fianna, led by Goll mac Morna [who killed Finn's father], were powerless to prevent it. Fionn arrived at Tara, armed with his father's crane-skin bag of magical weapons. He kept himself awake with the point of his own spear, and then killed Aillen with it. After that his heritage was recognised and he was given command of the fianna: Goll willingly stepped aside, and became a loyal follower of Fionn, although in many stories their alliance is uneasy and feuds occur. Fionn demanded compensation for his father's death from Tadg, threatening war or single combat against him if he refused. Tadg offered him his home, the hill of Almu, as compensation, which Fionn accepted.

Love life

Fionn met his most famous wife, Sadbh, when he was out hunting. She had been turned into a deer by a druid, Fer Doirich. Fionn's hounds, Bran and Sceolang, who were once human themselves, recognised she was human, and Fionn spared her. She transformed back into a beautiful woman, she and Fionn married and she was soon pregnant. However Fer Doirich returned and turned her back into a deer, and she vanished. Seven years later Fionn was reunited with their son, Oisín, who went on to be one of the greatest of the fianna.

In *The Pursuit of Diarmuid and Gráinne*, one of the most famous stories of the cycle, the High King Cormac mac Airt promises the now aging Fionn his daughter Gráinne as his bride, but Gráinne falls instead for one of the fianna, Diarmuid Ua Duibhne, and the pair runs away together with Fionn in pursuit. The lovers are aided by Diarmuid's foster-father, the god Aengus. Eventually Fionn makes his peace with the couple. Years later, however, Fionn invites Diarmuid on a boar hunt, and Diarmuid is badly gored by their quarry. Water drunk from Fionn's hands has the power of healing, but when Fionn gathers water he deliberately lets it run through his fingers before he gets back to Diarmuid. His grandson Oscar threatens him if does not bring water for Diarmuid, but when Fionn finally returns it is too late; Diarmuid has died.

Death

Accounts of Fionn's death vary; according to the most popular, he is not dead at all, rather, he sleeps in a cave below Dublin, to awake and defend Ireland in the hour of her greatest need. Another legend states that Fionn, his wife and son were turned into pillars of stone in the crypt of Lund Cathedral, in Sweden.

So already in this myth of Finn we have Finn asleep under Dublin and ready to wake up, the salmon of knowledge similar to the Tree of Knowledge in the Garden of Eden, knowledge arising from death, strife among siblings, a love-duty conflict story like Tristan and Isolde and a continuation of influence in Dublin from a cave below the city, from the subterranean depths of the race. Joyce conceives of the Irish and Dublin as paradigms for the human experience. The name Finnegas suggests god's death fart. And most important, Finn is strongly individualistic, a successful leader of men, even though the son of a slave girl. He became independent despite his origins in dependency. He was fearless.

With these common blocks that appear in the many sources used by Joyce, we begin to uncover the foundation wall.

The Song of Tim Finnegan

Finn also lives in the song of Tim Finnegan, a song that resounds throughout the novel:

> Tim Finnegan lived in Walkin Street,
> A gentleman Irish mighty odd.
> He had a tongue both rich and sweet,
> An' to rise in the world he carried a hod.
> Now Tim had a sort of a tipplin' way,
> With the love of the liquor he was born,
> An' to help him on with his work each day,
> He'd a drop of the craythur every morn.
>
> *Chorus*
> Whack foIthe dah, dance to your partner,
> Welt the flure, yer trotters shake,
> Wasn't it the truth I told you,
> Lots of fun at Finnegan's Wake.
>
> One morning Tim was rather full,
> His head felt heavy which made him shake,
> He fell from the ladder and broke his skull.
> So they carried him home his corpse to wake,
> They rolled him up in a nice clean sheet,
> And laid him out upon the bed,
> With a gallon of whiskey at his feet,
> And a barrel of porter at his head.
>
> His friends assembled at the wake,
> And Mrs. Finnegan called for lunch,
> First they brought in tay and cake,
> Then pipes, tobacco, and whiskey punch.
> Miss Biddy O'Brien began to cry,
> 'Such a neat clean corpse, did you ever see,
> Arrah, Tim avoumeen, why did you die?'
> 'Ah, hould your gab,' said Paddy McGee.
>
> Then Biddy O'Connor took up the job,
> 'Biddy,' says she, 'you're wrong, I'm sure,'
> But Biddy gave her a belt in the gob,

And left her sprawling on the floor;
Oh, then the war did soon enrage;
'Twas woman to woman and man to man,
Shillelagh law did all engage,
And a row and a ruction soon began.

Then Micky Maloney raised his head,
When a noggin of whiskey flew at him,
It missed and falling on the bed,
The liquor scattered over Tim;
Bedad he revives, see how he rises,
And Timothy rising from the bed,
Says, 'Whirl your liquor round like blazes,
Thanam o'n dhoul, do ye think I'm dead?

Note that Tim was trying to raise himself up by carrying a hod up the ladder. This gives us Babel and the faustian/Eve desire for more. Note that the argument at the wake proceeds from a male commanding a female and quickly turns to violence. This is the spirit that wakes Tim, that keeps him going. The poem may remind you of Ibsen's **When We Dead Awake**.

The Finnegan in this poem owns his own wake—Finnegan's Wake with the possessive apostrophe, a possessive missing in FW. As with Tim Finnegan, our Finnegan in FW wants to wake up at his own wake. The spirits wake him up as an individual. But the mourners put him back under with promises of celestial paradise. This is the counterpart of putting individuality back under, anestheticizing the patient on the table of this life.

One of the main points of Joyce's title is that Finnegan just like Here Comes Everybody is not in charge of whether he wakes up. He does not possess his own Wake.

Dublin

As with Ulysses, the site of this universal drama is Dublin. For some facts about this ancient city, consider the following from Joseph Donnelly, Librarian, The Judges' Library, Dublin. July 2000:

Archeological & Historical Background
. . . Ptolemy (A.D. 140) referred to a settlement in the area of Dublin as Eblana. Later, in Christian Gaelic times, there were two settlements, one secular and one monastic, on the south bank of the River Liffey. The secular site, an agricultural and fishing community, was Ath Cliath, in the area around where St. Audoen's

Church now is. It took its name from a nearby ford on the river, made of hurdle-work (Ath Cliath - Ford of Hurdles), and gives us the modern Gaelic name for Dublin, Baile Atha Cliath (Town of the Hurdle Ford). That ford was near today's Father Mathew Bridge (Church St. Bridge), and was part of an ancient road system. The road continued north-west along present-day Stoneybatter, towards Tara.

Further down-river, close to where the river Poddle (now culverted under the city centre) joins the Liffey (near Parliament St.), a tidal black pool (linn dubh or dubh linn) formed on the Poddle (where the Castle Garden now is, on the south of Dublin Castle). A monastic settlement close by (around Aungier St.) took its name, Dubh Linn, from the black pool, and gives us the modern English name of Dublin (via Dyflin and Dyvelin).
***

In A.D. 841, Norsemen established a ship harbour (Longphort) at the confluence of the Poddle and the Liffey (around Lord Edward St.), and adopted the name of Dubhlinn or Dyflin for their settlement from the monastic settlement on the other side of the pool. These Vikings had arrived about three years earlier, marking their landing site with a long stone (commemorated today by a stone outside Pearse St. Garda Station at the junction of d'Olier St., Pearse St. and College St.). Their assembly point for discussions and judicial proceedings was a circular mound, the Thingmount (around the point where St. Andrew St. and Suffolk St. now meet).
. . . The town defences would in time extend from St. Augustine St. to Parliament St. (the base of a round fortification tower, known as 'Isolda's Tower' was recently excavated on Essex Quay, a few yards from the corner of Parliament St.), and the town grew out into the river, as quays were built up, channelling the river. Remains of the city walls can be seen in some places. St Audoen's Arch (1240) is the only surviving city gate, and the wall stands on each side of it in Cook St. (behind "Adam & Eve's" Church, or the Church of the Immaculate Conception (RC), on Merchants Quay). St. Audoen's Church (C of I), the oldest parish church in Dublin was founded in the 12th century. St. Patrick's Cathedral (13th century; C of I) and Christchurch Cathedral (12th13th centuries; C of I) have both been extensively restored, especially Christchurch, though much remains inside.

Two canals surround the Liffey, the Royal and Grand canals.
Several aspects of this history make their way into FW, including the name Eblana, the Ford of the Hurdles and the tidal black whirlpool, the saltwater tide pool of death. Ptolemy's name for the Liffey River was Libnia Labia. You can anticipate what Joyce does with that

74

name. Notice also the possibilities presented by the round mound used for group discussions and judicial proceedings called the "Thingmount."

Shekhinah

Since the Shekhinah figure cheerleads Tikkun in FW, puts things back together, some more about this concept from Wikipedia:

> *Shechinah* is derived from the Hebrew verb 'sakan' or 'shachan'. In Biblical Hebrew the word means literally to settle, inhabit, or dwell, and is used frequently in the Hebrew Bible. (See e.g. Genesis 9:27, 14:13, Psalms 37:3, Jeremiah 33:16), as well as the weekly Shabbat blessing recited in the Temple in Jerusalem ("May He who causes His name to dwell [*shochan*] in this House, cause to dwell among you love and brotherliness, peace and friendship"). In Mishnaic Hebrew the word is often used to refer to bird's nesting and nests. ("Every bird nests [*shechinot*] with its kind, and man with its like, Talmud Baba Kammah 92b.) and can also mean "neighbor" ("If a neighbor and a scholar, the scholar is preferred" Talmud Ketubot 85b). The word "Shechinah" also means "royalty" or "royal residence" (The Greek word 'skene' - dwelling - is thought to be derived from 'shekinah' and 'sakan'). The word for Tabernacle, *mishcan*, is a derivative of the same root and is also used in the sense of dwelling-place in the Bible, e.g. Psalm 132:5 ("Before I find a place for God, *mishcanot* (dwelling-places) for the Strong One of Israel.") Accordingly, in classic Jewish thought, the Shekhina refers to a dwelling or settling in a special sense, a dwelling or settling of divine presence, to the effect that, while in proximity to the Shekhinah, the connection to God is more readily perceivable.

Joyce's Shekhinah appears as a bird pecking at the mounds of history. The literary Shekinah dwells in the house of Joyce.

Sexual Intercourse

Sex has a prominent place in FW. Joyce seems to say that absent the Holy Spirit, sexual intercourse between consenting and loving male and female partners plays a small part of the role the Holy Spirit could. It is temporary unity and if it creates greater love it creates new possibilities.

Sex is only a small part of the potential of the Holy Spirit, the result of viewing love through death. Sex is good because it produces new ones. Sexual intercourse is one combination in which love can coexist with desire, desire being the hallmark of independence.

To repeat what was said 50 pages back. If the Father god is death and limitation, the Holy Spirit cannot be love and unlimited possibilities. The best she can do under these circumstances is to try to put the pieces back together. In the case of humans, this is through sex, the interest in which is unity for the female and possession for the male.

In K, sex under the right circumstances is thought to influence the behavior of the celestial beings, or put another way the degree of ES in TZTZ god. For Joyce, sex under the right circumstances points toward the unity and manifold possibilities inherent in ES:

> "[copulation is not the death of the soul because] there you are dealing with a mystery which can become anything and transform everything. Love-making can end in love, it often does, and so its possibilities can be limitless."[James Joyce as reported by Arthur Powers]

The importance of sex in connection with the inner essence of human experience was also emphasized by Schopenhauer:

> If I am asked where the most intimate knowledge of that inner essence of the world, of that thing in itself which I have called the will to live, is to found, or where that essence enters most clearly into our consciousness, or where it achieves the purest revelation of itself, then I must point to ecstasy in the act of copulation. [Manuscript Remains, vol iii]

Since our main character is named Earwicker, we should note the bug he is named for—the earwig. They earwig is like a lobster or crab in that the earwig has pincers but the pincers are at the tail end. These pincers suggest sex.

By contrast, Joyce's view of homosexuality, at least the kind that could exist in Ireland during his time, is ultimately tied up with rectal hair, excremental residue and the TZTZ creation. It is TZTZ god sex, park sex without possibilities and unification.

Spirits and Spirit

In both Ulysses and FW, Joyce uses alcoholic spirits in general and by brand name to make points about the human spirit. For example, Guinness beer easily morphs to genesis. This combination is justified on the basis of the positive effects of alcohol, the release of the user from limits, limits of socially approved behavior and limits of preconceived ideas. Individually controlled intake of alcohol breeds boldness and individuality within an increased appreciation of the immediate drinking group. As with TZTZ god, abused or addicted alcohol intake creates its own dependency.

In the case of the relation of the human spirit to the powers that be, the soaring human spirit, the Faustian spirit who dares to be great and reach god that way, is acting out in this grandest of versions the effects of alcohol. For Joyce the Faustian spirit is the holy spirit.

Primal Horde

Both Darwin and Freud, among many luminaries, believed that human society began with a type of organization known as the primal horde, a form of harem for one alpha male, a form of organization that links aggression and sexual drive. The primal horde still prevails among some mammals, such as the lion pride.

In the primal horde, the alpha male has exclusive sexual privileges with all the females in the survival group, including his sisters and daughters and granddaughters. The other males are either castrated or driven off in order to avoid competition. Revolts against the alpha produce uncertainty in the nest, where certainty is needed most for survival. This form of organization leaves possession as the fundamental motivation in the nest, not love and togetherness that could begin Tikkun progress back to unity.

Quoting Paul:

> Freud took his image of primordial human society from no less an authority than Charles Darwin, who put forward the following hypothesis in his Descent of Man: "The most probable view is that primaeval man aboriginally lived in small communities, each with as many wives as he could support and obtain, whom he would have jealously guarded against all other men. Or he may have lived with several wives by himself like the Gorilla. . . . The younger males, being thus expelled and wandering about, would, when at

last successful in finding a partner, prevent too close inbreeding within the limits of the family."

In terms of the group dynamics:

> He [Freud] elaborates in "Group Psychology and the Analysis of the Ego": the primal father's "intellectual acts were strong and independent even in isolation, and his will needed no reinforcement from others. . . . He loved no one but himself, or other people only insofar as they served his needs. . . . He, at the very beginning of the history of mankind, was the 'superman' whom Nietzsche only expected from the future" (1921, 123). In this essay, Freud goes on to distinguish between two different kinds of psychology, the one for the group and the one for the individual (the lone individual in primeval society being the primal father). The father, who is "of a masterful nature, absolutely narcissistic, self-confident" (123-124), is characterized by individual psychology, while the sons exemplify group psychology. This latter phenomenon is the result of the sexual privation the father imposes on the sons. Unable to give full expression to their own impulses, especially the sexual, the sons use their unspent and aim-inhibited libido to bond with one another and form a social coalition: the primal father "forced them, so to speak, into group psychology. His sexual jealousy and intolerance became in the last resort the causes of group psychology." (124)

The senior male has no interest in the development of the junior males and the senior's daughters are pressed into procreation service in the harem. The senior male wants offspring for his group but only his offspring, the ultimate expression of the selfish gene. This is a form of control of the future. The new lion alpha male kills the children of the former alpha in order to limit to his offspring the future of his world. The juniors are denied individuality which in this setting is equated with sexual privileges.

In this form of social organization, you can see the analog to the curse—the denial of full potential in humans by the senior god. The juniors are denied full realization by the alpha male, the counterpart of TZTZ god. The junior males are repressed and castrated or driven off. The females are valued only for breeding.

In this form of organization incest is natural. The junior males are reminded of their inferior position from time to time by ritual humping by the senior male, apparently the origin of the phrase "fuck you," a form of control grounded in disrespect. If you think this practice died out long ago, consider that in the Middle Ages prisoners of warfare were frequently sodomized by their captors. Freud also thought that the memory of the treatment of the junior male by the alpha survived in the ritual of circumcision.

Freud believed that after the death of the father all of the sons banded together and agreed on pain of death not to try to replace the father, and that that experience originating in the band of brothers funded all of our human notions of law and religion. Incest was renounced and sisters were traded to other groups. These rules were necessary to hold the group together and for survival. The strict rules regarding incest suggested to Freud that incest was prevalent before the rules were enacted.

With the primal horde in mind, it is not difficult to sense the source of the strife experienced in the human arena. In the effort to survive humans have to struggle in competition for reproductive resources and limited goods.

Oedipal Complex

According to Freud, memory of the primal horde experience survives to this day in the Oedipal complex, the desire of the child to supplant and replace the same sex parent in the affections of the opposite sex parent—the son for his mother. In FW, the daughter competes with her mother for the love of father H. C. Earwicker while the sons Shem and Shaun are constantly at odds. Dreams frequently feature an unresolved Oedipal complex.

It is easy to see how the Oedipal complex would be born of the primal horde. The junior male wants sexual privileges and to displace his father and at the same time has positive feelings for his father because he is the source of survival and abundance.

As the descendant of the primal horde, this complex of competition, strife and ambivalence is still with us. It is the serpent in the garden of the family, where love and togetherness could help Tikkun.

Primal Horde and Oedipal Complex in Myth

It was easy for Joyce to find the primal horde and its offspring in the Hebrew Scriptures and other prominent Jewish Legends. In the Garden of Eden God punishes Adam and Eve for disobeying the rules of the senior male. Through the serpent, God mates with Eve and buggers Adam, the junior male. Cain and Able fight for their sister. Noah's son Ham tries to castrate Noah and copulate with his mother. Jacob tricks Isaac into giving him the blessing intended for

Esau. Joseph's brothers try to eliminate him as the successor to Jacob. Exodus can be read as the dethroning and murder of the Pharaoh father figure, who was considered divine by the Egyptians. Freud reads the wandering of the Jews in the desert to include the murder of the first Moses. The Greek Oedipus myth and the Egyptian Isis-Horus-Seth myth repeat the same basic story.

Fresh Water and Salt Water

Fresh and salt water are prime symbols in the first Genesis creation story and in FW. The untamed salt-water sea suggests death and destruction. Humans die if they drink much of it. Fresh water from above and from the earth is good for mankind. FW features the fresh water river Liffey flowing into the salt water Dublin Bay.

Reclaimed from the first creation story in Genesis, fresh and saltwater help float the plot in FW. Fresh water and salt water play a yes and no role as part of the celestial feminine and masculine. In the human "echoland," the fresh/female/Liffey River and the salt/male/Dublin Bay play as repetitive birth and death.

Salt water is featured in the description of TZTZ creation in the beginning of Genesis, in a long dependent clause in the first creation story:

> When God began to create the heavens and the earth—the earth being unformed and void, with darkness over the surface of the deep and a wind from God sweeping over the water—[Jewish Publication Society version of Gen 1:1-2]

The bad things are already there: Chaos, void, darkness and the deep salt oceans. The God referred to here creates from these, not from scratch. These bad things speak evil for humankind. The early deity Tiamat was the goddess of salt water and evil. Leviathan is the salt-water monster to be eaten by the elect on the day of judgment.

Now some Rashi commentary. First meet the noted Pentateuch commentator via Wikipedia:

> **Rabbi Shlomo Yitzhaqi**, (Hebrew: יקחצי המלש יבר), better known by the acronym **Rashi** (Hebrew: י"שר), (February 22, 1040 – July 13, 1105), was a rabbi from France, famed as the author of the first comprehensive commentaries on the Talmud, Torah and Tanakh (Hebrew Bible). Acclaimed for his ability to present the basic meaning of the text in a concise yet lucid fashion, Rashi appeals to both learned scholars and beginning students, and his

works remain a centerpiece of contemporary Jewish study. His commentaries, which appear in many printed editions of the Talmud and Torah (notably the Chumash), are an indispensable companion to both casual and serious students of Judaism's primary texts.

Back to Genesis. As Rashi notes, this first sentence in Genesis either does not indicate the order or time sequence of creation or, if it does, water came first—the earth being unformed in a sort of liquid mess. So Joyce also starts FW with water, a riverrun into the salt Dublin Bay.

After God makes light, a light not associated with the sun and moon, God separates the waters above from the waters below by means of the firmament—the dome or expanse meaning the sky. The word used for dome is literally a beaten piece of metal, a trope suggesting a future full of thunder. The waters above are the rainwaters, the fresh waters. The waters below are the salt waters, the waters of sea storms and drowning death. Most of the ancient near east people lived by rivers.

Fish

Now to the fish analogy. Joyce uses the image of the salmon throughout FW.

Christ the man-god was referred to by the sign for the fish. Fish live in water, some just in fresh and some just in salt and a few in fresh and salt. The salmon is one of the few; it starts in fresh as a par, changes into a smolt with scales and first migrates from fresh to salt water. Later as a grilse, it returns from salt water to the same stretch of fresh to spawn and die.

Now treat fresh water as life and salt water as death. The salmon are caught as they move from fresh to salt, from life to death. This is netting time for restrictive religions, when you are thinking about death. The salmon returns to fresh after salt to reproduce and die. In this phase the salmon is just like humans. They put it together in the home fresh waters. Like Christ, the salmon can return to the fresh water the second time. In this god-fish analysis we are to examine Finn's fins.

Garden Myth: The Tall Tale of Two Trees

Since FW is an endless riff on the Garden of Eden legend, let us read it again, carefully and with K as our inspiration. With K, the myth makes much more sense. TZTZ god tries to instill dependency with blessings and fear with curses. Eve strives for more possibilities with a god-like selfhood and independence as Adam stands by passively like a voyeur. The original sin for Joyce is Adam's passivity, his dependence.

In K there are two Gardens, the higher and the lower. The higher Garden is the place of Divine Nuptials from which the river of souls waters "offspring" produced in sanctified love pursuant to the Mystery of Sex. This is the river that comes from Eden into the Garden. In the ALP chapter, Joyce compares its sound to the sound of the mother's heart in the amniotic waters. During the action in the Garden myth, this river is quiet; it delivers no good souls. Like Joyce's river of repetition, it remains empty of new possibilities.

Sex plays an important role in the myth, especially in the K interpretation. The effect of sexual intercourse under the wrong circumstances [with the serpent] is registered as a prime example of a curse. As in human experience, the sexual interest creates independence from parents.

Note that Adam and Eve do not have sex in the Garden. According to K tradition, the serpent has sex with Eve after she eats from the Tree of Knowledge as Adam stands passively by, perhaps as a voyeur watching the serpent hump Eve. The serpent's scales would indicate lack of circumcision. This is bad sex and Cain is the result. This is union with lust and uninitiated excitement. Think of Eve as a 12 year old. In K's dramatic idiom, the serpent fills her sex organ with "defilement."

After Adam eats from the Tree of Knowledge too, the serpent also has sex with Adam and fills him with defilement as well. Presumably, the serpent sex with Adam was same sex, back to belly. Adam is first cuckolded and then sodomized. What a start for males! In order to emphasize this aspect, K has Samuel the angel of death ride the serpent [which will sponsor horse races in FW]. The serpent is Samuel's prepuce, the skin removed in circumcision. Samuel is an adverse angel, those angels known as impure, uncircumcised, wicked and crafty. Samuel is, of course, an aspect of TZTZ god and TZTZ creation. Samuel is already there.

Maimonides thought circumcision was an appropriate symbol of sanctity since it reduced the pleasures of sex by reducing the amount of time the male would require for ejaculation. This would relate circumcision to the right attitude about sex. Another way of making the same point is that sexual intercourse is such a potent force in creating relationships, it can even forge relationships albeit temporary with what are obviously bad partners. This potency is part of its heritage in the Holy Spirit.

Good sex between Adam and Eve had to wait for 130 years, and according to K the wait was worth it because the Sacred Mystery of Sex resulted in the procreation of Seth while the heavenly river of souls produced for him a special soul of virtue. Abstinence makes the heart grow fonder.

ES's TZTZ creation occurred before and is not registered in Genesis except for the first allusion to light, as in "let there be light." As Genesis makes clear in the later creation of the sun, the moon and the stars, this first light is light without source. This first light, never again mentioned, is in reference to the primordial light of ES that merges everything:

> At the beginning of the Creation of heaven and earth when the earth was without form and void and there was darkness, God said, "Let there be light."

Notice that the first sentence of Genesis as so interpreted does not say that this god created heaven and earth. Just that this god was there at the beginning and said let there be... Produced along with TZTZ creation by ES, the TZTZ god takes over from there and works on what ES produced, which was without form, void and dark.

So what is the first thing TZTZ god creates—why light of course, just like big daddy ES [this is my own gloss not K]. This is not the big ES light being created because ES light was already there in merged solution with everything else besides TZTZ creation in the hole. TZTZ god makes a baby finite version of the ur-unity light of ES, of big daddy light. TZTZ god wants to emulate the big god. This finite baby light version does not annihilate everything it touches and transcend separation. All this light does is separate night and day. Eventually the respect-hungry TZTZ god will also claim that he made all of creation. TZTZ god is the big forger, pretending to be something he isn't—a creator.

The opening of the Garden myth is connected to the prior creation material (creation over six days) by the storybook-type line "Such is the story of heaven and earth when they were created." As the curtain rises, TZTZ god is there. It takes over in the hole made by ES, the "hole affair." Note the dream aspects of the myth, unexplained events and lack of causation.

But before we get started, remember what happened before the Garden. Satan and other rebellious angels fell from grace in heaven as they tried unsuccessfully to take over heaven from god, an unsuccessful rebellion of the juniors against the alpha. They were jealous that god's son was promoted to the position of Messiah. The creation of humans was in some sense to replace the lost angels.

Phases I and II

In the first two phases of the myth, timelessness and integral wholeness prevail. Humanity has no consciousness separate from TZTZ god. In this TZTZ-based condition, humanity obeys the rules. Humankind has limited possibilities and is not afraid of death. Mankind is merged with TZTZ god in the ultimate dependency. The blessings of paradise produce dependency.

Phase I

In the first of four phases, TZTZ god is introduced. I use the pronouns Him, Him/Her and It indiscriminately to refer to god. God is referred to as *YHWH Elohim* (pronounced something like Ya **whha** Ee low **heem**) for most of the myth.

This Hebrew title *YHWH Elohim* is usually translated in English as YHWH God. This is the only time in Genesis that this dual name is used. Prior to this point, that is for the primordial acts of creation over six days, the name *Elohim* has been used. After this point in Genesis, either but not both are used.

Yahweh is in Hebrew a verb form of *haya*, which means the state of being or existence. The verb form suggests an active and dynamic immortal state of being that is always present. It can be translated as any or all of the following: "I am always with you"; "He who is"; and "I will be that I will be." Note that these names seem to proceed from a need to claim importance.

Elohim can mean either the plural form of god as in two gods or the singular godhead. As the feminine counterpart, it suggests the power manifested from whatever source in creation of our time-space continuum. The essential characteristic of that continuum is plurality—differentiation into things separated in time and space and as to living beings separation into male and female and subjugation to birth and death—becoming, being and dying.

The two special trees in the Garden symbolize the two gods ES and TZTZ. The Tree of Life represents ES the immortal presence of potentially unlimited life. The Tree of Knowledge of good and bad represents TZTZ god, the source of life restriction and creator of differentiation and being and dying in the finite TZTZ creation. Since this TZTZ god changes as humans change and with complete Tikkun will merge back into ES, it is subject to a kind of mortality. Just like humans. This is why the location of the Tree of Knowledge with reference to the Tree of Life is important.

At first the earth is barren of life because of the lack of fresh water rain and the lack of humankind to till the soil. Mist from an autonomous subterranean fresh water source [apparently an underground river] rises up to irrigate indiscriminately the entire arable surface of the earth. This is fresh water. Since this is autonomous, this spring must be residual ES, not a recent TZTZ creation.

TZTZ god is alone and apparently feels a lack. It also needs to manifest, just like ES. So without explanation as to why, TZTZ god creates humankind from the dirt or dust. The myth still refers to dirt or dust and not mud even though it must be wet because of the mist. The dirt is red clay and the act of creation is in the sense of "shaped," as a potter without a wheel or a child making mud pies according to childish whim. A critical ingredient in the Garden myth, mud plays an important symbolic role in FW. The killing fields at the Battle of Waterloo feature mud.

The point of using dirt for creation of the human is that something more substantial was not used. And dirt remains dirt through the centuries. The usual resting place for a dead human is a hole in the dirt, an echo of the TZTZ creation in a void.

Blowing life into the mud, TZTZ god creates a "living being." God instructs this being to till the soil. Note that right away TZTZ god gives instructions rather than allowing the new being to experiment with various possibilities and independently come up with something on its own. This mandatory agricultural training program seems to anticipate the expulsion from the Garden because tilling the soil is education in survival skills. The living being learns to remove the weeds from around the trees. Weed 101.

The important relationship of humankind to and dependency on the earth are indicated poetically by the similarity of the sound of the Hebrew words—*adam* for human (pronounced a **damm**) and *adama* for the soil (pronounced a damm **a**). *Adam* means humankind, and at this point is not the name of one male.

TZTZ god makes a special garden in a larger area named Eden. The garden is in the eastern part of Eden. The point here is that the parsimonious TZTZ god didn't make the whole planet into a paradise, just a little garden big enough for two people, a serpent, a few other animals and some trees. Nor are we told why TZTZ god makes a garden.

Rather than asking the new creature what it wants, God decides to place humankind in the garden. The garden has a wall around it— to keep creatures out rather than in. It has at least one entrance, at the eastern end. This entrance is always open as a physical matter. It may be blocked by an angel but the entrance itself is always open. [There is some hope]. When humankind is kicked out of the Garden, they are kicked out even further east, east of Eden. They are kicked out into the prime TZTZ creation, the land of survival and death, in FW the "weedworld" from which they make graffiti on the exterior of the walls keeping them out.

The Garden serves to satisfy humankind's basic needs but also to limit humankind's activities. Humankind doesn't try to get out. TZTZ god's interest seems to be paternal but exclusive, didactic and possessive. No intellectual development activities in Eden. No opera or Learning Company. Other than Weed 101, this god doesn't teach class. Individual development is not encouraged. Human possibilities remain at a low ebb.

Trees are important in the Garden. They are the only food source. No Irish potatoes in the Garden. God makes many trees grow in order to feed vegetarian humankind. And there are two special trees in the garden—the Tree of Life that is in the center or "midst" of the garden and the Tree of Knowledge of good and bad that is somewhere in the garden. Notice the unusual presentation concerning the location of the knowledge tree:

> YHWH God planted a Garden in Eden, in the east,
> And placed there the man [human] whom He had formed.
> And from the earth YHWH God caused every tree to grow,
> Desirable to see and good to eat,
> And the tree of life in the centre ["midst"] of the Garden
> And the tree of the knowledge of good and bad. [Wolde version]

The location of the knowledge tree is not specified. It just floats there at the end of the clause in ambiguous relation to the location of the life tree and the other trees. This presentation suggests that it is not secured to and can move away from the Tree of Life under some circumstances. In K, it is necessary for both trees to be together in order to achieve Tikkun. This initial loose connection of the trees is full of danger.

The kind of knowledge involved in the tree of knowledge, from the root *yada*, has the connotation of intimate personal possession, of individual subjectivity. Each person acquires the knowledge personally. The knowledge is of good and bad, not just good and evil. The original Hebrew apparently is not limited to moral implication. It can also be about theoretical and practical knowledge, discrimination or discernment in general and how to accomplish objectives. Knowledge of what is good in order to conceive a child would be one such subject.

Good and evil would be one subset of good and bad, and in the spiritual world the most important subset. Of course, the most fundamental way of gaining knowledge of good and evil would be to do both yourself. Since this knowledge is described as god-like, the suggestion is made that TZTZ god does both good and evil.

Moreover, note that the knowledge is framed as binary opposites, good and bad. Opposites and discrimination are the prime ingredients of TZTZ creation. And the main point is that with such knowledge human possibilities can be increased, at least in the TZTZ world.

Another aspect of the Tree of Knowledge is that for Vico, the phrase "knowledge of good and evil" refers to divination, that is anticipation of what god will do. Vico quotes Homer as using the phrase in this sense [par 364]. Vico concludes that this practice divination was prohibited to the Hebrews and that this prohibition was the foundation stone for their religion.

The emphasis concerning the trees is sensual; they are described as desirable to see and good to eat. This is apparently what the human creature would notice. At this point, desire is related only to eating, or biological needs. The human creature doesn't experiment with grafting.

For Pirke Eliezer, the trees had a very concrete meaning:

> "BUT of the fruit of the tree which is in the midst of the garden" (Gen. iii. 3). It was taught in a Baraitha, Rabbi Ze'era said: "Of the fruit of the tree"—here "tree" only means man, who is compared to the tree, as it is said, "For man is the *tree* of the field" (Deut. xx. 19). "Which is in the midst of the garden"—"in the midst of the

garden" is here merely an euphemism. "Which is in the midst of the garden"—for "garden" means here merely woman, who is compared to a garden, as it is said, "A garden shut up is my sister, a bride" (Cant. iv.12). Just as with this garden whatever is sown therein, it produces and brings forth, so (with) this woman, what seed she receives, she conceives and bears through sexual intercourse. (Sammael) riding on the serpent came to her, and she conceived; afterwards Adam came to her, and she conceived Abel, as it is said, "And Adam knew Eve his wife" (Gen. iv. 1). What is the meaning of "knew"? (He knew) that she had conceived. And she saw his likeness that it was not of the earthly beings, but of the heavenly beings, and she prophesied and said: "I have gotten a man with the Lord." (*ibid.*)

My take is that this sexual aspect of the trees is gloss or overtone at this point, suggesting and setting up what is to come. Note that in this interpretation Cain is the son of Eve and the "Lord." This father "Lord" is either TZTZ god or the serpent. Take your pick. The point may be that there is no difference.

The all-important fresh water comes into the Garden as one river from outside in Eden. It is underground. This is the river of souls. Then this river branches either inside or downstream from the Garden into four rivers, which are named. This is TZTZ in action, separating and discriminating. The Hebrew text provides that the one source river is separated (passive) and becomes four "heads." This is fresh water from ES, the water of life. In the Garden, it is unlimited.

At this point in the myth, humankind is at an elemental level. Adam/Eve is one creature. It contains both female and male in one body. It was made in the image of TZTZ god, and the question is to what extent are the activities in the Garden to be attributed to this god similarity. Even though Eve is not named at this point and Eve is not the name she eventually gets, I call the creature Adam/Eve to emphasize its combined or bisexual condition. The sexual aspect of TZTZ separation has not yet taken place.

The human creature is hermaphroditic. It presumably could propagate children by itself, as many plants, simple organisms and even some reptiles still do today. As a result, sexual interest would not arise, only some form of timely and narcissistic autoeroticism. Any offspring would be perfect clones from asexual reproduction or parthenogenesis. This is one form of immortality, that is "me forever." As indicated below, this is one interpretation of what it means to have access to the Tree of Life but not to eat thereof. At this point Adam/Eve has that access.

The creation of the unified creature is particularly poignant in view of the Jewish Legends of Lillith, the pre-unified human that TZTZ god created first and just female and then banished because she was too independent, would not accept the missionary position. You can view this background as involving no male just TZTZ god or another Adam just male. In any event, the unified creature creation is humorous after such an unsuccessful start. No need to ask permission.

The Garden contains plants that are good to look at and eat. No meat in the Garden. By implication, we learn that at this point the humankind creature is not interested in the fruit from the two special trees, the knowledge or the life tree.

Now comes the rub, or we should say the first of the rubs:

> And YHWH God commanded the human, saying,
> "Of every tree of the Garden eating you shall eat;
> but as for the tree of knowledge of good and bad,
> you must not eat of it;
> for on the day you eat of it, dying you shall die."

This TZTZ god acts like a human parent. This is a command—don't eat from this tree. TZTZ god doesn't say if you eat you shall surely die but it is up to you. The Big Boss issues a command. In this dream-like myth, TZTZ god doesn't have to indicate which tree is the knowledge tree.

The command begins the separation of the human creature from God as an apparently inevitable aspect of the TZTZ function. The separation begins before the human does anything "wrong." Adam/Eve is still merged in and **trusts** god. Adam/Eve does not **fear** god; there have been no curses yet. It doesn't worry about dying. Adam/Eve doesn't know for sure either way if it is immortal but doesn't care. It has god and that is all that matters. It doesn't know about or feel the need to eat from the Tree of Life. In short, it doesn't strive for more. It is dependent. In other words, the don't eat prohibition and penalty are not necessary. This is a written law that is not necessary because of the prevailing spirit, the difference in K between the spirit or oral law and the written law.

Adam/Eve must already have free will at this point. The don't eat rule assumes that humankind has free will. Otherwise, no warning would be necessary, except to prevent accidental eating. Contrary to many Sunday school interpretations, free will does not come with the serpent. It is already there before the serpent comes on the scene. Since there is no reason given for the command, the reason must be the natural one—TZTZ god doesn't want Adam/Eve to acquire knowledge or, if it does, to be mortal. In other words, TZTZ wants the creature to be dumb or mortal. What TZTZ god gets is a creature that is smart and mortal.

In K analysis, Adam/Eve is at this point immortal just because it is without doubt as to its immortality. Talk about mind over matter! In any event, it is clear just from the story line that Adam/Eve does not fear death at this point, and it must be because Adam/Eve is merged in god.

Notice that the penalty threat "dying you shall die," which is usually translated "you shall surely die," assumes that Adam/Eve would fear death. Otherwise the threat would not work to guard the tree. This is apparently because TZTZ god does fear death, does fear being merged back into ES. So TZTZ god fears death but at this point apparently the unified human doesn't. **Most interesting**. The unified human can at this point make perfect clones of itself. Subsequently this fear of death attitude of TZTZ god will be assumed by the humans. What is above will be below, in just a little while. TZTZ god is to make the humans fearful of death after separation when perfect copies are no longer guaranteed. The birth of Cain starts a mixing of the genes.

The don't eat rule is clearly designed to prevent development in the human since it refers to the tree of knowledge. Knowledge is, we learn later, one of two steps necessary to become fully god-like with greater possibilities. It is the one step necessary to become like TZTZ god. Two steps, eating from both trees, are necessary to become like ES god.

If Adam and Eve took both steps, that is ate from both trees, and became angels with knowledge of good and bad as well as immortal, they would become adjuncts of god. The question is which god? According to the alternative reading of translators Rosenbaum and Silbermann in the 1929 version of the Pentateuch and Rashi's Commentary, the TZTZ god says they would "become like the being who is One, unique among us." Unique among the gods who are speaking, the "us," would be ES god. If Adam and Eve were to become like ES, that would allow them to escape the control of TZTZ god. But TZTZ doesn't want that; it wants to keep them in his horde.

Rashi interprets the Tree of Knowledge in the context of creation. He believed that in order to play its part in the TZTZ world, the TZTZ god himself ate of the Tree of Knowledge, which gave TZTZ god the power to create and destroy, a power repeated in the human instincts of Eros and destruction. Whether the TZTZ god ate of the Tree of Life as well is the big question Rashi left unanswered.

Note there is no don't eat rule about the Tree of Life. In K, evil issues when the Tree of Knowledge is separated from the Tree of Life. So in K the potential for evil is already present in TZTZ creation in the separate treatment of the two trees. You can eat one without eating the other. Moreover, the knowledge tree does not have a fixed address in the Garden.

The exact type of fruit of the knowledge tree is never specified, as an apple, fig, grape or some other fruit. In K it is the grape with its potential for intoxication. The **fruit** of the knowledge tree naturally means the inevitable **result** of acquiring the knowledge, not the knowledge itself. Such fruit would include human children.

Knowing good and evil means in its most intense expression to do good and evil knowing it to be such. This is indirectly said to be godlike, for the TZTZ god is to knowingly do good and evil to humans. The curses are coming up.

Phase II

The second phase involves the physical separation of a female from the side of the creature. This separation by reduction makes the original bisexual creature into a male. This phase introduces the friction of opposites and the need for nurturing human relationships. This is yet another step in progressive separation and discrimination made by the TZTZ force during the course of the myth. At this point the relationships are still all good and simple.

With this step perfect copies in offspring can no longer be guaranteed. This is to be proved in spades as Cain is fathered by the serpent. This could not have happened to the combined Adam/Eve creature.

First, however, before the split off, God makes from the same soil the animals "of the field" and the human creature names them. This indicates the acquisition of language skills and the use of symbols. Language is associated with the development of consciousness and sense of self (Macphail, *Evolution of Consciousness*).

Then TZTZ god starts over. His first effort was not good enough. This god makes mistakes. For the second time He feels an unsatisfied need. He makes a change. This is another joke, perhaps based in the archaic traditions in K that god made several trial worlds [known as the Edomite Kings] before this one. This is allowed in dream-like myths.

TZTZ god decides that it is not good for humankind to be alone and that humankind needs a "helper corresponding to him." (The male "Him" is used rather than the neuter "it" because a Hebrew noun is either masculine or feminine never neuter.) Note that another combined bisexual creature could just as well satisfy these helper needs and be even more of a soul mate. TZTZ god doesn't seem to like unified creatures, particularly one able to make exact copies of itself and with no fear of death.

So with a penchant for separation and discrimination TZTZ god causes the separation of the one primeval humankind creature into two separate parts, or into two "heads," now male and female. This prepares the way for the development of human fear of death because two are necessary for procreation, Eve can procreate with other than Adam, and parthenogenesis of exact copies will no longer be guaranteed.

Each of the separate beings becomes a relational being, not a unified being. This is part of the separation and limitation involved in TZTZ creation. Procreation must now come from sexual intercourse, the ultimate relationship that temporarily suspends physical separation.

This is a big change. Each separated being would carry in his or her essential nature the "collective" memory of being joined together like Siamese twins. While not so described, this is the **first curse**. Because now you need to get along together in order to transcend death. Parthenogenesis is no longer possible. And Adam and Eve don't get along all that well, even in the Garden.

The separation sounds like a hospital operation. God puts the creature in a deep sleep (anesthetic foreshadowing love), and the female is sawed off from the creature's rib or "side." This is an acceptable explanation of what happened in a dream-like myth. Apparently the male and female aspects were side by side in Adam/Eve. The creature becomes male as the female creation is separated off. God does not breathe into her nostrils. She takes her life from the original creature Adam/Eve in whom God had already breathed life.

Notice that male and female are from the same DNA. She is a kind of clone, a twin sister. Their children would be clones of each of them. But remember that the serpent fathers Cain with Eve and

Cain is to be in the gene pool. So the ability **always** to make perfect copies has been lost.

The male likes what he sees:

> And He brought her to man. [from the beginning she is, but not just, an object of appearance]
> Then the man said,
> This one at last [literally "this time"], is bone of my bones and flesh of my flesh;
> This one will be called woman, for she is taken from man.

These lines change from prose to poetry; in the original the last two lines are a two-line strophe. The poetry registers the man's reaction to the woman. You could say that he sings his pleasure. The male's use of "at last" indicates that the creature or the male had been waiting for this development for some time, perhaps in connection with the creation of the other animals with mates or since his first wife Lillith left [mentioned in the Legends but not the Hebrew Scriptures]. Lillith must have been different, not bone of his bone and flesh of his flesh, not of the same DNA. Adam and Lillith didn't have children, unless the serpent is one. She was too independent for TZTZ god, having refused the missionary position in sexual intercourse.

The male now takes his identity as male in relation to her as female and vice versa. In Hebrew they are at this point called *ish* and *issha*, now man and woman and no longer *adam*. Each name carries the Hebrew root for fire, an inclusion that poetically portends desire. This would be the natural result of the friction of opposites. Commentators have YHWH God say that absent one of His vowels [H] in their names, they are left with just the root for fire.

The narrator intervenes didactically at this point in the story. This is the only such intervention in the myth. The narrator intervenes to explain that the original source of woman as part of combined humankind is the reason man parts from his parents and clings to his wife in one flesh:

> Hence a man will leave his father and mother,
> and will cling to his wife, and they will become one flesh.

By this reference, the narrator explicitly relates the story of the Garden to all humankind. The narrator is telling us that on the physical level, man and woman join in sexual intercourse to produce the same results that the original, unified creature could produce by itself. This makes sexual relations an imperfect avenue to the original unity. It is also the energy for independence from parents.

As far as sex is concerned:

> The two of them were nude, the man and his wife,
> Yet they felt no shame.

From our modern frame of reference, they are innocent like children, without knowledge of sex. Even though they have just experienced a Siamese twin type separation, they do not feel strange. They are separated physically but not psychologically. They are half of what they used to be, without clothes that would hide their new physical condition, but they are not ashamed. Their exposure is not indecent. They are not ashamed of their condition **because they are not separate emotionally or spiritually from each other or God**. They do not experience personal consciousness or subjectivity. They do not have "privates." They are nude not naked. Those changes come only with the fruit of the Tree of Knowledge. While reproduction must now be sexual, the two recently separated creatures don't know that yet. That knowledge is in the fruit of the Tree of Knowledge, or if you like the Tree of Death.

They are still totally dependent on TZTZ god. The condition is that of the primal horde. He is their larger reality. They are centered in Him. Child-like, they have only comfort and no anxiety since their Big Leader is in charge. Their possibilities are limited and to be governed by being merged with TZTZ god. They draw their strength and possibilities from within this dependency condition. Mortality is still not an issue; in their innocence and since they have no consciousness of themselves as separate, they reside in timelessness. They do not fear death. This is indicated poetically by their continuing lack of interest in the Tree of Life. They still **trust and do not fear** TZTZ god. They still do not seek more possibilities.

The male and the female are on the most equal of terms. They have free will but live in innocence. They could have sex at this point, but do not conceive a child. I believe any sexual arrangement would be estrus based (male and female activated only when female is in heat) rather than desire based (male and female activated all the time). That is because personal sexual desires are related to a sense of personal consciousness and individual separateness.

Phases III and IV

The third and fourth phases involve the serpent and the confrontation with God. The "disobedience" occurs as the woman develops personal consciousness as a separate being and strives to be an independent and more powerful individual, to become god-like with access to more possibilities and thereby compete with TZTZ god. As a result of this separation and increased knowledge, humankind begins to fear god.

Phase III

In this phase, the humans are no longer referred to as *is* and *issha*, woman and man, but as *ha-issa* and *isah*, or the woman and her husband. These names emphasize the separate identity of the woman and the relational identity of the man. This is a gender joke in favor of women. Fire is still present in the name.

The serpent is not introduced; it is just there all of a sudden:

> Now the serpent was the most shrewd
> Of all the animals of the field YHWH God had made.
> He said to the woman, "Even though God said: You are not to eat from any of the trees in the garden. . . " [the serpent's pregnant pause]

In the foregoing, the serpent is an animal of the field. Rosenbaum and Silbermann translate the same first line differently: "Now the serpent was more subtle than any animal of the field which the Eternal God had made." This translation leaves room for the serpent to be the child of Lillith left behind and not an animal of the field that God made. In any event, TZTZ god produces the serpent as part of his discrimination activities. In K the serpent is interdependent with TZTZ god.

In any event, all of a sudden the serpent is standing next to the woman. The text doesn't describe its approach or explain how it got there. This abrupt presentation is another illustration of the dream-like presentation.

The serpent is erect, must have feet and can talk, the first talking head. It is as tall as a camel. This serpent is highly unusual and is shrewd, more shrewd than the humans. This suggests the serpent has experienced access to greater possibilities than the humans. The serpent knows what will happen when she does eat from the Tree of

Knowledge, that her eyes will be opened to greater knowledge and she will not die, at least not right away—that TZTZ god spoke not in good faith or lied about death. And her teeth will be set on edge, which must be some kind of fear. The serpent is comfortable in the garden, not a stranger.

Clearly the serpent has already eaten from the Tree of Knowledge. I think this one serpent is different from all other animals and even all other serpents. This is the best of show. The serpent is an aspect of TZTZ god, perhaps god's son.

As the most shrewd of the animals, the serpent would consider the developing humans as potential competitors for the top spot. If so, we have the survival instinct in operation. And the serpent is deceptive, a forger as far as the truth is concerned. Just like TZTZ god.

The serpent seems impatient, impulsive and dissatisfied. He is talking to ha-issah who is as naked "as a jail bird." Perhaps the serpent is sexually aroused by her presence, suggested by his unusual erect condition. As I read the myth, sexual arousal would require knowledge from the tree. So the aroused serpent wants her to eat too so "they can get it on."

No preliminary discussion about the weather. The serpent dives right in. The alpha-like serpent takes command of the conversation with a provocative lead-in, making a statement but in effect asking a curious question. The question the serpent in effect asks is this—are you prevented from eating from *all* the trees? Perhaps this is the serpent's way of saying you look svelte.

To the serpent's curious statement/question, the woman dutifully repeats the rule she knows—that they the humans are free to eat of any of the trees except the one in the middle ("midst") and repeats the death threat. She does not specifically identify the knowledge tree, referring to it only as the one in the middle. Remember that the tree of life was the only one described as being in the middle. Apparently her attitude fixes the knowledge tree in the center.

Then the serpent's come-on:

> The serpent said to the woman,
> "You are not going to die, [literally "Die, you will not die."]
> for God knows that as soon as you eat of it
> your eyes will be opened
> and you will be like God, knowing good and bad."

The serpent uses the lesser title for God. This is the only time God is referred to as just *Elohim*. She follows this usage but does not seem to notice this very important signal. The usage of just *Elohim* signals a shift—that by comparison with the greater *YHWH Elohim*, the humans are, with this fruit, to become only like the lesser TZTZ god, being able to create life but subject to death.

The serpent's come-on creates desire in the woman to have greater insight and be god-like. Before the human creature within dependency had desire only for seeing and eating. But now, jump started by the serpent, the human woman is not satisfied with pure dependency. Her desire starts with seeing the knowledge tree, as if she hadn't noticed it before. She wakes up as an individual. Then the Hollywood-like motivational analysis:

> The woman saw that the tree was good to eat of and a delight
> To the eyes, and that the tree was desirable to get insight,
> And she took of its fruit and ate.

The woman's action is personal and independent. The description suggests she always had this potential. The woman makes an individual personal decision. She doesn't ask her mate what to do. Adam's presence or absence is not noted, which emphasizes the personal aspect of her decision. I think Issah is standing by her side all this time and hears all. What we do know that Adam doesn't do anything; he remains passive.

Ha-issah doesn't ask TZTZ god for a waiver of the rule. There is no sacred precedent for this action; indeed it violates the only announced rule, which she has happily followed up to this point. She acts independently and based on her own desire. She becomes manifest as an individual through desire. She wants to manifest into greater possibilities. Echoing earlier instances of God's sense of lack, she feels dissatisfied, that something is missing. There must be more to life than this. She wants to be different and better than she is, that is different from the dependent creature she had been. In the very first wave of feminism, mere "Help meet" becomes the prime mover.

The threat of death does not deter her action. In seeking god-like knowledge, she is not afraid of death. From the interpretation point of view, this is the most salient aspect of the myth and any convincing explanation must deal with it. The traditional Original Sin disobedience interpretation does not.

Having eaten, her eyes are opened. She knows the serpent was right. She is now to know good and bad personally. In fact she knows bad because she has done bad. Knowing these things, she has developed personal consciousness. Her personal and subjective desire is the signal that she has a sense of self separate from all else, the TZTZ attitude.

While she has access to greater possibilities, there are some adverse side effects from her new knowledge. She now feels separate from God and her husband. Her separate self is now capable of selfishness. She is no longer innocent in the sense that she is now capable of evil, knowledge that her selfish actions are causing harm. She has in fact done evil, evil as defined by god. She has created death. This is part of being god-like, creating evil. Now knowing what god can do, evil as well as good, she is afraid of god. Her teeth are set on edge. Fear sets in as the primal aspect of the relationship with god.

The Legends of the Jews are clear on the point that as part of her personal desire the woman has sex with the serpent. There are many hints to the same effect in the Hebrew Scriptures version. In the text, this possibility is communicated poetically through sound association in Hebrew. The words for naked and shrewd (the serpent is described as the most shrewd of the animals) sound the same, *arummim* for naked and *arum* for shrewd. Since the plural form of shrewd is also *arummim,* the two concepts are linked through subtle suggestion. Shrewd suggests knowing and knowing a woman in Hebrew Scriptures generally meant sexual knowing. Nakedness was apparently a near guarantee of sex in this ancient Hebrew culture. The sins of sex are referred to as the sins of nakedness. As with the primal horde and the Oedipal complex, disobedience in the Garden of Eden and the pursuit of independence have sexual overtones.

Again, if the serpent is the child of Lillith and Adam, we have the junior male on the make for an incestuous union with a woman whose genes are 50% identical with his own, the same percentage as any son and mother. If the serpent is the child of Lillith and TZTZ god, we presumably have no matching genes because immaterial god can't have DNA.

Sexual desire is now personal and subjective, not estrus or asexually based to serve only the species. Even the arrival of pregnancy does not stop it. It now serves selfish personal pleasure and, like the snake's skin, satisfies only short term.

It is important to note that TZTZ god lets all of this happen and does not intervene. It seems as if TZTZ god wants all this to happen. TZTZ god certainly wants humankind to fear death, just like TZTZ god does. Misery loves company.

The woman becomes pregnant with a child to be named Cain [in Hebrew *Kayin* which means smith as in blacksmith] and in the process of being in heat learns about human procreation. She learns most importantly that additional humans are not to be produced by God. They are to be produced exclusively by human sexual intercourse, as part of the separation process started by the TZTZ force. She now has the personal desire for sex and the knowledge of reproduction. She has the tools for existence without any god.

In a totally passive and apparently impotent role, "her husband" follows her into this condition:

> She also gave some to her husband with her and he ate.

No discussion. No indication of his motivation. He is just there "with her" and eats. He repeats her act. He follows behind her. Adam doesn't consider the rule either. Rashi believes that the now separate and possessive Eve wanted to make Adam mortal so he would not take another wife after she died—since she was now mortal and he wasn't until he ate.

In the Jewish Legends, the serpent also defiles Adam, buggers the passive Adam.

The humans' actions in the Garden are characteristic of the juniors in the primal horde and Oedipal complex; they disobey their parental figure in an effort to become like Him/Her, obtain His/Her power, to supplant Him/Her. They are challenging the Senior Male. As part of their effort to be god-like, they are moving away from dependency.

As part of their increased awareness of separateness and discrimination in the TZTZ creation, the woman and her husband realize their nakedness. They are now naked not nude. They consider their personal exposure indecent. This realization comes from looking at each other—they don't have full-length mirrors. Their reaction mimics the TZTZ creation itself, the first indecent exposure. In the Legends, they lose the sacred covering over their skin, a covering that was like fingernail material.

In response, they make loincloths (literally "aprons") of fig leaves. This is another joke—fig leave aprons would be very ticklish, producing the big itch. They feel exposed and cover. Like ES in the TZTZ creation, their garment covers something that is missing. The word "privates" carries the separate and subjective aspect of this reaction. They are hiding and protecting their genitals, those tools that are not self-sufficient for the job and need the other. Each is now separate and no longer complete physically or spiritually.

Most importantly, they now fear and distrust TZTZ god, and for good reason. TZTZ god administers death. As separate individuals, they now fear death. Feeling frightened and separated, the woman and her husband try to hide from God in the trees. They hide because knowing what TZTZ god can do, they are afraid of him.

In the evening, the breezy and cool part of the day, TZTZ god takes His usual walk around in the Garden, a very human-like activity. He finds them hiding from Him in the bushes and determines what happened. God asks them who told them of their nakedness. The text suggests that god didn't already know, is not omniscient. We are just about to learn that TZTZ god is not benevolent either. They don't answer but of course we know they told themselves with their new knowledge. TZTZ god reacts forcefully and negatively, you could even say cruelly.

Phase IV

The fourth phase is framed as the "penalty" phase. Merger with god is replaced by angry separation bridged only by an uncertain covenant. Certainty, splendor and unity have been lost. Fear governs the relationship with god. You can't trust this god without a covenant. And as Joyce is to note, you can't trust this god even with a covenant. The rainbow promised to Noah after the flood that even if humans were to sin in the future, god would not do harm in the world. The "bow in the clouds" was to be visible only if men were sinning. However, this covenant did not hold up. Harm was done on a grand scale again and again.

Separation increases, this time between the man and the woman and between the woman and the serpent. As TZTZ god investigates by asking questions, the woman and the man act independently, not as a team. Their human relationship suffers because their relationship with god has suffered. The man refers to the woman not as his wife but "as the woman you gave me," as if all this were God's fault. Which of course it is if god is the omnipotent Catholic god, but not if god is the TZTZ god "growing" with the humans. For the first time, the man refers to himself as "I" (in verse 3.10—four times in one sentence). The junior male begins to assert his independence with that famous barbell letter "I".

God questions the humans but not the serpent, even though the serpent can talk. The man blames the woman. The woman blames the serpent. Mankind does not readily accept the burden of freedom.

They play the blame game. After he blames her and she blames the
serpent, God comes down on the serpent:

> Because you did this, you are the most cursed of all the cattle
> And of all the animals of the field.
> On your belly you will crawl
> And dirt you will eat all the days of your life.
> I will put enmity between you and the woman,
> And between thy seed and her seed;
> They shall strike at thy head,
> And you will strike at their heel.

Interestingly, the serpent is not sentenced to death or knowledge
of death. Formerly erect, the serpent is now cursed and sentenced to
life in the prone position eating dirt. The serpent experiences a "fall"
to the prone position. In the Legends, his feet are cut off. That fall
promises less possibilities, less growth in awareness and loss of a
sense of balance. This will reverse the effect of eating from the
knowledge tree. The serpent even falls from its preeminent position
among the animals. By contrast, the humans remain upright, which
requires balance and promises further brain development in connection with manipulation of the arms and hands.

God creates enmity between the serpent and its seed and the
woman and her seed (male and female—this excludes only Adam).
This penalty of enmity suggests a prior attraction that could have
produced her pregnancy with Cain. Destined to become a different
species, the serpent will no longer have positive relations and mix
genes with human females. The woman and her seed are to strike at
the serpent's head, that shrewdest of heads. It is to strike at their
heels. In short, the humans leave the serpent in the dust.

And on the woman:

> I will greatly multiply the suffering of your pregnancy;
> in pain you will bear children
> For your husband will be your desire,
> And he will rule over you.

And on the man:

> [because you listened to your wife and not to me]
> Cursed will be the earth because of you;
> By toil you will eat of it, all days of your life.
> Thorns and thistles it will sprout for you.

The punishment includes more painful childbirth, painful hard work and poor crops with thorns and thistles—the "weedworld" that reinforces the fear of not surviving. These penalties are designed to produce fear, fear that god will deny children and ruin the harvests. This god can hurt us so we must placate this god. This exchange is mirrored in the human-to-human realm in tribute and in respect.

The process post-Garden involves repetition, repetition of childbirth to continue the species and repetition of food gathering as a necessity of individual survival. The energy and time necessary for these activities are to limit what humans can accomplish, what humans can become. This seems to be a continuation of the same motivation of god that was expressed by god's actions in the garden.

The two humans live on as Adam and Eve for several hundred years, so immediate death is not the penalty administered for eating of the knowledge tree. A long life is necessary for fear of death to develop its full acidity. That is why whom the gods love die young. Eventual death and knowledge of certain and total death are part of the punishment selected. How each human reacts to the fear of death, that corrosive condition, is the primary issue in spiritual life. It is the inevitable psychic residue of cosmic dependence. The only question is when and under what circumstances. In pain or in your sleep. Alone or with loved ones. Filled with cancer or just old age. TZTZ god is rough.

For the woman, the suffering of her pregnancy is increased. The suffering is increased, not imposed for the first time. This suggests that she is already pregnant with Cain. The woman is also sentenced to a different relationship with her husband. Formerly the first mover, Eve is now to take a secondary role. They are now separate, **yet** he is to "rule over" her: "For your husband will be your desire [literally lust] and ['yet' in some translations] he will rule over you." He wants and needs your sex but he is still the boss. You can't use your sex to be in control. She is now to assume the missionary position, the position Lillith refused.

This penalty reflects Eve's initial disobedience of TZTZ god's rule and restricts her life possibilities to those of the inferior and subservient sex. The prime mover is reduced in rank. This is the first instance of control over female reproduction. Note that all punishments involve corruption of relationships by reducing union and increasing separation.

After the punishments are delivered, the man names his wife *Chawwa*, the mother of all living beings. Her name focuses on the major development in the Garden of Eden, that human not divine procreation is to create additional humans, an addition in self-sufficiency that results from the fear of death. The man is not named. Later on in Genesis he is named Adam, taking over without comment as a proper name the word that means humankind.

God makes from animal skins full sets of clothes (not just aprons) for both the man and *Chawwa* or *Havva* (lets just call her Eve) and then drives them out of the Garden of Eden into Eden, east of the Garden. Apparently God kills animals for this purpose. As commander in chief God orders cherubim armed with swords (spinning 360 degrees like a propeller) to guard the eastern entrance to the Garden. Cherubim apparently don't mind repetitive work or get carpal tunnel syndrome. Who knows where the western entrance is.

Now for the critical point of the myth. The reason God drives the humans out of the Garden is so the man and Eve can't eat of the second tree, the Tree of Life, and live forever and thus be like the gods. According to the alternative reading of Rosenbaum and Silvermann, the TZTZ god says that if they ate from both trees they would "become like the being who is One, unique among us." That is, they would become like ES and independent from TZTZ god.

Note importantly that violating the rule about eating from the knowledge tree did not disqualify the humans from becoming god-like. Indeed, quite to the contrary: it was the necessary first step, one of the two requirements for full god-like status. What is convention-ally described as disobedience and Original Sin is an attempt to be god-like. This produces an internal disconnect in the Sunday School version of the myth.

Note also that having satisfied the two requirements the humans would not be just god-like but "unique among the gods"; this would seem to refer to the ES god and not the TZTZ god speaking. If they ate from both trees, Adam and Eve would merge back into ES and escape the control of TZTZ god. Note that TZTZ god didn't want that to happen. If all humans developed this way, TZTZ god would have to fold up shop and merge back into ES and die.

This move to keep Adam and Eve away from the Tree of Life along with rule designed to prevent access to the Tree of Knowledge are clear indications of a desire on the part of the TZTZ powers to reduce human potential, to make humans more like TZTZ god than like ES, and in the process to continue to manifest rather than fold-ing up shop. In addition, in K the barring of return to the Garden is designed to keep more evil from leaving the Garden and entering the world, not the other way around.

103

Since this aspect of the Eden dream-like myth comes closest to the latent content, it is put at the end of the story and is not emphasized. The censor is being more careful here, since it is close to the latent content that god cursed humans.

Note what has happened on TZTZ god's watch. Humans have been parted from god, from animals and from each other in sexual and equality terms. The myth has moved from unity and merger to separation and acrimony. This is what makes TZTZ god happy.

Closing off the Garden separates mankind from God. Normal time and history begin. The clock starts ticking. Knowledge and fear of inevitable death plague humankind—the base of Joyce's *secret cause*. Only children extend the game. The implied aspect is that these penalties are to apply to all of mankind in the future, not just these two Garden felons. These curses result in fear. Moving into FW, Thunder is a reminder.

So now the question: was Eve more god-like when she played by the rules and was satisfied to be unified with god or when she broke out and sought to be more? As you can see, this is now longer a simple question. Becoming more like ES is to do just what Eve did—strive for independence and be all that you can be regardless of posted limits. Becoming more like TZTZ god is to be what Adam and Eve were initially—totally aligned with and dependent on TZTZ god respecting his posted limitations. So the answer depends on which god you are talking about. You already know Joyce's choice.

Lillith

Note what does not happen in the Eden myth—God does not sentence Lillith to death, Lillith [pronounced something like Lil leet] the purported first wife of Adam. She is not mentioned in the Eden myth but lurks in the shadows and is showcased in Jewish Legends. Here is a summary from a recent review of what she became after she was banished:

> **Lilith** is a demonic creature, both rebellious and melancholy. As the art historian Daniel Arasse has pointed out, she is the 'first Eve', created by God from the same earth as Adam. Lilith asks to be considered as Adam's equal, but her request is refused. Outraged, she pronounces the Unspeakable Name of God, and is banished to the shores of the Red Sea. She is depicted in the various Judaic traditions as a female demon who seduces men and attacks pregnant women (in the Talmud), and as a corrupted, fallen woman, the queen of the forces of the evil (in the Zohar or Kab-

balistic Book of Splendour). In the Kabbalah, Lilith has dominion over all that is impure. She is also associated with Saturn, serpents (her attribute is a snake), lead, and people afflicted with melancholy.

The first desperate housewife and divorcee, Lillith was produced by god independently like Adam [not from his rib and with different DNA]. At this time there was no Adam and Lillith was an item with TZTZ god but was too independent in her relations with him or Adam was unisexual. In either event, She reportedly refused the missionary position. You can understand how after this start, TZTZ god would want to start over with a bisexual creature.

For this independent refusal, TZTZ god turned Lillith into an evil spirit that kidnaps children [or you could say in TZTZ creation her independence is a curse]. She is the personification of the curse that is opposite of the primary blessing in the Hebrew Scriptures, namely the blessing of offspring.

Free of TZTZ god's controls, Lillith reached her full potential, a potential for evil. **Since she is immortal, she denies children, children made necessary by mortality.** She is a pure expression of the super curse—both mortality and death of children. In my interpretation the serpent was her only child.

In FW, Lillith becomes the "prankquean" who is denied hospitality at the castle and challenges its authority by stealing its children. The unspeakable name of god that she uses is Mark the Wans, meaning the god of curses since wan means gloomy and dark, unhealthy, fearful, deadly, cruel.

Sequel—The Morning After

According to the Legends, once out of the Garden Adam and Eve become smaller in size and the surrounding Eden outside the Garden grows smaller in area, a dream-like presentation of a fall. They all fall to reduced status. Experiencing their punishment, a hungry Adam and Eve look for food after their eviction from the Garden. Unsuccessful, they plan to appease God in an effort to get back to food-full paradise. This, of course, is the wrong attitude, the dependent attitude. They should be planting rather than looking for welfare. But this dependency is the attitude TZTZ god wants, all humans on his welfare.

Adam suggests that Eve atone by standing in the deepest part of the Tigris River to wash herself clean, for in this version she has had intercourse with the serpent and they now know this may mean a child. For 37 days she is to remain in the water without saying anything, perhaps the first attempt at abortion by water and silence. Adam plans to fast (as if he could find food) for 40 days, and likewise stands in the Jordan to be cleansed. The woman can't talk and the man can't eat. The ultimate punishments.

Not happy with this development of remorse, Satan appears to Eve in the form of a counterfeit angel after she has endured 18 days in the Tigris. He convinces her that God has heard her lamentations (did she talk?) and has forgiven her. Once again she rises to the bait and has sex with what she thinks is an angel. This extra-curricular interest of the angel should have raised a red flag, but Eve didn't notice. Satisfied Satan leads her back to Adam at the Jordan. Adam berates Eve for falling again, losing her good name again. But Adam doesn't throw her out. He doesn't do anything to the serpent either. Adam is really accepting, the "whatever" man.

Interpretation

We are now ready for an interpretation of the Garden of Eden myth as it relates to the primal horde form of social organization and as it has been used by Joyce in FW. It is a biological interpretation based on the change from asexual reproduction or parthenogenesis to sexual reproduction. This isn't the only fertile interpretation of this legend, but it does frame a number of the important aspects. This is my very own personal midrash, so read it with a grain of salt.

This interpretation does explain the relationship between the two special Trees and the primal horde influence. It also explains why love becomes increasingly important as offspring move away from clones to mixed, when children are no longer in the image of the father. It may also explain the striking preference for the youngest son in the Genesis legends.

As far as the question of whether Genesis was written too early contain an understanding of these matters, consider that Horapollo in the 5th Century BCE spoke of what were even then "ancient" Egyptian hieroglyphs depicting parthenogenesis or "only begotten" by the scarabaeus beetle, a beetle considered sacred by the Egyptians. Virgin births in Ancient Egyptian mythology related to animals that could generate life without male impregnation. In nature and in myth, both male and female can possess the power of parthenogenesis.

106

Greek mythology featured virgin births, such as Athena from the forehead of Zeus. She was worshipped at the Parthenon. Thus Parthenogenesis. While this ancient understanding of parthenogenesis could not at Joyce's time have been expressed at the gene level, it would have been understood in power relationship terms and the primitive drive for "more like me" or for children "in my image," as male lions do to this day when they kill the children in the "pride" of the former alpha male. By restricting the gene package of children, this drive reduces the possibilities for the offspring and thus is a product in the image of the TZTZ god.

Adam or mankind is first produced male and female in the image of TZTZ god: "So God created the man in his own image, in the image of God created he him; male and female created he them." The sense of "image" used here is now used with respect to a photograph. Rashi explains the image as: ". . . the type that was specially made for him." *Adam* is in some sense a clone of god since produced in the same image. God doesn't need a mother for this first production. This is some sort of asexual reproduction issuing from the immaterial to the material plane in the TZTZ separated creation.

As Eliezer the Great said about the creation of Eve: "in order that people may not say that there are two Deities, the Holy One, blessed be He, the only One among the celestial Beings without a mate, and this one (Adam), the only one among the terrestrial beings, without a mate." The bisexual Adam/Eve has already been commanded to be fruitful and multiply. Note that the production of Eve from the body of Adam/Eve is also asexual. Looking at Eve for the first time, Adam expresses the primitive drive: "This is this time bone of my bone and flesh of my flesh." She has the same genes, the same likeness. Their children would be clones—as Seth is to be. But not Cain and Able for they are children of Eve and the serpent. They begin the gene mix.

As for reproduction, Adam/Eve the bisexual human would either contain both female and male aspects internally or would reproduce through parthenogenesis, a process in which an egg develops without male participation, without the mixing of genes from two participants. In either case, the offspring would be a clone of Adam/Eve, would carry only his/her genes. Many species of insects, reptiles and some mammals reproduce this way. Some even use both asexual and sexual preproduction.

Now two paragraphs from Wikipedia:

An asexual population tends to be genetically static. Mutant alleles appear but remain forever associated with the particular alleles present in the rest of that genome. Even a beneficial mutation will be doomed to extinction if trapped along with genes that reduce the fitness of that population.

But with the genetic recombination provided by sex, new alleles can be shuffled into different combinations with all the other alleles available to the genome of that species. A beneficial mutation that first appears alongside harmful alleles can, with recombination, soon find itself in more fit genomes that will enable it to spread through a sexual population.

Asexual reproduction is naturally a more efficient way to reproduce. It avoids all sorts of problems and the necessity of finding a mate at just the right time. There is no natural form of Cealis. It certainly would make you feel more independent and, as Woody Allen said, you wouldn't have to look your best. On the other hand, sexual reproduction provides a mechanism (through the recombination process of meiosis) to weed out harmful mutations that arise in the population.

As you can see, asexual reproduction would provide advantages in a stabile environment but sexual reproduction has advantages when the environment is changing and putting pressure on survival—when the build up of bad mutations would be a particular disadvantage. The birth of giants from sexual contact between angels and human females in Genesis 6:1 can be read as an echo of the build up of bad genes. And going from the Garden of paradise to the cruel weedworld is one huge environmental change to increased survival pressure.

Parthenogenesis would produce a form of immortality, since the offspring would be the same as the parent, a clone of the parent. This is the most selfish gene in action. And this, I believe, is the meaning of the availability and accessibility of the Tree of Life to *Adam/Eve* and *Ish* and *Isha* before and after they have been condemned to death for eating from the Knowledge Tree. Ejection and prohibition of return to the Garden of Eden were explicitly motivated by God's desire to avoid the humans' proximity to the Tree of Life and possible accidental eating of its fruit ["lest he put forth his hand, and take also of the tree of life, and eat and live for ever."] This is a striking use of "accidental" since our two humans are now imbued with the intelligence from the Tree of Knowledge. The accidental would be a slippage back to asexual reproduction. This is possible since some species do both.

In this interpretation, you would view the serpent [parthenogenesis relatively common in reptiles] as the then highest achievement possible with parthenogenesis and the corresponding build up of unusual genes: shrewdness, standing erect on feet and speaking. In the punishments, the serpent is not cursed to die. The serpent is to remain as before, still shedding its skin and reproducing asexually. It is denied sexual relationships with humans and mixing of genes.

Adam and Eve as beings who have achieved separate consciousness and individual desire including sex drive are ready for sexual reproduction. This occurs as the environment changes dramatically, when they are kicked out of paradise, when survival becomes difficult and painful. Cain is born out of paradise, the first child of sexual reproduction. Abel is born with Cain, and then Seth is conceived and born separately much later. Cain is not a clone of Adam and Eve because the serpent and not Adam was the father. Cain is different; he kills his brother. I can't see Adam killing Eve or Eve killing Adam or either killing Cain or Abel. This is further evidence that the serpent or TZTZ god fathered Cain [and Abel] with Eve, producing a different creature not in their image.

In the Garden, the knowledge of and desire for sexual reproduction are intimately and necessarily connected with fear of death. In this case one aspect of death is the loss of the possibility of clone immortality. The genes in sexual reproduction cannot be as selfish as in asexual reproduction. As human reproduction continues away from the first parents, the children will tend toward a mixture of 50-50 inheritance from the parents and even more diluted in relation to the grandparents. In other words, the children and grandchildren will be different from and not clones of the parents. These parents die in a deeper sense than parthenogenetic parents.

This is in one sense loss of control of the future by your particular genes, your selfish genes. It also increases the need for love of children, love of them as **individuals**, since in this non-clone case the father can no longer love his child as part of loving himself. The father must now love the child for the different individual that the child is, not as a chip off the old block but as new plywood.

Now for the primal horde, the first form of human organization, a form of organization suggested by the power arrangement between god and the humans in the Garden of Eden. The primal horde among humans can be viewed as an attempt of the senior male's selfish genes to obtain maximum control of offspring in the form of near-clone children and loving them only as an expression of self-love. Love of non-clones would not be consistent with the alpha's leader role. It would be a sign of weakness.

Note the effect of the primal horde, of a father having sex with his own daughters and granddaughters. Assuming his daughter is 50-50 in genes from this father and her mother, the child of the daughter and her father would be 75% genes from the father. Reproduction between the granddaughter and the father would produce offspring with 87.5% of the father senior male's genes. The same results obtain if a son reproduces with his mother.

In other words, the result of this process is moving back toward clone identity, toward a kind of immortality. The senior male would see more children "just like me" and in his image. This would produce a continued manifestation of the senior male. Think about the desire of fathers to name their sons by their same name: Seth, a child of Adam and Eve with identical genes, would be named Adam Jr. or Adam II.

You will recognize this desire as a form of repetition in the human arena, the loss of possibilities. It is a form of sexual possession of the future. Offspring are denied individuality.

This primal "just like me" desire is emphasized in Eliezer's analysis:

> "AND Adam lived an hundred and thirty years, and he begat in his own likeness after his image" (Gen. v. 3). Hence thou mayest learn that Cain was not of Adam's seed, nor after his likeness, nor after his image. (Adam did not beget in his own image) until Seth was born, who was after his father Adam's likeness and image, as it is said, "And he begat in his own likeness, after his image." (*ibid.*)

Note that the blessing is to follow the image. The more the son is like the father, the more likely to receive the blessing. The youngest sons would be most likely to be children of daughters and granddaughters of the father and thus nearest to clones. You will note the preference given to the youngest son in the Genesis legends: Isaac, Jacob, Joseph, Perez, Ephraim. This is often treated as a symbol of Israel as the youngest nation, the nation that is or should be the clone of YHWH.

And of course, FW, this most personal of art works, is Joyce's clone, his immortality. It is still living today, barely. But it produces offspring in creating readers.

HCE's Park Experience

The Garden of Eden legend returns in FW in HCE's experience in Phoenix Park, which leads to his political fall. While exactly what happened is shrouded in uncertainty, the basic outline is not. It involves two young girls and three soldiers.

The suggestion is that like Adam, HCE voyeur-like watched the two girls urinating and caught nothing more than sight of their sex organs, "knew" their sex organs. He may have been urinating at the same time himself. The suggestion is also made that the three soldiers knew HCE, caught him with his pants down. This would indicate soldier sex—anal sex associated with warfare, equally impersonal and lacking in individuality. Like Adam defiled by the serpent. HCE's interpretation of the proposal from the Cad as a homosexual one that makes HCE nervous in the very same park supports this interpretation. In both cases, HCE repeats Adam's crime of passivity.

The two girls remind us of Lillith and Eve and the three soldiers, in view of K, may stand for the three members of the trinity present in earthly affairs. The three soldiers could also suggest Noah's three sons, one of them sodomizing him. They "do him in."

These numbers [two females and three soldiers] bring us back to the mystical 231, or in Hebrew right to left 1 3 2, making reference to the self together with the 22 combinations of Hebrew letters and the 10 Sefirots.

Antidote—Temptation of Christ

The antidote to the Fall of Adam is the temptation of Christ by Satan in the wilderness. Christ fasted for 40 days among the beasts. Weakened physically but not in resolve to submission to the Will of God, Christ resisted Satan's temptations upon command to act like a god—turn stone into bread, fly off the roof of the Temple and under Satan rule all the Kingdoms of the Earth. This would be acting in accordance with Hebrew expectations of a Messiah and the people would rally to him. In other words, it first seems to be a temptation to be independent but ultimately can be seen as an invitation to dependency. Christ had seen what would happen to him. Christ could do miracles, but only within the will of god.

Cain and Able

The Cain-Able story is the first example of what happens right after ejection from the Garden of Eden and in life under the curse. Joyce viewed the fratricide of one twin by the other as the first example of warfare under the curse. And fratricide also extends the fear of death to within the family.

The Cain/Able competition is stated in the Hebrew Scriptures to be over the blessing of god. Apparently there was not enough blessing from TZTZ to go around. Cain and Able didn't join forces to produce a joint offering. TZTZ god likes competition.

In the Legends, Cain was conceived together with his twin brother Abel and his twin sister Awan. Cain kills Abel to take possession of his twin sister [same DNA], the first instance of competition and strife for possession of reproductive resources. Like a good senior male, Cain wanted all the women. Awan does not get to choose her life partner.

When Cain kills Abel, both god and Adam are nowhere to be seen. Cain and Awan go on to found the first city, the social organization in which the curse is paramount. Bad Cain founds the city that is bad inherently. Cain is frustrated in his apparent desire to control all future genes when Adam and Eve conceive Seth, their clone and likeness. Seth gets the blessing since he is their clone.

As Eliezer tells this story:

> Rabbi Zadok said: A great hatred entered Cain's heart against his brother Abel, because his offering had been accepted. Not only (on this account), but also because Abel's twin-sister was the most beautiful of women, and he desired her in his heart. Moreover he said: I will slay Abel my brother, and I will take his twin-sister from him, as it is said, "And it came to pass when they were in the *field*" (Gen. iv. 8). "In the field" means woman, who is compared to a field. He took the stone and embedded it in the forehead of Abel, and slew him, as it is said, "And Cain rose up against Abel his brother, and slew him." (*ibid.*)

The point of the Cain-Able story is that this curse-engendered strife for reproductive resources is capable of ripping through the fabric of the closest relationships in the family—twin brothers. Joyce's Shem and Shaun avoid fratricide but aggressively compete throughout FW. Note that TZTZ god set up competition between the brothers by denying acceptance of Cain's offering without explanation or encouragement—such as maybe next time big guy. Note

112

that Cain acted rebelliously but not individually. He was not satisfied with his own devotion but needed god to bless it. He did not honor Abel's individuality. He certainly did not honor Awan's wishes and moved to control her reproductive potential.

In FW, Shem the penman is aligned with the independent Cain and Shaun the postman is aligned with Abel.

Noah and Babel

Additional mythical coordinates for this novel are the stories in the Old Testament of triple X rated Noah and his sons, featuring drunkenness, sexual perversion and slavery and the Tower of Babel revolt against god, featuring city men who were like hard baked bricks rather than moist red clay.

In both cases, the motivation for the action is to become manifest, just as ES must have been motivated to make himself manifest in the TZTZ creation. The Primal Horde is the common denominator of these bible stories. Eventually a younger male tries to depose the aging or wounded alpha.

Just before the Noah story, Genesis 6 reveals aspects of the curse. First, "it came to pass" that "sons of the gods" [either sons of human rulers or angels] mated with the daughters of men, whomever they chose, and produced children who "were of old men of name." As angels, the sons of the gods are referred to as "fallen angels," the Nephilim. The Pirke interprets the daughters of men to be the daughters of Cain who walked around naked but with painted faces. In addition, if that weren't bad enough, there were giants "in the earth in those days." The angels, as aspects of TZTZ god, are copying the human males in sexual activity as part of the man-god-man interdependence.

Contemplating the evil of mankind, TZTZ god decides on two things: first, god will flood the earth and wipe out all of mankind saving only Noah and his sons; second, in order to avoid the necessity in the future for a big killing like the flood for humans' "backsliding," god will limit human life after the flood to 120 years. The humans will be killed off sooner than the old timers who lived to 500 years. This limitation makes the rainbow covenant easier to make.

Noah had a wife and three sons—Ham, Shem and Japheth. Having been blessed by Yahweh, they and their unnamed wives were the only survivors of the Flood which they rode out in the Ark. In this sense they are another set of first parents—another Adam, Eve, Cain, Abel and Seth.

That flood wiped out the rest of mankind, a curse by water. Joyce uses the Battle of Waterloo as Water Lieu—war as another method of curse in lieu of a water flood.

In Eliezer, the flood is viewed as a combination of fresh and salt water:

> Rabbi Zadok said: On the 10th of Marcheshvan all the creatures entered the ark; on the 17th of the same (month) the waters of the Flood descended from heaven upon the earth, for they were the waters (endowed with the) male (principle). And there came up the waters of the depths, for they are the waters (endowed) with the female (principle), and they were joined with one another, and they prevailed so as to destroy the world, as it is said, "And the waters prevailed exceedingly upon the earth." (*ibid.* vii. 19)

After the rain stops, Noah tests the situation by sending out birds, a raven that does not return and a dove that does [with a leaf]. After the Flood receded, the Noah clan came down from the mountains to the plain and Shinar, the name for the lower courses of the Tigris and Euphrates rivers. God promised to send a rainbow as symbol of covenant never to flood again. Note that the rainbow suggests TZTZ god, since it is made of separated colours not whole unified light. God apparently felt it was necessary to give a covenant. The "bow" was to appear when mankind was sinning, a kind of neon warning. While there was never the same kind of flood, there were plenty of other curses. With TZTZ god you need a lawyer. God has to give Abraham another covenant, that time about real estate.

Apparently at ease in post-Flood idleness, Noah cultivated the vine, brewed wine and became a drunkard—the curse of drunkenness. One time while drunk he took to the "tent of his wife" but passed out. According to the Legends, Ham happened along and, given the opportunity, either tried or did castrate his father and/or have sex with his mother. While Ham laughed at his prostrate and perhaps castrated father, the two good sons Shem and Japheth backed into the tent with a blanket and covered their father.

Here is the more blatant version by Eliezer that implicates a third party, Noah's grandson Canaan:

> Canaan [son of Ham] entered and saw the nakedness of Noah, and he bound a thread (a book mark that was at the passage about) the Covenant was, and emasculated him. He went forth and told his brethren. Ham entered and saw his nakedness. He did not take to heart the duty of honouring (one's father). But he told his two

brothers in the market, making sport of his father. His two brothers rebuked him. What did they do? They took the curtain of the east with them, and they went backwards and covered the nakedness of their father, as it is said, "And Shem and Japheth took a garment, and laid it upon both their shoulders, and went backward, and covered the nakedness of their father; and their faces were backward, and they saw not their father's nakedness." (*ibid.* 23)

Note that for the dirty deed Canaan uses the bookmarker for the Torah, a cloth marker that was settled at the page for the Covenant—presumably the rainbow covenant. You sense the irony—Noah would have taken his authority from the Torah and the family covenant should prevail. His blessing was cut short by his grandson at only three sons. Any sex involved in this incident would of course be defiling sex.

For this deed, this challenge to his alpha status, Noah cursed Ham's offspring to be the slaves of the offspring of the other two sons. They were cursed to have misshapen lips, twisted curly hair and to go about naked. Formerly among the blessed, the sons of Ham suffered slavery.

Carrying on the tradition of TZTZ god, Noah cursed his offspring. The ravages of the Noah story are sexual perversion and slavery, both elements of the primal horde and the clan. Slavery is ultimate fear/dependency relationship, a notable triumph of TZTZ god.

The Holy Book containing all celestial and all earthly knowledge—the take from the Tree of Knowledge—is given to Adam. But jealous angels steal the book and throw it in the sea. God retrieves it and gives it back to Noah. It is a book made of sapphires and enclosed in a golden casket. It alone provided lights for the ark. Noah entrusts it to Seth and he in turn to Abraham. It makes its way through the chain of blessed sons to Solomon. While the evidence chain is not certain, it apparently ends up with Enoch, and becomes his source of wisdom and that of Kabbalah. Its secular version is now enshrined in FW. ALP's letter that is lost during most of FW is a fallen version of the Holy Book.

The city and tower of **Babel** were built under the direction of Nimrod, a cursed grandson of Ham, who was famous as the Babylonian tyrant. Nimrod was under the curse put on Ham's children and their offspring. His name suggests rebellion, and he is first described in the bible as a "mighty hunter before god." In the anti-hunting Jewish culture, this description translates as a rebellious user of snares who was in god's face. Using false ideas, he snared the Babels into the city and into building the tower in defiance of god, a tower so high that it was in god's face. The tower was flood insurance in case god sent another flood. It was an attempt to be independent and secure in separation from god. The Babels would not have to fear god, not have to fear death from flood.

More detail from Eliezer:

> Rabbi Chakhinai said: Nimrod was a mighty hero, as it is said, "And Cush begat Nimrod, who began to be a mighty one in the earth" (Gen. x. 8). Rabbi Jehudah said: The coats which the Holy One, blessed be He, made for Adam and his wife, were with Noah in the ark, and when they went forth from the ark, Ham, the son of Noah, brought them forth with him, and gave them as an inheritance to Nimrod. When he put them on, all beasts, animals, and birds, when they saw the coats, came and prostrated themselves before him. The sons of men thought that this (was due) to the power of his might; therefore they made him king over themselves, as it is said, "Wherefore it is said, Like Nimrod, a mighty hunter before the Lord." (*ibid.* 9)

As Eliezer noted, the tower project builders became purely result oriented:

> Rabbi Phineas said: There were no stones there wherewith to build the city and the tower. What did they do? They baked bricks and burnt them like a builder [would do], until they built it seven miles high, and it had ascents on its east and west. (The labourers) who took up the bricks went up on the eastern (ascent), and those who descended went down on the western (descent). If a man fell and died they paid no heed to him, but if a brick fell they sat down and wept, and said: Woe is us! when will another one come in its stead [up 7 miles]?

The point about the fallen brick is that the higher the tower became the more difficult it was to build it higher. The purpose of the tower was to provide a safety zone in the case of another flood—to avoid another curse by water. While Yahweh had promised never to do genocide again and promised the rainbow as a special covenant for this purpose, the Babel group was not willing to trust Yahweh's promises as to the future. They believed in the past, not the new future promised by Yahweh. They wanted to control the future through their own efforts. They wanted to eliminate uncertainty through their self-reliance. They wanted flood insurance. For this

116

they dedicated their resources but without respect for the human unity.

Here is the story in Genesis 11, in the rather bland King James version:

> And the whole earth was of one language, and of one speech [more like one mind]. And it came to pass, as they journeyed from the east, that they found a plain in the land of Shinar; and they dwelt there.
>
> And they said one to another, Go to, let us make brick, and burn them thoroughly. And they had brick for stone, and slime [bitumen] had they for mortar.
>
> And they said, Go to, let us build us a city, and a tower, whose top may reach unto heaven; and let us make us a name. Lest we be scattered abroad upon the face of the whole earth.
>
> And the Lord came down to see the city and the tower . . . And the Lord said, Behold, the people is one, and they have all one language; and this they begin to do; and now nothing will be restrained from them, which they have imagined to do.

The tower is never finished. God scatters the people abroad and confounds their speech into different languages. This curse reduces what humans could do. The story concludes with a pun: Therefore is the name of it called Babel. Scattered, the people developed differently such that when they met, they would be naturally hostile.

The original of this myth is, of course, in the Hebrew language. The poetry of the original communicates much of the important message of the myth and doesn't come through in the English translation. Here is the take of Josephus, a Jewish historian who in the first century after Christ wrote the *Antiquities of the Jews*:

> Now the sons of Noah were three—Shem, Japeth and Ham, born one hundred years before the deluge. These first of all descended [after the flood] from the mountains into the plains, and fixed their habitation there, and persuaded others who were greatly afraid of the lower grounds on account of the flood . . . but they, imagining the prosperity they enjoyed was not derived from the favour of God, but supposing that their own power was the proper cause of the plentiful condition there were in, did not obey him [to disperse].
>
> [Nimrod] said he would be revenged on God, if he should have a mind to drown the world again; for that he would build a tower

too high for the waters to be able to reach and that he would avenge himself on God for destroying their forefathers.

The main emphasis in the Babel myth is on the kind of culture, city or rural, and the corresponding relationship to Yahweh. Noah's grandsons built a city culture, following the model set by brother-killer Cain. As cities then and now, this one featured inhuman values—pursuit of self-interest and a relative lack of concern for others. Sodom was a good example, Sodom the city that made hospitality to strangers illegal since the city sat on gold.

By contrast, Israel/Judah was largely a rural culture, and Judaism preferred smaller groups because of the belief that direct contact with nature led to humility and human values. In contact with nature, they took care of their widows and orphans.

This myth recounts the founding of a city and thus a bad culture in Babylon, the city on the plain between two rivers. This city culture is to be trouble on Israel's north and east for thousands of years to come.

The spiritual attitude of the Babel city dwellers is indicated by their choice to trust the future to themselves instead of to god and to devote their energies to building a tower to control their future in the event of another flood. Their hubris is codified in their tower, said in the legends to have been several miles high, high enough to be in god's face. This desire to control the future against god-driven evil reminds us of the desire to control the future through genes.

The Babel story emphasizes the bricks used to construct the tower and the bitumen used to hold the bricks together. Each brick was made from clay and, according to the Legends, had the name of a participating person inscribed on it, making a name for him or herself. Concert hall seats with donor names on the back are something of the same. Presumably only the names could use the tower in case of flood.

The Babels wanted to make a name for themselves, a name in the sense of a monument and immortal fame that would avoid the oblivion of death. In short, they wanted to manifest, just like ES. They became like dried bricks rather than moist red clay from which Adama was made. Like the hardened and dried [castrated] junior males in the primal horde, they were scattered.

The Babel builders used bricks and bitumen rather than the stone and mortar used by the Israelites. The bricks of clay had to be baked in order to remove the water that otherwise made the bricks unstable. As joinder material, bitumen sponsors the empathetic action "by two men" or "by t women."

Like others who try to control the future or fate and have the wrong attitude towards god, the Babel city dwellers were unsuccessful. Their building efforts were frustrated by god. TZTZ god came down, stopped the building and scattered the Babels to many lands and tongues, continuing TZTZ god's general inclination to separate. With many tongues and their general city inclinations, their natural tendency was division and strife. The tower remained unfinished. Despite their efforts, their names were lost to posterity. TZTZ god did not want humans to achieve too much in the way of building possibilities.

As Eliezer notes, after Babel reigned:

> And they wished to speak one to another in the language of his fellow-countryman, but one did not understand the language of his fellow. What did they do? Every one took his sword, and they fought one another to destroy (each other), and half the world fell there by the sword, and thence the Lord scattered them upon the face of all the earth, as it is said, "So the Lord scattered them abroad on that account, upon the face of all the earth." (*ibid.* 8)

Here is direct evidence of the guilt of god in producing war and strife. This is the latent content of the Babel myth. Because of this, tribalism developed and the word "like" in "I like you" stemmed from "like' as in likeness of his own race.

The word Babel means gate of god but sounds like *balal*, which means confusion. A related word is *tebel*, which means confusion as in incest. The Tower of Babel was in the shape of a ziggurat, a word that means tall or lofty. The ziggurat is generally in the shape of a pyramid but without smooth sides, a structure with serrated edges.

On the top level of the ziggurat rested a special room furnished with only a gold couch, a gold altar and, yes, a woman. The upper chamber seemed to be designed for renewal through contact with the ineffable and perhaps sex was the portal for the journey. The priest waited in the upper chamber for the gods to appear. If they didn't, he tried the summoning ritual again after resting up.

Our Finnegan is a hod carrier. In FW he carries bricks up the ladder for construction of tall buildings. He falls off the legendary equivalent of the Tower of Babel.

Jonathan Swift

While Joyce made much use of Swift in his book, he did not admire Swift's character. "He a mess of two women's lives," Joyce told Padraic Colum. These two women Stella and Vanessa are examples of restricted juniors in the primal horde, there only for the alpha.

As with so many of the characters used by Joyce in FW, JS was born fatherless. He was an insecure child without a settled home. His wet nurse stole him away to Ireland for several years and his real mother put him out to boarding school. Abused himself, he turned out to be an abuser as well.

Swift graduated from Trinity College in Dublin by special favor. He withdrew to England during the revolution of 1688 and worked as secretary to W. Temple in Moor Park, Surrey [think more park in Eden]. There he met Esther Johnson the future Stella when she was 8. She may have been the bastard child of Temple and his housekeeper Rebecca Dingley. The same can be said of the other girl Vanessa. Stella and Vanessa were probably half sisters, each fathered by Temple. Temple took care of them and in Moor Park they learned to worship Swift. As a surrogate father, he was to recycle with them the abuse of potential he experienced as a child.

Swift's treatment of Stella and Vanessa resulted in limiting their human possibilities. A monumental mind important in British politics in the early 1700s, Swift molded these two females to his requirements—that they worship him and give up any chance for a real emotional life of their own. In other words they were to be his cheerleaders. He seems to have done this in order to provide a constant source of praise he needed because his own childhood missed real love, the kind necessary for individual independence.

A bachelor his entire life, to both Stella and Vanessa Swift was part father and part lover/husband although there was no sex. He was apparently obsessionally adverse to the smells of the female nature. Swift went back and forth between Ireland and England and tried to keep his cheerleaders separate—Stella in Ireland and Vanessa in England. But one time desperate to be with him, Vanessa followed him to Ireland and eventually found out about Stella. With this discovery, that she was not even the only one, Vanessa died of anxiety. Swift didn't do anything to help for fear of scandal.

Swift was a major misogynist who encouraged women to be more like men, that is in his view ruled by common sense and not by the emotions. Molded and weakened by him, both Stella and Vanessa looked to him for approval. But as an egoist Swift could not trouble himself with their sufferings, even an illness leading to death. While he never formally objected to marriage proposals they received from others, he did not encourage them to seek an independent life. Given the many enemies his vituperative writings brought him, he sacrificed the happiness of his two cheerleaders to maintain his reputation in his drive for power and wealth.

Swift left Letters to Stella in his Journal. With her he used a kind of code to avoid any reputation-ruining scandal.

You will note the parallels with the treatment of Eve in the Garden myth.

Having debased Stella and Vanessa as individuals, Swift was qualified to write about debased coinage, a symbol of the Irish dependency on England. This coinage was a particular instance of the English debasing the Irish—on the model of TZTZ god debasing humanity. Swift wrote **Drapier's Letters** about the issuance of a patent to one Wood to issue half-pence coins in Ireland. These coins were debased by containing insufficient precious metal and too much brass instead. Inherently they were not as valuable as the stated value. Joyce refers to them as wood money.

Here is a summary by Temple Scott commenting on the Gutenberg e-text edition of Drapier's Letters:

> The matter of Wood's Halfpence was a trivial one in itself; but it was just that kind of a matter which Swift must instantly have appreciated as the happiest for his purpose. It was a matter which appealed to the commonest news-boy on the street, and its meaning once made plain, the principle which gave vitality to the meaning was ready for enunciation and was assured of intelligent acceptance. In writing the "Drapier's Letters," he had, to use his own words, seasonably raised a spirit among the Irish people, and that spirit he continued to refresh, until when he told them in his Fourth Letter, "by the Laws of God, of Nature, of Nations, and of your Country, you are, and ought to be, as free a people as your brethren in England," the country rose as one man to the appeal.
> ***
>
> The Irish people had again and again begged that they should be permitted to establish a mint in which coins could be issued of the same standard and intrinsic value as those used in England. English parliaments, however, invariably disregarded these petitions. Instead of the mint the King gave grants or patents by which a private individual obtained the right to mint coins for the use of the inhabitants. The right was most often given for a handsome consideration, and held for a term of years.
> ***

But even Coxe cannot hide the fact that the granting of the patent and the circumstances under which it was granted, amounted to a disgraceful job, by which an opportunity was seized to benefit a "noble person" in England at the expense of Ireland. The patent was really granted to the King's mistress, the Duchess of Kendal, who sold it to William Wood for the sum of £10,000, and (as it was reported with, probably, much truth) for a share in the profits of the coining. The job was alluded to by Swift when he wrote:

> "When late a feminine magician,
> Join'd with a brazen politician,
> Expos'd, to blind a nation's eyes,
> A parchment of prodigious size."

Note the connection with the Garden of Eden story—the woman selling out, the woman who was the mistress of the King. The Drapier is to return in Joyce's story in FW of the Norwegian sea captain, the tailor and the tailor's daughter.

Joyce's prime reuse is of Swift's **Tale of a Tub**, his satire on organized religion. In his public life Swift traced all dangers to irrationalities that disturb man's highest facilities—reason and common sense. The primary image in the Tub Tale is of a major source of disturbance—the hallow ideas and concepts used to distract us from the curse, the curse symbolized by the Leviathan in the salt water. Here it is in Swift's own words:

> To this end, at a grand committee, some days ago, this important discovery was made by a certain curious and refined observer, that seamen have a custom when they meet a Whale to fling him out an empty Tub, by way of amusement, to divert him from laying violent hands upon the Ship. This parable was immediately mythologised; the Whale was interpreted to be Hobbes's "Leviathan," which tosses and plays with all other schemes of religion and government, whereof a great many are hollow, and dry, and empty, and noisy, and wooden, and given to rotation. This is the Leviathan from whence the terrible wits of our age are said to borrow their weapons. The Ship in danger is easily understood to be its old antitype the commonwealth. But how to analyse the Tub was a matter of difficulty, when, after long inquiry and debate, the literal meaning was preserved, and it was decreed that, in order to prevent these Leviathans from tossing and sporting with the commonwealth, which of itself is too apt to fluctuate, they should be diverted from that game by "A Tale of a Tub."

Sailors hunting whales threw a tub into the ocean after a whale had been harpooned in order to confuse the whale and avoid damage to the real ship. The injured whale must think the tub is some kind of ship. When the whale is considered to be the leviathan, the evil creature of the deep salt water, its curse must be avoided and the Tub used for that purpose is religion.

In Swift's *Tale of a Tub*, Patter represented pattering Catholicism (St Peter), Jack represented the less formal Calvinism & Presbyterianism (Jean Calvin), and martin represented Lutheranism & Anglicanism (Martin Luther). These organized religions attempt to understand the relationship with the powers that be and instruct mankind. Their efforts amount to no more than the tub.

Here is a summary from Wikipedia:

> *A Tale of a Tub* is divided between various forms of digression and sections of a "tale." The "tale," or narrative, is an allegory that concerns the adventures of three brothers, Peter, Martin, and Jack, as they attempt to make their way in the world. Each of the brothers represents one of the primary branches of Christianity in the west. This part of the book is a pun on "tub," which Alexander Pope says was a common term for a pulpit, and a reference to Swift's own position as a clergyman. Peter (named for Saint Peter) stands in for the Roman Catholic Church. Jack (named for John Calvin, but whom Swift also connects to "Jack of Leyden") represents the various dissenting Protestant churches whose modern descendants would include the Baptists, Presbyterians, Quakers, Mennonites, and the assorted Charismatic churches. The third brother, middle born and middle standing, is Martin (named for Martin Luther), whom Swift uses to represent the 'via media' of the Church of England. The brothers have inherited three wonderfully satisfactory coats (representing religious practice) by their father (representing God), and they have his will (representing the Bible) to guide them. Although the will says that the brothers are forbidden from making any changes to their coats, they do nearly nothing but alter their coats from the start. Inasmuch as the will represents the Bible and the coat represents the practice of Christianity, the allegory of the narrative is supposed to be an apology for the British church's refusal to alter its practice in accordance with Puritan demands and its continued resistance to alliance with the Roman church.

We shall watch for the wonderfully satisfactory coats in FW.

St. Patrick

St. Patric (Latin: *Patricius*, Irish: *Naomh Pádraig*) also experienced early abuse and grew up to carry Catholic dogma to pagan Ireland. From the Catholic Encyclopedia:

> **St. Patrick**
>
> Apostle of Ireland, born at Kilpatrick, near Dumbarton, in Scotland, in the year 387; died at Saul, Downpatrick, Ireland, 17 March, 493. [Some sources say 460 or 461. --*Ed.*]
>
> He had for his parents Calphurnius and Conchessa. The former belonged to a Roman family of high rank and held the office of *decurio* in Gaul or Britain. Conchessa was a near relative of the great patron of Gaul, St. Martin of Tours. Kilpatrick still retains many memorials of Saint Patrick, and frequent pilgrimages continued far into the Middle Ages to perpetuate there the fame of his sanctity and miracles.
>
> In his sixteenth year, Patrick was carried off into captivity by Irish marauders and was sold as a slave to a chieftain named Milchu in Dalriada, a territory of the present county of Antrim in Ireland, where for six years he tended his master's flocks in the valley of the Braid and on the slopes of Slemish, near the modern town of Ballymena. * * *
>
> In the ways of a benign Providence the six years of Patrick's captivity became a remote preparation for his future apostolate. He acquired a perfect knowledge of the Celtic tongue in which he would one day announce the glad tidings of Redemption, **and, as his master Milchu was a druidical high priest, he became familiar with all the details of Druidism from whose bondage he was destined to liberate the Irish race.**
>
> * * * [He escapes Ireland]. He found a ship ready to set sail and after some rebuffs was allowed on board. In a few days he was among his friends once more in Britain, but now his heart was set on devoting himself to the service of God in the sacred ministry. * * * No sooner had St. Germain entered on his great mission at Auxerre than Patrick put himself under his guidance, and it was at that great bishop's hands that Ireland's future apostle was a few years later promoted to the priesthood. It is the tradition in the territory of the Morini that Patrick under St. Germain's guidance for some years was engaged in missionary work among them. When Germain commissioned by the Holy See proceeded to Britain to combat the erroneous teachings of Pelagius, he chose Pat-

rick to be one of his missionary companions and thus it was his privilege to be associated with the representative of Rome in the triumphs that ensued over heresy and Paganism, and in the many remarkable events of the expedition, such as the miraculous calming of the tempest at sea, the visit to the relics at St. Alban's shrine, and the Alleluia victory. Amid all these scenes, however, Patrick's thoughts turned towards Ireland, and from time to time he was favoured with visions of the children from Focluth, by the Western sea, who cried to him: "O holy youth, come back to Erin, and walk once more amongst us."

***[He comes back to Ireland]. It was probably in the summer months of the year 433, that Patrick and his companions landed at the mouth of the Vantry River close by Wicklow Head. The Druids were at once in arms against him. But Patrick was not disheartened. The intrepid missionary resolved to search out a more friendly territory in which to enter on his mission. First of all, however, he would proceed towards Dalriada, where he had been a slave, to pay the price of ransom to his former master, and in exchange for the servitude and cruelty endured at his hands to impart to him the blessings and freedom of God's children. He rested for some days at the islands off the Skerries coast, one of which still retains the name of Inis-Patrick, and he probably visited the adjoining mainland, which in olden times was known as Holm Patrick. Tradition fondly points out the impression of St. Patrick's foot upon the hard rock – off the main shore, at the entrance to Skerries harbour. Continuing his course northwards he halted at the mouth of the River Boyne. A number of the natives there gathered around him and heard with joy in their own sweet tongue the glad tidings of Redemption. There too he performed his first miracle on Irish soil to confirm the honour due to the Blessed Virgin, and the Divine birth of our Saviour. Leaving one of his companions to continue the work of instruction so auspiciously begun, he hastened forward to Strangford Loughand there quitting his boat continued his journey over land towards Slemish. He had not proceeded far when a chieftain, named Dichu, appeared on the scene to prevent his further advance. He drew his sword to smite the saint, but his arm became rigid as a statue and continued so until he declared himself obedient to Patrick. Overcome by the saint's meekness and miracles, Dichu asked for instruction and made a gift of a large *sabhall* (barn), in which the sacred mysteries were offered up. This was the first sanctuary dedicated by St. Patrick in Erin. It became in later years a chosen retreat of the saint. A monastery and church were erected there, and the hallowed site retains the name Sabhall (pronounced Saul) to the present day. Continuing his journey towards Slemish, the saint was struck with horror on seeing at a distance the fort of his old master Milchu enveloped in flames. The fame of Patrick's marvelous power of miracles preceeded him. Milchu, in a fit of frenzy, gathered his treasures into his mansion and setting it on fire, cast himself into the flames. An ancient record adds: "His pride could not endure the thought of being vanquished by his former slave".

Returning to Saul, St. Patrick learned from Dichu that the chieftains of Erin had been summoned to celebrate a special feast at Tara by Leoghaire, who was the Ard-Righ, that is, the Supreme Monarch of Ireland [the senior male]. This was an opportunity which Patrick would not forego; he would present himself before the assembly, to strike a decisive blow against the Druidism that held the nation captive, and to secure freedom for the glad tidings of Redemption of which he was the herald. As he journeyed on he rested for some days at the house of a chieftain named Secsnen, who with his household joyfully embraced the Faith. The youthful Benen, or Benignus, son of the chief, was in a special way captivated by the Gospel doctrines and the meekness of Patrick. Whilst the saint slumbered he would gather sweet-scented flowers and scatter them over his bosom, and when Patrick was setting out, continuing his journey towards Tara, Benen clung to his feet declaring that nothing would sever him from him. "Allow him to have his way", said St. Patrick to the chieftain, "he shall be heir to my sacred mission." Thenceforth Benen was the inseparable companion of the saint, and the prophecy was fulfilled, for Benen is named among the "comhards" or sucessors of St. Patrick in Armagh.

It was on 26 March, Easter Sunday, in 433, that the eventful assembly was to meet at Tara, and the decree went forth that from the preceeding day the fires throughout the kingdom should be extinguished until the signal blaze was kindled at the royal mansion. The chiefs and Brehons came in full numbers and the druids too would muster all their strength to bid defiance to the herald of good tidings and to secure the hold of their superstition on the Celtic race, for their demoniac oracles had announced that the messenger of Christ had come to Erin. St. Patrick arrived at the hill of Slane, at the opposite extremity of the valley from Tara, on Easter Eve, in that year the feast of the Annunciation, and on the summit of the hill kindled the Paschal fire. The druids at once raised their voice. "O King", (they said) "live for ever; this fire, which has been lighted in defiance of the royal edict, will blaze for ever in this land unless it be this very night extinguished." By order of the king and the agency of the druids, repeated attempts were made to extinguish the blessed fire and to punish with death the intruder who had disobeyed the royal command. But the fire was not extinguished and Patrick shielded by the Divine power came unscathed from their snares and assaults. On Easter Day the missionary band having at their head the youth Benignus bearing aloft a copy of the Gospels, and followed by St. Patrick who with mitre and crozier was arrayed in full episcopal attire, proceeded in processional order to Tara. The druids and magicians put forth all their strength and employed all their incantations to maintain their sway over the Irish race, but the prayer and faith of Patrick achieved a glorious triumph. The druids by their incantations overspread the hill and surrounding plain with a cloud of worse than Egyptian darkness. Patrick defied them to remove that cloud, and when all their efforts were made in vain, at his prayer the sun sent forth its rays and the brightest sunshine lit up the scene. Again by demoniac power the Arch-Druid Lochru, like Simon Magus of old, was lifted up high in the air, but when Patrick knelt in prayer the druid from his flight was dashed to pieces upon a rock.

Thus was the final blow given to paganism in the presence of all the assembled chieftains. It was, indeed, a momentous day for the Irish race. Twice Patrick pleaded for the Faith before Leoghaire. The king had given orders that no sign of respect was to be extended to the strangers, but at the first meeting the youthful Erc, a royal page, arose to show him reverence; and at the second, when all the chieftains were assembled, the chief-bard Dubhtach showed the same honour to the saint. Both these heroic men became fervent disciples of the Faith and bright ornaments of the Irish Church. It was on this second solemn occasion that St. Patrick is said to have plucked a shamrock from the sward, to explain by its triple leaf and single stem, in some rough way, to the assembled chieftains, the great doctrine of the Blessed Trinity. On that bright Easter Day, the triumph of religion at Tara was complete. The Ard-Righ granted permission to Patrick to preach the Faith throughout the length and breadth of Erin, and the druidical prophecy like the words of Balaam of old would be fulfilled: the sacred fire now kindled by the saint would never be extinguished.

Many aspects of St. Patrick's life make their way into FW, starting with his famous and rebellious fire. He joins in the culminating debate with the Arch Druid in the last chapter and once again appeals to the sun.

Patrick wore an unusual mitre, a circular cap supporting above a golden disc, something like the sun. Because of this unusual mitre, Patrick was known to some as "adzehead." That tool, the adze, was used to clear bark from a tree trunk. It may remind you of "crophead," Napoleon's nick name. In terms of the curse, Patrick did his part. Several of his converts were so taken with merging with Christ that they died immediately after conversion, even two young royal maidens. The literature doesn't say how Patrick managed this feat.

Even more influential in FW is St. Patrick's principal theoretical opponent within Christianity. Pelagius was originally from Scotland or Ireland. Condemned as a heretic by the Roman Catholic Church, he taught that humankind did not suffer from original sin, did not need baptism, and that man has the capacity to seek God in and of himself apart from any movement of God or the Holy Spirit. Augustine wrote four books to teach that mankind could be saved only by God's grace, which Pelagius thought [correctly] would result in automaton humans. As per Wikipedia:

> Pelagius taught that the human will, tempered in good deeds and rigorous asceticism, was sufficient to live a sinless life. He told his followers that right action on the part of human beings was all that was necessary for salvation. To him, the grace of God was only an added advantage; helpful, but in no way essential. Pelagius disbelieved in original sin, but said that Adam had condemned humankind through bad example, and that Christ's good example offered humanity a path to salvation, not through sacrifice, but through instruction of the will. Jerome emerged as one of the chief critics of Pelagianism, because, according to him, Pelagius' view essentially denied the work of the Messiah (Pelagius personally preferring 'teacher' or 'master' to any epithet implying divine power).

In the words of Pelagius:

> Whenever I have to speak on the subject of moral instruction and conduct of a holy life, it is my practice first to demonstrate the power and quality of human nature and to show what it is capable of achieving, and then to go on to encourage the mind of my listener to consider the idea of different kinds of virtues, in case it may be of little or no profit to him to be summoned to pursue ends which he has perhaps assumed hitherto to be beyond his reach; for we can never end upon the path of virtue unless we have hope as our guide and compassion…any good of which human nature is capable has to be revealed, since what is shown to be practicable must be put into practice." (The Letters of Pelagius and his Followers by B. R. Rees, pg 36-37, published by The Boydell Press)

Pelagius' views are very close to Joyce's faith in independent individuality.

Tristan and Isolde and King Mark

Joyce's use of this venerable story demonstrates that the common denominator in all the basic ingredients of FW is the power juice in the primal horde—the selfish human desire of the alpha male, desire blinded from the unity by the drive for survival of his image. This self-based desire wants to possess the other whether it is good for the other or not. It is to be contrasted with real love, the independent desire of the good for another. For Joyce, the hero of this story is the forgiving King Mark not the self-seeking Tristan.

The basic story takes the shape of the primal horde. Tristan is dispatched by his Uncle Mark the King to retrieve Isolde the Fair from Ireland to be the bride of King Mark, the King of Cornwall in England. Having drunk the love potion designed for the King and Isolde, Tristan and Isolde on the ship coming back fall into love-desire that is their life and death. Pointedly, they never conceive a child despite many conjugal engagements. They live an artificial life divided between duty and self. Their love is troubled by guilt and their duty is soiled by treachery. While they are heroes in modern romantic terms, in spiritual terms their souls are divided.

As retold by Joseph Bedier, the story goes like this. Mark is the King in Cornwall, southern England, at Tintagal Castle near a natural port. His sister Blachefleur is married to King Rivalin, the King of Lyonesse or Scotland. Rivalin is killed by Duke Morgan, so Tristan [means born in sorrow] is born fatherless from Blanchefleur. His mother dies soon. The orphaned Tristan is raised by Rohalt but kidnapped by Norwegian merchants. They encounter bad weather on the way home with their captive and, believing the weather and the captive are related, stop in Cornwall to let him off. He convinces the Cornwall Lords that he is of noble training by cutting up a stag properly. He is taken into the service of King Mark, who grows to love him as a son

Over in nearby Ireland, the King and the Queen have a child Iseult the Fair, a blonde of great beauty. As usual, the question is who gets the blonde. The Irish King demands tribute from King Mark and sends his giant Morholt to enforce the tribute requirement. The Irish King is married to Morholt's sister [apparently she is smaller]. Tristan overcomes Morholt the enforcer but in the process receives a wound laced with poison [foreshadowing other poison]. He is put out in a brier to die at sea, but the brier floats over to Ireland. There Isolde the Fair finds him on the beach, cures him with her magic herbs not knowing who he is, that he killed Morholt, who of course was her fiancée. Tristan makes it back home to Cornwall before anyone in Ireland finds out who he is.

While Tristan was in Ireland having his poison-laced wound healed by Isolde, he pretended to be someone else and went by the name Tantris, which reverses the first and last parts of his name. Reversed, it would mean sorrow in birth. Joyce uses this same reversal technique frequently.

King Mark is not married and the four bad Barons, who are interested only in their own welfare, convince Mark to seek a wife and heir so Tristan his favorite will not become king. These are the junior males in action. A swallow brings a strand of golden hair that is taken as a sign. Tristan is sent to find the maid of the golden hair, which of course turns out to be Isolde the Fair.

Tristan kills the dragon threatening the Irish kingdom and wins her "hand." But he takes her not for himself but for King Mark. Even after she recognizes him as Tantris, Isolde is put out that Tristan did not come for her personally. So much for feminine consistency.

On the ship bringing Isolde from Ireland back to Cornwall, Tristan and Isolde drink the love potion meant for King Mark and Isolde. They fall in love and consummate the desire of their sexual organs for each other.

The version used by Richard Wagner in his opera by the same name starts differently. From Wikipedia:

> ***Tristan had been allowed to leave, but had returned with the intention of marrying Isolde to his uncle, King Marke. Isolde, in her fury at Tristan's betrayal, insists that he drink atonement to her, and from her medicine-chest produces the vial which will make this drink. Brangaene is shocked to see that it is a lethal poison.
>
> At this point Kurwenal appears in the women's quarters saying that Tristan has agreed after all to see Isolde. When he arrives, Isolde tells him that she now knows that he was Tantris, and that he owes her his life. Tristan agrees to drink the potion, now prepared by Brangaene, even though he knows it may kill him. As he drinks, Isolde tears the remainder of the potion from him and drinks it herself. At this moment, each believing that their life is about to end, they declare their love for each other. Their rapture

is interrupted by Kurwenal, who announces the imminent arrival on board of King Marke. Isolde asks Brangaene which potion she prepared and is told that it was no poison, but a love-potion. Outside, the sailors hail the arrival of King Marke.

In the Wagner version, the relationship of love and death is more complex. Thinking that they have drunk death poison, Tristan and Isolde release themselves from love to passion, which they think is voluntary. However, they have in fact drunk the love potion, which suggests the survival instincts honed by death. From hereon, they are together only in the night, the Schopenhauer-inspired merger of all in unity of the Primal Will.

Back in Bedier's version: After arriving in Cornwall, Isolde and King Mark are married and Isolde's maid supplies the blood on the first night sheet, a forgery of Isolde's virginity. But Isolde and Tristan continue their now treacherous relationship. Tristan signals his coming to her at night by putting branches in a stream that flows through an orchard outside the castle and from there into the woman's rooms of the castle. With this signal they meet in the orchard under the cover of night.

The Bad Barons try to catch them together because Isolde does not become pregnant and Tristan is still set to be the heir, to receive the blessing. The Barons convince King Mark to lay a trap to catch them in the act, which is done with flour on the floor around Isolde's bed. Tristan's wound bleeds on the flour and they are discovered but never admit their wrong. King Mark reluctantly condemns them to death.

Tristan escapes the fire meant for him by leaping over a cliff, his fall broken by his cape acting as a parachute batman-like. Rather than burn Isolde, King Mark gives her to a group of lepers who are keen to share with her their oozing desire [another symbol of the effect of this kind of love]. Tristan rescues her from the lepers and together they escape and hide from the King in the nearby Woods of Morois. There they don't have enough to eat but hippy-like have each other. Still she doesn't get pregnant. A wood ascetic Ogrin recommends penance but denial is not for them. Hodain, Tristan's selfless dog, joins them in the woods and learns not to bark and give their location away.

King Mark discovers the lovers asleep in their simple bower in the forest, clothed and with a sword between them. Believing the best in both of them, Mark believes them to be pure at heart and in conduct. Tristan arranges for Isolde to be returned to Mark and his

131

own banishment from the Kingdom to Wales. After hiding out and meeting Isolde several times for one last time, he finally leaves.

While the lovers are separated for quite awhile, they begin to doubt each other. This kind of love requires frequent draughts of love potion. Tristan marries the daughter of a local knight whose king he helped, this one Isolde of the White Hands. He never consummates this marriage, and her vengeance is the final poison. Without a love potion, Tristan cannot get it up.

Tristan visits Isolde the Fair in disguise as a beggar/comic but she rejects him, thinking he has not been true. Rejected, Tristan goes on a long "knight about" fighting various places and finally is wounded with poison. He sends for Iseult the Fair and she comes. Tristan arranged a white sail as a message of yes she was on board and a black one for Isolde not aboard. Note the only purpose for this signal is for the "I can't wait" Tristan to know a little bit ahead of time. Isolde of the White Hands tells him the sail is black when it is white and he dies. Iseult the Fair arrives too late and dies too of a worn-out heart.

This story provides many references in FW, including a passage about the fateful trip over by Isolde and Tristan, who in Joyce's rendition is a soccer star. The Norwegian sailors who dump their bad luck cargo return in the story of the Norwegian captain and the tailor, which is redo of the ES TZTZ creation. The Four Bad Barons reincarnate in the four old men. The meaning of Tristan, born in sorrow, points to the TZTZ creation.

Thousand Nights and One Night

Joyce used the story "The Sleeper Awakened" from this collection of stories because that dream-like story involves waking up to have changed places with the King and back again. Finnegans Wake involves waking up to the kingdom self-mastery in the most fundamental sense. But Hasan's problem is that he believes he is king only when others tell him so. He takes his identity from others, not independently.

It is one of the many stories told by a young woman to the local alpha. This is the "framestory" for the Tales. As summarized by the EB:

> According to the story that serves as the collection's framework, the Sultan Shahryar found his first wife unfaithful, and, after deciding that he hated all women, he married and killed a new wife

each day. Scheherazade, daughter of his vizier, in an effort to avoid his previous wives' fate, related to him a fascinating story every night, promising to finish it on the following night. The sultan enjoyed the stories so much that he put off her execution indefinitely and finally abandoned the idea altogether.

You will sense why this story appealed to the alpha and reflects TZTZ god. Told at night, you sense the connection to dreams. It also suggests the role of art vis-a vis death.

The title of the collection is not "A Thousand and One Nights" as usually translated but "A thousand Nights and one Night." The girl storyteller pretends to be relating past events but in reality is predicting the future. Thus the title, indicating the latest night is the same as the previous thousand but could be different. The title A Thousand and One Nights suggests a continuous succession. The storyteller saves herself by inventing something new.

This adventure of Hasan took place because Hassan mistrusted friendship and would only invite strangers into his house. In this you will sense an improper relationship with others. One night he meets the Caliph who is out and about in disguise, another forged identity, and brings him home. Entertaining the disguised Caliph, Hasan expresses the wish that he could be Caliph for a day in order to bring down a bad sikh. For his own entertainment, the Caliph drugs Hasan and sets him up in the royal bedchamber where all are ordered to treat him as the Caliph.

After initial disbelief, Hasan is finally convinced after spending quality time with 28 women from the harem dressed in the colors of the rainbow. Drugged again, Hasan is taken back to his own home, but there he still thinks he is Caliph. This time it takes treatment in the madhouse to realize he is just Hasan not the Caliph.

Note that in this story, sex is the portal for Hasan to be convinced that he is the Caliph and social structures [the madhouse] are necessary to reduce him back to normal size.

After realizing the Caliph's role in this farce, Hasan and his wife stage for first the Caliph and then the Queen mock deaths and resurrections in order to gain a pension from the Caliph. The point here is that the ultimate authority figures want your death; that is when they help you—when you don't need it. Having gained the ability to trick the Caliph, Hasan is the Sleeper Awakened.

Huckleberry Finn, Mark Twain, and the Garden of Eden in Independence

Joyce makes frequent reference to Huckleberry Finn and Tom Sawyer. Indeed, Samuel Clemens is the one of the few authors I am aware of that in terms of a new language tried on a limited basis to accomplish what Joyce did in a major way.

The issue in the story of Huckleberry Finn is independence, self-realization. Huckleberry has it even though his parental support is limited to a single parent father who is drunk and gone whenever possible. Like Pelagius, Huck is free in spirit and mind and decides for himself whether the systems of thought he runs into make sense for him. For this reason, he is the one who helps Jim escape from slavery into freedom.

The image presented by Clemens of free mankind within the human unity is Huck and Jim on the raft floating down the Mississippi River. Set against this image of independence are many dependencies—drunkenness, respectability, fraud, superstition, gender dress, family blood feuds, egoism, a desire for adventure and style and cowardice just to name some. One of the worst is Tom Sawyer's insatiable desire for adventure thrills while playing with the life of Jim.

In this context of dependencies, Huck gets mixed with two professional frauds. They put on shows for locals in river towns in order to fleece them. In one show, Hamlet's "to be or not to be" speech is corrupted to a speech about the fear of death. This serves our TZTZ god theme.

One of their fraudulent shows is called the "Royal Nonesuch" or the "Kings Cameleopard." Suggestive of a failed good shepherd god, it features the frauds [nicknamed the King and the Dauphin, son of the King, or Duke—think father and son gods] naked on stage and

> . . .a-prancing out on all fours, naked; and he was painted all over, ring-streakeded-and-striped, all sorts of colors, as splendid as a rainbow.

This rainbow is all the paid audience gets and feels cheated. But this first audience doesn't warn the others in town who want to attend the second show, which is just the same. The first audience doesn't want to be the only ones to have been fooled. When the third show is planned and tickets sold by the frauds, all who attended previously buy tickets again and plan to run the frauds out of town and reclaim their money. But the frauds don't show.

You may get a charge out of interpreting these shows as the father, son and holy spirit—who doesn't show—and the rainbow covenant. I am sure Joyce did. In FW, Royal Nonesuch becomes **Royal Revolver**.

Finn of Huckleberry Finn yields Finn again. Berry in Huckleberry suggests the fruit in the Garden. The author's *nom de plume* Mark Twain connects with the Tristan and Isolde legend, Mark who kept the lovers twain.

What is less often appreciated is the connection of Huckleberry and Tom to Mormonism, the group of major iconoclasts in Christianity. Huck and Tom grew up in Hannibal, Missouri, which was on the **River Road** from Nauvoo, Illinois and then to Independence, the jumping off place for the Mormon move West. From Jamie Jennsen, the author of **Road Trip USA**:

> If you're passing through Nauvoo, you'll have plenty of opportunities to learn about Mormon history and religion. Nauvoo is Mecca for Mormons, or "Latter-day Saints" (LDS), as church members prefer to call themselves. In 1839, a dozen years after receiving their new gospel via the Angel Moroni, the Mormons purchased a large tract of swampy land along the Mississippi River, then set about draining swamps and building a city. Within a few years, Nauvoo was not only the largest LDS settlement in America, but the 10th-largest city in the United States. The emergence of such a powerful little theocracy (with its own well-armed militia) generated resentment among outnumbered neighbors, and even some internal dissent. The friction escalated to violence on both sides, finally culminating in the 1844 arrest of Joseph Smith Jr., church founder and president, for having sanctioned the destruction of printing presses used by some church members to question his leadership. While in the nearby Carthage jail, Smith was lynched by a mob and so became one of the Mormons' first martyrs. Amid ensuing disputes over church succession and renewed hostilities with non-Mormon neighbors, most residents followed Brigham Young across the Mississippi on the famous exodus to Salt Lake City.

Because of revelation to Joseph Smith, Mormons believe that the Mississippi River is the location of the Garden of Eden. The Garden is, as we know, where Eve took steps to be independent and god-like, to be like Huckleberry. In fact, Smith thought what is now **Independence** Missouri was the specific location for the Garden of

Eden. Like Pelagius, this independent-thinking Christian group also rejected the notion of original sin. These connections further the web between Eve's pursuit of god-like status and independence.

Note some similarities between Mormon doctrine and Joyce's version of Kabbalah. From the 15th EB edition:

> Mormon doctrine diverges from the orthodoxy of established Christianity, particularly in its polytheism, in affirming that God has evolved from man and that men might evolve into gods, that the Persons of the Trinity are distinct beings, and that human souls have preexisted.

Here is the interdependence of god and man as featured in the TZTZ creation in Kabbalah. Joyce would have approved each Person of the godhead being independent and the human potential to reach god status.

As for the Garden of Eden, read from **Was The Garden of Eden in Missouri?** by Sandra Tanner:

> The spot chosen for the Garden of Eden was Jackson County, in the state of Missouri, where Independence now stands; it was occupied in the morn of creation by Adam and his associates, who came with him for the express purpose of peopling this earth. (*Journal of Discourses*, 10:235)
> Brigham Young, also a close associate of the Prophet, testified similarly:
> In the beginning, after this earth was prepared for man, the Lord commenced his work upon what is now called the American continent, where the Garden of Eden was made. In the days of Noah, in the days of the Boating of the ark, he took the people to another part of the earth. (*Discourses*, p. 102)
> ***
> That is the position of the Latter-day Saints today, with respect to the much-discussed location of the Garden of Eden. Adam, after his expulsion from the Garden of Eden, lived in the vicinity of the great Missouri and Mississippi rivers. As his descendants multiplied, they would naturally settle along the fertile and climatically acceptable river valleys. When the flood came in the days of Noah, the Mississippi drainage must have increased to a tremendous volume, quite in harmony with the Biblical account. Noah's ark would be floated on the mighty, rushing waters, towards the Gulf of Mexico. With favorable winds, it would cross the Atlantic to the Eastern continents. There the human race, in its second start on earth, began to multiply and fill the earth.

136

Adam built an altar of rocks called Adam-ondi-Ahman. More from Tanner:

> Even after the Mormons moved west they continued to talk about the importance of Missouri. LDS Apostle Wilford Woodruff, writing in his journal on March 30, 1873, commented:
>
>> Again President Young said Joseph the Prophet told me that the garden of Eden was in Jackson Co Missouri, & when Adam was driven out of the garden of Eden He went about 40 miles to the Place which we Named Adam Ondi Ahman, & there built an Altar of Stone & offered Sacrifize. That Altar remains to this day. I saw it as Adam left it as did many others, & through all the revolutions of the world that Altar had not been disturbed. Joseph also said that when the City of Enoch fled & was translated it was where the gulf of Mexico now is. It left that gulf a body of water. (*Waiting for World's End: The Diaries of Wilford Woodruff*, edited by Susan Staker, Signature Books, 1993, p. 305)

Concerning the rocks as god's marks, which will appear in FW, this Mormon Oliver B. Huntington testified:

> Adam's Altar, which was mentioned, I have visited many times. I sat upon the wall of stone and reflected upon the scenes that had taken place thousands of years ago right where I was. There were the rocks that Father Adam used. I looked for marks of tools upon the rocks, but found none, not knowing then the command of God that there should be no mark of tool upon the rocks of an altar upon which sacrifices were be offered to Him.

The engraved golden plates in Mormon belief return in FW as ALP's letter buried in the mound of history. Here is Tanner on the plates:

> In western New York state in 1827, Smith had a vision in which an angel named Moroni told him about engraved golden plates. Smith allegedly translated these plates into English as the *Book of Mormon*—so called after an ancient American prophet who, according to Smith, had compiled the text recorded on the plates. The *Book of Mormon* recounts the history of a family of Israelites that migrated to America centuries before Jesus Christ and were taught by prophets similar to those in the Old Testament. The religion Smith founded originated amid the great fervour of competing Christian revivalist movements in early 19th-century America but departed from them in its proclamation of a new dispensation.

Through Smith, God had restored the "true church"—i.e., the primitive Christian church—and had reasserted the true faith from which the various Christian churches had strayed.

The Community of Christ uses Smith's unfinished translation of the Bible, which incorporates prophecies of his own coming and of the *Book of Mormon*. The church in Utah, however, prefers the King James Version. Of great importance to all Latter-day Saints is the *Book of Mormon*, which recounts the history of a group of Hebrews, led by the prophet Lehi, who migrated from Jerusalem to America about 600 BCE. There they multiplied and split into two groups: the virtuous Nephites, who prospered for a time, and the hostile Lamanites, who eventually exterminated the Nephites.

Joyce recycles this Mormon material in a different setting but with the same archetypical results.

FW as the Torah

FW is Joyce's Torah. The first chapter of FW is his Genesis. As the Torah was thought to be the mind of god, particularly in its esoteric or *sod* interpretation, Joyce structured FW to be the mind of mankind.

Both FW and the Torah are circular. In the Temple, the Torah is **sung** through the end of the book of Deuteronomy and then returns to the beginning of Genesis. Deuteronomy ends with the death of Moses. He dies after he was allowed to see but not enter the land of Israel, the promised land, from the top of Mt. Pisga. He died as he lived "at the mouth of YHWH." At the end of FW, the wife/mother river of life character Anna Livia Purabelle dies to the trident of the Angel of Death. But she too has seen the promised land of independence, and she is not afraid of the angel of death at the end of the River Road.

Moses had seen YHWH face to face, the only human to do so and live. Moses is said to have written the Torah. Joyce our modern Moses is to die shortly after writing FW. He is the only author to have seen face to face the full human condition.

The Torah is said to be built on the ineffable name of ES and to be encoded with esoteric knowledge. FW is built on the effable names HCE and ALP. It likewise is encoded with esoteric knowledge. Both are expositions of the man-god-man relationship. Both have inner layers of meaning and both are living organisms, both living bodies. They are what you make of them, just like your life and your god. They contain almost infinite possibilities. As language was the method of creation in Genesis [as in let there be light], Joyce's new language continues the creative process of god.

In K the Hebrew letters have mystical significance and properly used can create even material objects, for example a golem. The first letter of the Torah is *bet* and the last letter is *lamed*. The magic number 32 is written *lamed bet*. The first letter of FW is r for *resh*, the signal for the curse.

The Torah is written without vowels, perhaps to limit understanding to those who knew Hebrew well and didn't need vowels. Thank goodness Joyce didn't decide to do that. He used his own form of shorthand.

If Joyce's language could reach back to the ur-unity of Ein-Sof, then it would all be one big compound word. As it is, the longest words depict the sounds of thunder, the fear-mongering sound, the sounds of TZTZ god. These shorter compounds reflect the limited and discriminated character of TZTZ god.

Death

FW views death as the end of separate existence, of separate individuality, the final step in the process of attack on individuality begun in the Garden of Eden myth. The spiritual issue is whether release from individuality results in nothing or reconciliation in unity.

We humans are given glimpses of the eternal [means without regard for time and does not mean forever in time] in moments of art experience and love or care for the suffering of others [thank you Schopenhauer]. Buddha taught relief from desire in compassion and active help for others. The resulting permanent satisfaction and relief from separate desire in these all too fleeting moments suggests that unification is important somehow. These moments of real satisfaction seem to be minor episodes in something larger and important.

Unification in FW, as in the human experience, lies hidden below the surface. It offers hope of something. Meaningless death would be FW without underlying unities.

Quinet

Several times in FW Joyce mimics a famous sentence originally penned by one Edgar Quinet (1803-75). Here is the original in French and as translated by Ellmann:

Aujourd'hui comme aux temps de Pline et de Columelle la jacinthe se plaît dans les Gaules, la pervenche en Illyrie, la marguerite sur les ruines de Numance et pendant qu'autour d'elles les villes ont changé de maîtres et de noms, que plusieurs sont entrées dans le néant, que les civilisations se sont choquées et brisées, leurs paisibles générations ont traversé les âges et sont arrivées jusqu'à nous, fraîches et riantes comme aux jours des batailles.

Ellmann's translation: Today as in the time of Pliny and Columella the hyacinth disports in Wales, the periwinkle in Illyria, the daisy on the ruins in Numantia and while around them the cities have changed masters and names, while some have ceased to exist, while the civilizations have collided with each other and smashed, their peaceful generations have passed through the ages and have come up to us, fresh and laughing as on the days of battles.

The point of all this is that flowers don't fight with each other even though they are competing for reproduction.

Here is Joyce's version in the chapters covered by this book:

FW14-15 [qv]: Since the bouts of Hebear and Hairyman the cornflowers have been staying at Ballymun, the duskrose has choosed out Goatstown's hedges, twolips have pressed togatherthem by sweet Rush, townland of twinedlights, the whitethorn and the redthorn have fairygeyed the mayvalleys of Knockmaroon, and, though for rings round them, during a chiliad of perihelygangs, the Formoreans have brittled the tooath of the Danes and the Oxman has been pestered by the Firebugs and the Joynts have thrown up jerrybuilding to the Kevanses and Little on the Green is childsfather to the City (Year! Year! And laughtears!), these paxsealing buttonholes have quadrilled across the centuries and whiff now whafft to us, fresh and made-of-all-smiles as, on the eve of Killallwho.

Title and Names

The title Finnegans Wake carries many meanings. Let's start with some that create meaning because they don't apply.

Note the lack of an apostrophe in Finnegans. It is not possessive. Finnegan does not own his own wake. He does not own his own resurrection, his own life. Being dependent on others, he is not in control of whether he wakes up. TZTZ god is in control of death. Also the title does not mean Finnegan **is** awake. The major point of the dream structure of the novel is that he is not awake. He is trapped in the past, in the possibilities of the past, not free in the additional possibilities of the future. The Here Comes Everybody characters are dead to the world in sleep and while awake.

Finnegan separates into Finn and again since all have the same experience, finn or death again. Wake is a funeral ritual but waking up suggests a restoration. Wake in the water suggests movement in the life current as a result of Finnegan having been alive. Joyce's heroes left a big wake in the water of life.

Annie Livia Plurabelle suggests the plurality of life strands that she must put together. Her major effort at putting together is to mix genes in conception and to teach children love of others. Livia suggests life and the River Liffey. Plurabelle suggest the beauty of additional possibilities. The additional possibilities point the way to ES through the Tikkun of independent individuality.

HCE for "here comes everybody" suggests the group behavior sponsored by TZTZ god attitudes. Group behavior restricts possibilities. "Comes" is also slang for ejaculation and suggests procreation by sex. Humphrey Chimpden Earwicker: Humphrey for hump or hill. Chimpden for the den of the chimp or the primitive survival instincts. Earwicker for an ear cleaner and a bug that visits and buzzes in the ear. Earwicker plays against the Holy Spirit, the Virgin Mary's fertilizing ear visitor.

The earwig is a common European nocturnal insect that was believed to enter human ears at night. The wiggling bug in the ear and buzzing dreams are a poor substitute for the Holy Spirit, who is absent. From Wikipedia:

> Earwig is the common name given to the insect order Dermaptera characterized by membranous wings folded underneath short leathery forewings (hence the literal name of the order—"skin wings"). The abdomen extends well beyond the wings, and frequently, though not always, ends in a pair of forceps-like cerci. With about 1,800 recorded species in 10 families, the order is relatively small among Insecta. Earwigs are, however, quite common globally. There is no evidence that they transmit disease or otherwise harm humans or other animals, despite their nickname *pincher bug*.

> Earwig may also be used as a verb to mean: "to fill the mind with prejudice by insinuations" or "to attempt to influence by persistent confidential argument or talk".

> The name *earwig* comes from Old English *eare* "ear" and *wicga* "insect". It is related to the fanciful notion that earwigs burrow into

the brains of humans through the ear and therein lay their eggs. This belief, however, is false. Nevertheless, being exploratory and omnivorous, earwigs probably do crawl into the human ear; even if they are only looking for a humid crevice in which to hide, such behavior provides a memorable basis for the name.

Earwigging - also known as eavesdropping - means to overhear another's conversation.

All of these meanings play a role in FW. Humans have the pincher bug, sexual instinct, rather than the Holy Spirit. The human spirit is defeated by prejudicial insinuations about the debased human condition. You are only human. Eavesdropping spreads the word about HCE's original sin, the crime in the Park.

Sigla

Here is John Barger on the sigla, signs Joyce used as abbreviations for the primary elements in FW:

> "E" = Earwicker (rotated E makes M for Mark) also Roderick O'Conor
> [a triangle] = his wife Anna Livia Plurabelle
> "[" = his son Shem (a stylized C, for Cain) also Berkeley the druid
> "/\" = Shem's brother Shaun (A for Abel) also Kevin the saint
> "T" or "/[" = Tristan, Earwicker's son and successor, combining /\ and [
> "I" (or a rotated T) = E's fair daughter Isolde, or her dark twin
> "X" = the four historians, Mamalujo (Matthew Mark Luke John)
> (These are conventionally designated as sigla via a prefixed "$": $E, $A, $[, $/\, etc.)

Just for starters, note that the E for Earwicker is open and looks like a male—head, penis and feet marked by the horizontal bars forward. The triangle for ALP indicates a bringing together and stability.

The sigla E, linked to HCE, is used in various positions through the novel—turned on its back with the bars up or upside down with the open spaces down. When the E is placed with the spaces down and linked with other E's below and to the right, the picture makes a pattern that looks like the Hurdles of the Ford.

142

Vico

The theories of Giambattista Vico, an 18th Century Italian philosopher, put forward in his *New Science* provide important patterns for this novel, just as it did for Ulysses.

Joyce indicated he did not believe in this or any other "science" but did acknowledge that he used it for all it was worth and that it made sense of certain of his life experiences. Joyce admired the breadth of synthesis accomplished by Vico—it gave him [Bishop]:

> . . a psychology of the unconscious, an account of dream formation, and a system of dream interpretation which, because they were synthetically integrated into a social history and a linguistic vision . . .

Just imagine one professor of history, linguistics, psychology, and something like archeology of mentality. Talk about integrated studies.

Vico also gave Joyce a pattern based on a history of social and political institutions and language of the mental development of the gentile humans—the Romans, Greeks, Egypt, Teutons, the Arabs and other pagans. Vico pragmatically excluded Jews and Christians from the analysis because of the power of the Catholic Church at the time. Vico rationalized that unlike the pagans, the Hebrews and Christians had infinitely free minds. While we must forgive him this deference to the Church, it does set up the notion of the ultimate K god ES.

Vico's explanation reveals development of human consciousness from earliest times. FW's dream language illustrates the mentality of primitive man. This is one illustration of "double ends joined," current man dreaming as first man thinking.

Per Vico, first man had experience only of his body and his desires, which were unrestrained. Bisexuality and bestiality would be the natural choices for lust—have sex with anyone and anything that moved at any time. Like these ancestors, today's infants are not born with a sense of sexual identity, just urges. Development of discrimination in targets of the urge is a later development. Each of us during our personal development in a sense traces the development of humanity as a whole. Here Comes Everybody.

Vico started with the notion that our first forbearers were [in Joyce's terms] "furbears," totally primitive and hairy [watch in Joyce for Tom, Dick and *Harry*]. Human consciousness was a variable, changeable with society, and at any time depended on what had gone before. As Bishop put it:

> Nature gives Vico's man the mind of an unconscious animal; Vico's history is the process by which man, of his own blind, stumbling power, slowly builds that natural mind toward consciousness, interdependently with language and civil institutions.

Vico guessed that these original men would have thought much like today's infants pre-training. But modern infants soon have the benefit of parental teaching [language, customs, morals, identity, family] based on hundreds and thousands of generations. By contrast, the first children were abandoned at weaning.

In Vico's story, the descendants of Ham, Japeth and Shem [Noah's children so after the flood] became a race of giants. They were nursed by their mothers and then abandoned at weaning time. In the forest alone these brutes killed to survive and the survivors grew to great size. This was in part because they were in constant contact with filth, Joyce's sign of the curse. Note that under these circumstances each giant would have independent mentality but no compassion. They mated with anything that would do.

Like a sleeper, these giants could only know their own desires. And when they did not understand, they like dreamers identified things by reference to themselves, understood by analogy to body parts—the foot of the rock, the mouth of a river, the head of a hill, the eye of the storm. Vico called this "poetic wisdom." Words related to body parts are called "carnal etymons" by Bishop.

Vico believed that as far as being is concerned, these originals thought that the ground of being that sustained human life resided in the heels, at the base of the feet. [While Vico doesn't make this point, note the heel supported erect posture which in turn led to greater mental development.] This was why Achilles' fate rested in his heels.

Initially these primitives had no fear of father or god [v 369]. According to Vico, these are the giants referred to in Gen 14:5, the offspring of human females and angels. They practiced unrestrained lust. As tribes the giants were called Emim and Zomzommin [suggests TZTZ] and included Nimrod, who later organized and directed the building of the Tower of Babel.

Several hundred years after the flood, these giants were frightened by thunder and lightning that began only then [following a long

144

dry period after the flood]. Frightened, they took to caves for protection, the strongest of them on mountaintops. Fear was no to desire's yes. Each giant who could took to a cave for protection and brought with him what he needed, a few women, so he would not have to go out much where the lightning bolts landed. In the cave he ruled as a alpha by brute strength, ruled his women and children with violence. Individual realization of the support cast was not an issue.

Thus fear of god was the first organizing principle. The original primitives gave us fear of god and celestial punishment. And caves were the first have or have not, those with caves were in tension with those who were without and lurking about just waiting for a chance.

These primitives spoke in symbols and gestures and considered observed nature to be the language of the lightning hurler. By divination they tried to determine the future intentions of the gods, that is what good and evil god would do in the future [v 379]. Vico comments that the Hebrew religion was founded on the principle that humans were not to divine god's future intentions—presumably this referred to prohibition about eating from the Tree of Knowledge of Good and Bad.

Per Vico, these first people developed through frightful religions, offerings to appease the gods and violence-reinforced patriarchal authority much like the religions. We still bear the marks of this beginning. As does FW.

The connection with the past is in the nature of continuous formation. Again Bishop:

> If consciousness is a man-made property that changes in historical time, then each individual owes the way in which he thinks to the generation of this parents; yet his parents owe their thinking and behavior to the generation of their parents; and so forth, in a chain extending back to the beginnings of the gentile world. Those crude choices made by Vico's giants, then, inform all minds born out of them . . .

These original beasts, living in a state of nature, inform the alleged crime in the park by HCE. With the two girls he was in a "state of nature," presumably with his pants down, and in this condition of "indecent exposure" he was done in by the three soldiers. The park sits under the influence of the Wellington memorial, the big stone penis always in the state of ready.

Joyce's language in FW records the ideas of Vico about the development of language—originally signs, then grunts for the passions, then words from the body to designate unknown objects and the merger of several words to mean new objects: ". . . in order to build new words and concepts that always lie just beyond his slowly growing, conscious grasp." The original combinations would have been distorted blurs until the users got accustomed to them. Because of this method of development, all language carries a subliminal record of the past.

In the cave culture, the social structure was the primal horde. It was ruled by an alpha male who exclusively had sex with all the women, his "wife," daughters, grand daughters and captives. Additional persons were allowed in to the protective and cooperative benefits of the cave and its society at the cost of being a slave. The children of the patriarch eventually became freedmen within the concept of a family. One cave group related to others in terms of conflict or trade. These groups eventually became tribes and then nation states. These beginnings in the family cave group are why FW is centered in a family.

Vico noted changes in words from their Indo-European roots, such as "Gen" for to beget, bring forth or conceive and "ar" for join together. Gen eventually developed into the notion of knowing and reflects the connection in the Eden myth between shrewd and sex. Ar eventually meant many things including arts, the skill of joining together. Joyce was particularly attracted to Vico's use of etymology to seek meaning.

Vico also presented a theory of recurring patterns. He viewed as inevitable four stages of history: (1) mythical age of the gods or theocratic (2) heroic or aristocratic (3) human or secular and (4) chaotic to be followed by a *recorso*, a return to the first stage. Each Vico stage has a language, character, jurisprudence and method of reasoning in tune with a basic mindset. In this system, language and history are parts of the same whole, the basic mindset. By contrast with these cycle-controlled mindsets, Vico believed that both Hebrews and Christians could break out of the cycles because of their belief in the divinity of an infinitely free mind [v334]. This is definitely Joyce's god.

In this system, you will sense the fundamentals that historical reality is cyclical. This meant repetition. For Vico, religion, marriage and funeral rites were instrumental in assessing gentile societies.

In the Vico cycle, the first stage is the theocratic or mythical age of the gods. This stage features a powerful deceit of the imagination, weak reasoning, inability to generalize and tendency to assign natural powers to the gods. Most importantly, subject and object are merged

146

in this mentality. Subject Zeus and object lightning are the same thing. Natural law is divine and government theocratic. Authority and reason are divine and the characteristic institution is birth and baptism. The balance of tenses is the past tense. In Vico's theocratic or mythical age, myths and metaphors reign in art, words are concrete not abstract and the prose is discontinuous.

The second Vico stage is the aristocratic or heroic age of paternal authority. In this stage, control is predominant in governance and subject and object are more separated in thought. This stage sponsors the primal horde and its expression the Law of the Fathers. Customs are choleric, law is by force, government is aristocratic, language is by heroic blazonings, writing is about heroic characters, the characteristic institution is marriage and the balance of tenses is the present.

The human or secular cycle features human values, duty, human reason, democratic societies, articulate speech but vulgar writing, facts, individual reason and the funeral as the characteristic institution.

The ricorso is the interlude of chaos that brings society back to the beginning, to the age of the gods.

Now take another look at the same ideas, this time from the mind of Samuel Beckett, one of the acolytes chosen by Joyce to present approved understanding of FW:

> It is first necessary to condense the thesis of Vico, the scientific historian; In the beginning was the thunder: the thunder set free Religion, in its most objective and unphilosophical form - idolatrous animism: Religion produced Society, and the first social men were the cave-dwellers, taking refuge from a passionate Nature: this primitive family life receives its first impulse towards development from the arrival of terrified vagabonds: admitted, they are the first slaves: growing stronger, they exact agrarian concessions, and a despotism has evolved into a primitive feudalism: the cave becomes a city, and the feudal system a democracy: then an anarchy: this is corrected by a return to monarchy: the last stage is a tendency towards interdestruction: the nations are dispersed, and the Phoenix of Society arises out of their ashes. To this six-termed social progression corresponds a six-termed progression of human motives: necessity, utility, convenience, pleasure, luxury, abuse of luxury: and their incarnate manifestations: Polyphemus. Achilles, Caesar and Alexander, Tiberius, Caligula and Nero.

In terms of the relationship of the individual to history:

> Individuality is the concretion of universality, and every individual action is at the same time superindividual. The individual and the universal cannot be considered as distinct from each other. History, then, is not the result of Fate or Chance - in both cases the individual would be separated from his product - but the result of a Necessity that is not Fate, of a Liberty that is not Chance (compare Dante's 'yoke of liberty'). This force he called Divine Providence, with his tongue, one feels, very much in his cheek. And it is to this Providence that we must trace the three institutions common to every society: Church, Marriage, Burial. This is not Bossuet's Providence, transcendental and miraculous, but immanent and the dull itself of human life, working by natural means. Humanity is its work in itself. God acts on her, but by means of her. Humanity is divine, but no man is divine. This social and historical classification is clearly adapted by Mr. Joyce as a structural convenience - or inconvenience. His position is in no way a philosophical one.

Beckett also gave us a summary of the four-part organization of FW:

> Part I. is a mass of past shadow, corresponding therefore to Vico's first human institution, Religion, or to his Theocratic age, or simply to an abstraction - Birth. Part 2 is the lovegame of the children, corresponding to the second institution, Marriage, or to the Heroic age, or to an abstraction - Maturity. Part 3 is passed in sleep, corresponding to the third institution, Burial, or to the Human age, or to an abstraction - Corruption. Part 4 is the day beginning again, and corresponds to Vico's Providence, or to the transition from the Human to the Theocratic, or to an abstraction - Generation.

So here we go with Part I, the "mass of past shadow." We start with **riverrun**, the river being the product of the past, past rain, in a repetitive, circular moisture process.

Riverrun Symbolism

The first word in Joyce's work is important. In Ulysses, it was Stately, an emphasis on externals for other approval, in the usurper chapter. In FW, the first word is **riverrun**.

Joyce starts with **riverrun** in order to introduce the concept of repetition. The point of this emphasis is the restriction on possibili-

148

ties resulting from repetition. Restriction on possibilities means restriction on individuality.

What runs in the river is water, and the emphasis on water comes from the second act of creation in Genesis, which gave us waters above and waters below. In the human experience they do not remain separated; the waters above become the waters below. Rain falls from above, gathers as rivers, drains to the ocean. There it evaporates to become rain again. And riverrun again. The run of the river is part of the repetitive process of moisture. This repetitive process images the equally repetitive process of the flow of birth and death by humans and other life forms.

The relationship of the waters above and the waters below is a cyclical one. The two waters are interdependent. There would be no ocean without rain and no rain without the ocean. Salt water is "redeemed" by evaporation. It rises as fresh water moisture [the spirit of water if you will], falls in rain as fresh water, and then still as fresh flows to the ocean again. The process is constantly repeated. Repetition repetition repetition. The river is always becoming, always dying into the ocean [here Dublin Bay]. Note the same fresh, salt, fresh, salt and on and on water pattern in the life of the salmon, a fish featured in FW.

The repetition results from the never-ending curse. The individual river dies when it enters the ocean or bay. It is no longer a river with its own identity, no longer fresh water. The fresh water riverrun must go to its saltwater death in the Bay. It can't change its mind and go uphill away from the Bay. Conceived like the sefirots and channels of flow from ES, this riverrun is blocked by death. Occasionally the salt water in the bay will enter the river on the tide and mix the salt and fresh waters, just as the male semen occasionally enters the female. In this case the banks guide the semen in.

The Liffey is in contrast to the sacred river that watered the Garden of Eden and is the source of special souls. These souls would be new souls with new possibilities. This Joyce repetitive riverrun is the averse river, the river of repetition and less possibilities. Few special souls flow down this river in Dublin.

Riverrun is deliberately a noun form rather than a noun and verb [the river runs] in order to correspond to Vico's analysis. Vico thought that in primitive language nouns must have been invented first because their objects have a permanent trace whereas verbs reflect impermanent motion and change. In dream language, it is a semi-condensation.

Joyce invented the word "riverrun" to start the novel because it repeats the letter "r". In Hebrew script the letter "r" is known as "resh" and looks like a bent over human, a human under a curse. This is particularly so in the Rashi version of the letters, mentioned in Joyce's notes.

The redactor of the Hebrew Scriptures went out of the way to start the Torah with a "b," a *beit*, in *Bereshit*—in the beginning. The first letter had to be something other than alef because of alef's association with *arar* and curse [Ginzburg]. Deliberately going against the grain of Genesis to make his point, Joyce goes out of his way to start FW with an "r" for curse.

The first word riverrun with its many "r's" is connected with the many loose "a's" at the end of this a circular novel. This combination of "a" and "r" suggests *ARAR*, Hebrew for "to curse." Arur is the past participle, cursed. Arura is the feminine past participle. The sound of the combination of "a" and "r" in English is "are," or being. To be is to be cursed.

In its various forms *arar* is used hundreds of times in the Old Testament. The etymology is to snare or bind--"to bind with a spell or hem in with obstacles, render powerless to resist." This original magic-associated meaning of *arar* supports the notion of curse as the limitation of human possibilities. Since *arar* also means "to punch a hole in," it reminds us of the TZTZ creation by ES in the big hole, the "hole affair." In K the consonants in riverrun stand for head, hook and fish, subjects that appear often in FW. This is the kind of play with language sponsored by K practices.

Because the beginning of FW plays against the beginning of the Torah, we note that the word in the Torah corresponding to "riverrun" in FW is "*Bereshit*." The beginning words of Genesis are "*Bereshit bara Elohim*." Bereshit means "in the beginning." "*Bara*" means the concealed mystery from which all extends and *Elohim* means the mystery that supports all below. The Zohar interprets the meaning of this opening phrase as "With reshit it created Elohim, the mystery that supports all below." [Zohar i 312]. K interprets this reference to creation "by it" to imply ES. TZTZ god is in the creation below. *Bara Shit* also is interpreted to mean "he created six," as Joyce does in his second paragraph with six examples of the curse.

Joyce's first sentence based on riverrun sets out the subject of repetition for the novel and aligns repetition in human experience with TZTZ god. And its counterpart in the Torah indicates what is to be repeated: reshit, that is literally shit again in English.

Ending and Beginning: The Aristotelian Whole is Missing

First some general comments. The ending of FW circles around to the beginning and the beginning needs the ending to make sense. The double ends are joined.

Since Joyce was intimately familiar with Aristotle's standards of art set forth in **Poetics**, we should measure the ending and beginning of FW by those standards. What we find is that by those standards FW is notably "incomplete," deliberately and pointedly "incomplete" as a "whole." And with this deliberate gesture Joyce says by implication that modern TZTZ dependent "riverrun" man is also incomplete because all the possibilities of independent individuality are not realized. Wow!

Here are the rules per Aristotle:

> A tragedy is a presentation of a whole action—a whole is what has beginning, middle, and end. A beginning is what does not necessarily come after something else, but is so constituted as to have something else come after it; and end, on the contrary, is what is so constituted as to come after something else but to have nothing after it: and a middle is what is so constituted as to come after something else and also to have something else after it—for beauty depends upon size [so the relationship of the parts may be appreciable] and order. [quoted from Bosanquet]

As we will see, FW breaks these rules for the purpose of making a point. Both the first and last materials fail the test. The opening material is not a beginning as defined and the last material is not an ending as defined. The first material of FW does necessarily come after something else; it is not independent. Riverrun must necessarily come after rainfallgather. And the last material is constituted to have something else come after it—namely the first material. Both the first and last materials are middles as defined by Aristotle, constituted so as to come after something else and to have something else after it. They do not stand alone, just like a TZTZ man is incomplete.

FW is deliberately incomplete in this sense because designed to indicate through form as well as content all psycho-spiritual history is in a cycle and depends on what has gone before. Nothing can be linear and complete in and of itself. Without a breakout, nothing is independent.

Note in more general terms that in Aristotle's theory the parts must be different in order to constitute a whole by reason of their relationship. The beginning, middle and end must be different in a certain way and lined up in a certain sequence in order to make a whole. Several parts that are all the same do not make a whole. The different parts must be individual.

Let us keep this in mind as we traverse the Joycean landscape of possibility nurturing independence and possibility limiting dependence. Wholeness of the human experience would suggest more possibilities related as different parts in a whole or unity.

Section III: Textual Analysis

Text of Ending and Beginning

First the ending [using the common meaning not Aristotle's], which is necessary to set up the opening. For the ending, Joyce reduced the dream distortion element of the language because in this scene ALP is coming into freedom from fear of death. Latent content is close to the surface; god is death. God wants death as a fisherman wants fish.

Here we have the fresh water feminine river of life [ALP] flowing like a fish into salt-water male Dublin Bay of death. ALP speaks to her husband who eventually morphs into the Angel of Death, the Angel who awaits her arrival downstream with his trident poised to fork her. As with the senior male in the primal horde, he wants to get rid of the old woman and get a new one from inventory. He wants his daughter, for repetition of his likeness. This is fairly obvious dream-like symbolism for the curse of limited possibilities, which as latent dream content is becoming manifest.

As stated in the Pirke:

> All rivers flowing on the earth, as soon as they flow on the earth, they are blessed and good and sweet. There is some benefit to the world through them; (when) they flow into the sea they are bad, cursed, and bitter, and they are of no benefit to the world.

ALP is flowing from the fresh water of possibilities of life into death, the death of possibilities. No choices after death. The fresh water river of individuality is to perish in the bay. Long-term terminal patients report loss of individuality as death nears.

Like a dream, this action is basically fluid. The river is manifest content and god as the angel of death is what would normally be the hidden content. Bolstered by images of unity and unlimitedness, she unmasks god as death as she loses here fear of death.

ALP thinks the Angel of Death has already dismissed her and, as in the primal horde and the desire for repetition, is thinking of a new daughter/wife as new rain falls in the hills. ALP notes, promoting her own desirability, that her hind spot, her hind most spot, the point of most intimate and important contact, is still moist. No dry wall yet. Nonetheless she is ignored by her husband for her daughter, and she reminds the old man that he too will soon be replaced, replaced and cheated by a child, his son. She would have been happy to stay alive longer. She thinks about having been in the womb, the great blue bedroom.

Here she is speaking to her husband. She issues a Freudian slip referring to him as son/husband. Daughterwife is a natural composite here. My comments are in [comments]:

> **[627] up and tightening down** [the motion of the wave or wake]. **Yes, you're changing, sonhusband, and**
> **1**
> **you're turning, I can feel you, for a daughterwife from the hills**
> **2**
> **again. Imlamaya** [fullness of delusion]. **And she** [younger wife] **is coming. Swimming in my hindmoist** [hind most moist].
> **3**
> **Diveltaking on me tail** [the devil is on my tail]. **Just a whisk brisk sly spry spink spank**
> **4**
> **sprint of a thing** [describing the young woman swimming behind the hindmost] **theresomere** [there so mother]**, saultering. Saltarella** [word for Virgin Mother combined with salt] **come to her**
> **5**
> **own** [coming into her own]. **I pity your oldself I was used to. Now a younger's there** [a son].
> **6**
> **Try not to part** [that is be whole together—don't fight or separate]! **Be happy, dear ones! May I be wrong! For she'll**
> **7**
> **be sweet for you as I was sweet when I came down out of me**
> **8**
> **mother** [when I was really young and all was possible]. **My great blue bedroom** [womb]**, the air so quiet, scarce a cloud.**
> **9**
> **In peace and silence. I could have stayed up there for always only.**
> **10**

Notice that the language of regular English is employed for this scene. Joyce's language is gradually leaving the dream-distorted and returning to regular English, the language of day-time, because she is losing her fear of death.

Try not to part! Be happy dear ones! Here the selection of the word **part** recalls the spirit of TZTZ god, the spirit that always separates and discriminates rather than unifying. TZTZ god is the spirit of dissension and acrimony. Here that spirit separates husband and wife, mother and daughter, father and son. It separates whole into part.

At this point, we could say she undergoes a transformation. First, she remembers fondly her last taste of real unity, the realm of ES, when she was in the unlimited and unified womb of her mother. All possibilities were still available. The dream carries her to her primal experience of unity and unlimitedness.

Then the formula of life. We feel and then we fall, like Eve and then Finnegan, because god fails us and has fallen before us. She becomes disgusted with the male function, the slime machine:

> **[627] It's something fails us. First we feel. Then we fall. And let her rain**
> 11
> now if she likes [new rain new river new woman]. **Gently or strongly as she likes. Anyway let her**
> 12
> rain for my time is come. I done me best when I was let. **Think-**
> 13
> ing always if I go all goes [I hold it together]. **A hundred cares, a tithe of troubles and**
> 14
> is there one who understands me? One in a thousand of years of
> 15
> the nights [Thousand Nights and One Night]? **All me life I have been lived among them** [males] **but now**
> 16
> they are becoming lothed to me. And I am lothing their little
> 17
> warm tricks [male tricks]. **And lothing their mean cosy turns** [hugs and kisses]. **And all the**
> 18
> greedy gushes out through their small souls [self- interested ejaculations]. **And all the lazy**
> 19
> leaks down over their brash bodies [semen and prostate grease]. **How small it's all** [only one teaspoon per ejaculation]!

And me
20
letting on to meself always [espressing my emotions]. **And lilting** [speech with cadence] **on all the time.**

Note the fundamental differences expressed here between the women from Venus and the boys from Mars, the female unifiers with ES and the male separators with TZTZ. She is the spirit of unity that holds it all together. But the TZTZ separation spirit means that no male can even understand her, much less sympathize with her. The repetition in male behavior is indicated by sets of alliteration, repetition of first letters—**small souls** and **brash bodies**. The temporary unification provided by sexual intercourse in the case of men must be motivated by self-interest based lust rather than love and given all the ick involved lacks elegance and continuing satisfaction that genuine unification would provide.

Now she belittles the Male principle/Angel of Death further identified with TZTZ god, the god of guilt and glory. She reaches independence from TZTZ god as she denies death's due—fear:

[627] I thought
21
you were all glittering with the noblest of carriage. You're only
22
a bumpkin. I thought you the great in all things, in guilt and in
23
glory. You're but a puny. Home! My people were not their sort [guilty and limited]
24
out beyond there [in death] **so far as I can. For all the bold and bad and**
25
bleary[the independent ES people] **they are blamed, the seahags. No! Nor for all our wild**
26
dances in all their wild din [rebellious]. **I can seen meself among them, alla-**
27
niuvia pulchrabelled. How she was handsome, the wild Amazia,
28

when she would seize to my other breast! And what is she weird,
29
haughty Niluna, that she will snatch from my ownest hair! For
30
'tis they are the stormies. Ho hang! Hang ho! And the clash of
31
our cries till we spring to be free. Auravoles, they says, never heed
32
of your name! But I'm loothing them that's here and all I lothe.
33

ALP identifies with independence: the boldness of Eve, with the Amazon female warriors who cut off one breast so they could draw the bow better and caress the one remaining of their lesbian lover, and with the Niluna—the River Nile that in its changes of flow suggests all or nothing. It is not limited by the banks; it overflows and brings a new planting. It is pregnant annually. These are examples of ES inspired independence. Auravolves for aureole, the aura or halo around virgins who through independence from males overcame the world and the devil. She springs to be free. Since ES remains concealed, he cannot help her. She will inevitably die into dependent oriented TZTZ god, but she dies without fear. TZTZ god has lost his hold.

Now she is passing out of consciousness beyond the banks, as the river reaches the salt bay, the bitter salt bay and her son/husband mutates into the Angel of Death:

[627] Loonely in me loneness. For all their faults. I am passing out. O
34
bitter ending! I'll slip away before they're up. They'll never see.
35
Nor know. Nor miss me.

And here is the giant, old, sad and weary Angel of Death—the cold mad feary father—with his trident of death, like Neptune with his trident spearing a fish:

157

And it's old and old it's sad and old it's
[628] sad and weary I go back to you, my cold father, my
cold mad
1
father, my cold mad feary father, till the near sight of the
mere
2
size of him, the moyles and moyles of it [big angel of death],
moananoaning, makes me
3
seasilt saltsick and I rush, my only, into your arms. I see
them [the prongs]
4
rising! Save me from those therrble prongs! Onetwo
5
moremens more. So. Avelaval.

Feel the resignation in the rhythm of this sentence resulting from
repetition of key words: old old sad cold cold mad father cold mad
father. Note the pattern of connections that mimics Vico dependent
origination: old; old and sad; old, sad and weary; cold; cold mad; cold
mad feary. What has gone before conditions the future.

The Big Angel of Death is owning moaning [**moananoaning**].
Therrble merges terrible and treble for three prongs. **Onetwo
moremens more** is the male formula—in the RCC even the Holy
Spirit is male. Joyce genders it female given his experience with characteristic human males and females.

Moremens is more men [ironically with a reference to Mor-
mons] but also more moments in time. **Avelaval** is hail and farewell
and downstream. **Cold father** because the father of death. **Feary**
[fairy, feared, feathered] father because a feathered angel of death
causes fear. The curse, fear of death, is pressed into the word fairy.
This is the TZTZ god of death come to spear the plurabelle, to hold
down the additional possibilities in life. His trident echoes the trinity
and the three soldiers in the park.

Now ALP goes back into the Garden of Eden. Joyce here takes
the position that dying is like going back into the Garden. What does
she find? Inescapable dependency.

As she was last with god in the Garden of Eden with her fig leaf
on her privates, here she has her **lff**—fig leaf becomes life with the
"I" removed. She is losing her leaves, her individuality, in the process. Leaf becomes leave this life. As she experiences increasing dependency, God becomes **taddy**, the big daddy like the senior male

TZTZ god whose name carries the double "t's". She is back in the Garden after eating from the Knowledge Tree, the toy fair:

> [628] My leaves have drifted from me.
> 6
> All. But one clings still. I'll bear it on me. To remind me of. Lff!
> 7
> So soft this morning, ours. Yes. Carry me along, taddy, like you
> 8
> done through the toy fair! If I seen him bearing down on me now
> 9
> under whitespread wings like he'd come from Arkangels, I sink
> 10
> I'd die down over his feet, humbly dumbly, only to washup. Yes,
> 11
> tid.

Death is pure dependency. Death eliminates individuality. In the Garden, life with Big TZTZ Taddy is like the dependent life of the young girl at the toy fair, a child dependent on Taddy to carry her around. Toys, the **lff** of distraction, help avoid thinking about death. I could dive down to avoid the trident but would only **washup**. She doesn't try to avoid being speared. Having conquered fear, she stares death in the face.

Now the last part—the curse of death. Beginning with a reference to the bush, the *malbush* in K, the garment of TZTZ god. God is not love but death. After she passes behind the garment, out of life and into death, she passes through **grass behush the bush to**. What does she see behind the garment? Why of course God's rectal hair— the grass behind the garment—that is the source of the excrement of TZTZ creation. Death is God shit:

> [628] There's where. First. We pass through grass behush the bush
> 12
> to. Whish! A gull. Gulls. Far calls. Coming, far! End here. Us
> 13

then. Finn, again! Take. Bussoftlhee, mememormee! Till
thous-
14
endsthee. Lps. The keys to. Given!

Note **mememormee** as memory that is distorted to me me
more me, the past converted to memory and me. Memory is related
to the Male Angel of Death as St. Augustine identified memory in
the human mind trinity of memory, understanding and desire as the
counterpart of the father in the father, son and holy spirit trinity.
Memory is of course repetition in some sense. All of this combines
to say that the father god is death. It also characterizes the TZTZ
god as a me me more me spirit, a selfish spirit. Behind becomes **behush** in order to indicate the classified nature of what is there.

Bussofttlhee for kiss of death by YHWH for Moses. TZTZ god
ended Moses' life by kissing him. Death for thousands ends with
thee. **Lps** for lips, the keys to the kingdom of life, receiving food and
kisses, food giving survival and kisses leading to procreation. Note
the letter "I" for individuality is missing in lips. **Finn, again** for end
again, death again. Feel the resignation and peace as she enters the
waters of death unafraid.

Then the last segment:

> **A way a lone a last a loved a**
> **15**
> **long the**

THEN BACK AROUND TO THE OPENING:

> **[3] riverrun, past Eve and Adam's, from swerve of shore to
> bend**
> **1**
> **of bay, brings us by a commodius vicus of recirculation back
> to**
> **2**
> **Howth Castle and Environs.**
> **3**

Don't miss the death theme imbedded in this procedure—the ending
is the beginning. This is the message of Joyce's method.

Chapter 1.1: The Fall

The entire sentence, separated into an ending segment [in italics] and a beginning segment, reads in full:

A way a lone a last a loved a long the riverrun, past Eve and Adam's, from swerve of shore to bend of bay, brings us by a commodius vicus of recirculation back to Howth Castle and Environs.

This ending/beginning sentence starts four sections that take us from the curse of repetition, to restriction on individuality, to the fall, and to strife. These four sections are presented as an inexorable progression, an inexorable progression of dependent origination that limits possibilities. This is the TZTZ god template: limited possibilities and repetition supported by dependence. The Fall is the fall to less possibilities.

Now back to that text. As to the ending fragment _in italics,_ notice how impersonal and sluggish the repetitive use of "a" makes this sequence. Life is **a** way, **a** lone, **a** last, **a** loved **a** long. "A" is the signifier for impersonal. Compare that with the resulting four straight words beginning with the letter "L"—lone last loved long. The upright, tall and capability suggesting "L" symbolizes her independent ES spirit. Its Hebrew counterpart _lamed_ is the tallest and the middle letter in the Hebrew alphabet. The independent way is lonely, loving, lasting and long. But this upright "L" is about to give way to the bent over "r."

The separated "a's" give this sequence an impersonal aura, as in "a person" rather than "the specific person." This is what happens in TZTZ god's precinct--impersonalization. The key to the kingdom is death. From death at the ending to falling asleep at the beginning, we have the twin brothers of the Night, the permanent and temporary restriction of voluntary, free will possibilities.

The word "away" is separated away into **a way,** "at last" into **a last**, "a loved one" into **a loved**, and "along" into **a long. This is TZTZ god separating even the words as it spears Plurabelle.** She is so far away the word "away" separates. She is so alone the word "alone" separates.

This separation frees the "a's" so the floating and unattached and impersonal "a's" can go with the "rr" implied by riverrun. Guided by the process of repetition through the ending back to the beginning, the floating "a's" attach and combine with the "r's" as *arar*, Hebrew for curse. Repetition becomes curse. Impersonal, average not individual behavior is the result of the curse.

Note also that the "a's" are floating just like ALP is floating in the River Liffey and that "riverrun" has three "r's," just as the Angel of Death has three prongs on its trident. The Hebrew r or *resh* looks like a bent over man, a man under a curse.

Dream displacement or separation of the "a's" gives way to condensation or intensification in **riverrun**. The focus in the beginning segment is loose and slightly obscure, coming off the relatively clear ending. Eve and Adam's is a distorted name [the correct name of the church is Adam and Eve's]. The name is distorted to bring in the Garden of Eden myth in which Eve is the prime mover. Swerve of shore and bend of bay suggest the maternal ammonic waters, procreation being an important subject in the Eden myth. The subjects are the type of involuntary ideas that emerge as we fall asleep. Freud:

> As we fall asleep, involuntary ideas emerge, owing to the relaxation of a certain deliberate (and no doubt also critical) activity which we allow to influence the courses of our ideas which awake. . . As the involuntary ideas emerge they change into visual and acoustic images.

Repetition in form and content points to death as the latent content. Note that the first paragraph is built on repetition—both in word selection as well as explicit subject matter. Repetition is common in dreams, at least in mine. To start with, the "r's" repeat in riverrun, three of them. Word selection features alliteration of first letters and construction is a series of phrases set off by commas. **Swerve of shore** and **bend of bay** give repetition in alliteration with double s's and b's [perhaps to suggest in Hebrew *Bere*S*hit*]. It also gives repetition in the use of single syllable words, a limitation that restricts possibilities. **Comodius vicus of recirculation**, water circling in the Bay, is repetition personified with Vico [**vicus**] thrown in for good measure. This word selection and subject matter point attention to the repetition of the moisture process—the process that mimics the human birth life and death process and incarnates TZTZ god, the god of limitation.

In Joyce's Torah, god says let there be death, repetition and limitation.

With "vicus" [a Roman word meaning the smallest municipal unit of administration], Vico's cyclical theory of human history is laid in and on the repetitive moisture process. By analogy, it becomes a municipal unit of administration in this world by the powers that be in this world. In other words, the curse administers the cycles. And with the first letters of Howth Castle and Environs, HCE is laid in the landscape, the finite world of time and space. Engraved in the text throughout the novel, his initials serve as the main subject of repetition. Moreover HCE is the product of repetition. He is "here comes everybody" because of repetition. Just to make the point, heroes are not HCE; they are not like everybody else. They are independent. They can break free from what went before.

The tone of the ending fragment is calm resignation slowed down by the repetitive use of "a" and "l" while the beginning fragment accelerates with the alliteration of S and B. The first fragment starts fast but then ends slowing down. This mimics the river water movement, rushing between the narrow banks to the Bay and then slowing down in the big Bay. It also mimics the process of individuation, rapid early in life and then slowed down as age advances.

Like the serpent whose skin is our world, this opening fragment is sinuous. It slips and slides on scales of alliteration. As the "a's" are detached in the ending fragment, the opening fragment slips out of the dead skin of the ending fragment and then undulates along in a new sheath, a sheath that is new but always the same as the old and must eventually wear out as well. Compare it to the full-page size, snake-like S that opened the original edition of Ulysses.

In terms of voice, the singular voice of ALP the female principle of the plurality has left the ending sequence in favor of an unidentified narrator who refers to the reader and itself as "us." She the individual brave one is gone, and the group is back in charge.

Riverrun is a runonword that flows like the river. Past Eve and Adam's—there is a church on the Liffey in Dublin called not Eve and Adam's but Adam and Eve's, also known appropriately enough as the Church of Immaculate Conception [Virgin Mary as the second Eve]. **Past** the church brings in with just one word both time and space—past in time and past the space of the spot. The "'s" on Adam brings in possession. Note it is missing on Eve, the one demoted to second-class citizenship by TZTZ god in the Garden. Since the correct name of this church is Adam and Eve's, the river is running right to left relative to the name that is read left to right. This is a signal to be attentive to Hebrew based implications [Hebrew read right to left]. Joyce's name Eve and Adam's also indicates that males own the church.

Swerve of shore and **bend of bay** are mirror images of each other—the shape of the joined land and water—suggesting the mirror images man-god-man. **Swerve of shore** suggests movement, undulating movement. *S'r* is the Hebrew root of leaven and derives words meaning fullness, satisfaction, plenty and satisfied. **Bend of bay** suggests pregnancy. The Hebrew root *Ben* refers to sons. *Barak* is the blessing. In TZTZ creation the main blessing is reproduction. Everyone ends up in the salt death bay so new ones must be floated. And any other version of death is another Tale of a Tub, and that tub won't float.

And now moving on inexorably and without explanation to the next paragraph, which consists of six instances in the primal horde setting of limitation of the independence, individuality and human possibilities of the junior members. Six for six days of creation and six examples record Bara Shit.

This use of multiple examples is another instance of repetition and a kind of repetition caused by the curse set forth in the first paragraph. With the curse, the limitation set forth in these instances was inevitable. The broad sweep of the examples in this second paragraph through time, place and source indicates that same forces have been active from the earliest times to the present, apply internationally and are registered in history and legend.

Here the curse/warp of the god-man relationship is echoed in the warp of the man-man relationship. Senior males continue the role of TZTZ god in the garden—they rule by creating fear, dividing and conquering. The primal horde warps the senior/junior male relationship. As a result the females like the Holy Spirit do not issue into freedom. In this material the use of many languages or many tongues recalls Babel, the second time in Genesis humans were explicitly denied god powers.

Unlike the first paragraph, this second paragraph is in a kind of semi-dream language. In terms of dream technique, these examples constitute a chain of association held together by a non-sensical time element: not yet. The common element is sexual energy: penisolate, rocks, gorgios, buttended, wroth and pa's malt. As in the primal horde, the sexual energy of the juniors is frustrated unless they can break free. They cannot be individuals.

The six examples are merged together. The language starts in story book mode and morphs to a kind of poetry. The latent content is still the same, restriction of possibilities.

Here are the six cases of abuse:

164

[3] Sir Tristram, violer d'amores, fr'over the short sea, had passen-
4
core rearrived from North Armorica on this side the scraggy
5
isthmus of Europe Minor to wielderfight his penisolate war: nor
6
had topsawyer's rocks by the stream Oconee exaggerated themselse
7
to Laurens County's gorgios while they went doublin their mumper
8
all the time: nor avoice from afire bellowsed mishe mishe to
9
tauftauf thuartpeatrick: not yet, though venissoon after, had a
10
kidscad buttended a bland old isaac: not yet, though all's fair in
11
vanessy, were sosie sesthers wroth with twone nathandjoe. Rot a
12
peck of pa's malt had Jhem or Shen brewed by arclight and rory
13
end to the regginbrow was to be seen ringsome on the aquaface.
14

The first draft went like this:

> Howth Castle & Environs! Sir Tristan had not encore arrived from North Armorica nor stones exaggerated themselves in Laurens County, Ga, doublin all the time, nor a voice answered mishe mishe to tufftuff thouartpatrick. Not yet had a kidon buttended Isaac not yet had twin sesthers played siege to twone Jonathan. Not a peck of malt had Shem and Son brewed & bad luck to the regginborew was to be seen on the waterface.

For this material, we have a partial explanation by Joyce from a letter reprinted by Ellman:

. . . he [Joyce] sent a key:

Howth (pron Hoaeth) = Danish Hoved (head)

Sir Armory Tristram 1st Earl of Howth changed his name to Saint Lawrence, b in Brittany (North Armorica) ,

Tristan et lseult, passim

Viola in all moods and senses

Dublin, Laurens Co, Georgia, founded by a Dubliner, Peter Sawyer, on r. Oconee. Its motto: Doubling all the time.

The flame of Christianity kindled by S. Patrick on Holy Saturday in defiance of royal orders

Mishe = I am (Irish) i.e. Christian

Tauf = baptise (German)

Thou art Peter and upon this rock etc (a pun in the original aramaic)

Latin: Tu es Petrus et super hanc petram

Parnell ousted Isaac Butt from leadership

The venison purveyor Jacob got the blessing meant for Esau

Miss Vanhomrigh and Miss Johnson had the same christian name

Sosie = double

Willy brewed a peck of malt

Noah planted the vine and was drunk

John Jameson is the greatest Dublin distiller [Jameson whiskey]

Arthur Guinness is the greatest Dublin brewer

rory = Irish = red

rory = Latin, roridus = dewy

At the rainbow's end are dew and the colour red: bloody end to the lie in Anglo-Irish = no lie

regginbrow = German regenbogen + rainbow

ringsome= German ringsum, around

When all vegetation is covered by the flood there are no eyebrows on the face of the Waterworld [TZTZ god the lesser countenance had eyebrows unlike ES]

exaggerare = to mound up

themselse = another dublin 5000 inhabitants

Isthmus of Sutton a neck of land between Howth head and the plain

Howth=an island for old geographers

Passencore=pas encore and *ricorsi storici* of Vico

Rearrived=idem

Wielderfight=wiederfecten=refight

Bellowed=the response of the peatfire of faith to the windy words of the apostle.

This seems like a partial list.

Note that given the curse, each one of these six instances is in the form of a "not yet"—it had not happened yet—**passencore**. To say that something has not happened yet is a backhanded way of saying that it is bound to happen. It is in the future but cannot be changed, the normal attribute of the future. So this is a weird tense, a dream tense.

Given the first paragraph, the curse of repetition, these instances of limitation were bound to happen, were destined to happen, even though they have not happened yet. They are prototypes yet to be realized. Moreover, **passencore** literally means not again, not again yet. Note also that happily "again" separates into "a," the prefix of denial, and gain. Again produces no gain. Since these are all historical or legendary events in various degrees of the past, the text is speaking from the beginning.

Here is the line up of juniors and the curse limitation function in action through the primal horde restricting individuality, restricting completeness:

1.   The first is the basic primal horde set. Tristan is the junior male with King Mark as the senior male and Isolde the Fair as the sex prize. Instead of life as a honest lover and knight to his king, the junior male Tristan is consigned by Mark's legitimate primacy with Isolde the Fair to a life of treachery, a life of forgery. He only pretends fealty to his King and hides his on-going affair with the Queen. His individuality is restricted by these circumstances. He leads a derivative life. He is a forger.

For this opening, Joyce selected material from later in Tristan's life, that part that inevitably unfolds with him as a mercenary warrior. While he readily raises his sword, he cannot without the love-death potion even get it up with the second Iseult, Iseult with the White Hands to whom he is wedded. Pointedly, he never fathers a child. All he can do with his penis is to fight.

This is a classical case of the limitation of the junior in the primal horde and frustrated sexual energy.

2.   The second instance follows the juniors that are driven off. In this case, they are Irish sons who escape English control by venturing to America, to Georgia. They are in the other Dublin, Dublin in the state of Georgia in the U.S. There they are free from the alpha and get it on.

Repeating the same process, they consider success to be many children—doubling [Dublin] their number all the time—what Daddy would not let them do in the horde. They are too busy surviving and procreating to achieve individuality. They even name their new colony after where they came from—Dublin,

Ireland. Not feeling a new identity, they don't come up with a new name for their new home, not even New Dublin.

3. **Mishe mishe** is the desire of the junior male for individuality—it means I am I am. I want to be who I am. I want to be able to press my individuality. I want to manifest myself. I want sex so I can be an individual, the legacy of the primal horde.

4. The next example involves succession among the juniors. Junior male Jacob competes against his older male brother Esau. Jacob uses fraud to obtain the blessing from the senior male Isaac. He is forced to use fraud since without the blessing he is nothing, nothing just as an individual. He can only be made important on a derivative basis by his father's blessing. He is incomplete, dependent and not an individual. The independent and individual Esau loses out.

5. The next example shows equal non-realization treatment for females in the primal horde. Two half-sister junior female cheerleaders [Vanessa and Stella] compete for Jonathan Swift, whose possessive interest in them restricted their life possibilities. They have no sex with him because he can't stand the smell. They do not exist as individuals separate from Swift and got no sex.

6. The last example shows lack of spirit in our forbearers, those left after the flood. Neither of Noah's loyal sons Japeth nor Shem [combined as Jhem] had brewed any "spirit," here viewed as wine and individuality. Their names are corrupted and combined as Jhem to indicate their lack of individuality. Only papa got to pass the malt to the females. No sex, no individuality.

Note that the first five cases of these instances of individuality repression are joined by colons, the punctuation word that also means the human organ that processes excrement. The last instance is set off with periods. Perhaps creation of the human on the sixth day rules this choice. Perhaps it suggests a menstrual period and comments on the lack of child bearing by the ladies who are the subject of the fifth instance.

Now one at a time in more detail:

> **[3] Sir Tristram, violer d'amores, fr'over the short sea, had passen-**
> **4**
> **core rearrived from North Armorica on this side the scraggy**
> **5**
> **isthmus of Europe Minor to wielderfight his penisolate war:**

Sir Tristram joins the legendary Tristan from Tristan and Isolde and the historical character Sir Armory Tristram [note the military arms in his middle name]. The joinder spins the Vico cycle to a repetition.

Tristram contains "tris" for sad and "tram" for a repetitive travel schedule. Trams always stop in the same places [death]. North Armorica contains armor as well as amore, war and love. The North Armorica reference is to old Brittany [where Tristan first came from in some versions], not to new North America, so the reference has the effect of forgery. It is only a short sea away.

This example is a reference to the latter part of Tristan's career when he was a mercenary knight and couldn't get it up with the second Isolde. All he could do was **wielderfight his penisolate war.** Tristan is incomplete.

The curse is operating the cycle. **Passencore** [not again] and **rearrived** for repetition. More and more of the same.

Violer d'amores is to violate love or violate by love—as in Tristan violating his duty to King Mark by cavorting with Isolde and violating real love by unrelenting self-fulfilling sexual possession of Isolde. King Mark gives Tristan the benefit of the doubt, much as the sympathetic, extra strings on the viola d'amore are excited by bowing of the main strings. Denied continuing access to Isolde by the senior male Mark, Tristan makes war—secret penis war **penisolate war**—for Isolde and indiscriminate mercenary warfare. **Wielderfight** through German is fight again. Denied genuine life, denied an undivided and complete soul, all Tristan does is fight.

Penisolate is a condensate word: penis and isolate—separate and sex, the TZTZ activities. Spinning the Vico cycle from legendary Tristan to the 19th century, Peninsular war gives us Waterloo and cheerleaders, who are coming up shortly. Howth is a peninsula. A penis is howth it happens.

The second:

[3]. . . nor
6
had topsawyer's rocks by the stream Oconee exaggerated themselse
7
to Laurens County's gorgios while they went doublin their mumper
8
all the time:

This refers to an actual historical example with a suggestion of the Mormon experience.

Topsawyer's rock is an actual rock formation on the river Oconee in Georgia, U.S. There one Sawyer founded a town of Irish immigrants. Their motto was doubling their number. Mumper gives the phrase a rabbit overtone, the rabbit being an excellent procreator. A little history:

> **Laurens County History by Harriett Claxton**
> The town of Dublin was incorporated by the Assembly on December 9, 1812. It may have been the smallest town ever created by the Legislature: "The incorporation shall extend to and include all the inhabitants living within 250 yards of Broad Street and within 400 yards of the Court House." Legend has it that Jonathan Sawyer, a pioneer citizen of the county was granted the privilege of naming the new county seat, and he named it Dublin in honor of the capital of his native land, Ireland. The site chosen has been proved to be a good location with many advantages for growth and development.

The name Dublin leads to doubling their number, their mumper. Cutting a log by topsawyers involves cooperation by the band of brothers, one on top and one on the bottom of the huge log being cut. They are sawing a log after felling it, which suggests castration of the father, a popular event among god families in Greek myth and the crime of Ham. Rocks fill in for testicles. Topsawyer easily becomes Tom Sawyer, and Mark Twain points to separation and back to the Tristan saga [Tristan and Isolde kept twain by Mark].

In this immigrant environment away from the senior male back in Ireland, success is many children in order to defeat death. These birthing and survival activities would limit the possibilities of individual realization. Or as Joyce put it in another context: "The economic and intellectual conditions that prevail [in Ireland because of the British] . . . do not permit the development of individuality."

Lauren County's gorgios would be the Indians in the same area of Georgia. The Irish immigrants "exaggerate" themselves to the local Indians, that is manifest themselves by pointing out their differences [the heritage of Babel] and their importance. This fosters separation among groups of humans. So TZTZ activities continue to repeat, even in the New World. This group can't even think up a new name for their settlement, not even New Dublin.

[3]: nor avoice from afire bellowsed mishe mishe to
9
tauftauf thuartpeatrick:

With the meaning in Hebrew and sound in English of *mishe mishe*, you have *I am* and *me she*, which together suggest *give me a she*. Mishe is from the burning bush, the senior male YH talking to Moses and giving him orders and courage. Moses was dependent on TZTZ god for power and dependent on Aaron for speech since Moses was a stutterer.

The voice from the fire *has not yet said* thou art an individual, you are your own peatrick, your own peat trick, your own fire, referring to the Paschal fire built by St. Patrick in defiance of the King's orders, Patrick's own individual fire. As a man Patrick was heroic and independent. He left his parents responding to an internal call to mission to Druid Ireland. His Paschal fire was a bold move in the face of royal authority.

As a Christian, Patrick was a loyal Catholic and not an independent thinker—a fact featured here in the repetitive **tauftauf** and eventually in the culminating debate. **Tauftauf** suggests stuttering and repeated baptism, taufen meaning to baptize in German. Repeated baptism would be necessary in god's water closet.

[3] not yet, though venissoon after, had a
10
kidscad buttended a bland old isaac:

Shortly after Moses, Jacob and Esau competed for the blessing of Isaac. Jacob used fraud pretending to be Esau while Esau was out looking for venison at the request of his father, prepatory to giving the blessing to Esau the first born. Thus venison and very soon combined as **venissoon**. Venison forces its way into the word because the deer must be killed and death visits all very soon.

Kidscad is the cad Jacob in the skin of a kid, the younger son. The cad is hidden in the word as Jacob was hidden in the skin. **Buttended** for the ritual act of dominance—what the senior male does to the junior males to remind them of their inferior position.

Jacob and Esau competed for head of the family and a larger share of worldly goods. The derivative Jacob was nothing without the blessing, nothing just by himself. So he used fraud to forge his identity for dad. But Jacob couldn't even do this fraud by himself. His mother Rebeka the wife of Isaac was a co-conspirator in this effort. He used concealment in sheepskin in order to mimic the hair of Esau. Forced to use a forged identity and lie to his father, Jacob lost his integrity. This is what happens with TZTZ god.

Against the grain as always, Joyce doesn't treat Jacob as a hero but as a heel. You remember that he tried to come out of his mother first but ended up second holding the heel of Esau. Esau was Joyce's choice between these two, Esau who was sufficiently independent to marry three non-Jewish wives and skip the Torah lessons. Esau and his other name "Edom" mean red.

> **[3] not yet, though all's fair in**
> **11**
> **vanessy, were sosie sesthers wroth with twone nathandjoe.**

This band of sisters, at least half sisters, is angry with Jonathan [revise order of Jonathan to **nathandjoe**] because Swift kept both of them secret from the other [**twone**] as long as he could and discouraged their other emotional possibilities and sexual satisfaction. He wanted them as his personal cheerleaders, but not as sex partners. When each of them found out that they weren't the only one, weren't quite so manifest in Swift's affection, when one became two—**twone**—they were quite put out, quite **wroth**. One of them died from depression. Swift didn't help for fear of scandal that could hurt his precious career. Swift is **nathandjoe** in this regard because he is just like any nath and joe.

I don't know why this one example ends with a period rather than a colon unless it indicates the sisters' lack of pregnancy. Because of Swift's treatment of them, neither bore a child.

Now the 6th one, the one after the period or the red menstrual flood:

> **[3] Rot a**
> **12**
> **peck of pa's malt had Jhem or Shen brewed by arclight and**

After the flood, Noah's good sons remaining true to the Noah primal horde [combined Japeth and Shem as **Jhem**] had not created any spirit of individuality—not a peck of pa's malt. Pa had all the malt—wine and sperm delivery—but Ham cut him short on more children. **Rot** for not since Noah's testicles and the junior sons' spirits rotted.

Neither had **Shen**, the she hen or the Shekhinah, brewed any spirit—no Holy Spirit who issues only when the father/son relationship is proper. The Shekhinah is God's dwelling within his people and bright light and glory—in Kabbalah the female presence of god. She and her built-in light are not present so Noah & Sons must use arclight. The arc in arclight suggests the arc of a rainbow, the weak separated light from TZTZ god as opposed to the strong light of ES blessed individuality. The rainbow shines when mankind sins but supposedly promised to more flood.

The suggestion is that the only son who brewed any individual spirit was Ham, the son who violated his father. Ham not being nearly dependent enough, TZTZ god consigned Ham's offspring to ultimate dependence, to slavery. Leave it to Joyce to make Ham the hero.

So in the absence of spirit.

[3] rory
13
end to the regginbrow was to be seen ringsome on the
aquaface.
14

so there was no full rainbow [ringsome] on the face of the waters [aquaface] even though promised to Noah by god by way of covenant. Instead of a bow there was a **brow**, the "r" added to bow for *resh* and curse and bent over. Instead of seven colors, there was only red, the last color in the rainbow **the rory end to the regginbrow**, blood on the waters of the king's eyebrow [the Lesser Countenance of TZTZ god]. Red for judgment. Only a curse instead of a covenant—not a rainbow but only an eyebrow continuing to watch humans in the spirit of Din, of harsh judgment, and a prophecy of killing.

The first two paragraphs tell us that from the curse of repetition the limitation of individuality and human possibilities was inevitable. The third paragraph takes us to the fall, which comes inexorably with the limitation of individuality. Joyce gives us a Fall from a tower, a tower of Babel kind of tower, and a Fall of Finnegan to his death.

Since there was no rainbow on the waters, no indication of god's covenant-promise of never flooding again and only **the rory end to the regginbrow**, the tower of Babel was built as flood insurance— high to avoid the next floodwaters and the wrath of god. God did not like this cooperative effort at reaching higher because a mankind that did not have to fear god's wrath would be too independent, too courageous and not fearful enough. God cursed mankind once again by scattering them geographically and by language. This once again limited mankind and the differences born in diaspora- promised strife.

So in this third paragraph we have in one big brown thunder word a Fall into fear of thunder, excrement and death: The fall:

[3](bababadalgharaghtakamminarronnkonnbronnto   nner-
15
ronntuonnthunntrovarrhounawnskawntoohoohoorden
enthur-
16
nuk!)

According to a Joyce letter, this big word is about noise, thunder, defecation and fear. Thunder is god's fart that threatens more curses, the fall of more excrement, more impurity from the godhead. As with a dream, this long Fall word is a combination of words from different languages thus incorporating the Babel curse. In K, thunder is the *Din* or harsh judgment aspect of god ES that produced the limited and finite TZTZ creation. Din is for thunder. Note for pictorial symbolism that this long word contains many [11] bent over "r's" and even more [19] really bent over "n's" but only one "l."

Fear was the first organizing principle in Vico's vision of primordial humanity post-flood. The continuing human desire for greatness and lack of fear of god manifested in Nimrod and the Tower of Babel. God separated and divided the people and in the process set up the small differences that produce conflict in a survivor-based environment.

Joyce's primordial giant, his version of Admon Kadmon and Adam, is Finnegan the hod [brick] carrier. During the construction of the last of many Babel-like high towers he worked on, Finnegan, even though an experienced hod man, falls off scaffolding and dies. Bricks are the Hebrew symbol for suffering since the Egyptians forced the Hebrews to make them. Finnegan carries suffering on high and then falls. The long fall word is the sound of his fall.

Climbing a ladder is a common dream symbol for an erection and falling for loss of erection. This merges or condenses two images that produce less possibilities, that of erectile dysfunction and fear of god-heights.

Like Adam whose giant fallen body lies in Jerusalem, Finnegan's giant fallen body lies beneath Dublin. Given the Fall as an continuing aspect of every human condition, he remains in Dublin, in the subspace. Our FW dreamer falls asleep dreaming of Finnegan falling to his death. The dream starts with death and godshit hidden in a fall word.

Breaking the big Fall word

(babababadalgharaghtakamminarronnkonnbronntonnerronntu onnthunntrovarrhounawnskawntoohoohoordenenthurnuk!)

down into its parts:

Bababa—stuttering produced by fear of the thunder and of the overwhelming senior male. Jove's thunderbolt was three furrowed [Vico v 391] thus three ba's. Read backwards as in Hebrew, it is aba-bab, suggestive of the beginning and infant speech and means father in Hebrew--*aba*. Father equals fear.

Dal—Irish *dail* for divide as in separation. So far the feared father separates.

Gharagh— Hebrew *gur* for be afraid, fear, stand in awe. Grrhh. Hindu *Karak* for thunder. Father separates and we fear him.

Takammin—I take, it is mine. Hebrew *Tame* for unclean. Impurity was considered the actualized form of demonic forces. Japanese *Takaminari* for thunder. Afraid of father, we take when we can.

Arronn—Aaron brother of Moses, who often spoke for Moses the stutterer. Arronn is one way Moses would stutter his name. We the ones afraid of our fathers are dependent on others.

Konnbronn—the French General Pierre Combrone at Waterloo and his famous surrender exclamation "merde." Dependence is surrender is Godshit in TZTZ creation.

Tonnerron— French *tonnerre* for thunder. Look out for more.

Tuonn— Italian *tuono* for thunder.

Thunn-- Old Rumanian *tun* for thunder.

Trovarr-- Portagese *trovaro* for thunder.

Hounawn—yawn for repetition? Thunder, thunder, thunder.

Skawn--?

Toohoohoordenen— Danish *tordemen* for thunder. Word expands to toor hoo hoo denen.

Enthurnuk—Thursday is Thor's day

God's thunder, god's fart, creates fear and fear creates dependency. A fart suggests more merde is coming, more curses in TZTZ. Fear reduces what humans can be. TZTZ god wants humans to be less, to have less human possibilities. So our dreamer dreams of a fall to death, both the dream and death functions denying full human possibilities.

Going on in the paragraph about the fall:

> **[3] The fall . . . of a once wallstrait oldparr is retaled early in bed and later**
> **17**
> **on life down through all christian minstrelsy. The great fall of the**
> **18**
> **offwall entailed at such short notice the pftjschute of Finnegan,**
> **19**
> **erse solid man, that the humptyhillhead of humself prumptly sends**
> **20**
> **an unquiring one well to the west in quest of his tumptytumtoes:**
> **21**
> **and their upturnpikepointandplace is at the knock out in the park**
> **22**
> **where oranges have been laid to rust upon the green since dev-**
> **23**
> **linsfirst loved livvy.**

Wallstrait is for the straight, high wall of the Garden of Eden and the fall of stock prices on Wall Street in 1928. In dreams it is connected with the father, whose chest is flat without mammary glands. The fall of stock prices started or was part of the Great Depression, an echo of the Fall in the TZTZ creation when the world had to make do with less. **Old Parr** is the stage of the salmon while young with spots on its sides. Old *par* suggests repetition of the average—as in par for the course.

The Fall is retold [**retale**] early in bed. Here Joyce suggests the early dream is of the fall, the early dream in this case being the Garden of Eden myth. And it is retold by Christians all through history—repetition of the doctrine of Original Sin to continue to emphasize dependence on the Church. **The great fall of the Offwall** suggests the fall of offal or refuse, the subject of waste matter leeking into the dream from its latent curse content. The Fall of Finnegan off the wall resulted in his death, a death like the sound of **pftjschute**—the end of the breath of life.

Like Adam laid out in Jerusalem, Finnegan is laid out in Dublin, his head at Howth and toes in Phoenix Park. Like Humpty Dumpty, his humpty head is a hill. All the King's horses and all the King's men couldn't put Humpty Dumpty back together again because they didn't want to—they wanted him separated. Note the King is not involved in the effort. Finnegan laid out is like our immobilized dreamer. He doesn't know where his toes are; he is not in touch with them.

Then the letter "u" in **humself** and **prumptly**, "u" or the group dependent "you" rather than the independent upright letter "i" in "himself" and rather than the complete "o" in "promptly." The pursuit of the toes [**tumptytumtoes**] by the **unquiring** one reflects the legend of Adam Kadmon and the measure of his body. His toes are the lowest emanation—matched by lowest awareness and thus the "unquiring" or non-inquiring dependent one. The children's story atmosphere animates **tumptytumtoes**. In the lowest emanation and awareness, the toes are joined with military instruments—**pike** and **point. Knock Out** suggests more strife and is the name of a gate in Phoenix Park, Dublin's proxy for the Garden of Eden.

Rust for rest suggests death as a form of corruption, which in turn suggests the TZTZ connection. Like dream content, rust is a connection with the past.

The curse restricts individuality that in turn produces the Fall that produces strife, so next in the Joyce chain of dependent origination we have violence in all lands and all ages:

[4] What clashes here of wills gen wonts, oystrygods gaggin fishy-
1

gods! Brékkek Kékkek Kékkek Kékkek! Kóax Kóax Kóax! Ualu
2
Ualu Ualu! Quaouauh! Where the Baddelaries partisans are still
3
out to mathmaster Malachus Micgranes and the Verdons cata-
4
pelting the camibalistics out of the Whoyteboyce of Hoodie
5
Head. Assiegates and boomeringstroms. Sod's brood, be me fear!
6
Sanglorians, save! Arms apeal with larms, appalling. Killykill-
7
killy: a toll, a toll. What chance cuddleys, what cashels aired
8
and ventilated! What bidimetoloves sinduced by what te-gotetab-
9
solvers! What true feeling for their's hayair with what strawng
10
voice of false jiccup! O here here how hoth sprowled met the
11
duskt the father of fornicationists but, (O my shining stars and
12
body!) how hath fanespanned most high heaven the skysign of
13
soft advertisement! But was iz? Iseut? Ere were sewers? The oaks
14
of ald now they lie in peat yet elms leap where askes lay. Phall if
15
you but will, rise you must: and none so soon either shall the
16
pharce for the nunce come to a setdown secular phoenish.

These are dream-like, highly charged images in a chain of association related by violence. Taking each one:

What clashes here of wills gen wonts, oystrygods gaggin fishy-
1
gods!

Wills gen wonts-- I will on one side against I won't on the other. The basic argument and pointedly about nothing at all. The free will of Eve and Adam versus god's rule against eating from the one tree. "Gen" is the Indo-European root for to fit or join and here is pulled up out of the collective consciousness of man.

Oystrygods gaggin fishygods—Oystrygods are Ostrogoths combined with oyster. Fishygods are the Visigoths. They were rival Gothic tribes. In each of these names the Goth has been changed to god because of the black hole affect of the curse. Because TZTZ God is violence, because violence and strife were built into the TZTZ creation. Fish eat each other. **Gaggin** is eating, gagging on food, combined with *Gaggen* German for "against." Christians were known by the sign of the fish, a fishygod as mongered by the institutional church.

Brékkek Kékkek Kékkek Kékkek! Kóax Kóax Kóax! Sounds of frogs in Hades in Aristophanes ***The Frogs***. Note **Brekkek** sounds like break, **kekkek** sounds like kick and **koax** like coax. What is it that coaxed a male to break and kick, to violence? Why it's sex.
More on ***The Frogs*** from Wikipedia:

> *The Frogs* tells the story of the god Dionysus, despairing of the state of Athens' tragedians, and allegedly recovering from the disastrous Battle of Arginusae. He travels to Hades to bring Euripides back from the dead. He brings along his slave Xanthias, who is smarter, stronger, more rational, more prudent, braver, and more polite. To engage the audience, their first scene consists of a battle of potty humor jokes, and Xanthias subtly wins each round.

> * * * When Dionysus arrives at the lake, Charon ferries him across. Xanthias, being a slave, is not allowed in the boat, because he was unable to take part in the Battle of Arginusae, and has to walk around it. As Dionysus helps row, he hears a chorus of croaking frogs (giving the play its name). Their chant - Brekekekex ko-ax ko-ax is constantly repeated, and Dionysus joins in. When they arrive at the shore, Dionysus meets back up with Xanthias, and they get a brief scare from Empusa. A second chorus composed of spirits of Dionysian Mystics soon appear.

The chorus of the frogs is always the same; it repeats and it covers up the fart of Dionysus who is pretending to be Hercules and brave. Like TZTZ god, Dionysus is a forger, pretending to be brave. Potty humor jokes remind us of TZTZ creation.

Moving on in the Joycean encyclopedia of strife:

[4] **Ualu**
2
Ualu Ualu! Quaouauh
3

This is, according to Campbell, a Welsh lament that sounds like "you are a lu." Lu as an ending in Welsh apparently means something like an organization. Lu is to give us the Loo, the water closet, and an organized Loo, the Battle of Waterloo, nationally organized death in lieu of another flood. The curse is pulling on the dream.

More:

[4] **Where the Baddelaries partisans are still out to mathmaster Malachus Micgranes and the Verdons cata-**
4
pelting the camibalistics out of the Whoyteboyce of Hoodie
5
Head.

These refer to famous quarrels among Celtic clans and invaders. **Mathmaster** is a compound word that means to cut down men and annihilate their homes and monasteries [Campbell]. As the Norse did in Ireland. As mastering the science of math it is ironic. Math gives us counting at the simplest level, counting that assumes separation as in one two three different things. The white boys were religious fanatics who like the KKK went around in groups with individual identity subsumed and hidden by robes in order to do their dirty work to the unbelievers. TZTZ god hides his role in death.

More strife:

[4] **Assiegates and boomeringstroms. Sod's brood, be me fear!**
6
Sanglorians, save! Arms apeal with larms, appalling. Killykill-
7
killy: a toll, a toll. What chance cuddleys, what cashels aired
8

and ventilated! What bidimetoloves sinduced by what te-
gotetab-
9
solvers! What true feeling for their's hayair with what strawng
10
voice of false jiccup!

More violence. On and on. Over and over. Sieges at the gate. Boo-
merangs. Booming storms of canon. Violence is in TZTZ god's
blood [**Sod's brood**]. All of this without glory—**sanglorians**. *Sans*
means "without" in French. What chance love [**cuddleys**]. What bid
me to loves [compounded together as **bidimetoloves** for together-
ness] were sin seduced by what **tegotetabsolvers**? In the original
draft this word was "egosetabsolvers," which apparently means an
ego control absolver or ego control destroyer, a separator. The final
word must mean something similar in terms of absolving the tet, the
head. In other words, why all this violence? Where is mental control?
Where is Truth as a value when Jacob the identity forger fools his
father, fools him with **hayair**, that is false hair of hay and straw, and
a falsely strong-like Esau voice—the false gyp or jiccup. Jacob is a
chip off the old block of the forger god. False cup for the K metaphor of the vessels that broke.

[4] **O here here how hoth sprowled met the**
11
duskt the father of fornicationists but, (O my shining stars
and
12
body!) how hath fanespanned most high heaven the skysign
of
13
soft advertisement!

Back to the rainbow covenant. God and Adam and Noah are the
fathers of fornicationists, the primal horde system that relies on violence. **O here here how hoth sprowled met the duskt**—here at
this place Howth [stuttered] laid out, met the dust, died—this is presumably Finnegan. **the father of fornicationists**—fornication in
architecture means an arch, and so the reference is to the rainbow
arch of which TZTZ god is the architect. This may also mean that in
view of all the violence fornication was sent as covenant of survival.
The **skysign of soft advertisement** would be the rainbow on the
aquaface promising the blessing after the flood. But the rainbow is

fanespanned, that is scattered and without fame like the people of Babel. Sexual love is now the temple [**fane**] of the soft advertisement. More:

> [4] But was iz? Iseut? Ere were sewers? The oaks
> 14
> of ald now they lie in peat yet elms leap where askes lay.
> Phall if
> 15
> you but will, rise you must: and none so soon either shall the
> 16
> pharce for the nunce come to a setdown secular phoenish.

Now the dream narrator asks where was the rainbow that promised blessing—**But was iz?**. He asks **Iseut**, Isolde with a suggestion of insult, and also asks her where the sewers were, the sewers needed to take away the excrement after the TZTZ creation. We got excrement rather than a rainbow.

Now about the secret preserved in the human soul:

> The oaks
> 14
> of ald now they lie in peat yet elms leap where askes lay.

Continuing the excrement metaphor we have peat [vegetable matter] rotting in the bog. The oaks of old [**ald**] have fallen and remain trapped in peat, preserved in peat bogs, but have no sun and no fire. [Spirit is needed; peat is not enough.] Nonetheless elms rise where ashes [**askes** suggesting questions] fell. Ashes of the Phoenix. In Norse mythology, the ash [ash from ashes] was the first man [Aksr] and the elm the first woman [Embla]. They lived in the middle world. From the Wikipedia:

> Odin and his brothers, Ve and Vili, were the creators of all nine worlds of Norse cosmology. They took driftwood from a beach and gave them human shapes. Odin then gave them the breath of life, Vili gave them wit and emotions, and Ve gave them senses and speech. These two people, Ask ("ash"), the male, and Embla ("elm"), became the progenitors of all humanity; they lived in Midgard.

Note that Odin or Woden [read wooden] made the first humans from driftwood. Note that elm the female is to do the leaping, the restoring. She thrives where the oak dies. She is to restore, to put the separates back together, starting with the sperm and egg, which were separated when Eve was sawed off.

> **[4] Phall if**
> **15**
> **you but will, rise you must: and none so soon either shall the**
> **16**
> **pharce for the nunce come to a setdown secular phoenish.**

You will fall if you exercise free will [**Phall**—fall of penis] but you must rise and very soon [become erect]. And the only way to rise in these circumstances, circumstances ruled by TZTZ god, is your own secular phoenix, through the birth of children: *that is the production of more possibilities for the human race*. This phoenix is your finish, your end, your **setdown**. Your Phoenix is a **phoenish**, a finish.

Now under these circumstances caused by TZTZ god [curse, limitation on individuality, fall and strife] what does mankind do? What is the solution to the curse? Our savior, Mankind's proxy, the giant Finnegan gives us the answer. He reaches for the heavens in the process of building the counterpart of the Tower of Babel. This is a reach for the ultimate and the manifestation of more individual spirit in pursuit of more possibilities. He climbs the ladder without the fear of god or fear of death. This is the Faustian spirit, the spirit that took us to the moon. We would now say reaching higher for more possibilities by technology:

> **[4] Bygmester Finnegan, of the Stuttering Hand, freemen's mau-**
> **18**
> **rer, lived in the broadest way immarginable in his rushlit too-far-**
> **19**
> **back for messuages before joshuan judges had given us numbers**
> **20**
> **or Helviticus committed deuteronomy (one yeastyday he sternely**
> **21**
> **struxk his tete in a tub for to watsch the future of his fates but ere**
> **22**
> **he swiftly stook it out again, by the might of moses, the very**

wat-
23
er was eviparated and all the guenneses had met their exodus
so
24
that ought to show you what a pentschanjeuchy chap he
was!)
25
and during mighty odd years this man of hod, cement and
edi-
26
fices in Toper's Thorp piled buildung supra buildung pon
the
27
banks for the livers by the Soangso. He addle liddle phifie
Annie
28
ugged the little craythur. Wither hayre in honds tuck up your
part
29
inher. Oftwhile balbulous, mithre ahead, with goodly trowel
in
30
grasp and ivoroiled overalls which he habitacularly fondseed,
like
31
Haroun Childeric Eggeberth he would caligulate by multi-
plicab-
32
les the alltitude and malltitude until he seesaw by neatlight of
the
33
liquor wheretwin 'twas born, his roundhead staple of other
days
34
to rise in undress maisonry upstanded (joygrantit!), a waalworth
35
of a skyerscape of most eyeful hoyth entowerly, eri-
genating fromnext to nothing and celescalating
[5] the himals and all, hierarchitec-
1
titiptitoploftical, with a burning bush abob off its baubletop
and
2

> with larrons o'toolers clittering up and tombles a'buckets
> clotter-
> 3
> ing down.

This passage, some of the finest art in FW, is in babel language and says roughly as follows. Big Mister Finnegan of the Stuttering Hand [shaky hand like the shake of ES] lived big, far back in a cave [like Vico's giants] and too long ago to receive the benefits of TZTZ god's book the Hebrew Scriptures or the Old Testament. Operating without those benefits, he used direct divination instead of revealed scripture in order predict good and evil in the future. In this effort at divination he stuck his head in a tub one day in order to see the future of his fates [fixed already]. What he saw was that all would die. For this purpose the water in the tub evaporated.

Despite this revelation, Finnegan as a construction man climbed high to build many buildings. He wasn't afraid. He had sex with his wife and hugged their child. With his trowel in hand and wearing his favorite overalls he would calculate the attitude of all until he saw the mal spirit by which he was born. He would build skyscrapers with a burning bush on top.

Note that characteristic of Vico's first phase, the phase of the gods, Finnegan never says anything. Some of the images here are dream-like but the language is more Joyce joke than dream. It does reach back to earliest days. It is more like a myth.

Now in detail:

> **Bygmester Finnegan, of the Stuttering Hand, freemen's**
> **mau-**
> 18
> **rer, lived in the broadest way immarginable . . .**

Bygmester is master builder and big mister, pulling in the spirit of Ibsen who was a hero for Joyce and wrote a play *The Master Builder*. Master builder Finnegan was a freemason, a free thinker, and lived in the spirit in a big way, a Broadway show ["broadest way"] kind of spirit. He is a paragon of individuality. So big his spirit was that it was **immarginable**, like the universe without margin or end.

Finnegan sounds like an ES spirit. As with the builders of the Tower of Babel, he wished for immortality. And he was a unifier. He put buildings together. Finnegan lived in the ES template, unlimited possibilities and unity supported by independence. Put simply, he was not afraid of falling off the ladder.

Next, Joyce disses TZTZ god's book the Hebrew Scriptures by using its chapter titles as common words:

> . . . in his rushlit toofar-
> 19
> back for messuages before joshuan judges had given us numbers
> 20
> or Helviticus committed Deuteronomy. . .

This is priceless humor—Helviticus committed Deuteronomy, Deuteronomy being the chapter that contains all the rules, including the one against homosexuality. Given the rules, you don't have to think independently even about what to wear, what to eat or what to do on the Sabbath.

The master builder's spirit was lived in the **rushlit**, rushing light suggesting the spirit of ES. He lived **toofarback** [in time and in the cave, the combined word suggesting being confined in a cave] for spirit massaging messages from the Hebrew Scriptures and TZTZ god.

> . . . (one yeastyday he sternely
> 21
> struxk his tete in a tub for to watsch the future of his fates but ere
> 22
> he swiftly stook it out again, by the might of moses, the very wat-
> 23
> er was eviparated and all the guenneses had met their exodus so
> 24
> that ought to show you what a pentschanjeuchy chap he was!) . . .

Since he did not have the Hebrew Scriptures for guidance as to the future, he decided to plumb the future by divination—on a **yeasty-day**, a yeast or spirit rising day. Like Eve, he wanted god-like knowledge, knowledge of what would happen in the future. This involved washing watching [**watsch**] by sticking and strucking [**struxk**] his head in a tub of water [the confusing tub in this case is the purifying

186

waters of Baptism]. The tale of this particular tub was that all persons [**guenneses** or genesis spirits] would meet their exodus, their death. [This is much like Eve who acquired knowledge of death by acquiring additional knowledge.]

As with the fear of death, he did not see in this divination the multitude of possibilities he and others could accomplish in the interim but only their end, their fated death. Inevitable death is what the tub showed. As part of this soothsaying experience, the water in the tub evaporated and parted [**eviparated**], as the water parted for the Israelites fleeing the Egyptians. The tub went dry as life goes dry when the emphasis is on death. That connection to the miracle of the Exodus of the Hebrews shows you how much he was in tune with the Pentateuch [five books of the Torah] and juicy in the spirit [**pentschanjeuchy**]. In other words, he saw death under the influence of the TZTZ god who is registered in the Pentateuch.

> **. . . and during mighty odd years this man of hod, cement and edi-**
> **26**
> **fices in Toper's Thorp piled buildung supra buildung pon the**
> **27**
> **banks for the livers by the Soangso.**

During the mighty odd years depicted in Genesis prior to Abraham, Finnegan worked in construction erecting building upon building, a repetition of building. Finnegan used a hod to carry bricks, a hod being a v-shaped tray on the end of a long pole usually supported on the shoulder. This allowed him to deliver the bricks high up without climbing all the way up himself. He could reach higher using the hod. It also connects him with Lug of the Long Hand, another Irish hero. Bricks were the symbol of the suffering of the Hebrews in Egyptian captivity. The hod [shaped like the Bishop's mitre] also suggests religion as a tool to get higher up toward god than you can with your own efforts. You don't have to climb all the way yourself.

The hod was a personal technology much akin to the function of the Tower of Babel, to get higher. The V on the top of the hod would indicate victory of the individual human spirit over the curses of the gods, as the Babel builders tried to get close enough with their high building to be in god's face. A common language would cement them together for this effort.

In **Toper's Thorp**, that is in the effort to top others and drink in the spirit [tope means drink heavily], he piled education upon education and building upon building [**buildung** means education in German and sounds like building and dung in English]. The buildings were on the banks for those **livers** by the **Soangso**—that is, the spirit he drank was processed by his liver while he was singing. In other words, he tried to make the most of himself. Individuality is promoted by education and effort at making something new.

> . . . He addle liddle phifie Annie
> 28
> ugged the little craythur. Wither hayre in honds tuck up your part
> 29
> inher.

So now for the common, that is non-individual, part of Finnegan's life, which is given little space. He had a little wife Annie and hugged her like he craved drink of the spirit—the creature. With her hair in his hands [holding her head] he tucked up his penis **inher** [the word is a picture of the act]. Note the absence of a time factor or sequence in this material. Addle right to ugged. Then tucked inher. Notice how impersonal it is.

Back to his building effort:

> Oftwhile balbulous, mithre ahead, with goodly trowel in
> 30
> grasp and ivoroiled overalls which he habitacularly   fondseed,

Like Moses, he was often bare headed and stuttered [Tindall], more ES shaking, with his mitre [**mithre**] ahead of him in the form of his trowel. The mitre is suggestive here of the ritual headdress of a bishop or abbot [that is deeply cleft with a V] or in the Jewish religion by an ordinary priest. **Mithre** compared to mitre suggests the addition of myth. His overalls, that is what is over all of us and god gave to Adam and Eve as a Garden departure present, were **ivoroiled** or ivory coloured from the cement he carried and roiled. These are his vestments. He habitually fancied them particularly by habit [**habitacularly**], fancied being **fondseed** or fond of his seed. His seed sticks to the egg like cement to the brick.

> ... like
> 31
> Haroun Childeric Eggeberth he would caligulate by multi-
> plicab-
> 32
> les the alltitude and malltitude ...

Like HCE or the Caliph of Baghdad in Arabian Nights, he would calculate the ligulae [folds of the vulva] [**caligulate** is a compound of calculate and ligulae] by multiplication [procreation—1 times 1 equals 3] and would calculate what was capable or feasible given the cohesiveness of the people [**alltitude** is the attitude of all the people together] and high altitude of the building. **Malltitude** is the bad attitude of the gods for all.

> ... until he seesaw by neatlight of the
> 33
> liquor wheretwin 'twas born, his roundhead staple of other
> days
> 34
> to rise in undress maisonry upstanded (joygrantit!). ..

Until he saw back and forth [**seesaw**] by the light of the liquor or spirit he drank neat or naked the basics of survival by which he was born [human sexuality]. They were his **roundhead staple of other days**. The round headed penis "staples" the woman while staples are planted food necessary for survival in those **other days**—days after the Garden of Eden curse. His roundhead rose in undressed stone standing up or erect (grant us joy in sex or joy in granite). The tall building is now related to an erect penis.

Going on;

> ... a waalworth
> 35
> of a skyerscape of most eyeful hoyth entowerly, erigenating
> fromnext to nothing and celescalating
>
> [5] the himals and all, hierarchitec-
> 1
> titiptitoploftical. ..

He built a **waalworth of skyerscape**, a Woolworth kind of sky-scraper that was worth only a **waal** or wailing wall. **Skyerscape** is escape into the sky, what the babel builders tried to do. The building was an eyeful like Howth originating from next [**fromnext** is combined given the meaning of "next to" as proximity] to nothing [creation *ex nihilo*] and celestially scaling the heavens and all in hierarchy architecture tip top loftical. Up and up.

> [5] . . . with a burning bush abob off its baubletop and
> 2
> with larrons o'toolers clittering up and tombles a'buckets clotter-
> 3
> ing down.

The burning bush is now on top of the building rather than in the mountains. It said *mishe mishe* to Moses and he replied "here I am." Here the tall building with its burning bush on top proclaims mishe mishe I am I am. The sign of a bush in Ireland announces the sale of liquor within—liquor and the spirit. Here and on Mount Sinai TZTZ god says don't come any closer. Don't get too close to godly. Stay limited. Like the Hebrews at Sinai who wanted to scale the mountain to where god was, the patrons of Dublin were trying to climb up noisily while buckets were "clottering" down, falling buckets of clotted shit that made it hard to get higher. **Otoolers** are going up because of the independent **Saint Laurence O'Toole:** Archbishop of Dublin (1161-1180), and the city's patron saint who gave rise to Ireland's canonical independence from Canterbury. **Tumbles a'buckets** are going down because of Saint Thomas a Becket: Archbishop of Canterbury (1162-1170), the source of dependency for the Catholic Church in Ireland.

The next paragraph is a shift from Finnegan to a warrior in the second Vico phase heroic:

> [5] Of the first was he to bare arms and a name: Wassaily Boos-
> 5
> laeugh of Riesengeborg. His crest of huroldry, in vert with
> 6
> ancillars, troublant, argent, a hegoak, poursuivant, horrid, horned.
> 7
> His scutschum fessed, with archers strung, helio, of the second.
> 8
> Hootch is for husbandman handling his hoe. Hohohoho, Mister

9
Finn, you're going to be Mister Finnagain! Comeday morm and,
10
O, you're vine! Sendday's eve and, ah, you're vinegar! Hahahaha,
11
Mister Funn, you're going to be fined again!

This is a dream shift to a new scene modeled on the second phase per Vico, the phase of heroes, the age of the mute giants like Finnegan having passed.

Heroic-type sentences per Vico took one thing at a time as each new sensation cancelled the last one [v 265]. Heroic description was "as if things seen were actually taken possession of by sight" [v 266]. Heroes were close to the original giants, had limited understanding, vast imagination, violent passions and were "boorish, crude, harsh, wild, proud, difficult, and obstinate" but easily diverted particularly by women [v 457]. Accordingly, the last part of the foregoing sentence is a diversion. Being was eating [v 262] thus the pig. Their poetry would be about extremely disturbed passions [v 463] and normally spondaic as in shouts of all accented syllables. Ensigns were the first markers for private property [v 486]. Finn again is die again as wine becomes vinegar.

Campbell has the translation:

> He was the first to bear arms and a name: Wassaily Booslaeugh of Riensengeborg. His crest, green, showed in silver a he goat pursuing two maids, and bore an escutcheon with silver sun-emblem and archers at the ready.

This is the arena of conflict for limited survival resources, namely women. The pursuit of individual power is registered in heraldry.

Now notice how it is done:

Of the first was he to bare arms and a name: Wassaily Boos-
5
laeugh of Riesengeborg. His crest of huroldry, in vert with
6
ancillars, troublant, argent, a hegoak, poursuivant, horrid, horned.

191

7

His scutschum fessed, with archers strung, helio, of the second.

Heraldry is individuation in warfare. Heroes fought individual battles to decide wars, a sort of sudden death decider. This kind of guy is caught up in violence but violence that at least saves others.

The name **Wasaily Booslaeugh** is all about booze, a big boozy passionate name ringing of drink, drunk and giant. Composed in hero-type language, the second sentence takes one thing at a time as you might see it and without overall organization or meaning—the separates in TZTZ creation, the husks containing the sparks. **Huroldy** combines heraldry with hure for whore and hurry. The two maidens are **Ancillars**, as in ancillary. The signs are **troublant** or perturbed. The **hegoak** is the he-goat combined with the seminal oak in Norse mythology. Like the he-goat, the hero is horrid and horned in his get-up. The **scutschum** is the type of escutcheon referred to as scutum, which has square corners rather than round ones and is made in the form of the bony plate. [v564]. **Helio** is the sun-emblem and archers are strung at the ready, apparently to shoot the sun.

Then easily distracted, the sentence suddenly shifts to Finnegan:

> **Hootch is for husbandman handling his hoe. Hohohoho, Mister**
> **9**
> **Finn, you're going to be Mister Finnagain! Comeday morm and,**
> **10**
> **O, you're vine! Sendday's eve and, ah, you're vinegar! Hahahaha,**
> **11**
> **Mister Funn, you're going to be fined again!**

The first sentence is all or nearly all spondees [each word has accented syllables only]. It says: so Wasaily, before you get too big for your britches, remember that just like Finnegan you are going to die. Be afraid and smaller says TZTZ god. Not so bold. The language is children's sing song, a dream technique.

Finn is going to die again, that is be ended or fined again. His **Funn** is done. The vine or hootch of the spirit will soon be turned to vinegar. Four for repetition in **hohohoho** and **hahahaha**.

Now for some big questions and shards from other spiritual systems, as the Thousand Nights and One Night brings us to Muslim land and the Prophet Mohammed. The title reminds us of the dream of the night. And since Islam promotes submission and predestination, it like the dream is based on and limited by the past. Joyce views Allah as the Arab version of TZTZ god. Note that inevitable death is the most potent predestination:

[5] What then agentlike brought about that tragoady thundersday
13

this municipal sin business? Our cubehouse still rocks as earwitness
14

to the thunder of his arafatas but we hear also through successive
15

ages that shebby choruysh of unkalified muzzlenimiissilehims that
16

would blackguardise the whitestone ever hurtleturtled out of
17

heaven. Stay us wherefore in our search for tighteousness, O Sus-
18

tainer, what time we rise and when we take up to toothmick and
19

before we lump down upown our leatherbed and in the night and
20

at the fading of the stars ! For a nod to the nabir is better than wink
21

to the wabsanti. Otherways wesways like that provost scoffing
22

bedoueen the jebel and the jpysian sea. Cropherb the crunch-
23

bracken shall decide. Then we'll know if the feast is a flyday. She
24

has a gift of seek on site and she allcasually ansars helpers,
the
25
dreamydeary.

This says that just like everyone else, the Muslims don't understand the relationship of mankind with the powers that be. The
camel might as well decide. The patriarchal line of Islam started with
Abraham through Ishmael, and you remember that Sarah convinced
Abraham to ban Hagar and Ishmael to the desert [competition in the
harem for succession].

Now in detail:

> What then agentlike brought about that tragoady thunders-
> day
> 13
> this municipal sin business?

Agentlike because dependent on others and because Satan is said to
have used the serpent in the Garden of Eden and because
Adam/Eve served as agent for all of us in original sin. **Tragoady** is a
combination of tragedy and goad, sex as the source and conduit for
original sin pressed into tragedy. **Thundersday** is the day of thunder—thors day or Thursday. **Municipal sin business** refers to Cain
killing Able in the first scene out of the Garden and then founding
the first cities.

> Our cubehouse still rocks as earwitness
> 14
> to the thunder of his arafatas but we hear also through suc-
> cessive
> 15
> ages that shebby choruysh of unkalified muzzlenimiissile-
> hims that
> 16
> would blackguardise the whitestone ever hurtleturtled out of
> 17
> heaven.

The Muslims are also on the receiving end of god's thunder—**the
thunder of his arafatas**. Fart in **fatas**. The **cubehouse** refers to the
Holy Ka'aba, the uniformly square house that is the center of Islam
and which the pilgrims circumnavigate seven times during the Haif

pilgrimage. Notice the repetition, seven times around. Note the uniformity—the cube.

The corner stone of the cubehouse is a black rock held together by a silver band. It is believed to have arrived from heaven during the time of Adam and Eve. Originally it was white but as it absorbed mankind's sin it subsequently turned black. The text suggests the rock originally came not white but black as part of the curse, that it was turned black by god's fart, his arafatas, an echo of our father.

The last part says that what the Muslims did themselves would turn the stone black [**blackguardise the whitestone**]. The Muslims are described as a shabby chorus of in-fighting [**chorusysh** is a combination of chorus and Quraysh the prophet's tribe that initially resisted him]. They are unqualified muslin wearing missile launchers with a Caliph or successor not agreed upon. Their fighting so much over succession would itself make any stone hurled white out of heaven turn black. Caliph means the successor, the militant issue between Sunni and Shiite. Fighting over succession to the Prophet reminds us that succession is the issue in the TZTZ creation and in the primal horde.

> **Stay us wherefore in our search for tighteousness, O Sus-**
> **18**
> **tainer, what time we rise and when we take up to toothmick and**
> **19**
> **before we lump down upown our leatherbed and in the night and**
> **20**
> **at the fading of the stars!**

Both Allah and Jove were referred to as "the sustainer." Muslims are enjoined to pray to Allah five times a day at specified times—so the next material says stay tight with us and steady us all the time—from the time we rise for first prayer and rise in the spirit, to when we take up the toothpick prayer right after lunch [the Prophet used toothpicks], to the prayer before siesta on the leatherbed [Prophet used one] and at dusk and at night. Stay tight with god, all day long and by implication from birth to death. Allah take care of us. In the Koran: "Prayer is the heart of Religion and Faith." Mohammed called it the "gate to heaven." Bow down, don't reach up. Submit. Ultimate dependency. This is TZTZ god in the cube house.

Now the text comments on the efficacy of prayer in reaching the powers that be:

**For a nod to the nabir is better than wink
21
to the wabsanti.**

This Joyce creation about the efficacy of prayer is modeled on the aphorism "A nod is as good as a wink to a blind horse"—that is the nod is no good at all; the blind horse, like the sleeper, can't see a nod or a wink and wouldn't know what either meant anyway. One futile gesture is equal to another futile gesture if the audience is unable or unwilling to pay attention. Interdependent with the FW dreamer, TZTZ god is asleep; the Lesser Countenance has eye lids.

Coming right after the reference to the five daily prayers, this reference would comment on the efficacy of prayer, particularly mandatory five times a day prayer. Required prayer can't be given in the right attitude, in free will, since it is required. Prayer would be a futile gesture if god is unable or unwilling to pay attention. Once again repetition is suggested by alliteration, of the letters "n" and "w," nod nabir and wink wabsanti.

Nod in this case refers to lowering the body in prayer. The **nabir** means the last of the prophets, a combination of nabi, prophet in Arabic, pressed together with nadir [which means end or last]. **Wabsanti** apparently means absent and refers [Atherton] by wab for web [OED] to a cave [on Mt. Thaur] where Mohammed hid during his flight from Meccah. This was before he was widely proclaimed as the prophet. A spider miraculously spun a big web across the opening of the cave so that it looked like no one had entered recently and Mohammed was successfully concealed. **Santi** apparently means saint or sanctified in Arabic. So like Vico's giants, Mohammed finds god in a cave because of fear of death.

The surface meaning of Joyce's aphorism would appear to be that an acknowledgment to the last prophet by regular devout prayer is as futile as a wink to the concealed saint that he can't see [since he is in the cave]. But **nabir** also seems in a deeper meaning to suggest death—that death is last real prophet. A wink is a sexual suggestion or more generally an attempt at connection.

Summarizing: As with the original aphorism, I think the deeper comparison of Joyce's aphorism is also to something that is no good at all—that the prayer is no good at all in terms of a communication to the concealed god and the only real connection is death.

> Otherways wesways like that provost scoffing
> 22
> bedoueen the jebel and the jpysian sea.

Otherwise, without the benefit of a connection to god, you will be adrift like the Prophet's coffin that is purportedly suspended in the air between heaven and earth. Like a Bedouin, His coffin is without a fixed home. **Bedoueen** combines between, Bedouin and queen. As the Bedouin have no true home, your spirit will be like a gypsy hung between the devil and the deep blue sea—or in the case of the Israelites, between Horeb and the Egyptian Sea.

Now to Mohammed's camel:

> Cropherb the crunch-
> 23
> bracken shall decide. Then we'll know if the feast is a flyday.
> She
> 24
> has a gift of seek on site and she allcasually ansars helpers,
> the
> 25
> dreamydeary.

So the critical issue of communicating with god will be left to Mohammed's camel, a delegation of means that Mohammed often used in social situations. In reacting to many requests for hospitality as he entered a town, Mohammed would declare that his camel would decide—to avoid personally offending any offered **host**. Where the camel stopped Mohammed would accept hospitality. Presumably the camel would also be fed.

Coming hard on the heels of the aphorism about the inefficacy of prayer in communicating with god, the camel deciding means that the Muslim religion like others is no better than a camel at this communication.

Cropear not **cropherb** was the name of Mohammed's favorite camel. A cropeared camel wouldn't hear too well. **Cropherb** would refer to grazing on grass. If cropherb decides, then the basic survival eating instinct would be in charge. In this material the meaning of the camel plays off against the blind horse in the original version of the aphorism discussed above.

The text goes on to state that when the camel decides then we would know if the feast day [day of eating the ritual **host**] is a Friday [flyday by L/R split] or day of the spirit, the day of flying. Muslims treat Friday as the holy day of rest for the week—as opposed to Saturday for the Jews and Sunday for the Christians. [Christ died on Friday and Easter Sunday was his flyday, his resurrection.] This is damning with faint praise, suggesting that deciding the rest day is about all organized religion can do. For this puny effort, it receives a L/R split, giving us the submissive bent over "r" in Friday instead of the erect "L" in flyday.

She the camel has a gift of prophecy, **a gift of seek on site** or secondary sight on sacred ground, and she quite casually answers helpers [**ansars** being Mohammed's helpers to whom he recited the Koran], so does the dromedary the dreamy one. In other words, the camel writes the Koran. In this context the camel is the dreamy one because Mohammed received his first injunction from the Archangel Gabriel to write the Koran while in a trance [during a fast in a cave]. While illiterate as a camel, Mohammed was able in the trance and under divine injunction to read from a scroll in his dream the words that start the Koran. In other words, Mohammed had a dream. Under these circumstances of divine injunction and help, the camel could just as well have written the Koran.

In this context of submission and human dependency, the text moves back to the Tower of Babel imagery and fault in humans:

> **Heed! Heed! It may half been a missfired brick, as**
> 26
> **some say, or it mought have been due to a collupsus of his back**
> 27
> **promises, as others looked at it. (There extand by now one thou-**
> 28
> **sand and one stories, all told, of the same).**

Why are humans so submissive, so lacking in individuality, so restricted in possibilities? Some thought humans may have [**half**—only partly divine] an inherent problem spiritually. Because of the curse humans would be limited to only one half divine. Or be equivalent to a misfired brick. Adam was made from red clay by god who blew life into the clay. The misfiring would be a fault in god's initial creation action—the TZTZ creation. Or it may be due to the collapse of god's back [previous] promise of the rainbow on the waters, a collapse of the bow or arch. The Babel humans didn't believe god's promise not to cause another flood or any other kind of harm on earth. The other reason the promise is a "back" promise refers to

198

god's statement that he only showed his backside and only to a fortunate few because the sight of his countenance would kill a human. But kill them is what god did, again and again. He showed his backside and delivered god shit.

Then the long sentence delivering a version of god shit in the city in a dream-like sequence:

[5] But so sore did abe
29
ite ivvy's holired abbles, (what with the wallhall's horrors of rolls-
30
rights, carhacks, stonengens, kisstvanes, tramtrees, fargo-bawlers,
31
autokinotons, hippohobbilies, streetfleets, tournintaxes, mega-
32
phoggs, circuses and wardsmoats and basilikerks and aeropagods
33
and the hoyse and the jollybrool and the peeler in the coat and
34
the mecklenburk bitch bite at his ear and the merlinburrow bur-
35,
rocks and his fore old porecourts, the bore the more, and his

[6] blightblack workingstacks at twelvepins a dozen and the noobi-
1
busses sleighding along Safetyfirst Street and the derryjelly-bies
2
snooping around Tell-No-Tailors' Corner and the fumes and the
3
hopes and the strupithump of his ville's indigenous rome-keepers,
4
homesweepers, domecreepers, thurum and thurum in fancymud
5

> murumd and all the uproor from all the aufroofs, a roof for
> may
> 6
> and a reef for hugh butt under his bridge suits tony) wan
> warn-
> 7
> ing Phill filt tippling full.

But as sure as Adam [**abe**] ate [**ite**] Eve's [**ivvys'**] holy red [**holired**] apples [**abbles**—this word suggests by reversing p to b and lowering the round part of the letter that the apple was taken down from the tree]. Then the long sequence: (what with the wallhall's Vahalla but with limitations of walls, horrors of all the cars, cabs, engines, tomes, trams, shouters, autos, hobbling horses, fleets for the streets, touring taxis, megaphones hogging the air, circuses, political meetings, serpents, castles in the air, and the noise and the laughing and the policemen in their coats and the whore bitch biting at his ear and the army barracks and his four old law courts for the poor mostly that were boring in repetition, and his black workingstacks at twelvepins a dozen and the noobibusses sleigh sliding along SafetyFirst Street and the ladies snooping around Tell no tales Corner and the smoke and hopes and the hump of the strumpet etc etc) without warning Phil [Tim] felt tippling full [in the song Tim was "rather full" the morning he died]. Tippling refers to drunk on alcohol but a tippler is also [OED] a revolving cage or frame in which a truck or other carrier is inverted to discharge its load. You can sense the TZTZ creation in this tippling image.

This long list is meant to be as deadening, mesmerizing and suffocating as the world of tangibles, noise and motion is, particularly in the city in TZTZ creation. No wonder Phill felt tippling full. The increasing distortion of the words used prepares the reader for a downward move into the lower intestine of myth—perhaps back to an image of Finnegan as Mohammed's camel staggering under his load:

> [6] His howd feeled heavy, his hoddit did
> 8
> shake. (There was a wall of course in erection) Dimb! He
> stot-
> 9
> tered from the latter. Damb! he was dud. Dumb! Mastaba-
> toom,
> 10

mastabadtomm, when a mon merries his lute is all long. For
whole the world to see.

His head felt heavy, **howd feeled** expressing that feeling. Perhaps
this is the FW dreamer with a hangover. His head shoke and with
that his hod [tool] it did shake, **hoddit** meaning head in Danish expressing the feeling and reminding us of ES shaking. There was, of
course, a wall in the course of construction, like an erection. Blind
[**dimb**] he was ineffective [**dud**] and he stutter-like fell from the ladder [ladder is rendered as **latter,** meaning previously mentioned—
namely Adam or god's previous fall]. Thud makes him a dud.
Damned and silenced [**Dumb**] by death, he was dud gone useless.
He fell and bounced bad into a mastaba-tomb. When a man marries
his penis [**lute**] his penis is long for all the world to see [a lust driven
long penis gets around for many to see]. Finn apparently died with
an erection. Death is like marrying your penis; both limit the unifying
possibilities.

Now to the Wake, the fall of Finn leading directly to the Wake.
First for some information about a wake in general and an Irish wake
in particular from Wikipedia:

> Traditionally, a wake takes place in the house of the deceased, with
> the body present; however, modern wakes are often performed at
> a funeral home.
>
> **The tradition stems historically from an ancient tradition of**
> **watching over the deceased's body in the hope that life**
> **might return and the term in many places is now synony-**
> **mous with viewing or funeral visitation.** The purpose of the
> wake has evolved so that now it is a time for the deceased's friends
> and loved ones to gather and to console the immediate family
> prior to the funeral. In Australia, New Zealand, and northern
> England, the wake commonly happens after the funeral service in
> the absence of the body and is often "wet" -- which is to say alco-
> hol and food are served and, as a result, the wake often resembles
> a party for the deceased as well as being of comfort for their fam-
> ily. In this way it follows the model of the traditional Irish wake,
> although there is a long tradition of feasting and celebration con-
> nected with funeral service amongst the Mori of New Zealand that
> predates European settlement. [emphasis added]

With this information we are given to understand that when the mourners of Finnegan find that he is about to wake up and convince him to go back to sleep *that they are denying the purpose of the wake with respect to the return of life*. We will also view this food and drink laced "wet" wake death through the trope of the flood. Now more about an Irish wake from the same source:

Irish wakes

The "Irish Wake" is a traditional mourning custom practiced in Ireland. An integral part of the grieving process for family, friends, and neighbors of the deceased, Irish wakes are occasions that mix gaiety and sadness. The custom is a celebration of the life that had passed, but the tone of the wake depended largely on the circumstances of the death.

***

Preparations for the wake began soon after death. All clocks in the house were stopped as a sign of respect, and women gathered to bathe and dress the body. The deceased often wore white garments, and if a man died, his face was shaved clean before being dressed. The body was then laid out for viewing on a table or bed and was attended until the burial. All mirrors in the household were also covered, removed, or turned around.

Immediately after they prepare the body, the women begin keening.

Further information: Caoineadh Airt Uí Laoghaire

This vocal lamentation [keening] is a display of mourning and sounds a bit like wailing to those who are not accustomed to it. Superstition holds that keening must not begin until after the body is prepared or evil spirits will surround the wake and body.

***

The Irish also celebrated the life of the deceased and shared food and drink throughout the wake. Music, dancing, and physical games made the wake feel more like a party. The Catholic Church has tried numerous times (unsuccessfully) throughout history to abolish the consumption of alcohol at wakes. Though it is a time of sadness, the presence of friends and family makes it more bearable and there is generally great joviality as the deceased is fondly remembered; indeed, there is tradition in some parts of the country to play a game of cards and include a hand for the deceased.

***

The Irish wake, in the sense of celebrating at a death, originated with the ancient Celts. In their belief system, once someone died in this world they moved on to the afterlife, which was a better world, and thus cause for celebration. Conversely, a birth was a time for sadness as it meant someone had died in the other world.

Those at the wake for Finnegan speak to his dead body and direct their attention to the liquid spirits at his head and feet. Those attending are mourning but also feeling license as at a totem meal. A mourner moans at the Wake for Finnegan:

> [6] Shize? I should shee! Macool, Macool, orra whyi deed ye diie?
> 13
> of a trying thirstay mournin? Sobs they sighdid at Fillagain's
> 14
> chrissormiss wake, all the hoolivans of the nation, prostrated in
> 15
> their consternation and their duodisimally profusive plethora of
> 16
> ululation.

One reveler identifies Finnegan with Finn Macool, a mythical Irish giant hero. The reveler says **shize** [shit in German]. I should see she [**shee**]. Why did you die? Why did you die on a trying thirsty Thursday [thunderday] mourning morning? They sighed and mourned at Finn's Fill again with Christ sorely missed [**chrissormiss**] at the wake, all the organized religions [**hoolivans**—holyvan or agents of holy] of the nation in false formality and sincerity (signified by tenor of the words) in their consternation and their **duodisimally** [12 of them] **profusive plethora of ululation** (the moaning of an owl).

> [6] There was plumbs and grumes and cheriffs and citherers
> 17
> and raiders and cinemen too. And the all gianed in with the shout-
> 18
> most shoviality. Agog and magog and the round of them agrog.
> 19

This material is based on an old song:

Chorus

> There was plums and prunes and cherries,
> And citron and raisins and cinnamon too,
> There was nutmeg, cloves, and berries,
> And the crust it was nailed on with glue.
> There was carraway seeds in abundance,
> Sure 'twould build up a fine stomach ache,
> 'Twould kill a man twice after 'ating a slice
> Of Miss Hooligan's Christmas cake.

Here Hoolivan, agent of the holy, is changed to Hooligan—a rowdy and destructive gang. TZTZ god is a hooligan. A Hooligan's Christmas suggests curses. In her hooligan cake a curse is hidden. There were plums to plumb the situation and prunes in lumps [defecation] and cherries as noblemen or sheriff and citrons with musicians and raisin raiders and cinnamon cinema men too. The hidden curse is that the crust is nailed on with glue. The crust that holds TZTZ creation together is glued together with a curse, not with unity.

And all joined in the giant [join and giant combined as **gianed**] with shouting joviality [**shoviality**] giving him a shove—keeping him dead, dead as an individual. Excited like giants and dodging the curse by using gog in place of god [Tindall], the round of them drunk with grog are treating Finn like old bricks broken up for new ones. License prevails. As the old song says, eating the father crust [the crust that holds it all together] will cause problems.

Now we zoom in on the totem wake as a feast on Finn's substance, his spirit symbolized by the alcoholic spirits served to the 12 revelers:

[6] To the continuation of that celebration until Hanand-hunigan's
20
extermination! Some in kinkin corass, more, kankan keening.
21

Now hooligan changes to **Hanandhunigan** or Han and Hun again. To the continuation of that celebration until Han and Hun again's death [Chinese and Hun warfare]. Some present are in "chorus" [**corass**—the core of us] and keening [moaning] as kin [**kinkin**] of

204

the deceased but more are present because they cancan keenly enjoy the food and drink.

More:

> [6] Belling him up and filling him down. He's stiff but he's
> steady is
> 22
> Priam Olim! 'Twas he was the dacent gaylabouring youth.
> Sharpen
> 23
> his pillowscone, tap up his bier! E'erawhere in this whorl
> would ye
> 24
> hear sich a din again? With their deepbrow fundigs and the
> dusty
> 25
> fidelios.

Building him up in speeches and laying him down. And then the first of the artificial speeches by the four old men, the authorities repeating the TZTZ basics—you are all the same, you are all here comes everybody. First old man: He is stiff but as steady as Priam the King of Troy was once [even Priam is brought down]. Second old man: he twas a decent youth who enjoyed his labor paid by the day [time before death]. Third old man: sharpen his gravestone that is like Jacob's stone pillow when he had his dream of the stairs to and from heaven. Close up his coffin like a beer keg. Fourth old man [doesn't even talk about Finnegan]: where in this whorl would you hear such a din again? The din suggests the unforgiving Din aspect of ES god in TZTZ creation.

With their serious profundity and the dusty old faith, the four old men consign the memory of Finnegan to an average human without heroics. They mention nothing about what he accomplished acting as an individual, just his common qualities, what he shared with everyone else.

Going right on:

> [6] They laid him brawdawn alanglast bed. With a bockalips
> 26
> of finisky fore his feet. And a barrowload of guenesis hoer his
> head.
> 27

**Tee the tootal of the fluid hang the twoddle of the fuddled, O
!
28**

In the TZTZ god life, spirit starts when you die, not while you live. So they laid him at last along his last bed [**alanglast**] for the dawn of his spirit life [**brawdawn** by *bradain* Italian for salmon and for brow-down]. He is between a bucketcalypse [**bockalips** suggesting apocalypse] of whiskey of the spirit finished [**finisky**] at his feet and beer **guenesis** start creation over his head. Between the sum total of these fluids, between finished in the spirit and starting in the spirit, hang the bewilderment of the human [**the twoddle of the fuddled, O.**] It hangs in between like the coffin of the Prophet.

Next Finn rolls over as the old **globe wheels in view**—as the cycle turns:

**[6] Hurrah, there is but young gleve for the owl globe wheels in
29
view which is tautaulogically the same thing.**

As the world turns and time rolls on, there is but a **gleve**, a young soldier armed with a sword. The young males become violent just like their fathers. The old wise globe wheels in view as the cycle turns, human experience always being the same thing necessarily [**tautaulogically**] since contained in the original TZTZ creation. The meaning is limitation above so necessarily limitation below. Man-god-man. In philosophy, a tautology is a redundant repetition [our limitation theme] and in logic a compound proposition that is unconditionally true for all the truth possibilities of its component propositions by virtue of its logical form. An example would be

> It is a sunny day and on a sunny day the rain does not fall so the rain does not fall.

This statement is true no matter what the truth value of the statements of which it is comprised. "It is a sunny day" and "The rain does not fall" may or may not be true as an empirical matter for that day but the statement is still true as far as it goes. Joyce's tautology is:

> God fell and if God fell man must fall so man fell.

After Finnegan turns over, those present at the Wake are not surprised about his movement and instead comment on Finnegan's bulk, his corporeal aspect:

> **[6] Well, Him a being**
> **30**
> **so on the flounder of his bulk like an overgrown babeling, let**
> **wee**
> **31**
> **peep, see, at Hom, well, see peegee ought he ought, platter-**
> **plate.** *Here an E on its back*
> **32**

With this they comment on how he lies—still concentrating on his body rather than his spirit. He looks like a flat flounder fish, an overgrown babel youngster. Flounder suggests failure at spirit. Let us peep and see Him [distorted to Hom for homme mankind]. He ought to pee, gee he ought to pee [projection of the mourners' own needs]. He lays there like a platterplate. He is like home plate. The E on its back is Finn lying down, or interred in the landscape with an erect penis [JJ letter].

Then there are four references to direction from west to east, suggesting the four chariot wheels in K and from death to birth. Each of these pairs makes reference to geographical locations where Finnegan **calmly extensolies**—which means lies extended and by way of extenuate gets smaller. But at the same time these references express main themes of the novel:

> **Hum ! From Shopalist to Bailywick or from ashtun to**
> **baronoath**
> **33**
> **or from Buythebanks to Roundthehead or from the foot of**
> **the**
> **34**
> **bill to ireglint's eye he calmly extensolies.**

One at a time:

From Shopalist to Bailywick: Shopalist suggests shopping your list and some degree of individuality. Shopalist sounds like Chapelizod, a village west of Dublin that is named after the Chapel of Isolde. Isolde's desires and shopping. Bailey is a light on Howth Head to the east of Chapelizod and Bailywick refers to the jurisdiction of a bailiff. In other words, the primal horde theme—Isolde and individual desire under the control of the senior male. In the big picture, the same pattern: TZTZ god in control in TZTZ creation.

From ashtun to baronoath: Ashtun is Ashtown a village to the NW of Dublin, west to east to baronoath—Howth Head and the castle thereon, where the baron lives and receives oaths of fealty. Or ashes by the ton [a curse by volcano] and control by the baron as a result of the curse.

Buythebanks to roundthehead: Buythebanks refers to a song about the River Lee in Cork, to the west of Dublin. Buythebanks also refers to the commercial life, living for material gain, and roundthehead recalls the last word of the first chapter of Ulysses, where Buck's round head in the distance suggested a seal's and the less resistance encountered in living for material rather than individual spiritual achievement. In other words, the commercial life to the lack of resistance to the compromise life.

Foot of the bill to ireglint's eye: Foot of the bill suggests the end of the bill or the total owed as well as foot of the hill. The debt owing would be the debt of death. **Ireglint's eye** refers to an island north of Howthhead. Ireglint would be the flash of anger or ire of the curse in TZTZ god's eye. In other words, from the debt of death to the angry god.

In the next material Finn is like Prometheus, the independent hero who disobeyed the commandments of the gods in order to steal fire for mankind, another Eve-like character who suffered because he dared to be great. He is rockbound where the winds in the bay wail him [as his relatives are keening at the wake]:

> [6] And all the way (a
> 35
> horn!) from fiord to fjell his baywinds' oboboes shall wail
> him
>
> [7] rockbound (hoahoahoah!) in swimswamswum and all the
> livvy-
> 1
> long night, the delldale dalppling night, the night of bluery-
> bells,
> 2
> her flittaflute in tricky trochees (O carina! O carina!) wake
> him.
> 3

From fiord to fall the baywinds' oboes [**oboboes** like the sound of the oboe] wail him, he who is **rockbound** like Prometheus. For stealing fire from the gods, Prometheus was punished by the gods for eternity, chained to a rock with his liver eaten out each day by a big bird. Another example of the curse. A big Hoho from the narrator because rockbound could also suggest testicle oriented—male testosterone oriented. Oboe because in French the word for oboe *hautbois* literally means high tree, for the tree of life and the tree of death. Dead he is in the present, the past and the past completed [**swimswamswum**]. In the night with a feminine aspect **delldale dalppling** [find ALP in this phrase]. The wind's musical bells and flute trochees [words with long and then short stresses like **ca**rina] wake him, the female principle. Trochees are used because when the stress is on the initial syllable or birth, you find the female principle. When the stress is on the last syllable or death, you find the male principle. Female principle wake him!

Now a major theme, the role of the female post-separation of Adam and Eve to take the sperm of the male and combine it with her egg in order to make a child, take the salt water from the male prostate that carries the sperm and make it into a miracle. This is the role of the female as unifier—to put things together, sperm and egg, and if necessary put back together again in peace making efforts things torn apart in male violence:

> [7] With her issavan essavans and her patterjackmartins about all
> 4
> them inns and ouses. Tilling a teel of a tum, telling a toll of a tea-
> 5
> ry turty Taubling. Grace before Glutton. For what we are, gifs
> 6
> à gross if we are, about to believe. So pool the begg and pass the
> 7
> kish for crawsake. Omen. So sigh us. Grampupus is fallen down
> 8
> but grinny sprids the boord.

Since the TZTZ religions place the spirit world in the death world, they place the cart before the horse, the last part before the first part. So mimicking the cart before the horse, **Essavans** is Vanessa rearranged with the last four letters first and suggests by sound "easy van" or easy transport. Similarly, **Issavan** is vanissa with the last four letters rearranged first and may refer to Issy, HCE's daughter as derived from Isolde, as well as a van to carry one away. These names also suggest what J. Swift did to those poor girls. He rearranged their lives to make things easy for himself. Essy or issy or easy for him.

Patterjackmartins refers to organized Christian religion [Peter **Patter** Catholic, Jack Calvinism, Martin Lutheranism in *Tale of a Tub*], organized religion that puts the cart post-death before the horse life. **Inns and ouses** are Inns and houses, souls and bodies, and birth and death—in and out. These religions ritualize birth and death, in and out, but not life while you are there. The house of life becomes mere **ouse**.

Tilling a teel of a tum, telling a toll of a teary turty Taubling: Telling a tale of a tummy [pregnancy] and telling of the toll [curse] of Teary [suffering] or Dirty Dear or turd-like Dublin.

Grace before Glutton: Higher aspirations please—dare to be great—grace before a meal. Normal form of grace: For what we are about to receive. A distorted form of grace: **For what we are, gifs a gross if we are, about to believe**. We thank you for what we are, which you gave us, which are big **gross** gifts if we believe in you. **Gross** carries the suggestion of gross versus refined.

So pool the begg and pass the kish for crawsake. Omen. So pool the fish and pass the basket for fish-Christ's sake. Christ was often referred to by the sign of the fish. Since Christ participated in both god and man, he is a meeting of the powers that be and mankind, of the salt and fresh waters. He is the host; he is in the ritual host. As a fish, he would have to be a salmon. The Greek word *ichthys* was a backwards acronym [backronym] for Jesus Christ, Son of God, Saviour. Before that, the same symbol, two intersecting arcs reflecting the profile of a fish, was used worldwide as a symbol of the Great Mother Goddess, as an outline of her vulva [Wikipedia]. Christ died for others so they could be dependent; so they could lose their independence to others.

Grandfather is fallen down in splinters or pieces in the TZTZ creation but grandmother **sprids the boord**—puts it all back together in Tikkun. The primal Tikkun is childbirth. A grandmother is a grand mother indeed, a mother twice over.

Coming from Christ-fish, the next material explores the nature of what is eaten at the Wake, whether the body and blood of Finn the big and heroic individualist contain any god material. In this Christ-fish connection think fish fins for Finnegan. The reference is

210

to the Catholic Eucharist ritual in which transubstantiation converts the wafer and wine into the actual body and blood of Christ. Christ here is viewed as a victim of the requirements of the primal horde. Totem like, the eating repeats the killing of the giant father. He will not awake so let's eat him.

> [7] Whase on the joint of a desh? Fin-
> 9
> foefom the Fush. Whase be his baken head? A loaf of Sing-
> pan-
> 10
> try's Kennedy bread. And whase hitched to the hop in his
> tayle?
> 11
> A glass of Danu U'Dunnell's foamous olde Dobbelin ayle.
> 12

Who is on the dish? What is in the Eucharist? Mere bread or real god? The Eucharist ritual celebrates the death of Christ, the man-god. Joint suggests joinder of man with god. "Desh" suggests a dash and death, the die all-too-soon human condition. **Finfoefom** is from Jack and the Beanstalk: feefiefofom I smell the blood of an English-man. Children's stories are dream material. Here it is fin for the end, foe for the curse from god, and fom for death from god the First Mover to the man-god and man. **Fush** for flush. Where is his **baken** head, baked because the wafer is baked and represents his entire body including his head. His head contains a loaf or body from St. Patrick's wisdom, his Kennedy bread. And what is connected to the spirit in his tale? [**And whase hitched to the hop in his tayle?**] A glass of famous ["foamous"with foam for spirit] O'Connel Ale [from another son—that of Daniel O'Connell] Dublin ale, ale for all Dub-lin for Doublin their mumper. Reproduction is the only spirit left.

For more on **finfoefom,** note the following on its sound cousin teetotum:

> [From T-totum. Originally a teetotum was a kind of die used in a game of chance. It had a stick put through a six-sided die so that only four sides could be used. One of the sides had the letter T representing Latin totum (all), implying take the whole stake from the pot. Other sides had letters A aufer (take one stake from the pot), D depone (put one stake in), and N nihil (do nothing). A dreidel is a form of teetotum.]

Within TZTZ creation teetotum is understandable. Given the curses, the possibilities are limited—the stake through the **die** limits the possibilities of the roll. Only four not six results are available. Since you have bet one stake, that is bet your one life, you have the following possibilities: T—take all from the pot, take everything life has to offer; A—take one out, end a life; D--put one more in, that is create a child, and N—do nothing, waste your life.

Joyce converts teetotem to finfoefum, in order to eliminate the T result, of obtaining all. In the TZTZ system your possibilities are limited even more to just three: and death the fin is your foe and leads to fum, nothing.

From there the text moves to the claim that But eat thou you will, there is no god in that food, or in you. Finn your source is dead, he is no more "where," no more in space. He is finished, only a fading graph of a yesterday eastern scene [Christ]:

> **[7] But,**
> 12
> **lo, as you would quaffoff his fraudstuff and sink teeth through**
> 13
> **that pyth of a flowerwhite bodey behold of him as behemoth for**
> 14
> **he is noewhemoe. Finiche! Only a fadograph of a yestern scene.**
> 15

Quaffoff suggests ritual through repetition of the letter "f." The word **fraudstuff** refers to the claims for the Eucharist as the actual body and blood of Christ. **Behemoth**, the land monster like the water monster leviathan, unfolds as "be he a moth" and thus flutters away but is attracted to the flame. **Flowerwhite bodey** would refer to the flour in the Eucharist transubstantiated in this version into-flower. Noe of **noehwemoe** is Noah and the flood devastated generation—no we anymore. Like Noah, Finn is no more.

Now to the fish analogy. Christ was referred to by the sign for the fish. Christ was man-god. Fish live in water, some in fresh and salt, some just in fresh and some just in salt. The salmon is unusual: it starts in fresh as a par, changes into a smolt with scales and first migrates from fresh to salt water where it grows and spends most of its life. Later as the grilse stage, it returns to the same stretch of fresh to spawn and die. Like Christ the salmon can return to the fresh water the second time. A trout, by contrast, stays in fresh.

With this fish analogy in mind, we are invited to examine Finn's fins, Finn's death:

> [7] **Almost rubicund Salmosalar, ancient fromout the ages of the Ag-**
> 16
> **apemonides, he is smolten in our mist, woebecanned and packt**
> 17
> **away. So that meal's dead off for summan, schlook, schlice and**
> 18
> **goodridhirring.**
> 19

First we examine Finn as a salmon. Finn, almost a red salmon [**rubicund Salmosalar**]—the last grisle phase of procreation and death—ancient from the ages of the love feasts [**Apemonides**—a free love institution], he is in our midst **smolten**—with love, the counterpart of fresh and salt. The smolt is the second stage for a salmon, when it migrates downriver to the salt water. They would easily be caught on the way out. He is **woebecanned**, that is canned with woe like salmon who are caught. Like fish, he is **packt away**, that is packed away pursuant to a pact, the promise of death. So that meal is spoiled [**dead off**], that is to say there is no god in Finn. Finn is no good as fish, flesh or good red herring. The gods treat humans as humans treat fish: they catch, can and pack them away. **Summan** is the sum of mankind and **schlook** is a shoddy person. **Schlice** is cut as in primal horde castrating, which produces a shoddy mankind. **Goodredhirring** is good riddance as well as a good red herring or false clue.

In the view of Joyce, what the TZTZ god-based religious rituals involve is eating death, sanctifying god by eating death. Seeking sin-cleared life by eating death. For Joyce, eating is for life. Like the salmon that goes for salt water during its life cycle, the TZTZ religions preach death and dependence in the midst of life, producing a canned and shoddy life. The TZTZ religions would be like the oncologist who tells the patient after chemotherapy: "You are going to die, so worry about dying and don't bother making much of the rest of your life."

Now we examine Finn as a trout, a fresh water fish, a fish in life:

[7] Yet may we not see still the brontoichthyan form outlined
a-
20
slumbered, even in our own nighttime by the sedge of the
trout-
21
ling stream that Bronto loved and Brunto has a lean on.

That is, may we not still see the god fish in our dreams [but not in death but in life, in fresh water]. The dream scene would be by the edge plant [**sedge**] of the trout and trouble-bearing [**troutling**] stream that Bruno loved and **Brunto** [evil in TZTZ] had a **lean on**—lien on or influence. That is, the ES god can nonetheless still be seen in the stream of life described by Bruno's opposites even though the TZTZ god has a lien on it.

Now in the same paragraph with seeing the god image in dreams as fish in water, we now have the female principle in water:

[7] *Hic cubat*
22
edilis. Apud libertinam parvulam. **Whatif she be in flags or**
flitters,
23
reekierags or sundyechosies, with a mint of mines or beggar
a
24
pinnyweight. Arrah, sure, we all love little Anny Ruiny, or, we
25
mean to say, lovelittle Anna Rayiny, when unda her brella,
mid
26
piddle med puddle, she ninnygoes nannygoes nancing by.

The Latin *Hic cubatedilis. Apud libertinam parvulam* [bearing ALP] translates as "here sleeps the magistrate in the presence of the little freedgirl." The primal and concealed ES god provides the sleeping magistrate, and Eve breaking the rules in the Garden supplies the little freedgirl. What if she be in rags or tatters, reeking clothes or Sunday best, rich or poor. To be sure, **we all love little Anny Ruiny**—that is Eve ruining any and all with the Fall. Or we mean to say **lovelittle Anna Rayiny**, that is Anna raining, when under her undies umbrella [or protection by condom] with piddle and puddle of rain

214

[and sperm] she goes from a ninny to a mommy care giver nanny. In other words Eve is ok because she became a mother.

With rain, we note that Waterloo is coming right up, where torrential rain stalled the military action and insured the would-be hero's Napoleon's defeat through delay and hesitancy. Then:

> **[7] Yoh!**
> 27
> **Brontolone slaaps,. Upon Benn Heather, in Seeple**
> 28
> **Isout too. The cranic head on him, caster of his reasons, peer yu-**
> 29
> **thner in yondmist. Whooth? His clay feet, swarded in verdigrass,**
> 30
> **stick up starck where he last fellonem, by the mund of the maga-**
> 31
> **zine wall, where our maggy seen all, with her sisterin shawl.**
> 32

Still in the dream, the grumbler-thunderer slaps the thunder while you can only snore [**yoh snores**]. On Howth Head and Chapelizod too. Now about Finn's head and feet. First his head, where his reasoning is cast, appears yonder in the mist [remember the pre-Eden mist and Adam]. **Cranic** emphasizes and repeats head. **Whooth**: **Who** is **oth**-other, that is other oriented given the Fall of all. His feet of clay [suggesting fault] are covered in greengrass and stick up rigidly where he last fell in the fall for all fellowmen [**fellonem**]. He fell by the mound of the magazine in Phoenix Park, where our Maggy with her sisters by her shoulders [**sisterin shawl**] seen all.

Then a shift to Waterloo mixed with Eve's original sin, the initial human Fall being associated with modern battle death and the fall of Napoleon. The association is made through the phrase **belles' alliance**:

> While over against this belles' alliance beyind Ill Sixty, ollol-
> 33
> lowed ill! bagsides of the fort, bom, tarabom, tarabom, lurk the
> 34

ombushes, the site of the lyffing-in-wait of the upjock and
hock-
35
ums.

The **belles' alliance** would be the passage of original sin through the
female line as well as a reference to the village by that name in the
middle of the Battle of Waterloo. The Fall of Eve leads to Waterloo
and the fall of Napoleon. **Beyind** is beyond and behind. **Ill Sixty** in
military terms is Hill 60 near Ypres, which changed hands often during the Battle of Waterloo [and in WWI]. Wellington staged most of
his troops in defensive lines concealed behind the hill. Wellington
remained on the defensive in the battle such that the wet ground
conditions played to his advantage.

    Ill 60 also has something to do with illness into old age [60
years] or death. To the same effect is **Ollollowed ill**, Hallowed Hill
and allowed illness. All Hallows would be the female sex organ that
passes original sin. **Bagsides of the fort** would be the arse and the
fort the sex organ, **Bom and tarabom** are gunfire and thunder. The
ombushes are pubic hair, where the ambush lies, connected to
TZTZ god through AUM [**om**]. **Lyffing-in-wait** is lying in wait
combined with Liffey. **Upjock** suggests erection and **hockums**
worthless but mirth making. "Up guards and at them" was Wellington's command.

    The hero of the Battle of Waterloo, the Duke of Wellington [Ar-
thur Wellesley], was born in Ireland and was claimed by Irish as their
hero—thus the Wellington monument in Phoenix Park. He was born
in Ireland, but claimed English status with the quip: Just because you
are born in a stable doesn't make you a horse. Put in Joyce's terms,
just being born in TZTZ creation doesn't mean you have to be dependent.

    The losers at Waterloo were the French commanded by Napo-
leon and Cambronne. Cambronne serves Joyce by linking surrender
to merde, surrender to god under the curse to excrement. More from
Wikipedia on Cambronne, who will lead us to Waterloo:

> Pierre Jacques Étienne Cambronne, later Pierre, Viscount Cam-
> bronne (26 December 1770 - 29 January 1842), was a General of
> the French Empire. He fought during the wars of the Revolution
> and the Napoleonic Era. He was wounded at the Battle of Water-
> loo.

216

He became Major of the Imperial Guard in 1814, and accompanied Napoleon into exile to the island of Elba, where he was a military commander. He then returned with Napoleon to France in 1815 for The Hundred Days, capturing the fortress of Sisteron (5th March), and was made a Count by Napoleon when they arrived at Paris.

After the Battle of Waterloo, commanding the last of the Old Guard, he was summoned to surrender by General Colville. Cambronne reputedly answered: *La garde meurt mais ne se rend pas! (The Guard dies, but does not surrender!)* Though historians still argue whether he actually ever said it, and it has been ascribed to General Claude-Etienne Michel.

The word of Cambronne
He then, it is claimed, in the face of British insistence, gave an answer today known as "The Word of Cambronne": *Merde!* ("Shit!")

Merde and death are the principal substance of the TZTZ creation. Waterloo is one of god's watercloset, or perhaps god's bidet. Shit is to surrender your independence.

So in Dublin, the city of merde, there is a Waterloo museum [Wallinstone National]. So now to the Museum:

> **[7] Hence when the clouds roll by, jamey, a proudseye view is**
> **[8] enjoyable of our mounding's mass, now Wallinstone national**
> **1**
> **museum, with, in some greenish distance, the charmful water-**
> **2**
> **loose country and the two quitewhite villagettes who hear show**
> **3**
> **of themselves so gigglesomes minxt the follyages, the prettilees!**
> **4**

Hence when the rain clouds roll by a view through a proud eye [proud is slang for in heat] is afforded of the mass of our hill [suggestive of the mound of Venus], now named the Wallinstone national museum. It is contained in the mound of history. Wallinstone combines Wellington and wall and stone. In the distance is a charming and harmful [**charmful**] "water loose" country, one with more water than can be absorbed [which echoes the elements not absorbed by

217

ES]. It suggests waterloo and the water closet. Here there are two young girls from nearby villages [**two quitewhite villagettes**] who display themselves giggling and minx-like mid the folly foliage like Eve, the pretties.

More on the museum:

> [8] **Penetrators are permitted into the museomound free. Welsh and**
> **5**
> **the Paddy Patkinses, one shelenk! Redismembers invalids of old**
> **6**
> **guard find poussepousse pousseypram to sate the sort of their butt.**
> **7**
> **For her passkey supply to the janitrix, the mistress Kathe. Tip.**

Male penis penetrators are permitted into the museum mound free of charge—perhaps as veterans. [The museum has become a female sex organ displaying war and sex.] Non-veteran Welsh, Irish and English are charged one old shilling. The invalids of the old guard [Napoleon's crack troops and veterans in general] revisit their own dismembering and wounds and find a pushpush push-pram [a kind of wheelchair] to sit down on. For the passkey apply for supply [army provisioning terms] to the female janitor Kathe [**janitrix** suggests tricks]. Tip. Kate Strong was an official in Dublin in charge of clearing the streets of horse manure. Here she is in charge of showing god manure, the results of war.

Now Kathe guides us in the museum and Wellington becomes "willing done," or free will devoted to destruction. Sex and war are combined as the inheritance from TZTZ creation and its successor the primal horde. We have the leaders and their cheerleaders. At the Battle of Waterloo, wives and even children accompanied the soldiers. A disproportionately large number of Wellington's troops were Irish.

> [8] **This the way to the museyroom. Mind your hats goan in!**
> **9**
> **Now yiz are in the Willingdone Museyroom.**

Mind your head, your seat of reason, going into the musey room, which has a wax museum type display, a dream-like display. Now

218

you [Irish] are in the Wellington willingly done musey room. Musey suggests muse, the god of war.

Let us start with the history of the Battle from EB:

(June 18, 1815), Napoleon's final defeat, ending 23 years of recurrent warfare between France and the other powers of Europe. It was fought during the Hundred Days of Napoleon's restoration, 3 miles (5 km) south of Waterloo village (which is 9 miles [14.5 km] south of Brussels), between Napoleon's 72,000 troops and the combined forces of the Duke of Wellington's Allied army of 68,000 (with British, Dutch, Belgian, and German units) and about 45,000 Prussians, the main force of Gebhard Leberecht von Blücher's command. After defeating the Prussians at Ligny and holding Wellington at Quatre-Bras in secondary battles south of Waterloo on June 16, Napoleon's marshals, Michel Ney and Emmanuel de Grouchy, failed to attack and annihilate either enemy while their armies were separated. Grouchy, with 33,000 men, nearly one-third of Napoleon's total strength of 105,000, led a dilatory pursuit of Blücher. On the 18th he was tied down at Wavre by 17,000 troops of Blücher's rear guard, while Blücher's main force escaped him, rejoined Wellington, and turned the tide of battle at Waterloo, 8 miles (13 km) to the southwest. At Waterloo, Napoleon made a major blunder in delaying the opening of his attack on Wellington from morning until midday, to allow the ground to dry; this delay gave Blücher's troops exactly the time they needed to reach Waterloo and support Wellington.

The four main French attacks against Wellington's army prior to 6:00 PM on June 18 all failed in their object—to decisively weaken the Allied centre to permit a French breakthrough—because they all lacked coordination between infantry and cavalry. Meanwhile, a secondary battle developed, in which the French were on the defensive against the 30,000 Prussian troops of Karl von Bülow's corps of Blücher's army. The Prussians arrived at Waterloo gradually and put pressure on Napoleon's eastern flank. To prevent the Prussians from advancing into his rear, Napoleon was forced to shift a corps under Georges Mouton, Count de Lobau, and to move several Imperial Guard battalions from his main battle against Wellington.

Finally, at 6:00 PM, Ney employed his infantry, cavalry, and artillery in a coordinated attack and captured La Haye Sainte, a farmhouse in the centre of the Allied line. The French artillery then began blasting holes in the Allied centre. The decisive hour had arrived: Wellington's heavy losses left him vulnerable to any intensification of the French attack. But Ney's request for infantry reinforcements was refused because Napoleon was preoccupied with the Prussian flank attack. Only after 7:00 PM, with his flank secured, did he release several battalions of the Imperial Guard to Ney; but by then Wellington had reorganized his defenses, aided by the arrival of a Prussian corps under H.E.K. von Zieten. Ney led part of the guard and other units in the final assault on the Allies. The firepower of the Allied infantry shattered the tightly packed guard infantry. The repulse of the guard at 8:00 PM, followed in 15 minutes by the beginning of the general Allied advance and further Prussian attacks in the east, threw the French army into a panic; a disorganized retreat began. The pursuit of the French was taken up by the Prussians. Napoleon lost 25,000 men killed and wounded and 9,000 captured. Wellington's casualties were 15,000 and Blücher's were about 8,000. Four days later Napoleon abdicated for the second time.

Several connections bring Waterloo into FW. The name Ney gives us a seguey to the sound of horses neighing as well as the negative. Horses typically symbolize the passions, the main subjects of dreams. Waterloo is symbolic of the end, a climatic end. Waterloo brings us end by water as in the flood, the water closet or TZTZ toilet. The names Wellesley and Duke of Wellington, the "allied" commander, give us water from the well, as the big Flood came from below and above. He had a servant Ali the Mameluke, meaning slave or the ultimate dependent. Bonaparte translates literally as "good apart" or separate, associating him with TZTZ god. Bonaparte fails in the Battle of Waterloo because he hesitates and fails to unify or coordinate his ground and horse troops. He was known as *le petit tondu* or little crophead—remember Mohammed's camel cropear and the Lesser Countenance. Crophead also describes the dreamer's brain activity.

On the French side the Emperor's best troops were the Old Guard, as in the primal horde of the father. They wore large bear sky hats, sported tattoos and earrings and generally were subhuman veterans [think bikers]. They the "furbears" sponsor the use in FW of "Hebear," the male killing machine. Hebear and *bereshit*, the first word [Hebrew] in Genesis are natural associates.

In the Battle of Waterloo many were killed by friendly fire since some of the uniforms were similar. The battle was supposed to result in peace and prosperity and did usher in an era dominated by English mercantilism. It was in turn swept away by WWI.

Now with that as some background, back to Kathe the janitrix, the female who cleans up. She begins to point out some of the objects in the museum display:

220

> [8] This is a Prooshi-
> 10
> ous gunn. This is a ffrinch. Tip. This is the flag of the Prooshi-
> 11
> ous, the Cap and Soracer. This is the bullet that byng the flag of
> 12
> the Prooshious. This is the ffrinch that fire on the Bull that bang
> 13
> the flag of the Prooshious.

This is a precious Prussian [important allies of Wellington whose arrival won the day] gun [a long gunnnnn]. This other gun is French but short [frrinch]. Guns and penises. Tip again. This is the flag [slang for licentious woman] of the Prussians, bearing the Cap and Sorcerer. This is the bullet that banged [General Byng and fornicated] the Prussian flag [flags or standards were shredded by the volume of fire]. This is a French shell that was fired on the English [Bull] that banged the Prussian flag.

> [8] Saloos the Crossgunn! Up with your
> 14
> pike and fork! Tip. (Bullsfoot! Fine!)

Salute the crossgun [**saloos** the **crossgunn**], the gun that is cross or angry. Crossgunn suggests crossbow that in turn suggests failure of the cross and failure of TZTZ god's rainbow promise. Raise your weapons, **your pike and fork**. Fork also refers to Napoleon eating elegantly before the battle and reputedly saying victory would be as easy as eating breakfast. Tip again. Bullseye turned into **Bullsfoot** for lower order behavior. **Fine** for the end.

Now for our two leaders—**Lipoleum** for Napoleon [linoleum for a hard surface to be walked on and crop head] and **Willingdone** for Wellington. First Napoleon:

> [8] This is the triplewon hat of
> 15
> Lipoleum. Tip. Lipoleumhat.

Since Napoleon wore a two-corner hat, triplewon hat must refer to his head being turned by military victories. **Lipoleumhat**—he is now his hat and his victories.

And now for Willingdone in his very best dress:

> **[8] This is the Willingdone on his**
> 16
> **same white harse, the Cokenhape. This is the big Sraughter Wil-**
> 17
> **lingdone, grand and magentic in his goldtin spurs and his ironed**
> 18
> **dux and his quarterbrass woodyshoes and his magnate's gharters**
> 19
> **and his bangkok's best and goliar's goloshes and his pullu-pon-**
> 20
> **easyan wartrews. This is his big wide harse. Tip.**

Arthur Wellesley, Duke of Wellington, continues the water symbolism. For the big wide horse, see this from Wiki:

> cf. a joke quoted by Sigmund Freud in his *Wit and Its Relation to the Unconscious*: "Von Falke brought home a particularly good example of representation by the opposite from a journey to Ireland ... The scene was a wax-work show ... A guide was conducting a company of old and young visitors from figure to figure and commenting on them: 'This is the Duke of Wellington and his horse,' he explained. Whereupon a young lady asked: 'Which is the Duke of Wellington and which is the horse?' 'Just as you like, my pretty child,' was the reply. 'You pays your money and you takes your choice.'" → compare this with Wellington's assertion (on being "accused" of being Irish) that one is not necessarily a horse merely because one happened to be born in a stable.

If you can pay and take your choice, there is no independence in the presentation. Regardless of his claim to the contrary, Willingdone has become his horse. This is his big wide horse, the symbol of the passions.

In battle, Willingdone is his horse—his mount and his passions—and Lipoleum is his hat or his ego. The name of Wellington's horse was Copenhagen, which means merchants' harbor—suggestive of the promotion of mercantile interests as a result of the victory over Napoleon. And the distortion from Copenhagen to Cokenhape suggests the fortune that falls to one.

As to the

> big Sraughter Willingdone, grand and magnetic in his gold-tin spurs and his ironed dux and his quarterbrass woody-shoes and his magnate's gharters and his bangkok's best and goliar's goloshes and his pullupon-easyan wartrews,

Straughter is slaughter and Arthur combined, and **magentic** is majestic and magnetic combined. The combined metal **goldtin spurs** will show up in HCE's wardrobe [check out that word]. It is a combination of more value and less value. His ironed dux instead of tux for the iron leader; he was known as The Iron Duke. **Quarterbrass woodyshoes** refer to a battle at Quatre Bras and brass money and wooden shoes. **Magnate's gharters** would be a powerful man's garters. **Pulluponeasyan wartrews** for the Peloponnesian War and also pull upon easy waters.

Over in the French camp:

> [8] This is the three
> 21
> lipoleum boyne grouching down in the living detch.

The three boys, Napoleon I, II and III [II and III are the future] are crouching down in the ditch and grouching about their condition. They are not accustomed to privation. The Emperor's brother Jerome did lead one army group in the battle. Grouchy was a French general away from the main battle. The ditch is death [**detch** as ditch and death combined].

Now for more emphasis on horses, horses being featured since the passions are in charge:

> [8] This is an
> 22
> inimyskilling inglis, this is a scotcher grey, this is a davy, stoop-
> 23
> ing.

Royal Inniskilling [**inimyskilling**—in my skill at killing] Fusiliers: an enemy-killing English regiment of the British army from Enniskillen,

223

County Fermanagh, Ireland; they fought at Waterloo. **Scotcher grey** is kind of a horse and Scotch Greys a regiment of the British army; they also fought at Waterloo. A **davy stooping** is a reference to buggering, the wartime same-sex substitute among soldiers.

> [8] This is the bog lipoleum mordering the lipoleum beg. A
> 24
> Gallawghurs argaumunt. This is the petty lipoleum boy that
> 25
> was nayther bag nor bug. Assaye, assaye!

Waterloo was **bog**ged down in mud the days and night before the battle on June 18, 1815, and it was the mud that cost Napoleon the victory. With the rain, the Big outhouse Napoleon [**bog lipoleum**] is murdering [**mordering**] the hopes of little Napoleon [**lipoleum beg**], the would-be conqueror and massive egoist. Another interpretation of this same sentence suggests the primal horde: the big Lipoleum murders the junior Lipoleum. **Gallawghurs** [suggests gallows or death ggrrs]: Gawilghur was a fortress in northern India involved in the Battle of Gawilghur, 15 December 1803, in which Wellington took the fortress, as part of the Second Anglo-Maratha War. **Argaumunt** is argument and Argaum—a village in northern India involved in the Battle of Argaum, 29 November 1803, in which Wellington was victorious, as part of the Second Anglo-Maratha War.

This is the short Napoleon boy [from Corsica] that was neither small nor inconsequential [**bag** or beg from *beag* Italian for small]. I say, easy easy, try try and **Assaye**—a village in southern India involved in the Battle of Assaye, 23 September 1803, in which Wellington was victorious, as part of the Second Anglo-Maratha War. Note the suggestion by language that war is an ingrained human experience, just like argument.

Now the three boys, Tom Dick and Harry combined with references to female genitalia. Sex and war:

> [8] Touchole Fitz Tuo-
> 26
> mush. Dirty MacDyke. And Hairy O'Hurry. All of them
> 27

Touchhole refers to the canon's mouth and is slang for a homosexual. **Tuomush**—too much mush. **MacDyke** is son or offspring of a hair-ringed hole and futher homosexual reference. A dyke also holds back the flood. Hairy O'Hurry is quick soldier sex in the hair guarded anus and inadequate wiping after defecating. All of them are bellicose ass [**arminus**] stuck varmints [**varminus**]. Homosexual soldier sex without love. Amorous becomes arms and minus. The word connecting dash, **arminus-varminus,** punning as quick, is the connection, a limited connection indeed. That is the point, war the most powerful of separators separates even sex into a non-unifying act.

Now on to mountains:

> [8] **This is Delian alps. This is Mont Tivel,**
> **28**
> **this is Mont Tipsey, this is the Grand Mons Injun. This is the**
> **29**
> **crimealine of the alps hooping to sheltershock the three**
> **lipoleums.**
> **30**

The three mountains are references to battles. Why mountains and generals and horses? To mount is to ride a horse and slang for sex. Mons. This is the hoped-for skirt of the alps [ALP] hoping and **hooping** to shelter from shock the three Napoleons.

> [8] **This is the jinnies with their legahorns feinting to read in**
> **their**
> **31**
> **handmade's book of stralegy while making their war undis-**
> **ides**
> **32**
> **the Willingdone. The jinnies is a cooin her hand and the jin-**
> **nies is**
> **33**
> **a ravin her hair and the Willingdone git the band up.**

This is [notice the impersonal singular] the girls with their horned legs [**legahorns**]. Leghorn was a battle Napoleon won while females with horned legs suggest the dangerous sirens in *The Odyssey.* The Sirens hid their raptor legs and seduced sailors to jump ship by singing about the old days, necessarily limiting their future possibilities. See the Sirens chapter of Ulysses. They are **feinting** pretending [and fainting] to read in their **handmade's** handmaid's book of strategy [**stralegy**—the sex attraction strategy of the bare leg] while making their war **undisides** Willingdone, that is taking sides with their undies or underpants. Undies also suggests "never dies" since females produce offspring. The word **undisides** also points to undecided since Napoleon was famous for maneuvering in battle at the last minute and undecided about strategy for this Battle of Waterloo. Undecided takes us back to hesitancy and forgery.

In a singsong style, the jinnies is [singular verb used] cooing in her hand and the jinnies is rapine her hair and willingdone got excited—got up the band. [bander means get an erection]. Sex and war. The jinnies are the cheerleaders.

> [8] This is big
> 34
> **Willingdone mormorial tallowscoop Wounderworker obscides**
> 35
> **on the flanks of the jinnies. Sexcaliber hrosspower. Tip.**

This is a big Wellington memorial in wax [see Freud joke]. The thighs of the jinnies work as a rectal obstacle remover. Wonderworker was a product to solve rectal complaints; just as female thighs stop soldier same sex. Sex and gun horsepower—sex and horses [**sexcaliber hrosspower**]. Tip again.

> [9] This is me Belchum sneaking his phillippy out of his most Awful
> 1
> **Grimmest Sunshat Cromwelly. Looted.**

The narrator at the museum now identifies Belchum, the Belgian or non-English soldiers on Wellington's side allegedly sneaking away from the fight on their horses [philly or women or Battle of Philippi] but with loot. They are sneaking their horses out of sun shit celestial curse [**Sunshat**]. **Cromwelly** because like TZTZ god Oliver Cromwell directed genocide against Irish Catholics as Lord Protector of Ireland for England.

Now the jinnies, the cheerleaders in war and the primal horde prize, forge [forgery theme] a dispatch from Lipoleum to Willingdone:

> [9] This is the jinnies' hast-
> 2
> **ings dispatch for to irrigate the Willingdone. Dispatch in thin**
> 3
> **red lines cross the shortfront of me Belchum. Yaw, yaw, yaw!**
> 4

226

The dispatch is in haste [**hastings**—a battle] like all the passions and is to irritate [**irrigate**—water waterloo] the Willingdone. The dispatch is written in thin red lines [name of military unit] across the shirtfront of their stomach [the belch place for Belchum]. This sounds like a bare midrift, currently a popular place for posting messages to males. The message said:

> [9] Leaper Orthor. Fear siecken! Fieldgaze thy tiny frow.
> Hugact-
> 5
> ing. Nap.

This message mimics German:

> *Lieber Arthur. Wirsiegen! Wie geht's deiner kleinen Frau?*
> *Hochachtung:*
> (translating from the German) Dear Arthur.
> We conquer! How's your little wife?
> Yours faithflly. Nap.

This is in German to rub in the fact that Willingdone doesn't yet have his German troops. How's your little wife—**This would be like saying we claim your wife**. At this point he was married but did not get on well with this wife. Willingdone must read this message through his telescope as he stares at the cheerleaders.

Now a discussion of what the jinnies did:

> [9] That was the tictacs of the jinnies for to fontannoy the
> 6
> Willingdone. Shee, shee, shee! The jinnies is jillous agin-
> courting
> 7
> all the lipoleums. And the lipoleums is gonn boycottoncrezy
> onto
> 8
> the one Willingdone. And the Willingdone git the band up.

These were the tactics [**tictacs**—blind chess game] of the jinnies to fountain-annoy [**fontannoy**] the Willingdone. The jinnies forge a message from Lipoleum. She laugh she laugh she laugh about he [**shee** as she hee hee hee]. The jinnies are trying to use jealousy [letter to Willingdone] to court once again all the lipoleums [**Agincourt** a famous battle is again court]. And the lipoleums is going [**boycot-**

toncrezy] gun boy boycott heavy cotton crazy—firing canon—on the one Willingdone. And Willingdone responds by getting the troops up, with an erection.

Willingdone:

> [9] This
> 9
> is bode Belchum, bonnet to busby, breaking his secred word with a
> 10
> ball up his ear to the Willingdone. This is the Willingdone's hur-
> 11
> old dispitchback.

Willingdone is obsessing on the fact that Blucher has not arrived with the Prussian troops as soon as promised. So Willingdone says this is bad old Belgium-Blucher [**bode Belchum**], whose head is gone from **bonnet to busby**, a furtail hat suggesting the female sex organ [in other words Blucher must have stopped in a village]. Belchum is now Blucher not the Belgians. The strict and unforgiving Willingdone believes that Blucher has broken his sacred secret [**secred**] word given in a prior message to the Willingdone—the message that he would be there soon. [Sacred because of Blücher's famous statement to his troops that they must go on, as he had pledged his word to Wellington—as if the ethics of keeping one's word were more important than not killing.]

Here is some history about Blucher from EB:

> After Napoleon's return in 1815, Blücher again assumed command of the Prussian troops in Belgium, with August von Gneisenau as his invaluable chief of staff. Blücher immediately set about coordinating his force with that of the British and Allied forces under the Duke of Wellington. At Ligny (June 16, 1815) he was defeated by Napoleon; but, in order to ensure cooperation with Wellington later, he withdrew his army toward Wavre, although by so doing he endangered his own communications. His troops took no part in the early stages of the Battle of Waterloo (June 18, 1815); but, urged on by Gneisenau, they made an exhausting countermarch and appeared on the French right flank at a critical stage of the battle. This action, together with a general advance by the British, completed Napoleon's defeat. Blücher's cavalry continued the pursuit of the French toward Paris throughout the night.

So Willingdone writes on his ass to the jinnies, which they would see only with field glasses:

> [9] Dispitch desployed on the regions rare of me
> 12
> Belchum. Salamangra! Ayi, ayi, ayi! Cherry jinnies. Fig-
> treeyou!
> 13
> Damn fairy ann, Voutre. Willingdone.

Salamangra is a former Wellington victory—I will do to you what I did to them. I I I yes yes yes [**Ayi, ayi, ayi!**] Willingdone senses the forgery of the message by the **cherry jinnies;** as virgins, they would be forgeries. **Fig tree you**—up yours and Garden of Eden source of all evil. Continuing the Eve reference, **Damn fairy ann** sounds like Willingdone's attempt at the French *ce ne fait rien* for that doesn't matter. Presumed reply—what you said doesn't matter. Yours faithfully and fuck you. Willingdone. We don't know if the jinnies see this message.

Now an echo of the curse:

> [9] That was the first joke of
> 14
> Willingdone, tic for tac. Hee, hee, hee!

The first joke of ES was TZTZ creation. Tactics and a child's game. Laughter for he he he.

> [9] This is me Belchum in
> 15
> his twelvemile cowchooks, weet, tweet and stampforth fore-
> most,
> 16
> footing the camp for the jinnies. Drink a sip, drankasup, for
> he's
> 17
> as sooner buy a guinness than he'd stale store stout.

This is me Blucher in his rubber boots moving 12 miles toward the jinnies. Drink up soldiers [brandy rations] for he Wellington is less likely to buy a Guinness [for us] that steal stout from a store. Stout here must refer to courage. In the K context, it must mean he would rather start creation than let Eve steal god-like powers in the Garden.

Now more directions from the museum guide:

[9] This is Roo-
18
shious balls. This is a ttrinch. This is mistletropes.

More War and Sex. These are Russian cannon balls and testicles. This is a trench and a female sex organ [**ttrinch**], two "t's" for the lips of the vagina. These lips are mistletoe to encourage kissing and Irish Missile troops.

[9] This is Canon
19
Futter with the popynose. After his hundred days' indul-
gence.
20

This is cannon fodder with the Pope's nose—French Catholic troops? The French king was absent from the capital for 100 days after Napoleon's return and before his defeat at Waterloo. An indulgence is a Catholic concept, to purchase from the Church a reduction in the amount of time to be spent in Purgatorio. This is the King's indulgence—allowing him to be absent. Like ES in the "French leave."

More from the guide apparently referring to pictures or wax statues:

[9] This is the blessed. Tarra's widdars! This is jinnies in the
bonny
21
bawn blooches. This is lipoleums in the rowdy howses.

The wounded French are the blessed [since not killed]. The Tarra widows are the widows of Irish soldiers who fought and died for Willingdone. These are the jinnies [rendered singular as a force] in the pretty, fortunate short boots [bluchers] that show their legs. This is the French in the red hose and rowdy houses [**howses**].

More in the museum:

[9] This is the
22
Willingdone, by the splinters of Cork, order fire. Tonnerre!
23
(Bullsear! Play!) This is camelry, this is floodens, this is the
24

solphereens in action, this is their mobbily, this is panick-burns.
25

This is the Willingdone ordering canon fire [cannons use cork]. Thunder as the sound of cannon. **Bullsear** is bullseye in the ear of sound. Play. This is calvary by camel [**camelry** of Mohammed], this is the **floodens**, the counterpart of the curse flood, this is the **solphereens**—soul for reens [reens is a large ditch—sex organ—or soul for sex]. This is Thermopylae [**their mobbily**], this is their **panickburn**, their panicked Battle of Bannockburn [June 23, 1314, in which Robert Bruce of Scotland defeated Edward II of England]. Notice the run-on-compound sentences—it just continues to be the same.

Now the narrator gets excited herself:

> [9] **Almeidagad! Arthiz too loose! This is Willingdone cry. Brum!**
> **26**
> **Brum! Cumbrum! This is jinnies cry. Underwetter! Goat**
> **27**
> **strip Finnlambs! This is jinnies rinning away to their ouster-**
> **28**
> **lists dowan a bunkersheels. With a nip nippy nip and a trip trip-**
> **29**
> **py trip so airy. For their heart's right there. Tip.**

Excited by battle and sex herself, the guide exclaims **Almeidagad**: Almighty god. Battles like **Almeida** in Wellington's peninsular war. **Arthiz too loose**—is this to loose Toulouse! Touloose is a city in southern France [Battle of Toulouse, 10 April 1814, in which Wellington defeated the French, was the last battle of the Peninsular War]. In the Battle of Waterloose from the curse flood, Toulouse is too loose with the water. **Brum brum**—fog and mist in the fall. Flood and fall. **Cumbrum** Cambrone: Shit falls. Zimzum. Retreating from the Battle of Waterloo, the jinnies cry my pants are wet with excitement [**Underwetter**]. The goat god strips Finn's innocence—**Finnlambs**. The jinnies are running **rinning** away to their **ousterlists**, Austerlitz being an early battle Napoleon won, but here their place to go in Paris when they are ousted. They go down into **bunkersheels**, holes made by shells. The jinnies are running lightly and quickly. For their heart is in the bunker [sex organ]. Tip.

[9] This is me Bel-
30
chum's tinkyou tankyou silvoor plate for citchin the crapes in
31
the cool of his canister. Poor the pay! This is the bissmark of
the
32
marathon merry of the jinnies they left behind them.

This is me Blucher thinkyou thankyou s'il vous plais for catching the buckshot in the cool of his but—[The **Canister**: a house at the intersection of Main St and Napoleon St in Jamestown, on the island of St Helena, where Napoleon was imprisoned after Waterloo.] The pay is poor when you fight pour la pays, for your country, so we steal silver plate. War sex and greed. At the Battle of Waterloo Napoleon had his own personal treasury of gold in his personal carriage. This is Bismark or the bite mark of the Marathon battle spirit that the jinnies left behind them when they cut out.

[9] This is the
33
Willingdone branlish his same marmorial tallowscoop Sophy-
34
Key-Po for his royal divorsion on the rinnaway jinnies. Gam-
35
bariste della porca! Dalaveras fimmieras!

And now an unusual museum piece. As the French are running away, every man for himself: This is Willingdone brandishing and masturbating [Sophy Key-Po sounds like French every man for himself] his memorial sperm for his royal diversion on the memory of the jinnies who had runaway. Masturbation is independence without connection. Royal diversion for Royal Divorce, a play about Napoleon's divorce and also about the concealment of ES behind the TZTZ creation. **Gambarist della porca** refers to the author of "The Rival Brothers." [Lord] Deliver us from errors [**Dalaveras fimmieras**].

More in the wax museum:

[10] This is the pettiest of the lipoleums, Toffeethief, that spy on the Willingdone from
1
his big white harse, the Capeinhope. Stonewall Willingdone
2

232

is an old maxy montrumeny. Lipoleums is nice hung bushel-
3
lors.

This is the petty lipoleum spying on Willingdone who is on his big
white horse, now known as the Capeinhope, the cape being the end
of a land mass, so the end of hope. Stonewall Willingdone is an old
and blundering man and monster married together [**montrumeny**].
Lipoleum has big genitals, good for a bachelor collecting women by
the bushel full for temporary liaisons.

The guide points out additional characters:

[10] This is hiena hinnessy laughing alout at the Willing-
4
done. This is lipsyg dooley krieging the funk from the hinnessy.
5
This is the hinndoo Shimar Shin between the dooley boy and
the
6
hinnessy. Tip.

This is a red French [**hinnesy**--Hennessy] character [cartoon characters Dooley Irish-English and Hennessy French created by Finley
Peter Dunne] laughing aloud [**alout**] at the Willingdone. The meaning is Dunne—death is laughing. This is the Leipzig [German] character warring the funk from the French character [German troops on
Willingdone's side]. This is Wellington's Hindu boy **Shimar Shin**
between the German and the French characters. Napoleon called
Wellington the general of sepoys. Tip.

[10] This is the wixy old Willingdone picket up the
7
half of the threefoiled hat of lipoleums fromoud of the blud-
dle
8
filth.

This is the waxy old Willingdone picking up half of the three- corner
hat of Lipoleums from out of the puddle of filth. Humans in war are
using only one-half of their head. The other half is in the filth. More:

[10] This is the hinndoo waxing ranjymad for a bombshoob.
9
This is the Willingdone hanking the half of the hat of lipoleums
10
up the tail on the buckside of his big white harse. Tip. That was
11
the last joke of Willingdone. Hit, hit, hit! This is the same white
12
harse of the Willingdone, Culpenhelp, waggling his tailo-scrupp
13
with the half of a hat of lipoleums to insoult on the hinndoo see-
14
boy. Hney, hney, hney! (Bullsrag! Foul!)

This is Willingdone's Hindu servant [**hinndo** is Hindu himdo] wax-ing ranga mad for a bomb shoob—sounds like he wants in on the action. This is Willingdone hanging hankering the half Lipoleom hat on the tail of his big white horse's arse. Tip. With this act the hat and head of Lipoleum become the arse of a horse. That was the last joke of Willingdone, reminding us of the Irish horse joke. Hit it hit it hit it—the tail wagging and banging the hat on its ass. This is the arse of the same white horse of the Willingdone, this time named Culpen-help—help for the fault or culpa. It is waggling whipping his tail crupper with the hat to insult the Hindu Sepoy. In other words wip-ing his ass with the hat. A sense of sin and fearful dependency cause our mentality [our hat] to scrape like a windshield wiper across the filth in TZTZ creation; it keeps us there rather than the unlimited of ES.

The Sepoy is insulted because having your head in excrement-laced TZTZ creation is a violation of Hindu practice of non-violence. He ney he ney he ney or he is a horse. A dirty rag to make a bull mad. Foul indeed. The Sepoy removes the hat apparently kill-ing the horse in the process [remove ego remove passions]:

This is the seeboy,
15
madrashattaras, upjump and pumpim, cry to the Willing-done:
16

Ap Pukkaru! Pukka Yurap! This is the Willingdone, bornsta-
ble
17
ghentleman, tinders his maxbotch to the cursigan Shimar
Shin.
18
Basucker youstead! This is the dooforhim seeboy blow the
whole
19
of the half of the hat of lipoleums off of the top of the tail on
the
20
back of his big wide harse. Tip (Bullseye! Game!)   How
Copen-
21
hagen ended.

This is the Sepoy, the see boy, mad as a hatter in Indian sounding
language, jumping up and pumping, crying to the Willingdone: just
like at the battle of Aboukir Bay in Egypt and for sure Europe not
nonviolent India. The Hindu Sepoy hates the violence in TZTZ
creation.

This is the Willingdone tendering his matchbox and burns away
at his maximum botch of the human condition to his curse again
Shimar Shin. Suck your own ass instead [**Basucker youstead**]; apparently Sepoy said something like clean the horse's ass. This is the
servant [**dooforhim**] sepoy blowing the half hat off the top of the
tail on the big wide horse arse apparently with a gun. Shimar Shin's
religion would separate the spirit from the body. This is how Copenhagen Willingdone's horse ended up dead. This is the breath of
death, which god also breathed into humankind. **How Compenha-
gen ended** gives HCE one more time.

[10] This way the museyroom. Mind your boots goan
22
out.
23
Phew!
24

The guide says this way back to the museum [repetition]. Joyce says
this way, the way of death, is the way of the museyroom, the room of
the Muses, of the gods. Another way goes out. Mind your boots on
your way out—as if they had been made dirty by the subject matter.

235

Boots are stolen from dead men. **Phew**—an imitation of puffing combined with pew, referring derisively to the breath of limited life breathed by god into mankind in the church [pew].

Remember Kate's job to remove horse manure from the streets. Here the horse manure of conflict is the subject in the museum. The presentation in wax figures stands for some kind of static art.

Now for an additional take on the museum scene. The fit for this interpretation is not perfect but it is substantial. In this interpretation, Willingdone represents the forces of free will and independence and Lipoleum the forces of dependence, such as egoism and a desire to dominate and control—the alpha male attitude. Free will and the forces of ES can always send dependency and TZTZ god into exile if free will is exercised within and consistent with the human unity. This connects with the basic facts of the Battle. Wellington's forces achieved unity with the disciplined Prussians at the last second and Napoleon's remained separated. Willingdone, like ES, remained concealed behind the hill, the hill where the Battle took place.

Read Willingdone as free will, acts done willingly, the gift from ES god who willingly made the TZTZ creation. Read Lipoleum I, II and III as the Trinity TZTZ god working in the mud of TZTZ creation. Bonaparte was famous for his ego and desire to control all of Europe. Bonaparte translates as "good part" or good to separate, TZTZ god's discriminating function and Bonaparte's to take. He is called Lipoleum to suggest the linoleum, which is on the floor and walked on, the dependent floor. Potential free will is walked on and made dependent by the alpha male attitudes.

Cambrone's expression "merde" in connection with surrender equates the merde of TZTZ creation to surrendering your independence. The booms of the canon are Din, Din from the Iron Duke ES acting just in Din and without the Sefirots of compassion. His allies are the strictly disciplined Prussians. Napoleon lost the Battle because he was not able to separate Wellington's forces from the Prussian and because of his TZTZ god aspects—he hesitated and failed to unify his own infantry and horse troops.

The Iron Duke wears an odd combination of opposites, such as goldtin spurs, suggesting the reconciliation of opposites by ES. The message from the jinnies jeers him for **not having a wife**, as ES was without spouse. Lipoleum wears a three cornered hat like the Trinity [Napoleon's hat was actually two cornered].

In this context, the joke about being born in a stable and not being a horse means being independent [particularly of the passions] in a dependent based creation. Lipoleum is hesitant and a forger as Emperor. The Royal Divorce is TZTZ creation. Even ES's Sepoy servant acts independently, by blowing the hat off the tail of the horse, by removing the higher functions off the anus of the representative of the passions. Paying your money and taking your chance refers to which god you apply. Getting the band up is leading the band, a form of unity.

Men are allowed free into the museum because they are the principal actors in the TZTZ world. This scene is made from images in a museum as TZTZ creation.

The **Ill 60** and **ollolowed ill** refer to the ill built into this TZTZ world. The hill suggests the concealed nature of ES, concealed by the TZTZ creation. The water that is loose on the battlefield is water that was not absorbed, like the TZTZ creation excreted by ES. The belles' alliance is the compact of females to transmit original sin. Grouchy is an attitude, perhaps the attitude of ES that motivated the TZTZ creation. The looting by Willingdone's allies suggests this kind of world was looted from the unity. **Cromwelly** because Oliver Cromwell directed genocide against Irish Catholics as Lord Protector of Ireland for England. Just like the Lord Protector ES. TZTZ creation was the first joke of ES. The King's indulgence—allowing himself to be absent, refers to ES god as well.

Now back to the text and out of museum, the guide speaks of the sex-aggression connection:

> **[10] What a warm time we were in there but how keling is here the**
> **25**
> **airabouts! We nowhere she lives but you mussna tell annaone for**
> **26**
> **the lamp of Jig-a-Lanthern! It's a candlelittle houthse of a month**
> **27**
> **and one windies. Downadown, High Downadown.**

The reference to a **warm time . . in there** suggests more intimate places as well as the museum. The museum of war affects even the air around it. The air is **keling**, killing and drilling a hole in a hat [Kelly].

Now the guide speaks of a **she**, a she that they apparently see from right outside the museum. This she has no name and no fixed abode, that is we know she lives **nowhere**. The condensate **nowhere** splits into either "no where" or "now here" or "know here." Note in this phrase that **nowhere** serves to say all of us now here know here she lives nowhere. **now here** is the eternal right here right now. With this legerdemain, Joyce says the Holy Spirit/Shekhinah lives in knowledge in the present.

But the guide cautions the guided group [more dependency] that they must not tell anyone about her [about Anna the one—**annaone**] because she is only a temporary insubstantial will of the wisp, a ghost. She is immaterial in the world that recognizes only the material. She is also bad for business at the war museum. In other words, don't spread the word about unity and love in the world.

We sense the she ghost without permanent habitation as the Holy Ghost or the Shekhinah [both referred to as the "HSS"]. Here in the vale of wars, the HSS is picking over the mound of history devoted to the battlefield instead of ruling the world with god's love. She is putting things back together hopefully for new possibilities, after former ones have been separated by strife. She could be doing a lot more if times were better, if the father and son relationship were in charity.

In the Old Testament the Holy Spirit was symbolized as breath or wind, an unseen life-giving force. It is the Spirit that enlivens the community with hope for the future and was known in the New Testament as the paraclete, or defense counsel [apparently TZTZ god is prosecuting]. At the apostles' Pentecostal experience, the HSS spirit manifested as forked tongues of fire. She was often portrayed as a dove, the dove of peace. Here she lives in a little house lit only by candles, a faint glimmer of those forked tongues of fire. Her house has 29 windows, which is somehow related to the menstrual and birth cycle for human females. Procreation is the only opening for the HSS.

Low and down, but high low and down—the above below [**Downadown, High Downadown**]. For an interpretation of down and high, more about the Holy Spirit from the EB:

> The definition that the Holy Spirit was a distinct divine Person equal in substance to the Father and the Son and not subordinate to them came at the Council of Constantinople in AD 381, following challenges to its divinity. The Eastern and Western churches have since viewed the Holy Spirit as the bond, the fellowship, or the mutual charity between Father and Son; they are absolutely united in the Spirit. The relationship of the Holy Spirit to the other Persons of the Trinity has been described in the West as proceeding from both the Father and the Son, whereas in the East it has

been held that the procession is from the Father through the Son. He proceeds, not by way of generation, but by way of spiration, from the Father and the Son together, as from a single principle.

Proceeding through the son [eastern interpretation] would be **downadown**, a double down—from father to son and from son to HSS—while proceeding from father and son both [western interpretation] would be **High downadown**. The spiration is the reason for the wind [**one windies**]. The male dominated RCC made the HSS male, but in Joyce and in Kabbalah the Holy Spirit is the female aspect of god putting it back together in Tikkun, fixing the broken vessels and gathering the sparks from the husks. For Joyce, this gendering is justified by the characteristic difference between human females and males.

And now the guide spots a bird, perhaps the **she** referred to:

> [10] And num-
> 28
> **mered quaintlymine. And such reasonable weather too! The wa-**
> 29
> **grant wind's awalt'zaround the piltdowns and on every blasted**
> 30
> **knollyrock (if you can spot fifty I spy four more) there's that**
> 31
> **gnarlybird ygathering, a runalittle, doalittle, preealittle, pouralittle,**
> 32
> **wipealittle, kicksalittle, severalittle, eatalittle, whinealittle, kenalittle,**
> 33
> **helfalittle, pelfalittle gnarlybird. A verytableland of bleak-bardfields!**
> 34

And **nummered quaintlymine.** And numbered [counting assumes separates] in merde [same letters as **mered**]. Only one bird, **quaintlymine**—uniquely or bizarrely I or one. The HSS is an individual not a group experience. With reasonable weather [Father and Son in conjunction] there should be more. The vagrant wind/bird is waltzing around on the piltdowns peat and on every blasted rock with proterubances. The guide says she can spot 54 rocks. There are 54 portions in the Torah. The bird of life, the HSS with proterubances, has so much to do: is gathering, running a little, doing a little, praying a little, pouring a little, wiping a little, kicking a little [6], severing a little [7], eating a little [8], whining a little [9], kenning a little [10], that half a little pitiful little gnarlybird. A veritable table land of fields bleak for a bard. The bird is now identified with female and the bard. Both put things back together, the bard reprocessing experience into art. Peace.

> [10] Under his seven wrothschields lies one, Lumproar. His glav toside
> 35
> him. Skud ontorsed. Our pigeons pair are flewn for north-cliffs.

> [11] The three of crows have flapped it southenly, kraaking of de
> 1
> baccle to the kvarters of that sky whence triboos answer; Wail,
> 2
> 'tis well!

Speaking of the bard's field of experience, the bleakbardfield, there lies underneath even wealth accumulation [Rothschilds] only one force, the roar of the testicles [**lumproar**], the roar of the lump from TZTZ creation. ["Money is for keeping score."] Like Tristan in the forest, his sword is beside him [**His glav toside him.**] The sword has been shot out of his hands, like a horse under him. Unlike the knarlybird, the pigeons have flown north for the cliffs and the three crows [three ravens] have taken off for the south, proclaiming to all quarters of the sky the debacle of warfare where three boos echo in answer. It is good that these birds wail.

Now more about the gnarlybird, this time about what she doesn't do:

> [11] She niver comes out when Thon's on shower or when
> 3
> Thon's flash with his Nixy girls or when Thon's blowing toom-
> 4
> cracks down the gaels of Thon. No nubo no! Neblas on you liv!
> 5

> Her would be too moochy afreet. Of Burymeleg and Bindme-
> 6
> rollingeyes and all the deed in the woe. Fe fo fom! She jist
> does
> 7
> hopes till byes will be byes.

The peaceful gnarlybird Holy Spirit never comes out when the gods make thunder or lightning with the salt sea goddesses [sex by lightning bolt] or when the god of thunder is blowing cracks of toom down his girls. **No nubo no**—no gods as husbands. Not on your life, which would be threatened. She would be too much afraid. Of the demons. She must keep her legs buried and her roving eyes bound to avoid the woe producing deed, the curse. The giant god Nephilim [one of the angels that mated with human females—mimicking human male behavior] smells her [**Fe fo fom**—I smell the blood . . .] But she just in justice hopes that what is past is past, bygones will be bygones. And will not be repeated—that the curse will end. Remember that the Holy Spirit issues when the spirit between the father god and the son human kind is right, which it isn't the case when the curse is on.

Here she comes, the gnarlybird, the Holy Spirit weathered by difficulties:

> [11] Here, and it goes on to appear now,
> 8
> she comes, a peacefugle, a parody's bird, a peri potmother,
> 9
> a pringlpik in the ilandiskippy, with peewee and powwows
> 10
> in beggybaggy on her bickybacky and a flick flask fleckfling-
> ing
> 11
> its pixylighting pacts' huemeramybows, picking here, peck-
> ing
> 12
> there, pussypussy plunderpussy.

Here comes the unity bird under whose influence alliteration serves unity. **Peacefugle** is an example for peace, ironically dressed in military language. **Parody's bird** riffs on bird of paradise and the failure of paradise in the Garden of Eden. **Peri potmother** refers to **peri**— in Persian Mythology, one of a race of superhuman beings, originally represented as having an evil or malevolent character, but subsequently as good genii, fairies, or angels, endowed with grace and beauty. She serves as a pinprick in the landscape, the **ilandiskippy**, the "I land disk kippy" [perhaps female salmon during breeding season, kipper is male]. She is a lapwing for peace. A lapwing pretends to be injured to draw prey away [Christ and TZTZ god]. Note parallel construction suggesting peace and unity. She has a big bag on her big back [**beggybaggy on her bickybacky**]. And like a flash of arrows her **lighting** pact's counterpart of the rainbow covenant of peace, her rainbow is pixillating [remember when this was written] or fading [**and a flick flask fleckflinging its pixylighting pacts' huemeramybows**]. Then pixillating meant confused or intoxicated theater characters whose movement appears to be artificially animated. The rainbow was the pact of peace. In the absence of the rainbow, Her light of peace is flickering. The alliterated letter "f's" give a sense of the flickering. **Pussypussy plunderpussy**—the Holy Spirit being consubstantial with the thunderer father must be like the blunderbuss, the thunder box in Dutch.

The gnarly bird is pecking on the mound of human detritus. This is what she does when the spirit of the father and son is not right. As Joyce put it in Ulysses, this is History, the nightmare from which I am trying to awake. Awake to new possibilities other than competition and strife.

> **[11] But it's the armitides toonigh,**
> **13**
> **militopucos, and toomourn we wish for a muddy kissmans to the**
> **14**
> **minutia workers and there's to be a gorgeups truce for happinest**
> **15**
> **childher everwere. Come nebo me and suso sing the day we**
> **16**
> **sallybright.**

Given the presence of the Holy Spirit of peace, it is the armistice tonight, the tide of amity, peace poco in war [**militopucos**], and for many mornings we wish for a trench muddy kissman [**kissmans**] for the **munutia** workers [wives picking up mundane minutia or bits and pieces] and there is to be a gorgeous gorge up truce for happiness with [the men "coming" from war to their women] and they **childher** pregnant **everwere**—"everywhere" for place and "ever were" for time. Come put me on the mountain [ecstasy] between your

242

knees and sing [stutter] the day we celebrate sally sudden activity bright light of the Holy Spirit.

This HSS had to borrow a light, had to emanate from the father and son:

[11] She's burrowed the coacher's headlight the better to
17
pry (who goes cute goes siocur and shoos aroun) and all spoiled
18
goods go into her nabsack: curtrages and rattlin buttins, nappy
19
spattees and flasks of all nations, clavicures and scampulars, maps,
20
keys and woodpiles of haypennies and moonled brooches with
21
bloodstaned breeks in em, boaston nightgarters and masses of
22
shoesets and nickelly nacks and foder allmicheal and a lugly parson
23
of cates and howitzer muchears and midgers and maggets, ills and
24
ells with loffs of toffs and pleures of bells and the last sigh that
25
come fro the hart (bucklied!) and the fairest sin the sunsaw
26
(that's cearc!). With Kiss. Kiss Criss. Cross Criss. Kiss Cross.
27
Undo lives 'end. Slain.
28

The bird picks up off the battlefield objects that can be put to good use in everyday life. She borrows the coach god's headlight the better to pry open the ground (who goes cute-clever gives succor and shoes around) and spoiled goods go into her nabsack, not knapsack—nab for grab. The items include cartridges and bullet cut rags [**curtrages**], rattling buttons, fuzzy stockings, drunk or wavering flags of all nations, keys and flasks, woodpiles of hay or half pence [base currency], moon colored lead clasps with bloodstained trousers in them, boasting a ton Knight garters [**nightgarters**] for the Order of the Garter [an order of Knighthood in Britain whose motto means "shame upon him who thinks evil of it."], lots of sets of shoes, knickknacks, and fodder for St. Michael all mighty and an ugly parson interested in choice food [curate tried to abuse Joyce's future wife Nora], and howitzer cannon much in the ears and flies and maggots, unfortunate men and women [**ills and ells**] ill with lots of love and tears of bells and the last sigh that came from the heart deer dear and the fairest sign sin the sun saw the rainbow. The hen as the ark, the savior, the Holy Spirit. With kiss, kiss the cross of Jesus [**With Kiss. Kiss Criss. Cross Criss.**] Undo **lives 'end**. Slain. That is undo death. A call to the Holy Spirit to undo death as Christ was supposed to overcome death.

Now for metaphysics and the Holy Spirit:

> [11] How bootifull and how truetowife of her, when strengly fore-
> 29
> bidden, to steal our historic presents from the past post-propheti-
> 30
> cals so as to will make us all lordy heirs and ladymaidesses of a
> 31
> pretty nice kettle of fruit.

She is beautiful like boots full and how true to a wife she is, supporting us, when it is strictly forbidden for her to steal our present by way of past prophecy, that is deprive us of free will, and as a result has bequeathed to us a nice kettle of fish, an difficult situation. That is, the Holy Spirit is prohibited from bringing about entirely on her own what was promised in prophecy, the era of the Holy Spirit in love on earth. Humans must do this themselves in Tikkun.

As it is:

> [11] She is livving in our midst of debt and
> 32
> laffing through all plores for us (her birth is uncontrollable), with
> 33

a naperon for her mask and her sabboes kickin arias (so sair! so
34
solly!) if yous ask me and I saack you. Hou! Hou! Gricks may
35
rise and Troysirs fall (there being two sights for [12] ever a picture)
for in the byways of high improvidence that's what makes life-
1
work leaving and the world's a cell for citters to cit in.

She is living [**livving** for long life] in the midst of our debt owed to death and laughing and crying through all her pores for us [her compassion is uncontrollable] with an apron [Garden of Eden] for her mask and her shoes kicking the head of the serpent. Next is a suggestion that the Holy Spirit impregnated Abram's wife Sarah as well as the Virgin Mary [through the ear]. [**if yous ask me and I saack you.**] So Sarah so sorry for your late age pregnancy [when birth pains are greater]; if you ask me and I Isaaac you [**I saack**—impregnate you with Isaac for an extended stomach] **Hou Hou** for how how and Ha Ha [Sarah laughed when told Abram would have a son by her and Isaac means laughter]. Greeks **Gricks** may rise and Troy sirs may fall (there being two interpretations for every picture) for in the annals of the malign powers that be [**high improvidence**] that is what makes life worth living-leaving [death] and the world is a cell for sitters to sit in.

The Trojans would rise in the alternative interpretation(**there being two sights for [12] ever a picture**) since they were defeated and died. This discussion of the Trojan War seems to refer to the irony of Christ defeating death by dying. He had to be resurrected in order to win. The 12 apostles were the only ones to witness [**sight**] the resurrection. Defeat in death was one sight and resurrection defeating death was another sight. Two sides to every story, one side punctured by a spear and one not.

[12] Let young
2
wimman run away with the story and let young min talk smooth
3

behind the butteler's back. She knows her knight's duty while
4
Luntum sleeps. Did ye save any tin? says he. Did I what? with
5
a grin says she. And we all like a marriedann because she is mer-
6
cenary.

And let young women [**wimman**—win man to avoid **woe**man] run away with the story [Eve in the Garden of Eden] and let young **min** [not a "man" with an "a" but **min** with an "i" so the erect and individualized serpent not the passive Adam] talk smooth [the serpent was smooth and seduced Eve to be god-like] behind god's back, god the **butteler** who ushered them in and then butted them out of the garden. She now knows her sexual duty at night to her knight while Luntum the slow rising smoke of the Holy Spirit sleeps. Now to a conversation between Adam and Eve. Adam: Did you save any money [**tin** as contrasted to gold and silver] from having sex with the serpent? Did I what, she says with a grin, having enjoyed it. And we all like a married Anne [**marriedann**] or Mary Anne mother of Jesus because she is mercenary—uses marriage with Joseph [in which she remained a virgin] to insure support for her children.

[12] **Though the length of the land lies under liquidation**
7
(floote!) and there's nare a hairbrow nor an eyebush on this glau-
8
brous phace of Herrschuft Whatarwelter she'll loan a vesta and
9
hire some peat and sarch the shores her cockles to heat and she'll
10
do all a turfwoman can to piff the business on. Paff. To puff the
11
blaziness on. Poffpoff.

Though the land lie under a flood because of a broken pact with god [the flood] and there is neither a **hairbrow** [much less a rainbow not

246

even any of god's hair] nor an **eyebush** [instead of eyelash] on this smooth [back to the serpent] place phase of this Lord created rolling ocean. In Norse myth after the flood Ymir's body became the world—his hair the trees and his eyebrows the grass and flowers. Nonetheless she the Holy Spirit will loan a match of the eternal flame and hire higher some peat to burn and search the shores for some hearts to heat with love and she will do all that is necessary for a turfwoman [peat] to keep the fire business going [**to piff the business on**]. She gives the breath of life—**Paff. To puff the blaziness on. Poffpoff.** In the absence of charity between the father and son gods, the Holy Spirit acts as the sexual love impulse. This is the mix of unity from ES conditioned by the separation required by TZTZ creation.

So here is the formula: absent love in the world due to the improper conjunction between the father and son aspects of god, the Holy Spirit will concentrate on sex heat for procreation. At least that much love. It makes for future possibilities and keeps love possible.

And even if some die, she is there to make new ones, the Holy Spirit as sex and birth:

> **[12] And even if Humpty shell fall frumpty**
> **12**
> **times as awkward again in the beardsboosoloom of all our grand**
> **13**
> **remonstrancers there'll be iggs for the brekkers come to mourn-**
> **14**
> **him, sunny side up with care. So true is it that therewhere's a**
> **15**
> **turnover the tay is wet too and when you think you ketch sight**
> **16**
> **of a hind make sure but you're cocked by a hin.**

And even if Humpty Dumpty the egg shell shall [**shell**] fall forty times as awkward again in the beards and booze on the loom [in our annals of wisdom and spirit–**beardsboosoloom** sounds like Jerusalem] of our grand pronoucers of abuses [**remonstrancers** or religious authorities on original sin] there will still be more eggs Iggy births [**iggs**] for the ones doing the breaking come to mourn Humpty, the eggs prepared sunny side up optimism mixed with care. So true is it that where there is [reversed as **therewhere's**] a turnover [death or eggs over easy] the tea is ready too [female   fertile] and when you think you catch sight of a bare behind make sure you are cocked by [have an erection for] a hen not a him [**hin** is part of hin**d**]. That is when you have sex make sure it is with the opposite sex, not soldier sex, and she is ready to get pregnant—the tea is wet.

> **[12] Then as she is on her behaviourite job of quainance bandy,**
> 18
> **fruting for firstlings and taking her tithe, we may take our review**
> 19
> **of the two mounds to see nothing of the himples here as at else-**
> 20
> **where, by sixes and sevens, like so many heegills and collines,**
> 21
> **sitton aroont, scentbreeched and somepotreek, in their swisha-**
> 22
> **wish satins and their taffetaffe tights, playing Wharton's Folly,**
> 23
> **at a treepurty on the planko in the purk. Stand up, mickos!**
> 24

Then as she is engaged in her instinctive job of providing for others, reaching for first born fruit [**fruting for firstlings**] and taking her share [with echoes of the fruit of the tree of good and bad] we the narrator may take our review of the two mounds [testicles buttocks breasts] to say or see nothing of the heaven-nipples [**himples**] viewed by him where in a disordered state [by 6s and 7s] like so many boys and girls [with a suggestion of gills to indicate primordial behavior] sitting around bashfully and smelling good and dressed up in their satins and tights swishing a wish and playing the preliminaries to the umbilical cord [**Wharton's** jelly part of that cord] and pregnancy at a tree party on the ground in the Park [where the **Wharton's Folly** fortress is]. Sex and birth is the necessary folly given the curse of death. Be erect you Irishmen, you descendants of the militant Michael. Defeat death with your penis, make love not war.

[12] Make strake for minnas! By order, Nicholas Proud. We may see
25
and hear nothing if we choose of the shortlegged bergins off
26
Corkhill or the bergamoors of Arbourhill or the bergagam-bols
27
of Summerhill or the bergincellies of Miseryhill or the coun-try-
28
bossed bergones of Constitutionhill though every crowd has its
29
several tones and every trade has its clever mechanics and each
30
harmonical has a point of its own, Olaf's on the rise and Ivor's
31
on the lift and Sitric's place's between them.

Now for some hill-mountain, female and music terms, that is the theme of making music on the female mounds traced through the conventions of music [harmony triad based—suggests Holy Trinity in full charity and the sigla E]. By the order of the horny Devil [**Nicholas Proud**] Irish men make straight for the Irish women [**minnas**]. We may see and hear nothing [not do much] if we choose to begin with the violins, the smallest viol [**shortlegged bergins**— short women] from Corkhill [street in Dublin], or begin with the viola d'amore [**bergamoors** or unfaithful women—more more] of Summerhill [street in Dublin], or begin with the cello [**bergincellies** of sell easy women] of Miseryhill [street in Dublin], or begin with the contrabass [**bossed bergones** or old bossy women] of Constitution-hill [street in Dublin]—these are women to be avoided—though every crowd chord has its several tones [is different] and every trade triad composer has its clever mechanics and each harmonical togeth-erness has its own point of view. That is, sexual attraction is individ-ual and subjectively based. The ISO chord [Ivar, Sitric and Olaf and the triad of tonic third fifth] consists of the tonic under the sub-dominant [3rd] under the dominant [5th]. This relationship suggests missionary position sex with the third interval penis in between [pun-ishment in GE—he will rule *over* you]. Olaf, Sitric and Ivar were Norse brothers who founded Dublin accord to legend. It seems that

Ivor is the tonic on the left, Olaf is the dominant fifth and Stitric is in between in the triad [tric]. Chromatic and twelve tone music that rejected triad or even key based composition and created more possibilities and their analogs different sexual persuasions are on the way.

> **[12] But all they are all**
> **32**
> **there scraping along to sneeze out a likelihood that will solve**
> **33**
> **and salve life's robulous rebus, hopping round his middle like**
> **34**
> **kippers on a griddle, O, as he lays dormont from the macroborg**
> **35**
> **of Holdhard to the microbirg of Pied de Poudre.**

But they the males are there all scraping along and bowing badly [dependent on boss] in order to squeeze out a likely livelihood that will solve and placate life's coarse rebus-like mystery and hopping [contrast hoping] like a herring still alive in the middle of a hot pan. As he lays dormant [in the frying pan ready for the fire] from the macrocosm of **Holdhard**—the TZTZ god that reigns reins in human potential like a horse held hard by the reins—to the microcosm of feet of dust, that is death [**Pied de Poudre**]. As penalized in the ejection from the Garden of Eden, mankind struggles to survive in the context of a god who limits human potential and demands death. Men have to work and women have to bear children. Both can limit potential.

Human servitude under TZTZ god is now compared with the Irish under the English. God picked human kind bare and England has done the same in Ireland:

> **[12] Behove this**
> **36**
> **[13] sound of Irish sense. Really? Here English might be seen.**
> **1**
> **Royally? One sovereign punned to petery pence. Regally? The**
> **2**
> **silence speaks the scene. Fake!**
> **3**

250

So This Is Dyoublong?
4
Hush! Caution ! Echoland !
5

This music of the mounds, the sounds of the mounds, behold this Irish common sense—have sex since you will die. The Irish are to the English as humankind is to god. **One sovereign punned to petery pence**: a donation to the Roman Catholic Church is Peter's Pence so **petery** would refer to watery and death, death being god's pence. Are the English made regally, that is in the image of god? No answer only silence, no contact with god. It is a fake. So this is Dublin that doubles the gods, where the history of the gods is repeated [**Dyoublong**]. Hush so you can hear. But be careful because this land is only an echo of the gods. Their thunder is the echo of the curse.

And now for some tagging and graffiti on the walls of the Garden of Eden:

[13] How charmingly exquisite! It reminds you of the out-washed
6
engravure that we used to be blurring on the blotchwall of his
7
innkempt house. Used they? (I am sure that tiring chabel-shovel-
8
ler with the mujikal chocolat box, Miry Mitchel, is listening)
I
9
say, the remains of the outworn gravemure where used to be
10
blurried the Ptollmens of the Incabus.

HCE. **How charmingly exquisite** it is to repeat the history of the gods [exquisite means precise in this context]. It reminds you of the washed out engraving [**engravure** contains grave for death] that we formerly painted on the wall of his ill enclosing house [Garden of Eden and HCE is an innkeeper]. These engravings were painted on from the outside as in graffiti since we couldn't get back in—to paradise, to god. The wall around the Garden of Eden is death. Man has tagged death. Inside the wall everlasting life is possible. A life lived out of time.

These engravings on the wall would be a copy below of the ES engravings above in the TZTZ creation. Did they? (I am sure that muddy Michael, the tiring choveller for graves with the musical chocolat box, is listening.) Chocolat would be the food of the resurrection. I say, the remains of the worn-out grave wall where formerly were buried the giants mentioned in Genesis created by human sex with the angels [[**ptollmens of the Incabus** suggest ritual stones or death [the toll on mankind] buried [**blurried**] in the Garden walls by devils having sex with human females]]. Sex with god leaves inanimate objects such an inkblot [**incabus**] on the wall of the Garden of Eden—**incabus** being an echo of the serpent. In this interpretation the serpent acting for god or god disguised as the serpent, not an independent Satan, impregnated Eve not only with Cain and Able but also with death. The angel with the chocolate music box that plays mechanically suggests reaching resurrection and heaven only by mechanical predestination—which is god chocolate.

Now for some more about Michael, the warrior angel, from the EB:

> *Hebrew Mikha'el, Arabic Mika'il, or Mikha'il,* in the Bible and the Qur'an, one of the archangels. He is repeatedly depicted as the "great captain," the leader of the heavenly hosts, the warrior helping the children of Israel; and early in the history of the Christian church he came to be regarded as helper of the church's armies against the heathen. He holds the secret of the mighty "word" by the utterance of which God created heaven and earth and was "the angel who spoke to [Moses] on Mount Sinai" (Acts 7:38). The numerous representations of Michael in art reflect his character as a warrior: he is shown with a sword, in combat with or triumph over a dragon, from the story in the Book of Revelation (Apocalypse).

Contrast militant Michael with the peaceful Holy Spirit. Going on the same vein:

> **[13] Used we? (He is only pre-**
> **11**
> **tendant to be stugging at the jubalee harp from a second ex-**
> **isted**
> **12**
> **lishener, Fiery Farrelly.) It is well known. Lokk for himself and**
> **13**
> **see the old butte new. Dbln.**

252

Here is the spirit of this material: Did we leave a mark on the wall of Eden? Are we being used merely to repeat the experience of the gods [**used we**]? Does the mere repetition or doubling [**old butte new. Dbln**] result in predestination?

Now Michael and the jubalee harp—the harp of forgiveness that would short-circuit predestination. Given his allegiance to predestination, Michael is only pretending with a dash of his important but attendant nature [**pretendant**] to be tugging struggling [**stugging**] at the jubalee [forgiveness] harp to keep it away from a second listener Fiery Farrelly—the devil in the form of a dragon slain by Michael. As with predestination, this is well known. In predestination the devil gets a guaranteed flock, a quota, so the devil is against the jubalee forgiveness harp. Look lock for himself and see the **old** but **butte new**, the same old story Dublin Doubling, the same old royal ass in TZTZ creation in the **butte new**.

> [13] W. K. O. O. Hear? By the mauso-
> 14
> lime wall. Fimfim fimfim. With a grand funferall. Fumfum fum-
> 15
> fum. 'Tis optophone which ontophanes. List! Wheatstone's
> 16
> magic lyer. They will be tuggling foriver. They will be lichen-ing
> 17
> for allof. They will be pretumbling forover. The harpsdischord
> 18
> shall be theirs for ollaves.

Using radio signs and K Gematria number code, this is DBLN for 32 and WKOO for 64 or WK for 1132 backwards. These are the constant call signs in this god's universe. Do you hear it? Listen by the mausoleum lime [**mausolime**] wall, where death dwells. **Fimfim** repeated. Tzimtzum repeats in the excreted world where only "I" in fim saves us from fum. With a grand funeral fun for all [**funferall**]. Fumfum repeated as tutti. It is a process [let there be light] by which speech is converted to light and light is converted into being [**Tis optphone which ontophanes**.] Listen! The magic lyre liar invented by Wheatsone, a lyre that would pick up vibrations from an adjoining room thus appearing to play itself—an analog of the human condition in relation to god particularly in predestination.

Then a series of four pronouncements: First, they will be tugging forever in the river of life: the divel and Michael. Second: they will be listening covered as with lichen for all of humanity. Third: they will be falling prematurely for ever over—[**pretumbling forover**] transmission of original sin. Fourth: the music of discord [**harpsdiscord** not harpsichord] shall be theirs forever sagely. Constant strife.

Now after these four pronouncements:

> [13] **Four things therefore, saith our herodotary Mammon Lujius**
> **20**
> **in his grand old historiorum, wrote near Boriorum, bluest book**
> **21**
> **in baile's annals, f t. in Dyffinarsky ne'er sall fail til heathersmoke**
> **22**
> **and cloudweed Eire's ile sall pall. And here now they are, the fear**
> **23**
> **of um. T. Totities!** *Unum.* **(Adar.)**

Against the guaranteed doom of predestination, the text takes us to the New Testament and the historians [Herodotus] of Christ—Matthew, Mark, Luke and John combined as **Mammon Lujius** with Mammon thrown in on top. Christ and forgiveness suggest predestination does not rule. Mammon is the angel interested in material gain—perhaps a dig at the wealth of the RCC. Boreum was Ptolemy's name for Donegal, where *The Annals of the Four Masters* was written. **Boriorum** suggests boredom and intoxication—rum. The true bluest book in human history—the Annals. Four things ["f.t."] in Dublin shall never fail until heathersmoke and cloudweed shall not rise pall in Ireland. **Sall pall** suggests soft rising smoke.

And these are the things we have to fear! The predicted and thus predestined four things. These are placed in Adar—in the 6th month of the Jewish civil and 12th month of the religious calendar. Adar is associated with the 9th plague, the curse, that struck the Egyptians for their refusal to release the children of Israel from slavery—a thick darkness that blanketed the land so that "no man saw his fellow, and no man could move from his place" (Exodus 10:23)—commenced on the 1st of Adar, six weeks before the Exodus.

Now on to the four things to be feared: the thick darkness on the land—war from politicians, poverty among the people, adultery

254

and desertion among couples, and the ineffectiveness of written materials [adultery or subjectivity in art]:

> [13] A bulbenboss surmounted up-
> 24
> on an alderman. Ay, ay! *Duum.* (Nizam.) A shoe on a puir old
> 25
> wobban. Ah, ho! *Triom.* (Tamuz.) An auburn mayde, o'brine
> 26
> a'bride, to be desarted. Adear, adear! *Quodlibus.* (Marchessvan.) A
> 27
> penn no weightier nor a polepost. And so. And all. (Succoth.)
> 28

War from politicians: A cannon mounted on the back of an alderman, a politician representing many jurisdictions—as in god. Ay ay! [the sign of the four] Of two powers that be. **Duum** for Din and thunder. (**nizam** is the seventh month or order in the Jewish religious calendar). Poverty: A shoe on a poor old woman wobbling. Ah, ho! [another sign of the four] Of three. (**Tamuz**, the 10th month and dying god of Mesopotamia). Adultery and desertion: An auburn maid having been made, a bride of the salt sea [bride of semen], to be deserted after the start—pregnancy [**desarted**]. Ah, ho! [the sign of the four]. What you please. (**Marchessvan**, the 2nd month of the Jewish religious calendar). Ineffective art: A pen or art no heavier nor more aesthetically oriented than the post—the post, the newspaper, is written to be wanted and received by others. In Joyce's view, the post is pornographic art. This is the reason Shaun who panders to the views of others is called the postman. (**Succoth**: movable shelters used by Jews as they wandered in the desert suggest ineffective art). **And so. And all** have only temporary life. Death rules. Life is just a tent, being put up and taken down, with only pegs in the ground for stability.

> [13] So, how idlers' wind turning pages on pages, as innocens with
> 29
> anaclete play popeye antipop, the leaves of the living in the boke
> 30

255

of the deeds, annals of themselves timing the cycles of events
31
grand and national, bring fassilwise to pass how.

The Holy Spirit wind or breath of god was known as the paraclete. Joyce has changed the word to **anaclete**. Para as a prefix means nearby. **An** as a prefix means lacking or without. The anaclete is what you get with the curse, the paraclete is what you get with the blessing. So the only wind is an idler's wind, not the Holy Spirit. The idler's wind is one without purpose to protect, as innocent human beings [**innocens**] with only the anaclete in the world play looking for god through the eye of the Pope [**popeye antipop**]. The Pope is the strong man ["popeye" the cartoon character] of the church and anti-father, the man without children in the flesh. Human children are the leaves or result of living in the vomit [**boke**] of the deeds, historical annals of their own gauging the cyle of grand and national events, showing how fossils come to pass, how men die. Men are passed over for immortality.

Now for some history and mystical numbers. The Annals listed events year by year as does this material. First we go backward in time:

[13] 1132 A.D. Men like to ants or emmets wondern upon a groot
33
hwide Whallfisk which lay in a Runnel. Blubby wares upat Ub-
34
lanium.
35
566 A.D. On Baalfire's night of this year after deluge a crone that
36
[14] hadde a wickered Kish for to hale dead turves from the bog look-
1
it under the blay of her Kish as she ran for to sothisfeige her cow-
2
rieosity and be me sawl but she found hersell sackvulle of swart
3
goody quickenshoon ant small illigant brogues, so rich in sweat.

4
Blurry works at Hurdlesford.
5
(Silent.)
6

1132 is the number representing the total of possible combinations of any two of the 23 Hebrew letters, which is 231. Reading from right to left as in Hebrew gives 132 and adding an extra 1 for yourself to manifest arrives at 1132. In K, this is the number of ES's garment.

The year 1132 has many meanings in FW, as it did in Irish history. Among other things the independent Irish church was taken over by the RCC in that year, creating more dependency of the spirit. During that year men acting like ants and not like the brave Robert Emmet wandered wondered upon a great big white whalefish that lay in a rivulet [salt water whale in fresh water rivulet]. The image of this stranded whale gives off echoes of the leviathan to be eaten by the blessed on judgment day. This whale fish came from saltwater ocean and tried to swim upriver but died apparently in the fresh water of life. Blubber bloated wares up at the shore in Dublin. The inhabitants ate from the saltwater whalefish, the **blubby wares** of death.

In the year 566 [one-half of 1132 or the folded garment of ES] on Mid-summer's Eve after a flood [curse] an old woman had a wicker basket in order to carry dead **turves** or turds from the bog [the TZTZ creation]. She was looking at them under the small fish in the basket [Christ] as she ran in order to satisfy curiosity— [**sothisfeige**] so this is a fig shell currency [**cowrieosity**]. Eve and curiosity. Currency to buy transport. But by my soul [**be me sawl**] she like Eve found herself full of goody child and in small inelegant shoes, so rich in sweat [in other words pregnant and poor]. This created Blurryworks at Hurdlesford or Dublin, known as the Ford of Hurdles, which is one of Gaelic names for Dublin. This name refers to a ford of hurdles [osiers or woven connectors] used as foot stepping bridge across the river Liffey. The meaning seems to be this: Sex and pregnancy are the blurry vision of god whose image is his half folded garment of time. In Joyce's vision, the garment is half folded by ES as It bends over to defecate.

Now time in the opposite direction from 566 to 1132 A.D., the point here being that direction doesn't matter in terms of what will happen:

> **[14] 566 A.D. At this time it fell out that a brazenlockt damsel grieved**
> **7**
> **(*sobralasolas!*) because that Puppette her minion was ravisht of her**
> **8**
> **by the ogre Puropeus Pious. Bloody wars in Ballyaugha-cleeagh-**
> **9**
> **bally.**
> **10**

This time it fell out [the fall or birth] that a brazen damsel grieved (over the waves) because her youth [her doll-**minion**] was raped by the ogre of Priapus the Pious [RCC Pope or father figure in general]. **That is to say the role of the senior male was played by the institutional church**. The result was bloody wars in Baile Atha Clliath—the Town of the Ford of Hurdles.

> **[14] 1132. A.D. Two sons at an hour were born until a goodman**
> **11**
> **and his hag. These sons called themselves Caddy and Primas.**
> **12**
> **Primas was a santryman and drilled all decent people. Caddy**
> **13**
> **went to Winehouse and wrote o peace a farce. Blotty words for**
> **14**
> **Dublin.**

Still in the garment of time at 1132 CE. Two sons were born each hour. This refers to the many brother struggles in myth. For example Abel/Cain, Romulus/Remus, Castor/Pollux and here in FW Shem/Shaun. These particular archetypical sons called themselves Caddy and Primas. Cad and prime, the primal horde sons, the competition already present in the names—the Prime brother calls himself prime and his brother a cad. Like Saint Patrick, Primas Shawn was a sentry and drilled, that is instructed, in how to behave like all decent people. They were dependent and obeyed his reflection of the rules. Caddy Shem Joyce went to Paris [winehouse—spirit house—muses] and wrote a piece peace of farce [Ulysses]. Smeared [**blotty**] words for Dublin like the smears on the wall of the Garden of Eden.

Now for some more history, and some more about words:

[14] Somewhere, parently, in the ginnandgo gap between antediluvious and annadominant the copyist must have fled
with his
17
scroll. The billy flood rose or an elk charged him or the
sultrup
18
worldwright from the excelsissimost empyrean (bolt, in sum)
19
earthspake or the Dannamen gallous banged pan the bliddy
du-
20
ran. A scribicide then and there is led off under old's code
with
21
some fine covered by six marks or ninepins in metalmen for
the
22
sake of his labour's dross while it will be only now and again
in
23
our rear of o'er era, as an upshoot of military and civil en-
gage-
24
ments, that a gynecure was let on to the scuffold for taking
that
25
same fine sum covertly by meddlement with the drawers of
his
26
neighbour's safe.

Somewhere sometime, apparently the original source parent, in the
emptiness [**ginnandgo gap**—gin and go gap or sex organ] between
the devious pre-flood [**antediluvious**] and the removal of the Lord
[**annadominant** instead of Anno Domini the year of the Lord] the
copyist must have fled with his scroll, leaving us without a clue as to
the relationship of god to man. What was left was a debt owed by
man to god, the debt of death. The debt came in various forms: The
billy flood [bill] rose or a giant **elk charged** [charge] him or the sa-
trap world maker [**sultrup worldwright**] god the secondary demiurge [TZTZ god] from the most high heaven [zohar layers] caused
the earth to speak [natural disasters] or the Danish men foreigners to

259

bang pan the Hen [Holy Spirit]. A murderer of a writer [**scribicide**—perhaps Moses killed by god] then is let off under the old code with a fine of only six marks or nine metal money for his deed [writer not worth much] while it will be only now and again at the end of our era, as a result of strife, that a woman cure [**a gynecure or** abortionist] was let on the scaffold for taking that same amount [a life] from the **drawers of his neighbor's safe**—neighbor's wife. This may mean that making the Virgin Mary a virgin was like taking a life.

> **[14] Now after all that farfatch'd and peragrine or dingnant or clere**
> **28**
> **lift we our ears, eyes of the darkness, from the tome of** *Liber Li-*
> **29**
> *vidus* **and, (toh!), how paisibly eirenical, all dimmering dunes**
> **30**
> **and gloamering glades, selfstretches afore us our fredeland's plain!**
> **31**

The four writers of the Annals of the Four Masters are woven into **farfatch'd**, **peragrine**, **dingnant** and **clere**. Now after all that far-fetched and outlandish or indignant or clear, we lift our ears and our eyes from the darkness recorded in the Annals [constant warfare] and from the blue book Leviticus [all the rules of the Jewish religion making for *Tikkun*]. And look what we see: how possibly and ironically peaceful does our freeland's plain stretch before us in dunes that dimm and glades that gloam. In other words the strife does not come from the earth.

In a trite romantic style, more about nature in Ireland, nature that is peaceful and contrary to warfare:

> **Lean neath stone pine the pastor lies with his crook; young pric-**
> **32**
> **ket by pricket's sister nibbleth on returned viridities; amaid her**
> **33**
> **rocking grasses the herb trinity shams lowliness; skyup is of ever-**
> **34**
> **grey. Thus, too, for donkey's years.**

In a phrase that identifies the province of Ulster, the pastor [St. Patrick] lies with his sheepherding crook beneath the stone pine; in a phrase that identifies the province Leinster, a young [2nd year] deer [**pricket**] stands by his sister and nibbles on new grass [**viritidies**— with a suggestion of truth in death]; amid a made maid's rocking grasses the clover [**herb trinity**] shams lowliness by being lower but symbolizing the trinity and used by St. Patrick; in a phrase identifying the province of Connaught, the sky above is always gray. It is also gray in Tara [formerly the fifth province where the High Kings of Ireland ruled]. So the gods rule with gray, with *Tzimtzum*. In the culminating debate, St. Patrick is to wear gray and fold his garment in order to defecate.

Now for some more history *a la Quinet*:

> **[14] Since the bouts of Hebear**
> **35**
> **and Hairyman the cornflowers have been staying at Bally-**
> **mun,**
> **36**
> **[15] the duskrose has choosed out Goatstown's hedges, twol-**
> **ips have**
> **1**
> **pressed togatherthem by sweet Rush, townland of**
> **twinedlights,**
> **2**
> **the whitethorn and the redthorn have fairygeyed the mayval-**
> **leys**
> **3**
> **of Knockmaroon, and, though for rings round them, during a**
> **4**
> **chiliad of perihelygangs, the Formoreans have brittled the**
> **too-**
> **5**
> **ath of the Danes and the Oxman has been pestered by the**
> **Fire-**
> **6**
> **bugs and the Joynts have thrown up jerrybuilding to the**
> **Kevan-**
> **7**
> **ses and Little on the Green is childsfather to the City (Year!**
> **8**
> **Year! And laughtears!), these paxsealing buttonholes have**
> **quad-**
> **9**

rilled across the centuries and whiff now whafft to us, fresh and
10
made-of-all-smiles as, on the eve of Killallwho.

This is the first use in FW of Edgar Quinet, the use of the structure of one of his famous utterances combining flowers and violent human history. The implied point is that if you argue that human strife is just a natural part of competition for sexual resources, how do you explain flowers? They are also sexual resources and do not produce violence but instead compete with color. You competitive readers need to forget about the strife between plants for sunlight and minerals.

Here is Joyce's use of the same idea. It starts in time at the beginning, that is since the trials of an ancient Milesian leader in Ireland [Heber in **Hebear**] and his brother [Eremon in **Hairyman**]. The animal hair references of **Hebear** bring in he the bear [the bear skin hats of the Old Guard at Waterloo] and Bear Shit for *bereshit*. **Hairyman** brings in the Zoasterian god of evil Ahriman or hairyman opposed to the good god Ahura Mazda. And of course Vico's first men. Since then, since the beginning of evil, the cornflowers have been staying at Ballymun [village north of Dublin], the duskrose has chosen to thrive in Goatstown's hedges [village in south of Dublin] with a suggestion of chewing like goats; tulips and lovers kissing with two lips have pressed together to gather them at sweet Rush [village in east Dublin famous for tulips], the townland of entwined lights; the whitethorn and redthorn [red and white] have decorated like fairies in May the valleys of Knockmaroon [means the Hill of the Corpses which is located in the west of Dublin in the corner of Phoenix Park]. And notwithstanding all this continuing natural beauty, the historical Irish—the Formians, the Tuatha de Danan, and the Oxmen—have pestered each other during thousands of years while the sun blessed the plants and have been pestered by the fire lovers Firblogs while the Juts built only shabby buildings without faith in the future and only commercial markets not culture were built by the original fathers of the City of Dublin [Danes]. (**Year! And laughtears!** years around the sun with tears). Meanwhile these peace sealing buttonhole flowers have danced across the centuries and now waft to us smiles on the eve of the final dissolution, the Apocalypse, the kill of all who. The wars have not stopped the flowers, the women keep on blooming. Pun intended—for bloomers.

[15] The babbelers with their thangas vain have been (con-
fusium
12
hold them!) they were and went; thigging thugs were and
hou-
13
hnhymn songtoms were and comely norgels were and pollyfool
14
fiansees.

This history of strife is traced to the Tower of Babel [**babbelers**], viewed as [**thangas vain**] vanity or inability to communicate [effort would be vain] because of different languages resulting from geographical displacement. Vanity stems from the Babel practice of placing names on the building bricks as symbolic of personal importance and the corresponding sense of separation. Separation of races to different environments would produce slightly different human traits that in turn would create suspicion when they meet. With a sequence of Irish, Italian, French, and Norwegian based names, the babbelers with their language vain [both not effective and proud] have been in the past (confusion continue to hold them!); they were in existence and then went; in the past came [into Ireland] food stealing thugs, horse-like [from Gulliver's Travels] singers of songs, comely Norse and French [**pollyfool**] fiancées.

Now repeating the Babel-like linguistic sequence:

[15] Menn have thawed, clerks have surssurhummed, the
15
blond has sought of the brune: Elsekiss thou may, mean
Kerry
16
piggy?: and the duncledames have countered with the hellish
fel-
17
lows: Who ails tongue coddeau, aspace of dumbillsilly? And
they
18
fell upong one another: and themselves they have fallen.
19

Men have warmed up, clerks have sucked up humming sir sir, blond Norse have sought out brunette Irish women: [the crude Norse says] May I kiss you you Kerry piggy, you Irish pig? And the dark Irish lasses have countered with the Norse: where is your gift of tongue [French kiss], you silly dumbbell? But sexual attraction overcame differences, and they fell upon **upong** one another; and in that process they have fallen themselves [into original sin].

Now back to love and flowers and short-term life of flowers and humans:

> **[15] And still nowanights and by nights of yore do all bold floras of the**
> **20**
> **field to their shyfaun lovers say only: Cull me ere I wilt to thee!:**
> **21**
> **and, but a little later: Pluck me whilst I blush! Well may they**
> **22**
> **wilt, marry, and profusedly blush, be troth!**

And still at the present moment in the night [**nowanight**] and by nights of yore do the bold flowers of the field say to their shy faunlike lovers: cull me [remove my virginity] before I wilt and lose my freshness for you!: and, but a little later: pluck me while I can still blush. Well may they get older [wilt], marry and blush profusely! Norse men and Irish women are still part of nature, being males and females.

This sexual binder, though, does not prevent war and raiding. This is an old truth:

> **[15] For that saying is as**
> **23**
> **old as the howitts. Lave a whale a while in a whillbarrow (isn't**
> **24**
> **it the truath I'm tallin ye?) to have fins and flippers that shimmy**
> **25**
> **and shake. Tim Timmycan timped hir, tampting Tam. Fleppety!**
> **26**
> **Flippety! Fleapow!**
> **27**
> **Hop!**

For that saying [men are men and women are women whatever nationality they may be] is as old as the hills [**howitts** are mountains in

264

Australia] that is how it is [**howitts**]. If you leave a whale awhile in a wheelbarrow, it will shimmy and shake its fins and flippers. It is part of its nature, just as sexual attraction between human females and males, even Irish and Norse, is part of nature. Tim, because he could, tempted her; Tim was tempting Tam [female Tam to male Tim—names built the same except for what is in the middle]. Tim and Tam undulated in sex like the flips of a whale in a wheelbarrow. A whale out of water, humans out of paradise. Both about to die. Hop! The spirit of beer. Sex is the spirit of mankind, the big hops.

Now a new presence comes on the FW scene, the "invading" Jute who comes on Mutt. Perhaps this encounter will explain the reasons for warfare. This encounter is designed to speak as an arche-typical meeting in order to demonstrate the basis for strife. Once again, the basis for strife is separation, the curse of Babel, people in different areas with different languages and cultures developing differently. That is to say, the strategy of TZTZ god in scattering the population at Babel worked. The separated populations are different and don't cooperate. Small differences lead to strife. As the enemy they must be demonized. Their only form of interaction is imperialism—when one wants to take from the other:

> [15] **In the name of Anem this carl on the kopje in pelted thongs a**
> **29**
> **parth a lone who the joebiggar be he? Forshapen his pigmaid**
> **30**
> **hoagshead, shroonk his plodsfoot. He hath locktoes, this short-**
> **31**
> **shins, and, Obeold that's pectoral, his mammamuscles most**
> **32**
> **mousterious.**

In the name of the name [same letters in **name** scrambled in **Anem** to indicate the two races involved are made of the same stuff], there is this northern **carl**, this churl, this commoner. Note on the part of Mutt the instinct for aggression rather than an instinct for hospitality.

This **carl** appears on the small hill [**kopje**] in pelt covered thongs and all alone like the Parthalon, the mythical post flood colonizer of Ireland [separated as **parth a lone** and remember **a lone** at the end of the novel]. Who be he? Note the first impression is that carl is subhuman. The narrator notes Carl has a protruding forehead and acts like a pig or a hog. His plodding feet are small [like a pig or hog].

He has locked or crossed toes, short legs and a large chest most mysterious and monstrous. More cultural facts about Jute:

> **[15] It is slaking nuncheon out of some thing's brain**
> **33**
> **pan. Me seemeth a dragon man. He is almonthst on the kiep**
> **34**
> **fief by here, is Comestipple Sacksoun, be it junipery or fe-**
> **brew-**
> **35**
> **ery, marracks or alebrill or the ramping riots of pouriose and**
> **froriose. What a quhare soort of a mahan.**

It [notice the impersonal pronoun] is different culturally, eating brains out of a cranium, with suggestion of cannibalism. To me he seems like a dragon man. He is almost on the kiep fief near here [he is invading]. He must be a rough [**comestipple**] Saxon because they come in January, February, March, or April or the ramping rigors of May and June—in other words at any time during the cold months way up north. What a queer sort of bear-man [**mahan**].

> **[16] It is evident the mich-**
> **1**
> **indaddy. Lets we overstep his fire defences and these kraals**
> **of**
> **2**
> **slitsucked marrogbones. (Cave!) He can prapsposterus the**
> **pil-**
> **3**
> **lory way to Hirculos pillar.**

It is evident that as a subhuman he represents a fork [a **michindaddy**] in the human tree. Note the judgments being made by Mutt through the narrator about Jute on the basis of looks alone. Mutt is profiling. In secret Joyce Torah code, Mutt treats Jute like a fork daddy, suggestive of the male angel of death at the end of the novel ready with its trident to spear ALP in the female waters. Now, as if stepping into his camp, the narrator now expanded to "we" notices Jute's burning fire. Mutt assumes it is a defense [fire to keep animals away rather than to keep warm]. Mutt notices containers of marrowbones from which the marrow has been sucked through the slit in the bones [now *osso bucco*]. **Marrongbones** gives the practice a gog

impression. Caveman he. He can make it on the **paspsposterus** preposterous [means reversed or inverted, having last what should be
first, as well as contrary to nature] way of punishment [**pillory**—the
stock] to the pillars of Hercules [at Gibraltar]—the end of the earth.
Substituting prap for pre in **prasposterus** suggests that Jute practices
sex in the posterior—back to belly—with his pillar. Remember that
Hercules had to clean the Aegean stables.

Now more:

> **[16] Come on, fool porterfull, hosiered**
> 4
> **women blown monk sewer? Scuse us, chorley guy! You tol-
> ler-**
> 5
> **day donsk? N. You tolkatiff scowegian? Nn. You spigotty an-**
> 6
> **glease? Nnn. You phonio saxo? Nnnn. Clear all so! 'Tis a
> Jute.**
> 7

And now the not so friendly greeting to the new one. Come on you
fool full of porter. Do women blow your monk sewer—give you a
blow job, fellatio or French love? The same sounds in French mean
like how are you today, my fair sir [come on is comme and monk
sewer is monsieur]? What a difference a language makes. Excuse us,
you chorley [Charlie? Chori means apart or sunder] guy. You speak
Danish? Norwegian? No. You speak [with a low connotation] English? You understand Saxon? No. Then you must be a Jute.

This series of questions is based on an old joke. It is a classic
German joke about Jutes [Jutland is modern Denmark]. The joke
goes:

> A German is walking in Jutland and loses his way. There are two
> Jutes leaning on a fence and so he goes over to them. "Sprechen
> sie Deutsch?" he asks. They shake their heads. "Parlez-vous Fran-
> çais?" Again no. "Do you speak English?" No. And so it goes on.
> In the end the German gives up in disgust and walks on. First Jute:
> "You know, we should really learn some foreign languages." Sec-
> ond Jute: "What would be the point? That man knew ten, and look
> where it got him!"

The point is that the Jutes don't get the point. They could be more accommodating. They could unify with others by learning another language. They have shifted the blame.

Going on:

> **[16] Let us swop hats and excheck a few strong verbs weak oach ea-**
> **8**
> **ther yapyazzard abast the blooty creeks.**

Let us swap hats and exchange a few threats. I am happy to hazard violence about the bloody looting at the creeks [rivers in Eden and Creek Indians in Ochonee Georgia and the site of the Battle of Clontarf].

Now for the archetypical conversation between Jute the invader and Mutt the local. Mutt suggests mute. The historical background is the Battle of Clontarf, which was fought in 1014 CE on the Talka Creek where it flows into Dublin Bay. Brain Boru lead the Irish forces that defeated the occupying Danes.

> **[16] Jute.— Yutah!**
> **10**
> **Mutt.— Mukk's pleasurad.**
> **11**
> **Jute.— Are you jeff?**
> **12**
> **Mutt.— Somehards.**
> **13**
> **Jute.— But you are not jeffmute?**
> **14**
> **Mutt.— Noho. Only an utterer.**
> **15**
> **Jute.— Whoa? Whoat is the mutter with you?**
> **16**
> **Mutt.— I became a stun a stummer.**
> **17**
> **Jute.— What a hauhauhauhaudibble thing, to be cause!**
> **How,**
> **18**
> **Mutt?**
> **19**
> **Mutt.— Aput the buttle, surd.**
> **20**

First Jute speaks in a strange tonque. He says something like Utah or you tah. Mutt of the cartoon characters Mutt and Jeff responds. Like the cartoon, this is to be dream-like caricature.

The language reported is what Jute hears. Mutt apparently says something like Mutt is pleasured to meet you [**Mukk's pleasured**] but Jute doesn't understand it. The Jute then asks Mutt if he is jeff, which means tedious or boring. In the context of Mutt and Jeff, Jute would be Jeff so confusion about identity reigns. Mutt responds **Somehards.** We expected "sometimes" for the answer rather than **somehards**.

Now apparently understanding each other since veiled insults are involved, Jute asks Mutt if he is **jeffmute**, instead of the expected deaf-mute, a question he could not hear if he were. To be **jeffmute** would be not to understand Jute. Mutt responds that he is only an **utterer**, that is a stutterer without the first s. Ututterer also means one who passes counterfeit coins, to connect us to the forgery theme. Utter means to make a sound but also as an adverb it means to be apart. Note the "ute" in Jute for overlooked common substance with Mutt the utterer.

Now with common substance in play Jute shows some concern for Mutt—what is the matter with you? Mutt responds that he became **a stun a stummer**. Stun is an unfermented grape juice, that is partially civilized. Stummer is Norse for stumble. Jute laughs at this and asks how he came by the stuttering. Mutt replies after the battle [of Clontarf reminding the Jute of their loss] and calls Jute a surd, which means stupid and suggests turd. The battle caused fear and stuttering, like TZTZ god's curses that are disguised in Dungtarf.

But Jute doesn't hear the slight:

> [16] Jute.—— Whose poddle? Wherein?
> 21
> Mutt.—— The Inns of Dungtarf where Used awe to be he.
> 22
> Jute.—— You that side your voise are almost inedible to me.
> 23
> Become a bitskin more wiseable, as if I were
> 24
> you.
> 25
> Mutt.—— Has? Has at? Hasatency? Urp, Boohooru! Booru
> 26

Usurp! I trumple from rath in mine mines when I
27
rimimirim !
28

To connect with flood imagery and Waterloo, Joyce has Jute hear
puddle rather than battle or buttle, **Poddle** apparently means Erin in
Danish. And Jute asks **wherein** [where in Erin or place is seemingly
the most inconsequential aspect of a battle but wherein in the sense
of what context is more important for the TZTZ theme]. Mutt replies the **Inns of Dungtarf.** This word combines Clontarf with
Dung in the TZTZ creation. These Inns did not provide hospitality.

Clontarf means the bull meadow. The historical battle of Clontarf in 1014 CE was on the north side of Dublin Bay near where
Dublin castle rose later. **The Used awe to be he** spoken by Mutt
refers to the loss by the occupier Danes of political control [**awe**] of
the area as a result of the battle. The victorious ruler gets the awe.
Mutt is dissing Jute. And Joyce is dissing the god of TZTZ creation.
What awe is due Him?

Jute responds, so as to avoid the necessity of dealing with the
insult, that he can't hear Mutt and suggests that he wise up–a denial
of the separation. He uses bits and kin together [**bitskin**] for this
suggestion. You can sense the sparks of unity and separate shards in
this reference.

Mutt then builds up to **hasatency** through **Has** and **Has at**,
the primordial elements of history—the past, violence and where.
Hasatency suggests a tendency in history: Has atency. This word as
misspelled with an "e" rather than an "a" [hesitency] also played a
famous role in the trial of Parnell, the Irish freedom patriot. Joyce is
suggesting that in this TZTZ world the relation to god is something
like a forged letter resulting is less human potential—hesitency rather
than bravery.

Mutt goes on to lay it on and rub it in. He mentions the victorious Brian Boru, the leader of the Irish against the Norse occupiers.
Boru becomes **Boohooru**, incorporating "boohoo" the childhood
fear taunt. On a roll, Mutt says there was usurpation in Rathmines [a
District in Dublin and the mine of rath] when I rim him [**rimimirim**
for repeated licks]. Rim from ream means oral sexual stimulation of
the anus—oral anal. Try saying **rimimrim** without a great deal of
tonque action. In other words, your kind sucked our shit at Clontarf.
TZTZ.

[16] Jute.—— One eyegonblack. Bisons is bisons. Let me fore
all
29
your hasitancy cross your qualm with trink gilt. Here
30
have sylvan coyne, a piece of oak. Ghinees hies good
31
for you.
32
Mutt.—— Louee, louee! How wooden I not know it, the intel-
33
lible greytcloak of Cedric Silkyshag! Cead mealy
34
faulty rices for one dabblin bar. Old grilsy growlsy!
35
He was poached on in that eggtentical spot. Here
36
[17] where the liveries, Monomark. There where the mis-
1
sers moony, Minnikin passe.
2

Now the Jute says that loss was one black eye, but he doesn't know
English slang for sure so he says **One eyegonblack**. Then he coun-
sels peace: Let bygones be bygones. This becomes let **bisons be bisons**—in other words let the two sons [bi-son] that we are remain
two sons and not kill each other [Cain-Able]. In view of your hesitancy and qualms about me, let me cross your palm. Hestitancy becomes has it ancy—he is ancy to have it. He offers a piece of oak,
sylvan coyne—a half pence in Wood's money [not actually wooden
money] introduced by the British in Ireland. Like Guinness beer,
wood coin is good for you. Mutt responds Louee—French [incor-
rect] for it is we [c'est oui] or Italian for it is him [c'est lui]. These
play with the Buddhist phrase "Thou are that," an indication of the
primal unity.

Mutt continues with the rejection: Wooden money I know not;
it is like the **intellible** grey great cloak of Cedric [remember time and
space as the garment of ES]. Cedric was the King of the Danes at
Clontarf, the King of the losers. His grandson was Sigtrygg Silkbeard
Olafsson, whom Joyce makes into Silkyshag, the garment of unity.
These northerners worshipped oak trees. The Irish replaced the
Danes as TZTZ god replaced ES.

Mutt continues with a thousand welcomes rise for one **dabblin**,
a small coastal fish around Britain but referring to dabbling [means

271

dipping in water or hitting lightly] in Dublin. The next sentence [**Old grilsy growlsy!**] returns to the salmon motif with a grilse, a salmon that has returned to fresh water after the smolt stage and one year in the ocean. Punning on poaching fish or intruding, Mutt says Cedric was poached on in that identical [**eggtentical**—egg tent] spot. Here is where the horse servants [war captured slaves such as your kind] go, Mr. One Mark. Right there where the misers of compassion go crazy [under the influence of the moon], become mere manikins or dwarfs of humans [**Minnikin passe**].

Now Jute speaks of history from the pen of Tacitus, Tacitus the writer with the concise style [thus **Taciturn**]:

> [17] Jute.—— Simply because as Taciturn pretells, our wrong-story-
> 3
> shortener, he dumptied the wholeborrow of rubba-
> 4
> ges on to soil here.
> 5
> Mutt.—— Just how a puddinstone inat the brookcells by a
> 6
> riverpool.
> 7
> Jute.—— Load Allmarshy! Wid wad for a norse like?
> 8
> Mutt.—— Somular with a bull on a clompturf. Rooks roarum
> 9
> rex roome! I could snore to him of the spumy horn,
> 10
> with his woolseley side in, by the neck I am sutton
> 11
> on, did Brian d' of Linn.
> 12

Using pretell, Jute disses Ireland or that part at least as the rubbish heap, the dump. Mutt boasts that it was good enough to make the conglomerate rock in the brook near the riverpool—the whirlpool in the Liffey River. Showing a green conscience, Jute deplores the load of garbage in the marsh, the field of battle of Clontarf. [Waterloo has become the marsh.] What was it like for the Norse, Jute asks. Mutt responds that the Norse experience was similar to the experience of a bull on a clompturf, a muddy ground difficult to maneuver in to catch the cows. The rooks were roaring in the king's room [men trapped in mud like chess rooks trapped in the back row of the los-

ing King and the TZTZ god]. Remember we are speaking of
Howth's Head—how did the head get into this mess. Mutt says that
he could bore Jute with an explanation of the spumy horn, the flowing penis, with his wooly side in, where Brian of Linn moved [in the
battle] by the land neck [Sutton joins Howth and mainland].

Now Jute is offended:

> **[17] Jute.**— Boildoyle and rawhoney on me when I can beu-
> raly
> 13
> forsstand a weird from sturk to finnic in such a pat-
> 14
> what as your rutterdamrotter. Onheard of and um-
> 15
> scene! Gut aftermeal! See you doomed.
> 16

Becoming angry [**boildoyle** and **rawhoney**—sound like districts of
Dublin], Jute tells him to go to hell and that he can't stand to hear
this weird tale from start to finish about **rutterdamrotter**—
Gotterdammerung recast with rutting, being a combination of death
of the gods and rotting waste. It is unheard of and obscene [**um-
scene**]. Jute says you will eat after I do [**Gut aftermeal**]—the primal
sign of dominance.

Mutt responds:

> **[17] Mutt.**— Quite agreem. Bussave a sec. Walk a dun blink
> 17
> roundward this albutisle and you skull see how olde
> 18
> ye plaine of my Elters, hunfree and ours, where wone
> 19
> to wail whimbrel to peewee o'er the saltings, where
> 20
> wilby citie by law of isthmon, where by a droit of
> 21
> signory, icefloe was from his Inn the Byggning to
> 22
> whose Finishthere Punct. Let erehim ruhmuhrmuhr.
> 23
> Mearmerge two races, swete and brack. Morthering
> 24
> rue. Hither, craching eastuards, they are in surgence:
> 25

hence, cool at ebb, they requiesce. Countlessness of
26
livestories have netherfallen by this plage, flick as
27
 flowflakes, litters from aloft, like a waast wizzard all of
28
whirlworlds. Now are all tombed to the mound, isges
29
to isges, erde from erde. Pride, O pride, thy prize!
30

First a surprise. Mutt agrees. He will eat second. Then Mutt says wait a second [save a second—into the eternal]. Walk around this almost island [penisula means that—penis almost brings together—remember the pier-peer as a disappointed bridge in Portrait]. You shall skull see the old plain of my elders [old plain of Elta where the Parthalonians died of plague, next to Howth], free of Huns [invaders in general]. This is now ours, where whimbrel and lapwing birds fly over the salt meadow [tide], where by will a city was made under the law of ismas man [Christians—connected to god by an isthmus], where by the right of the senior male ice flowed from his Inn the Beginning to be finished there punctually—Norse creation legend involves escape from ice. Mutt now dreams the impossible dream— to merge the races that have fallen on this field of battle [**livestories have netherfallen by this plage**]: let him be the first one— **erehim**—to remember [rue murder—**ruhmuhrmuhr**]. Merge undiluted or as one [merged unity—the nature of ES] two races, sweet and brackish—fresh and salt water, female and male cosmic sexuality. Mothering the rue—the pity and compassion. [HCE] Here crashing on the estuary [eastuards—east wards—out of Eden—salt and fresh]. Now the could-be-merged humans are all tombed in the mound [a death mound being no substitute for a unity in ES], and ashes to ashes [**isges to isges**] is the royal route of death planned for celestial hospitality. And **erde from erde** or merde from merde— excrement from excrement. Pride, the original sin, this is your prize—excrement.

[17] Jute.—— 'Stench!
31
Mutt.—— Fiatfuit! Hereinunder lyethey. Llarge by the smal
an'
32

274

everynight life olso th'estrange, babylone the great-
33
grandhotelled with tit tit tittlehouse, alp on earwig,
34
drukn on ild, likeas equal to anequal in this sound
35
seemetery which iz leebez luv.
36
[18] Jute.— 'Zmorde!
1

Jute replies that the mound stinks. Mutt responds philosophically. Instead of luxfuit that means "there was light," we have an arbitrary order "there was" [**Fiatfuit**]. Let it be it was, the TZTZ command of time past. They the dead buried in lye in the mounds lie lethe forgetting [**lyethey**] hereinunder. Large—so large it has two l's [**Llarge**]—by the small—so small it has only one l [**smal**]—and also the estranged human experience [small humans removed from ES], giving us night life in Babylon where the great and grandhotel was built as the Tower of Babel with titles on the bricks [**tit tit tittlehouse**], giving us alp on earwig, giving us drunken on fire id. This estranged human experience is like an equal to a non-productive equal [male] in this sound cemetery of seeing space [sleep as **sound seemetery**] which Issie loved. Jute exclaims **zmorde**—a combination of shit and death. Perhaps the inevitable death of both of them will bring about some form of reconciliation.

[18] Mutt.— Meldundleize! By the fearse wave behoughted. Des-
2
pond's sung. And thanacestross mound have swollup
3
them all. This ourth of years is not save brickdust
4
and being humus the same roturns. He who runes
5
may rede it on all fours. O'c'stle, n'wc'stle, tr'c'stle,
6
crumbling! Sell me sooth the fare for Humblin! Hum-
7
blady Fair. But speak it allsosiftly, moulder! Be in
8
your whisht!
9

Mutt cautions softly and gently with *mild* and *leise*, words from Wagner's **Tristan und Isolde**, previously referenced in Issy loves. These words begin the last singing in the Opera, by Isolde, about how peaceful and quiet Tristan looks when he is dead, when he is finally reconciled. Mutt gains confidence as Jute displays no knowledge of these subjects. Mutt continues his cultural references, gaining superiority through knowledge like an academic. **By the fierce wave behoughted** refers to a song by the name *By the Feal's wave benighted*. Feal means constant and loyal. So this must refer indirectly to Tristan fetching Isolde across the sea as his duty to King Mark. Hough in **behoughted** means heel or hamstring, suggesting the weakness of Achilles' heel, Tristan's susceptibility to sexual attraction. Mutt's next reference is to **despond's sung** [about the love potion's effects]. And then a reference to the deadly **thanacestross** [ancestor] mound that has swallowed them all swelling pregnant-like in the process [**swollup**]. Tristan and Isolde die. This earth of years is not worth brickdust [Tower of Babel and Adam from clay] and being earth born to the same returns [**roturns**] in death. He who reads the magic symbols may read it on all fours—that is even when a baby. Then in Hebrew style without vowels, Oldcastle, Newcastle and Tricastle are crumbling. Please send me the fare to get to humble Dublin [Humblin]. **Humblady Fair**. But speak it all so softly, mister-mother. Be in your wish it.

Jute asks why shit:

> [18] Jute.— Whysht?
> 10
> Mutt.— The gyant Forficules with Amni the fay.
> 11
> Jute.— Howe?
> 12
> Mutt.— Here is viceking's graab.
> 13
> Jute.— Hwaad !
> 14
> Mutt.— Ore you astoneaged, jute you?
> 15
> Jute.— Oye am thonthorstrok, thing mud.

Mutt explains the shit as a result of the giant earwig [**gyant Forficules**] laying with **Amni the fay**—a river with overtones of the fairy or sorcerer [fay]. Amni was also the Roman Goddess of the ring of the year, fortune for the coming year. The giant earwig is a symbol of the TZTZ god's mental influence on humans resulting in repetition. The giant earwig with its rear-end pincer is to be contrasted with the Holy Spirit, who in Roman Catholic doctrine impregnated the Virgin Mary through the ear.

Jutt asks **howe** does it happen—a howe is a burial mound, a type of barrow, sometimes referred to as a cairn circle. So the question is how does shit death happen. Mutt explains with a reference to a grab by the king of vice [viceking's graab], which combines TZTZ god and vikings. Mutt in Danish asks what say? Mutt replies with exasperation: Are you [with reference to dumb as rock] from the stone ages, knock you? Jute thinks that Mutt has asked him if he is made of rock and responds: I am thunder struck by Thor [Din], thing mud man as wet clay. In other words, I am mortal. This ends the conversation.

Now the narrator asks us some questions that apply to FW as well as other matters:

> [18] (Stoop) if you are abcedminded, to this claybook, what curios
> 17
> of signs (please stoop), in this allaphbed! Can you rede (since
> 18
> We and Thou had it out already) its world? It is the same told
> 19
> of all. Many. Miscegenations on miscegenations. Tieckle. They
> 20
> lived und laughed ant loved end left. Forsin.

Stoop to the mud clay of mankind if you are minded to read the history of this world in letters [Torah], to this book of man of clay, what curious signs are in this **allaphbed**, the ALP alphabet of the alpha first bed? Can you read the world of the letter? It is the same story of all. Many. Miscegenations by the gods on mankind. The macro and the micro. Given what was possible, they lived, laughed and like ants loved and in the end died [**end left**]. Note the progressive change from "and" to **und** and then **ant** and then **end**. Those under TZTZ domination are characterized by "and," signifying just another one, who will become ant-like worrying about the end. Death was ordained by the first sin, the **forsin** [with a word play on foreskin being removed].

Some scriptural reference seems to be in play here. From Daniel:

> And this is the writing that was inscribed: MENE, MENE, TE-KEL, and PARSIN. This is the interpretation of the matter: MENE, God has numbered the days of your kingdom and brought it to an end; TEKEL, you have been weighed on the scales and found wanting; PARSIN, your kingdom is divided and given to the Medes and Persians. (Daniel 5:25-28)

Which is to say, things are going to be bad.

Carrying on with this quote:

> [18] **Thy thingdome is**
> 21
> **given to the Meades and Porsons. The meandertale, aloss and**
> 22
> **again, of our old Heidenburgh in the days when Head-in-Clouds**
> 23
> **walked the earth.**

In other words god ends lives and kingdoms. They are repetitions of the old meandering tale, of repeated loss, of our old stone age man in the days the giant Adam Kadmon [**Head in Clouds**--HC] walked the earth.

Now for the Buddhistic twelve step chain of dependent origination. This formula is an attempt to understand human existence. The sequence is modified by Joyce:

> [18] **In the ignorance that implies impression that**
> 24
> **knits knowledge that finds the nameform that whets the wits that**
> 25
> **convey contacts that sweeten sensation that drives desire that**
> 26
> **adheres to attachment that dogs death that bitches birth that en-**
> 27
> **tails the ensuance of existentiality.**

Note in Joyce's sequence the repeated use of alliteration implying repetition: III KK FF WW CC SS DD AA DD BB EEE. Feel the razor sharp disappointment in the mood of Joyce"s sentence. Dependant origination of humans from a curse of the gods is the backbone of FW.

From the EB:

> The Buddha, according to the early texts, discovered the law of dependent origination (*paticca-samuppada*), whereby one condition arises out of another, which in turn arises out of prior conditions. Every mode of being presupposes another immediately preceding mode from which the subsequent mode derives, in a chain of causes. According to the classical rendering, the 12 links in the chain are: ignorance (*avijja*), karmic predispositions (*sankharas*), consciousness (*vinnana*), form and body (*nama-rupa*), the five sense organs and the mind (*salayatana*), contact (*phassa*), feeling-response (*vedana*), craving (*tanha*), grasping for an object (*upadana*), action toward life (*bhava*), birth (*jati*), and old age and death (*jaramarana*). According to this law, the misery that is bound with sensate existence is accounted for by a methodical chain of causation. Despite a diversity of interpretations, the law of dependent origination of the various aspects of becoming remains fundamentally the same in all schools of Buddhism. The primary ignorance is the desire for life, for repeated lives.

Joyce's sequence goes ignorance-sensation-knowledge-name and form-desire-attachment-death-birth-existence.

The main message of the Buddha is that desire makes one incomplete, dissatisfied, while compassion can help make one complete. This message will be featured in the Prankquean story coming up shortly.

Now into other forms of understanding human existence:

> **[18] But with a rush out of his**
> 28
> **navel reaching the reredos of Ramasbatham. A terricolous**
> **vively-**
> 29
> **onview this; queer and it continues to be quaky.**

This is the image of Vishnu floating on the endless snake Ananta on the primeval waters with the temporary world issuing out of his navel. Translating: From his **navel** grew a lotus, in which the god Brahma was born reciting the four Vedas with his four mouths and creating the "Egg of Brahma," which contains all the worlds. **Reredos** means repetition of the worlds. The multicolored world so supported is **queer** and **quaky**—the earth moved for the Buddha. The Buddha summons the earth witness to confirm his enlightenment:

> **[18] A hatch, a celt,**
> 30
> **an earshare the pourquose of which was to cassay the earth-crust at**
> 31
> **all of hours, furrowards, bagawards, like yoxen at the turn-paht.**
> 32
> **Here say figurines billycoose arming and mounting. Mounting and**
> 33
> **arming bellicose figurines see here. Futhorc, this liffle ef-fingee is for**
> 34
> **a firefing called a flintforfall. Face at the eased! O I fay! Face at the**
> 35
> **waist! Ho, you fie! Upwap and dump em, ace to ace!**

This describes the process the earth mounts to confirm the Buddha's enlightenment: a hatch [from an egg] a birth, a smelt celt, an earshare [earwig] that has the purpose to essay the earth at all hours, forwards and backwards like yoked oxen back and forth in the field. She the watcher will find warlike figures **arming and mounting**, aiming their weapons and mounting their sex. Then like the oxen reversing direction [**bagawards**]—they are **mounting and arming**. In the Futhorc runic-based alphabet this little effigy [**effigee**] is a **firefing** called a **flintforfall**, strike for fire for all with the sex instinct. Face east! O I fay. **Face at the waist** [belly to belly]. Ho, you fie. Up and dump them, face to face with the E turned 90 degrees clockwise. Put them in the dump of death. The end cry is reminiscent of Wellington's on the Waterloo battlefield: Up boys, and at them.

Now for some macro and micro, part and whole, with a pun on whole/hole:

> **When a**
> 36
> **[19] part so ptee does duty for the holos we soon grow to use of an**
> 1
> **allforabit. Here (please to stoop) are selveran cued peteet**

peas of
2
quite a pecuniar interest inaslittle as they are the pellets that make
3
the tomtummy's pay roll.

When a part so petite—so small the word is reduced to **ptee**—does duty [acts as a synecdoche] for the infinite whole the **holos** [TZTZ creation does duty for ES who made the hole and female sex organ does duty for TZTZ god who made the hole], we soon grow used to words made of letters standing for things [**allforabit**]. Remember the claims for the Torah. And in the same sense of substitution, the sex instinct in which all are for a bit of ass there in that petite [**peteet**] experience you find the gods. Here, if you stoop to understand, are several cued small peas of quite a peculiar pecuniary interest— money—since they are the pellets bullets that make the soldiers' pay-roll—rape sex is their pay for killing [**tomtounny's pay roll**].

Now death extends to the gods—the death of the gods of the Norse. The letter "r" does duty for the Hebrew *resh* based word for curse [*arar*] and bent dependent humans whose repetitious activity alliterates the entire sentence:

[19] **Right rank ragnar rocks and with these**
4
rox orangotangos rangled rough and rightgorong. Wisha, wisha,
5
whydidtha?

Ragnorokr, a word loaded with "r's," means the destruction of the Norse gods as the orangutan-like humans played rough with rocks. Did you wish it, why so?

Now alliteration with t's:

[19] **Thik is for thorn that's thuck in its thoil like thum-**
6
fool's thraitor thrust for vengeance. What a mnice old mness it
7
all mnakes!

Thick is the thorn, given the penalty for life outside the Garden of Eden. **Thik** is also tik for Tikkun slowed down or unfinished. That is **thuck in its thoil**—remove the h for tuck in its toil—work required after garden removal. This penalty is like a thumfool's traitor thrust for vengeance, god acting the same as humans. God thumbed Adam and Eve out of the Garden. Then add m to n's and n's to ms: **What a mnice old mness it all mnakes!** What a nice old mess it all makes. The added letter makes the mess. The letters are a mess themselves. Snake seems to hide in "mnakes."

Now the mess as a middenheap:

> [19] A middenhide hoard of objects! Olives, beets, kim-
> 8
> mells, dollies, alfrids, beatties, cormacks and daltons. Owl-
> ets' eegs
> 9
> (O stoop to please!) are here, creakish from age and all now
> 10
> quite epsilene, and oldwolldy wobblewers, haudworth a wipe
> o
> 11
> grass. Sss! See the snake wurrums everyside! Our durlbin is
> 12
> sworming in sneaks.

More objects and letters. The midden is a dung heap hiding a hoard of objects, objects hoarded by a desire for possession. The list of objects mimics the start of the Hebrew and Greek alphabets. The symbol of Athens is the owl, and its eggs are here, grating with age and now quite low grade [epsilon]. We also have old-world snakes—**wobblewers**—to cause to shake or wobble. Like the shaking in ES preparatory to TZTZ creation. Snakes like excrement are hardly worth a wipe of grass. Sss for hissing snakes. See the snake worms [**wurrums** for were rum or past spirits] on every side. Our Dublin dustbin is swarming in sneaky snakes. S alliteration is used because an "s" looks like a snake [and is the first letter of Ulysses]. Wurm is a pun meaning both snake and evil and evil in the land is the subject here, except K teaches that evil is part of TZTZ creation and cannot be removed with removal of the snakes.

But St. Patrick came to help [that he rid Ireland of snakes is apparently a false legend]:

[19] They came to our island from triangular
13
Toucheaterre beyond the wet prairie rared up in the midst of
the
14
cargon of prohibitive pomefructs but along landed Paddy
Wip-
15
pingham and the his garbagecans cotched the creeps of
them
16
pricker than our whosethere outofman could quick up her
whats-
17
thats. Somedivide and sumthelot but the tally turns round the
18
same balifuson. Racketeers and bottloggers.
19

They, Patrick and St. Brigid and St. Columba, the three of them—the
trinity [**triangular**]—came from Angleterre disguised as **Toucheaterre**. In other words, they came selling religion with original sin.
With remarkable efficiency, this one word **Toucheaterre** captures
the punishment of death for eating or even touching the fruit of the
knowledge tree [touch eat terror terroir]. Eve did eat and experienced terror or terroir the ground in death—her teeth were set on
edge and to dust you shall return. Patrick and company came from
beyond the wet prairie [Garden served by underground rivers] having
been raised in the midst of the cargo of prohibited fruits [of the Tree
of Knowledge]. But along came Paddy [Patrick] Wippingham and he
caught the creepy serpents in his garbage cans quicker than our outofman [out of man or Eve] could quick up her question what is that
[what are the snakes]? Some divide and some sum the whole but the
tally, the result, turns round the same balifuson—the fusion of the
balls [**balifuson**], whether males can get along. Males generally turn
out to make racket and log from the bottle.

Now for writing:

[19] Axe on thwacks on thracks, axenwise. One by one place
one
20
be three dittoh and one before. Two nursus one make a
plaus-
21

ible free and idim behind. Starting off with a big boaboa and three-
22
legged calvers and ivargraine jadesses with a message in their
23
mouths. And a hundreadfilled unleavenweight of liberorum-queue
24
to con an we can till allhorrors eve. What a meanderthalltale to
25
unfurl and with what an end in view of squattor and anntis-quattor
26
and postproneauntisquattor! To say too us to be every tim, nick
27
and larry of us, sons of the sod, sons, littlesons, yea and lealittle-
28
sons, when usses not to be, every sue, siss and sally of us, dugters
29
of Nan! Accusative ahnsire! Damadam to infinities
30

Now to marks left by humans. Perhaps the relationship of human writing to humans will teach us about the relationship of mankind to god. First the first writing of mankind—the Garden of Eden, the one by one place.

With alphabets in mind, first came marks made by axes on wood and rocks [**thwacks on thracks**] in an effort to plumb the gods. Numbers indicate separation [1 2 3 separate items], and these numbers tell the story of the Garden of Eden in terms of unity versus multiplicity. The first important sign was the separation place, the **one by one place,** when the Garden was created as a separate place apart from ES. In the Garden, separation ensued. One became three in separation—first Adam, Eve and the serpent and dittoh the Trinity: Father, Son and Holy Spirit. This all compared to the unity of one that existed before—one before. [**One by one place one be three dittoh and one before.**] Total dittoh means it was done before.

These machinations take us to the important number 1132. This number is Hebrew [right to left] for 231 1—the summary in numbers of the relationship between the TZTZ god and mankind. First Adam the combined creature and god [2], then Adam, Eve and god [3] and then Adam and Eve separated [1 1]. They are all separated from god, separated by the garden and then further by choices.

Then the formula [**Two nursus one make a plaus-ible free and idim behind.**] Two or separation instead of one with god makes freedom plausible with **idim** or "I am dim" left behind with the increase in personal consciousness [her eyes were opened].

This Garden legend was prophecy of the continuing separation in the relationship of god and mankind. So next we have other similar prophecies received in dreams or visions. These are a big snake [**boaboa** as Ananta and the periodic destruction of the world by Vishnu] and **three legged calvers** [a 3 legged calf as a prophecy in the life of Confucius] and **ivargraine**—ivory grained or Igraine the mother of King Arthur. They all have messages in their mouths [Confucius's mother saw images of a fabulous animal with a jade tablet in its mouth bearing prophecy]. And since then a hundred dread-filled experiences without leaven or redemption based on free will [**liberorumqueue**—liber rum spirit queue line] to con us. We can all see all the horrors free will produces right up to death. The Garden of Eden story is such a meandering Neanderthal tall tale, one that causes us to meander in thrall outside the Garden and gives us a promised end [the penalties] of fights among squatters, antisquatters and after the prone waters **eau** squatters [**postproneauntisquattor**]. The humans right out of the garden were inclined to strife.

To say to us all—to every Tim, Nick and Larry of us, sons of the earth, sons, littlesons, and even lea or fallow littlesons [Onan] when uses are not to be, every Sue, Siss and Sally of us, daughters of Nan! Nan from Onan. Transmission of original sin is through sex so the only way to stop it would be no sex by anyone, which in turn would eliminate the species. Accusative ancestors. Adam damned us to infinity.

Now from reproduction of humans by sex and on to paper and printing press:

> **[19] True there was in nillohs dieybos as yet no lumpend papeer**
> **31**
> **in the waste, and mightmountain Penn still groaned for the micies**

32
to let flee. All was of ancientry. You gave me a boot (signs on
33
it!) and I ate the wind. I quizzed you a quid (with for what?)
and
34
you went to the quod.

True there was in those days, in the teaching of the early Catholic Church [**nillohs dieybos** for *In illis diebus*—introduction to lesson & gospel in Mass], as yet no rag paper **in the waste** [of trees, of TZTZ creation], and the mighty as a mountain pen still groaned for mice to flee, that is didn't have much power [Horace: the mountains are in labour, a laughable little mouse is born]. Or more generally that is to say, pride and bluster, the desire for manifestation, bring forth an absurd product. That is the mountain of ES brought forth only the mouse of TZTZ creation. All repeated history. And you god gave me a boot and I [who?] ate the wind [the fart]. I quizzed you with a **quid**, what [what does all this mean?] and you went for the **quod**, the because. The answer is just because, because I wanted to.

Now to the concept of the world as one mind—the **quod**:

[19] But the world, mind, is, was and will be
35
writing its own wrunes for ever, man, on all matters that fall
36
[20] under the ban of our infrarational senses fore the last
milch-
1
camel, the heartvein throbbing between his eyebrowns, has
still to
2
moor before the tomb of his cousin charmian where his date
is
3
tethered by the palm that's hers.

The world, the mind of the world, is was and will be writing its own runes for ever, about mankind and all matters that fall under the ban of our infrared rational senses [all matters beyond rational comprehension such as dream work] before the last milchcamel is killed for a guest meal [Muslim rule that the last camel must be sacrificed rather than leave a guest hungry]. In other words mankind is hungry for this knowledge and will be looking for it until hospitality is the

286

norm. It the last camel dies with its heartvein throbbing [Mohammed had a prominent vein is his forehead] moored [you get it] before the tomb of his cousin charmian [Mohammed married to his cousin] where his date with death is tethered by her palm, that is preordained. Mohammed and his followers pledged to support each other to the death in "the Pledge of the Tree."

> **[20] But the horn, the drinking, the**
> **4**
> **day of dread are not now. A bone, a pebble, a ramskin; chip them,**
> **5**
> **chap them, cut them up allways; leave them to terracook in the**
> **6**
> **muttheringpot: and Gutenmorg with his cromagnom charter,**
> **7**
> **tintingfast and great primer must once for omniboss step rub-**
> **8**
> **rickredd out of the wordpress else is there no virtue more in al-**
> **9**
> **cohoran.**

Now for this world as a copy from the printing press of the gods— what is above is below and vice versa. The celestial form of self-publishing. If there is desire and incompleteness above, there will be desire and incompleteness below. But now is not the time of the end. Make art with bone, with stone, with ramskin; chip them, chap them and cut them all ways; leave them to cook in the mothering speaking muttering pot of the world's art; and Gutenberg with his original charter of progress printing fast [**tintingfast**] and the **great primer** [the first mover] must once as the boss of all [**omniboss**] make plain the rubric of the wordpress [that is, make the world experience understandable] or there is no virtue in the Koran **alchoran**— Mohammed said that little girls are made of alcohol—that is intoxicating spirit Gutenberg's printing press was based on the wine press. The connection of wine press and sexual activity is there for all readers to enjoy. The sex press prints faster and faster as humans multiplied.

More from Mohammed, continuing the connection between writing as a copy of the spirit of man and spirit of the world as a copy of god:

> **[20] For that (the rapt one warns) is what papyr is meed**
> **10**
> **of, made of, hides and hints and misses in prints. Till ye finally**
> **11**
> **(though not yet endlike) meet with the acquaintance of Mister**
> **12**
> **Typus, Mistress Tope and all the little typtopies. Fillstup.**

Mohammed stated: "O thou who art wrapped, rise up & warn." In this context the wrapping suggests the paper of the writing, the Koran, and the human as the writing of god. So here the rapt, the alcohol or the human spirit, warns that the gods are killers, just like the Muslims feuding over succession. The warning is to consider what the paper [in this analogy humans] are made [meed or spirit] of—which is to say the spirit of hides [killing] and hints and misses in print [hint of the imperfect gods in the imperfect human birth function].

The main human activities are killing and sex-birth. These activities are the wrapping of the human spirit and suggest the main attributes of the gods. Mohammed had a thing for young girls—witness his 6-year-old wife, marriage consummated at age 9. He said "A husband has sex with a wife as a plow goes into the field." So much for joint enjoyment. Soon we are to touch on the gods having sex with human females, which Joyce suggests is equally asymmetrical.

Back to the text: Consider this until you finally experience as to humans type or form, tope for place and all their offspring in spirit typtopies. Full stop—as if this were a telegram from on high [**fillstup** for fullstop because fill reminds us of pregnancy].

More:

> **[20] So you**
> **13**
> **need hardly spell me how every word will be bound over to carry**
> **14**

three score and ten toptypsical readings throughout the book of
15
Doublends Jined (may his forehead be darkened with mud who
16
would sunder!) till Daleth, mahomahouma, who oped it closeth
17
thereof the. Dor.
18

So [who is speaking?] you hardly need tell spell me how every word camel-like will be bound over to carry 70 top typical interpretations throughout the book of **Doublends Jined**—which refers to FW and two ends joined in the ending-beginning, birth-death, god-man, macro-micro (may his forehead be darkened with mud for Mohammed who would sunder the two ends!)—until death [the Hebrew letter *Daleth* suggests door and death] the big power that is— Mohammed as **mahomahouma** [ma home death], who opened life closeth the door, thus joining the ends. The period after "the" in **closeth thereof the. Dor.**" is an example of closing down a sentence early. Like FW with both ends joined, life and death are joined in god.

But don't cry about death because in Paradise;

[20] Cry not yet! There's many a smile to Nondum, with sytty
19
maids per man, sir, and the park's so dark by kindlelight. But
20
look what you have in your handself!

Don't cry! There is many a smile to Not Yet [remember passencore from the first page], that is many a pleasure thinking about death/paradise in the future, just thinking about 60 maids per man [more females than males in heaven?], sir, and the park of paradise is so dark by **kindleight** [candlelight plus fire] that there are plenty of opportunities. But look what you have in your hand, your own self [indicated by joined word **handself**]. In other words you have free will and the opportunity for self-abuse. The TZTZ creation would be self-abuse by ES. For Joyce, dependence is self-abuse.

Now for the plots of all stories:

[20] The movibles are scrawl-
21
ing in motions, marching, all of them ago, in pitpat and
zingzang
22
for every busy eerie whig's a bit of a torytale to tell. One's
upon
23
a thyme and two's behind their lettice leap and three's
among the
24
strubbely beds.

The movable types are scrawling in motion, marching ahead, all of them in movement in the past, in pitpat and zingzang sounds of press for every busy **eerie whig** earwicker has a bit of a **torytale** to tell. Now the garden story with food metaphors—used in the myth: One [Adam/Eve] is upon a time in a thyme [time] garden two [Adam and Eve] are behind [have already done] their let us leap into independence [**lettice leap**] and three [Adam, Eve and serpent] are among the strawberry stubble stubbeling difficulty [penalty] beds.

More of the Genesis stories:

[20] And the chicks picked their teeths and the domb-
25
key he begay began. You can ask your ass if he believes it.
And
26
so cuddy me only wallops have heels. That one of a wife with
27
folty barnets. For then was the age when hoops ran high. Of
a
28
noarch and a chopwife; of a pomme full grave and a fammy
of
29
levity; or of golden youths that wanted gelding; or of what
the
30
mischievmiss made a man do.

Angels such as Azazel and Shemhazi mate with human females and their children are evil giants and must be removed [**And the chicks picked their theeths**]. So the TZTZ god still can't get it right, first with Lillith, then with the giants produced by god/human miscege-nation. The dumbkey but the key, he must begin again—the first beginning now in past tense as distorted in **begay began**. You can ask Baalem's ass if he believes it—the humble ass that saw angels—and thus an example for us all. These giants were plunged into con-flict with each other by order of God—sound familiar? [god bless America]—so God sends the flood and warns Noah or *Noach* in He-brew. Joyce uses **noarch** to remind us that the rainbow promised in the covenant is missing—no arch.

Before the bad angels are destroyed [in the language of the Leg-ends of the Jews], "Azazel began to devise the finery and the orna-ments by means of which women allure men." So next we have heels and hoops—**only wallops have heels**—in other words those women are dangerous, they can wallop you. One woman wife had forty hoops or forty angels. Angels are hoops because of their halos. Hoops suggest high spirits. For then was the age when spirits hoops ran high—angels copulating with human females.

Noah's wife's name is not mentioned in the Hebrew Scriptures or Old Testament so here she is **chopwife**—just a cook. According to Jewish tradition her name is Naamah, a descendant of Cain. Her name, meaning "the beautiful" or "the pleasant one," reflects the worldly emphasis of the Canaanites, who looked for beauty rather than for character as the chief attraction in women.

Noah and chopwife had three sons, including Ham. This family was **of a pomme full grave and a fammy of levity**. Of a **pomme full grave** suggests the wine that Noah made [dry grave and his drunkenness as well as the grave for death]. Pomme means apple in French so Eve is not far away. Levity suggests Noah's son Ham, who laughed when born. Ham wanted to, tried and perhaps suc-ceeded in gelding his drunken father [and have his mother]; or of what the mischievousness [**mischievmisss**] in man with female made a man do. Contrary to God's rule for the Ark, Ham had sex on board with his wife just as the raven and the dog couples did. He mis-achieved his miss.

Noah's wife Naamah is a woman of beauty rather than character; so Noah is not married well. Given the emphasis on Eve in the Fall, following the flood the emphasis is placed on Naamah as one the four last women standing and thus the cause of evil:

[20] **Malmarriedad he was reverso-**
31
gassed by the frisque of her frasques and her prytty pyrrhi-

que.
32

Maye faye, she's la gaye this snaky woman! From that trip-
piery
33

toe expectungpelick! Veil, volantine, valentine eyes. She's the
34

very besch Winnie blows Nay on good. Flou inn, flow ann.
35

Hohore! So it's sure it was her not we! But lay it easy, gentle
36

[21] mien, we are in rearing of a norewhig. So weenybeeny-
1

veenyteeny. Comsy see! Het wis if ee newt. Lissom! lissom!
2

I am doing it. Hark, the corne entreats! And the larpnotes
3

prittle.
4

Malmarried to a descendant of Cain, Noah was reverse gassed [com-
pared to the breath of god or the gas-like Holy Ghost] by her friski-
ness and her pretty technique. Perhaps a sorceress [**maye faye**], she
dances like a snake! From her type expect a tonque lick [French kiss
with long snake tongue]. Dance of the veils, the volantine dance voluntary, valentine eyes. She is the very best southwest wind and she
blows bad on good [**Nay on good**]. Like the flood, flow into her
and flow again [**flou inn, flow ann**]. Ho whore. So we are sure she is
to blame for the evil behavior subsequent to the flood, thus exoner-
ating us or those in the present. But lay the guilt easily, gentlemen,
we are creating a norewhig—versus an earwig—a whig from the
north. So very small. Come see. It is as if he knew [**ee newt** suggesting animal level development]. Then her music. ["And our rabbis
said: There was another Na'amah, and why did they call her
Na'amah? She played melodies on the drum to accompany idolatry".]
Listen to her lithesome song. The come on entreats! And the
larpnotes prattle on.

Next is the story is of another woman and the gods after the
TZTZ creation. We transition from Naamah's desire causing beauty
to Lillith, represented by the prankquean ["PQ"]. Lillith was a male
Adam's or TZTZ god's first wife who was too independent and gave
birth to demons—perhaps the serpent. She is not mentioned in the
TZTZ god scripture [the Hebrew Scriptures or Old Testament]. She

was there in Eden but not allowed in the Garden. She is pure desire, selfish desire. She is incomplete.

Lillith was denied hospitality and kept out of or eliminated from the Garden of Eden because she was too independent and had too much potential. She was made independently by god, perhaps directly by TZTZ. Her removal was part of the curse to keep humans and particularly women down and limited.

Because she was denied hospitality in the Garden, her desires were frustrated. As a result, Lillith stole children at night and gave birth to demons to haunt mankind—the opposite of the blessing of many offspring. She is apparently immortal so she reaches her full potential. Her motive must be revenge and possession, desires without compassion. She is incomplete: no husband, no friends, no children.

The prankquean story owes much to several predecessors. It is built on the story of Grace O'Malley, the 16th century's most independent pirate. She was denied hospitality, dissed, by the Earl of Howth at his castle on Dublin Bay and kidnapped his son in order to force respect. The PQ story line is the same, and it is the lesson of the Buddha: **desire without compassion for the individuality of others makes one incomplete**. The framework of the story, the kidnapping of two sons and a daughter, is taken from Grimms' Fairy Tale *Our Lady's Children*. In that tale, human happiness in the form of return of two sons and a daughter is not achieved until the lady protagonist admits error in terms of opening the prohibited 13th door in Heaven and seeing the Trinity in action.

In the K story, ES is made incomplete by its desire to manifest in TZTZ creation. After that Fall, ES is incomplete in at least three ways—after this creation less than all of existence is contained within god; and ES's manifestation as TZTZ god is certainly less than ES could be. TZTZ god has no mate. Moreover TZTZ god needs humans—and humans need god. Also ES god lost many angels in the rebellion of Satan and his legions, a fall that takes place in the backdrop of the PQ story; ES's troop of angels were incomplete. In other words, this is how the gods become everybody. Like the gods, humans also selfishly desire and are incomplete as a result. Unfulfilled desire makes them frustrated and mean and lack of compassion makes them less than they could be. In the PQ story, the children of TZTZ god, two sons and a daughter making up a trinity, are kidnapped and trained by Lillith in desire. As trained in desire, they make up the characters in the celestial trinity and its earthbound counterpart the primal horde: the father who does what he wants, the son who is disappointed, and the daughter who is treated as a sex and reproductive object. In the celestial trinity, this means that charity is missing and the Holy Spirit of love will not issue. In the human arena, it means that possession is in charge.

In the PQ story, the characters include TZTZ god as Jarl van Hoother [JVH the initials for Javeh]. Hoother is the one who hoots. Or in a transposition to be used herein, "there hoo"—scaring mankind with thunder. The characters also include his twin sons Tristopher and Hilary and the "dummy." The twins and dummy represent the father, son and holy spirit gods in the celestial trinity, the essence of TZTZ god as conceived by humans post TZTZ creation. The holy spirit is Dummy in the sense that it can't speak independently since it is of the same substance. That is, when the relationship between father and son is not proper, the holy ghost or holy spirit does not issue, does not speak for god on earth. The children and JVH also make up a human one parent family like the primal horde: the father possesses all, the sons are frustrated and the daughter is a sex object. She doesn't get to speak her own mind.

In the original draft JH was Sir Howther [which is more in tune with an explanation of how it happened]. Remember now that this is a fairy tale or dream-like myth:

> [21] It was of a night, late, lang time agone, in an auldstane eld,
> 5
> when Adam was delvin and his madameen spinning watersilts,
> 6
> when mulk mountynotty man was everybully and the first leal
> 7
> ribberrobber that ever had her ainway everybuddy to his love-
> 8
> saking eyes and everybilly lived alove with everybiddy else, and
> 9
> Jarl van Hoother had his burnt head high up in his lamphouse,
> 10
> laying cold hands on himself.

It was late and a long time ago, in the old stone age, when Adam was digging delvining [Mohammed--"A husband has sex with a wife as a plow goes into the field."]. His angry spouse or Madame Eve [**Madameen**] was spinning water silts. Water silk is a tight weave. So a water silt would be used to keep out silts or salts, that is death. It could also be used for a condom.

Madameen performs several roles for the reader: **Ma damean**—Eve was demeaned as just a sex object in the Garden punishments; **Ma Da Meen**—Dad was mean to Ma; **M Adam Een**—Adam in the middle. Eve wants to do what she wants, eat from the knowledge tree, but not die. She wants to stop having children and be more of "her own person." She wants to be "centered," in herself. Her desires set up the meaning of the story as desires are the source of free will.

At this time Adam was as big as a mountain and the role model for every bully doing what he wants [giants in Genesis] and the first loyal rib robber Eve was the help mate who always had her own way [**ainway** reminding us of Ain Sof] and provided free will for everybody [this is in the spirit of parody since desires do not free one but imprison one]. She was buddy friend to Adam's lovesaking eyes. God and man lived above in love and unity.

Jarl van Hoother [ES's emanation as TZTZ god] had his burned head high up in his lamphouse, laying cold hands on himself—creating as an act of self-knowledge [that is "knowing" himself] but without the erotic connection necessary to produce unity in the gods to be. The TZTZ creation of the world is an act of cold masturbation, of self-abuse or being less than ES could be, of mere elimination, a mere sperm dump, incomplete. He has children but is without a mate. His undisciplined, mean and primitive-aggressive children are the product of his cold masturbation.

JVH's children are undisciplined since discipline requires compassion, wanting the good for the children:

> [21] And his two little jiminies, cousins
> 11
> of ourn, Tristopher and Hilary, were kickaheeling their dummy
> 12
> on the oil cloth flure of his homerigh, castle and earthenhouse.
> 13
> And, be dermot, who come to the keep of his inn only the niece-
> 14
> of-his-in-law, the prankquean.

And JVH's two little children jiminies-gemini twins are our father and son gods who are interchangeable in substance if not in person. The names Tristopher and Hilary suggest opposites in Bruno's phrase *In tristitia hilaris hilaritate tristis*—in sadness cheerful in gaiety sad.

So here we have stand-ins for father and son gods, who without parental guidance and following their father inherited primitive instincts are kicking their dummy sister holy spirit on the rug in the castle his earthenhouse [**homerigh, castle and earthenhouse**— HCE]. The heel is featured in this kicking since the serpent in the Garden was penalized to strike humans only at the heel. With many strikes, the heel would contain evil. Here father and son gods are twin boys about to claim sexual privileges with the dummy. An inconvenience in the primal horde.

The Prankquean's reception at the castle is an echo of Grace's being denied hospitality at Howth Castle and Lillith being denied hospitality in the Garden of Eden. Here anti-hospitality is another form of selfish desire—to tend just one's own requirements. Hospitality to a stranger is recognition of the unity. This aspect makes the PQ story Joyce's anti or averse Abram story. In that story Abram [later called Abraham] granted hospitality to strangers, god and two angels, a process that in Kabbalah is thought to bring forward the chesed sefirot. And the resulting blessing was the child Isaac in the old age of Abraham and Sarah. Some say Sarah got the bug in the ear, just like Mary.

Back to the text. And, be damned [the very process to be described] PQ as Dermot, the skin word or what you show to others, come to the door of his JVH's inn [with lack of hospitality it is more of an out than an inn]. The PQ is described as JVH's niece-of-his-in-law, that is the niece of the person who is TZTZ god's in- law. Lillith would be TZTZ god's in-law [daughter in-law] since Lillith was presumably married to TZTZ's son Adam. In order for Lillith to be TZTZ god's niece, she would have to be the child of a brother of TZTZ god, who in this interpretation could only be Satan.

[21] And the prankquean pulled a rosy
15
one and made her wit foreninst the dour. And she lit up and fire-
16
land was ablaze. And spoke she to the dour in her petty perusi-

17
enne: Mark the Wans, why do I am alook alike a poss of por-
ter-
18
pease?

And the PQ pulled a rosy one [urinated] and made her wit opposite
the dour door—that is urinated by or opposite the door that was
without hospitality [like the door of death]. She pisses where and
when she wants. Her urine is her wit as TZTZ creation is elimination. And she lit up [she lit the pool of her urine—alcohol not digested—without any external source of fire] and fireland hell was
ablaze. She apparently digests no spirit. She urinates all her spirit. She
turns spirit into urine, as in the TZTZ creation. And she spoke to the
dour door to announce her presence in her petty Parisian accent:
Mark the Wans [that is Mark the curse, Mark the pale] why do I look
like a **poss of porterpease**, a horror movie [poss] of porter [alco-
holic spirit and carrier vehicle like the spirit] pease [piss combined
with please or a corruption of piesporter]. That is, why is my spirit in
my urine, porter piss. Since this story is about corrupting the spirit,
PQ speaks in a corrupted way. She speaks of *one* poss of porterpease
because she is going to steal the father god, number *one* in the trinity.
She calls JVH Mark One. In asking why do I look like the father
god, she is forecasting that the father god will soon look like her.

So the PQ:

[21] And that was how the skirtmisshes began. But the dour
19
handworded her grace in dootch nossow: Shut! So her grace
20
o'malice kidsnapped up the jiminy Tristopher and into the
shan-
21
dy westerness she rain, rain, rain.

So that is how the skirmishes [because of a female—**skirtmisshes** or
skirt miss she or skirt mishe—I am a skirt] began. But the dour PQ
handworded [sign language—no verbal connection possible] her
grace van Hooter in Dutch Nassua—**nossow** or no sow. With this
She refers to JVH's lack of a female mate. **Shut** probably means the
door was shut or remained shut, a shut heart or lack of compassion
as well as shit in this world. Lillith's own door is shut because she
can not have her own children. In revenge her grace of malice [Grace

297

O'Malley the pirate] kidnapped the twin Tristopher [doesn't say how] and took him away into the west where she ran into the rain—the flood. That twin was apparently left outside. This is another way of depicting evil coming into the world—no help to stranger wayfarers. Remember the etymology of elimination—to remove out of doors.

JVH chases to no avail:

[21] And Jarl van Hoother war-
22
lessed after her with soft dovesgall: Stop deef stop come back to
23
my earin stop. But she swaradid to him: Unlikelihud. And there
24
was a brannewail that same sabboath night of falling angles some-
25
where in Erio.

So JVH war-lessed [free from war since TZTZ father god eliminated] telegraphed [wireless] after her with a soft love call [**dovesgall** for Dubh-hall a Danish love call]: Stop you deef one [she uses sign language] come back to me in the **earin** [Ireland] stop [communication]. But she answered [**swaradid** for Danish svarede] swore she did to him: Unlikely. And there was a fire wail that same Sabbath with angels falling somewhere in Erio. Here is Satan and his legion who fell because they did what they wanted, refused to bow down to mankind.

So how does the PQ treat the kidnapped Tristopher? She teaches him to do what he wants:

[21] And the prankquean went for her forty years'
26
walk in Tourlemonde and she washed the blessings of the love-
27
spots off the jiminy with soap sulliver suddles and she had her
28
four owlers masters for to tauch him his tickles and she convor-
29
ted him to the onesure allgood and he became a.

For forty years the PQ went for her walk in Tourlemonde [French for "all the world"] —as god walked in the Garden of Eden each day—and she washed the blessings of love [**lovespots**] off the twin with soap sulliver suddles [alliterated s's for the hiss of the serpent and suggesting mercury, the supposed cure for syphilis]. The mere presence of the Dummy HSS apparently caused love spots on the skin. In order to train him for desire, she had her four wise owl masters teach touch him his tickles [his desires] and she converted him to the one sure all good [omnipotent and beneficent] and he became a lazy idler funny man [**luderman**—suggestion of Lutheran with its emphasis on subjective religion, or believe what you want religion]. Tristopher became happy satisfying his desires. He wants and gets what he wants. That is why the father god looks like the PQ, like one **poss of porterpease**. Desiring, he became incomplete as suggested by the fragment—**and he became a.**

On with the tale. It rains again—evil in the world—so she visits the castle again:

> [21] So then
> 30
> she started to rain and to rain and, be redtom, she was back again
> 31
> at Jarl van Hoother's in a brace of samers and the jiminy with
> 32
> her in her pinafrond, lace at night, at another time. And where
> 33
> did she come but to the bar of his bristolry. And Jarl von Hoo-
> 34
> ther had his baretholobruised heels drowned in his cellar-malt,
> 35
> shaking warm hands with himself and the jimminy Hilary and
> 36
> [22] the dummy in their first infancy were below on the tearsheet,
> 1
> wringing and coughing, like brodar and histher.

So the PQ was back again while it was raining. At JVH's castle wearing a brace of samers and the Tristopher twin concealed in her pen frond, late at night in lace, at another time [corrupt sentence]. And where did she come but to the source of spirits—the bar of his bristolry—where JVH keeps his things from Bristol [slang for female breasts—in other words spirit and birth equipment].

This Bristol also bears the marks of substitution, of illicit substitution such as TZTZ god for ES. In the 12th century, Henry II taking charge of Ireland from the Pope made the city of Dublin the eternal property of the citizens of the English city Bristol. This is all about possession, the outer targets of desire.

JVH is down there with bruised heels from evil and drowned in his cellar malt, shaking warm hands with himself while the remaining twin Hilary the son god and the dummy holy spirit in their first infancy were below on the sheet of tears, **wringing and coughing**, like brother and sister. God's hands are warm in the macro. The sheet of tears is the TZTZ creation. Father JVH doesn't take care of his sick children, who are sick because the father god with the same substance has been corrupted.

So what does the PQ do at the bar of spirits:

> **[22] And the prank-**
> **2**
> **quean nipped a paly one and lit up again and redcocks flew flack-**
> **3**
> **ering from the hillcombs. And she made her witter before the**
> **4**
> **wicked, saying: Mark the Twy, why do I am alook alike two poss**
> **5**
> **of porterpease? And: Shut! says the wicked, handwording her**
> **6**
> **madesty.**

The PQ nipps a pale one, a beer [less spirits for the son god since partially human], and lights up again [with fire] which scares the birds [shekhinah] away. Then she makes water, urine from spirit again, saying: Mark the Second, why do I look like **two poss of porterpease**? Two for the 2nd person of the trinity. And: Shut again. PQ marks the fact the door has been shut by the dour in spirit. PQ is still speaking in hand signs. Turned away again, she grabs the other male twin, who apparently was left outside:

[22] So her madesty 'a forethought' set down a jiminy and
7
took up a jiminy and all the lilipath ways to Woeman's Land she
8
rain, rain, rain. And Jarl von Hoother bleethered atter her with
9
a loud finegale: Stop domb stop come back with my earring stop.
10
But the prankquean swaradid: Am liking it.

So with majestic malice aforethought, she sets down the one twin Tristopher and leaves him there since he is already treated with desire and takes up the other–Hilary the son god—and takes all the **Lilipath ways** to the Land of Woe running in the rain. JVH tries to stop her by crying out with a loud wind: in wind-like sounds—stop come back with my **ear ring,** my manifestation in the world conceived through the ring or echo ear of the Virgin Mary. Jesus as jewelry in time and space. The first cry by JVH was for the **earin**. Consider Earwicker in this connection. But the PQ refuses and justifies her actions as being what she likes—her desire.

So repeating as before in good fairy tale fashion:

[22] And there was a wild
11
old grannewwail that laurency night of starshootings somewhere
12
in Erio. And the prankquean went for her forty years' walk in
13
Turnlemeem and she punched the curses of cromcruwell with
14
the nail of a top into the jiminy and she had her four larksical
15
monitrix to touch him his tears and she provorted him to the
16
onecertain allsecure and he became a tristian.

More streaks in the sky from falling angels. So she converts this one, Hilary the son god, into a **tristian**, that is a sad Christian, the son god who must be sad given his duty to die to save mankind, make them dependent and not to take wife. In the human primal horde, he is the junior male who wants the females but is denied his desires. Note the father who desires and gets what he wants and the son who desires and doesn't.

Once again she takes her 40 years walk this time in Turnlemeem [turn him mean—desires frustrated—why have you forsaken me] and she punches the curses of Cromwell with a nail [crucifixion] into the top [Sefirot crown] of the twin and she had her four angelettes teach touch him his tears and she converted perverted him to the one certain all secure and he became a tristian [Tristan crossed with Christian]. He learns desire and tears for not being satisfied. No joy for Jesus of the common substance.

So now the third time, in the rain again:

> **[22] So then she started**
> 17
> **raining, raining, and in a pair of changers, be dom ter, she was**
> 18
> **back again at Jarl von Hoother's and the Larryhill with her under**
> 19
> **her abromette. And why would she halt at all if not by the ward**
> 20
> **of his mansionhome of another nice lace for the third charm?**
> 21

In the curse of the flood rain, She is back with Larryhill [Hilary last part first and Christ at Golgotha hill] under her apron. And why wouldn't she halt at the castle the third time [because she wants to], the third time being the charm. This time she seeks the daughter, the Holy Spirit, the charm. So where is JVH:

> **[22] And Jarl von Hoother had his hurricane hips up to his pantry-**
> 22
> **box, ruminating in his holdfour stomachs (Dare! O dare!), ant**
> 23
> **the jiminy Toughertrees and the dummy were belove on the**
> 24

watercloth, kissing and spitting, and roguing and poghuing,
like
25
knavepaltry and naivebride and in their second infancy.

JVH is eating and ruminating in his four holding stomachs—it must
be hard to digest. *Meanwhile* the twin **Toughertrees** is with his sister.
Toughertrees refers to the father god-Tristopher with the last part
"topher" placed first and revised as "tougher" and converted to evil
with reference to the tree of knowledge "her tree." It is also tough
because of withholding the tree of life. The father twin and the
dummy Holy Spirit were making love on the sheet, kissing and
frenchkissing, and another game or two—**roguing and poghuing**,
like a knave and a naïve bride in the second infancy provided by first
sexual love. Treated by the PQ's desire for possession, the desire-
based father god now heads the primal horde as the alpha male. Like
Cain, he has sex with his sister while her other brother is gone. Sex
as desire combined with love.

Now this is an important point about the relation of the gods
with mankind—which is what the trinity is all about. Joyce is talking.
The father god is desire and the son god is frustration. Does this
sound like the primal horde? In K, the primal horde in human relations is interdependent with the gods. The HSS is a "blank" and has
incest sex. While blank suggests "fill it up," it also suggests cancellation, cancellation of the desire and frustration already incorporated
by the father and son gods into the common substance of the trinity.
The normal love role of the female has been cancelled by desire and
frustration in the male two-thirds of the trinity. **The only outlet for
love through desire and frustration is sex**, and this is the only role
of the HSS on earth while the father and son gods are not in charity.

Now the PQ has come for the third person in the trinity, the
dummy, to deny god's love on the earth:

[22] And the
26
prankquean picked a blank and lit out and the valleys lay
twink-
27
ling. And she made her wittest in front of the arkway of trihump,
28

asking: Mark the Tris, why do I am alook alike three poss of
por-
29
ter pease?

For her third visit The PQ picks out a blank—the Holy Spirit is still
empty—love can not coexist with desire [except in sex]. And the PQ
lit out in the valleys that lay twinkling—with the sky falling-star
marks of the fallen angels. She made her wittest urination in front of
the arkway of triumph-hump [**arkway of trihump**—sexual allusion
on Arc de Triomphe and the rainbow covenant and humping the
third], asking this time: Mark the Tris [sad and threefold since now *a
trois*], why do I look like **three poss of porter pease**? In this case
pease is separated from **porter**, the carrier spirit, as the Holy Spirit
issues and separates from god in the theory of spiration. This time
JVH rises to the occasion, loss of his little human squeeze threatened. The Holy Spirit is saved from desire, she is not to have her
own desires as do the father and son gods:

> [22] **But that was how the skirtmishes endupped. For like**
> 30
> **the campbells acoming with a fork lance of-lightning, Jarl
> von**
> 31
> **Hoother Boanerges himself, the old terror of the dames,
> came**
> 32
> **hip hop handihap out through the pikeopened arkway of his**
> 33
> **three shuttoned castles, in his broadginger hat and his civic
> chol-**
> 34
> **lar and his allabuff hemmed and his bullbraggin soxangloves**
> 35
> **and his ladbroke breeks and his cattegut bandolair and his
> fur-**
> 36
>
> [23] **framed panuncular cumbottes like a rudd yellan grue-
> bleen or-**
> 1

304

angeman in his violet indigonation, to the whole longth of
the
2
strongth of his bowman's bill.

The old thunderer quickly comes out of his three castles [trinity of
forms] through the pike opened arkway [sexual allusions] in full human clothing and regalia, including snake proof pants. He is a very
human god. He is the TZTZ god. He is **Hoother Boanerges himself, the old terror of the dames,** the energy of the boa or serpent
who seeks human females. What does he do:

[23] And he clopped his rude hand to
3
his eacy hitch and he ordurd and his thick spch spck for her
to
4
shut up shop, dappy. And the duppy shot the shutter clup
(Per-
5
kodhuskurunbarggruauyagokgorlayorgromgremmitghund-
hurth-
6
rumathunaradidillifaititillibumullunukkunun!) And they all
drank
7
free.

He clopped his rude hand to his easy hitch [E C Haitch in First
Draft]. And he ordered-manured and in his thick speech [**spch
spck**—so thick it is without vowels like traditionally written Hebrew]
the dummy to shut up shop. This must involve the drawbridge to his
castle. His speech is thick because the common substance has been
issued into the three-fold trinity. And the dummy duppy [the Holy
Spirit] did shoot the shutter shut [which caused thunder thunder
thunder etc at least 12 times in various languages]. No more access
to god in the castle. No more access to love and unity.

Presumably both twins and the dummy and PQ are all outside
the shut up castle with JVH. Since they have joined her but not let
her in, the PQ finally has achieved some respect—independence has
received some respect. They have a drink of the spirit with her. And
they all drank free. JVH has taken on human clothes, as mankind
makes his god in *Tikkun*. **The gods no longer have to be different**

from humans; they no longer have the burden of individuality either. The result is [note this is out of order]:

> **[23] The prankquean was to hold**
> **12**
> **her dummyship and the jimminies was to keep the peace-**
> **wave**
> **13**
> **and van Hoother was to git the wind up. Thus the hear-**
> **someness**
> **14**
> **of the burger felicitates the whole of the polis.**

The resolution is phrased in terms of joint cooperation between the gods and independent humans with respect to the flood waters or the finite and evil condition: The prankquean remains in charge of dummyship, the ship of females in charge of the Holy Spirit. Females to bear love and unity in the human condition. The twins, father and son gods, were to keep the peacewave on the waters [maintain order] and JVH was to get the wind up—the wind of creation of the spirit that starts Genesis. Thus the ability to reach the burger god [the **hearsomeness** or the ability of the very human god to hear us] makes happy [**felicitates**] the whole polis of mankind. That is, we can't hear ES but we sure can hear TZTZ god, so we are happy with that.

This result comes about, that is Lillith brings god out of his castles, because

> **[23] For one man in his armour was a fat match always for**
> **any**
> **8**
> **girls under shurts. And that was the first peace of illiterative**
> **9**
> **porthery in all the flamend floody flatuous world. How kirssy**
> **the**
> **10**
> **tiler made a sweet unclose to the Narwhealian captol. Saw**
> **fore**
> **11**
> **shalt thou sea. Betoun ye and be.**

JVH in his **armour** [amour and armor] was no match for Lillith the PQ **under shurts** [undershirt and hurt]. This was the Fall of God, from the infinite primordial light of Ein-Sof to the Bible TZTZ god

JHWH, the god that was not concealed and related to and was heard by mankind, and the manure in this evil and finite world. And that [**poss of porter pease**] was the first peace-causing piece of alliterative illiterate door opening poetry [**porthery**] in all the flamend fire end floody flooded flatuous fart produced world [fire water air earth].

This story of Lillith corrupting the trinity produced by TZTZ god is here related to the story of how Kersse the tailor [curse the tailor TZTZ god] made a suit of clothes [this world as the garment of ES] for the humpbacked Norwegian captain [fallen ES]. From a fall, the captain was humpbacked and from neglect he had not married and had no clothes. Only so far shall thou see into the mysteries of this creation [that is ES fell while excreting TZTZ creation—the turd fell into the hole]. The rest must remain between you and the mystery of being [**Betoun ye and be**], that is to say not understood.

The fall of mankind that reflects the fall of the turd in the hole is blessed in St. Augustine's phrase O *felix culpa*, o happy fault that brought redemption through god's love and Christ. In view of the fate of dummy in the PQ story, this will ring false. For this phrase Joyce normally uses "o phoenix culprit," the rise of the culprit, but here it is this time:

> **[23] O foenix culprit! Ex nickylow malo comes mickel-massed bo-**
> **16**
> **num. Hill, rill, ones in company, billeted, less be proud of. Breast**
> **17**
> **high and bestride!**

O foe nixed culprit [nixed by Lillith]. From **nickylow**-nihilo—the devil-**malo**-evil [devil is d'evil]—comes Michael organized as the Mass, the bonum good of the Annunciation. Christ comes because of evil. Father god is frustrated by sin. The fallen giant—billeted like soldiers—in nature, in company with hill and rill [small stream not a flood] Hill of Howth and River Liffey. So be less proud of your own works. But these do not speak of the mysteries:

> **[23] Only for that these will not breathe upon**
> **18**
> **Norronesen or Irenean the secrest of their soorcelossness. Quar-**
> **19**

ry silex, Homfrie Noanswa! Undy gentian festyknees, Livia
No-
20
answa?

These—the fallen giant and nature—will not breathe upon the
Norse or the Irish the secrest [**secrest**—secret combined with crest]
of their sourcelossness [**soorcelossness**—loss of connection to their
source the Ein Sof—in K Adam's sin was cutting of the roots, the
lower sefirot from the higher]. The quarry, the original source for
human material, is silent, and home free is no answer [that is free will
at home is no answer to the connection]. What are you running away
from, Livia or life with no answers?

Now back to the often cloud-capped Hill of Howth, the legendary head of Adam or Adam Kadmon or Finnegan at the wake:

> [23] Wolkencap is on him, frowned; audiurient, he would
> 21
> evesdrip, were it mous at hand, were it dinn of bottles in the
> far
> 22
> ear. Murk, his vales are darkling. With lipth she lithpeth to
> him
> 23
> all to time of thuch on thuch and thow on thow.

His woolen cap-like cloud is on his head, and he is frowning, the
frown of the deef who cannot hear. If he could hear, he would
eavesdrop [listen to Eve], were it near [**mous**] at hand, were it just
the dinn of bottles [the human spirit as opposed to the din stern
judgment of ES] in the **far ear** [far year—distance in time]. Murky
his vales [empty void of creation] are **darkling** with evil. The female
river waters of life [coming into the bay] lips to him all through time
on such & such [**thuch on thuch** or such combined with "touch"]
and thou & thou [**thow on thow** or thou how combined with sow
for birth]. In other words, the spirit of human females no more than
touch and birth of new life is the only answer given on earth to the
ultimate mysteries.

The female waters speak:

> [23] She he she ho
> 24
> she ha to la. Hairfluke, if he could bad twig her!

308

Impalpabunt,
25
he abhears.

She speaks female to male, female garden to the male hoe [in the garden and take to your wife like a plow], female to **ha** [joy] to **la** [expression of surprise or pregnancy]. The curse of the Lord, if he could just understand-touch-extend his branch to her [**bad twig her**]. **Impalpabunt**—impalpable and bunt—imperceptible to touch and a bunt—he doesn't hear the river of life female voice or is distracted [**abhear** is literally hears away from].

So what keeps Adam-Finnegan's attention if he doesn't listen to the sounds of the river:

> **[23] The soundwaves are his buffeteers; they trompe him**
> 26
> **with their trompes; the wave of roary and the wave of hooshed**
> 27
> **and the wave of hawhawhawrd and the wave of neverheedthem-**
> 28
> **horseluggarsandlisteltomine.**

The thought of death bothers him. The salt water waves buffet his headland—the sounds of the waves [of violence] are his buffet or banquet [**buffeters**]; they deceive him with their trompes—an apparatus for producing a blast in a furnace by using falling water to displace air. In other words fire and the flood. Then the Four Waves of Ireland—the Four Annals of Ireland accounting for continuous warfare—for four points on the Irish Coast (Rory, Tuath, Cleena & Sceina)—the wave of roary [roar] and the wave of **hooshed** [who died] and the wave of **hawhawhawrd** [haw means an enclosure and hawhaw is an expression of hesitation] and the wave of **horseluggarsandlisteltomine**—a condensate word for never heed them horse pullers/passions and listen to mine.

If the headland Finnegan-Adam communal human consciousness could only hear:

> **[23] Landloughed by his neaghboormis-**
> 29
> **tress and perpetrified in his offsprung, sabes and suckers, the**
> 30

309

moaning pipers could tell him to his faceback, the louthly one
31

whose loab we are devorers of, how butt for his hold halibutt, or
32

her to her pudor puff, the lipalip one whose libe we drink at, how
33

biff for her tiddywink of a windfall, our breed and washer givers,
34

there would not be a holey spier on the town nor a vestal flout-
35

ing in the dock, nay to make plein avowels, nor a yew nor an eye
36

[24] to play cash cash in Novo Nilbud by swamplight nor a' toole o'
1

tall o' toll and noddy hint to the convaynience.
2

Joyce gives this material in one long, complicated and you might say landlocked sentence for emphasis. I have separated it like a good TZTZ author. The basic point is that with just the father god there would be no life.

Landlocked and loughed [a lake or strait] by his neighbor mistress [River Liffey] and petrified in his offspring, babes and sucklings with an "s" emphasis—dependents, the moaning pipers could tell some important things to Finnegan-Adam to his **faceback** [god's face seen only by Moses]. He the repository of human consciousness is the louthly rough one whose loab we eat—what we experience, [particularly in the night world].

Before the statement some exceptions: except for his bold halibut [**hold halibutt**—fish body in the world or Christ], or her to her **pudor puff** [Holy Spirit or Shekhinah wind spirit]. Wind spirit because after resurrection Christ blew on the faces of his disciples in order for them to receive the Holy Spirit. Without these exceptions, that is if we didn't have the Son and Holy Spirit and we had only the father god, there would be nothing.

The father god is referred to as the lipalip one whose libe ["pouring out" god kissed Moses to die] we drink at, that is drink death rather than life as the son god promised the Samaritan woman at the well. The father god is death. The HSS is life.

Without Eve, how but biff for her tiddywink of a fall in the spirit [windfall of free will and knowledge of sex], there would be no church in town [**our bread and blood givers**—mass] nor a virgin [Mary] floating dry in the dock [pure of the sin of insemination by the flood of evil], nor to speak plainly and truly, nor a you [**yew**] nor an I [**eye**] to play **cash cash** [economic life] in new **Nilbud** [no blossom or Nile source] by swamplight nor **a'toole o'tall o'toll** and no one aware of the convenience.

In other words, without Christ, the Holy Spirit and Eve there would be no life, no one to know about the convenience of life. [Eve leads to Christ and the Mass whose power is the Holy Spirit]. Father TZTZ god alone is the death god. The convenience of life is considerable understatement.

Here is Adam post-Garden, earning his bread by the sweat of his brow:

> [24] He dug in and dug out by the skill of his tilth for himself and
> 3
> all belonging to him and he sweated his crew beneath his auspice
> 4
> for the living and he urned his dread, that dragon volant, and he
> 5
> made louse for us and delivered us to boll weevils amain, that
> 6
> mighty liberator, Unfru-Chikda-Uru-Wukru and begad he did,
> 7
> our ancestor most worshipful, till he thought of a better one in
> 8
> his windower's house with that blushmantle upon him from ears-
> 9
> end to earsend.

Note that this material is connected by "ands" to suggest repetition. He survived by his tilling skills for his own and his own family [**all** belonging to him—his own] and he worked his crew for the future of the living and in the process of earning his bread he exhumed his dread or fear [**urned his dread**], that dragon of desire, and he made his successors a louse [dependent and fearful] and again delivered us to corruption like the boll weevil in the cotton bud [evil and death inside], delivered us to that mighty liberator Unfru-Chikda-Uru-Wukru [aboriginal god], our worshipped ancestor did, until he thought of a better god in his windower-widower's house [In Mark 12:40 widower's houses are devoured by the Jewish Scribes who pretend to be saintly—that is foreclose on mortgages] and then a better one yet with the burning bush experience upon him [Moses and YHWH] like a mantle from **earsend** [ear send] to **earsend** [ears end]. Man's TZTZ god changes, getting worse with foreclosing mankind.

Speaking now of Finnegan as a successor in the line of soul emanation from Adam Kadmon to Adam to Moses to Finnegan:

> [24] And would again could whispring grassies wake
> 10
> him and may again when the fiery bird disembers. And will
> 11
> again if so be sooth by elder to his youngers shall be said.
> Have
> 12
> you whines for my wedding, did you bring bride and bedding,
> 13
> will you whoop for my deading is a? Wake? *Usgueadbaugham!*
> 14

And [he may again find a better god, a new possibility] if whispering spring grasses wake him and may again [find a better god] when the Phoenix burns and rises from the ashes. And will again if truth be said from elder to younger. And then [in song rhythm] do you have the needs made by the curse, the needs for wedding, copulation and birth—to wake new life. Wake? Whiskey the water of life I am [***Usgueadbaugham!***]

With an emphasis on new gods, now Finnegan wakes:

> [24] Anam muck an dhoul ! Did ye drink me doornail?
> 15

Finnegan declares I am an an [**anam**]. Your souls from the devil in the filth [**muck an dhoul**]. Did you drink to my [**me**] death?   As in dead as a **doornail**.

But the wake group doesn't want Finnegan to wake up; they don't want Finnegan to be all he can be, for the Last Judgment to arrive, for death to end. We are reminded of the ending of Ibsen's *When We Dead Awaken*, when the courageous couple is killed by a thunder-driven avalanche high in the mountains:

> [24] Now be aisy, good Mr Finnimore, sir. And take your lay-sure
> 16
> like a god on pension and don't be walking abroad. Sure you'd
> 17
> only lose yourself in Healiopolis now the way your roads in
> 18
>
> Kapelavaster are that winding there after the calvary, the North
> 19
> Umbrian and the Fivs Barrow and Waddlings Raid and the
> 20
> Bower Moore and wet your feet maybe with the foggy dew's
> 21
> abroad.

Now be easy, good **Mr Finnimore** [that is die some more]. And take your leisure by laying sure like a god on pension [retired and dependent on the pension for work in the past] and don't be **walking abroad** like a ghost—that is don't be walking big. You would only lose your identity in the city of the healing sun [**Healiopolis**] given the way the roads in Buddha country are winding after Christ died on Calvary [that is you would be spiritually lost], for example the Roman roads North Umbrian, Fivs Barrow, Waddlings Raid and Bower Moore are new so perhaps you would just wet your feet there. **You wouldn't want the new possibilities of changes at home or what is abroad.** You wouldn't experience anything new, just the inconvenience of wet feet.

Abroad, you would be:

> [24] Meeting some sick old bankrupt or the Cottericks' donkey
> 22

with his shoe hanging, clankatachankata, or a slut snoring with an
23
impure infant on a bench. 'Twould turn you against life, so
24
'twould.

Like the young Buddha [the "awakened" one] coming out of his fa-ther-arranged reclusive leisure, you would if awake see suffering—disease, age and bankruptcy or financial suffering [**sick old bank-rupt**]. You would see the donkey with a bad shoe, horse named **clankatachankata** [combined names of Buddha's horse and Mo-hammed's horse containing clinging and attachment] and a slut with her diseased child sleeping on the sidewalk—it would turn you against life [parody of the doctrine of the Buddha—who strove for release from karmic reincarnation]. In this litany, poverty is the root of suffering. As Joyce said in a Trieste lecture about Ireland: "The economic and intellectual conditions that prevail [in Ireland because of the British] . . . do not permit the development of individuality."

Then for an incommensurate joinder to Finnegan—besides, the weather is as mean as life itself. The weather of course offers new possibilities each day against a prevailing average [mean]:

[24] **And the weather's that mean too. To part from Devlin**
25
is hard as Nugent knew, to leave the clean tanglesome one lushier
26
than its neighbour enfranchisable fields but let your ghost have
27
no grievance.

To part from Dublin-Ireland is hard as **Nugent** [the author of *Ode Written on Leaving Ireland*] knew; it is hard to become a new gent [**Nu-gent**]. It is hard to leave the Irish reservoir of souls for transmigra-tion [**tanglesome** of souls] clean of one who will have to reincarnate in another area [**neighbour enfranchisable field**] but let your spirit have no grievance of not coming back. Apparently all reincarnation, like politics, is local. This is geographic nirvana and new lives that are punishment for past-based karma. Even the possibilities of the new life through reincarnation are restricted—first by karma and second geographically.

314

They tell him you Finnegan are better off where you are:

> **[24] You're better off, sir, where you are, primesigned**
> **28**
> **in the full of your dress, bloodeagle waistcoat and all, re-**
> **member-**
> **29**
> **ing your shapes and sizes on the pillow of your babycurls**
> **under**
> **30**
> **your sycamore by the keld water where the Tory's clay will**
> **scare**
> **31**
> **the varmints and have all you want, pouch, gloves, flask,**
> **bricket,**
> **32**
> **kerchief, ring and amberulla, the whole treasure of the pyre,**
> **in the**
> **33**
> **land of souls with Homin and Broin Baroke and pole ole Lo-**
> **nan**
> **34**
> **and Nobucketnozzler and the Guinnghis Khan.**

You are better off here than abroad. In your Sunday best clothes, remembering your infancy like Osiris in the sycamore by the cold water, in innocence where the sacred ground [**Tory's clay**] will scare varmints evil away [Garden of Eden] and you have all you want— pouch, gloves, flask, bricket, kerchief, ring and umbrella—the treasure of sacrifice and you will be in the land of souls with celebrities such as **Homin** [Homer? Odysseus—Homing for home?] and Going Broke [**Broin Baroke**] and poor old Lonan [**ple ole Lonan**] and Nebuchadnezzar [**Nobucketnozzler** –no bucket to nozzle] and Genghis Khan [**Guinnghis Kahn**—getting his khan]. It will be noted these souls are unlikely to have achieved nirvana and rest.

This discussion suggests via the Egyptian Book of the Dead that like those who are not able to merge with Osiris [sounds like ES], you will have a second death and not be resurrected into eternal life. You will be annihilated.

And now promises for the Finnegan who continues to rest in death. The promises tell us more about those promising that about Finnegan:

And we'll be
35
coming here, the ombre players, to rake your gravel and bringing
36
you presents, won't we, fenians? And it isn't our spittle

[25] we'll stint
1
you of, is it, druids? Not shabbty little imagettes, pennydirts and
2
dodgemyeyes you buy in the soottee stores. But offerings of the
3
field.

It starts with **We fenians**. This is an ironical use of the name of U.S. supporters for Irish independence since these mourners are dependent oriented. We fenians will faithfully come here in groups of three [**ombre** is a game card game for three and the Trinity]. Like the Japanese rock gardens, we will rake your gravel. Like almost all gods we will bring you presents [so you will be nice to us]. We won't stint on the magic spittle we anoint you with like Druids and other medicine men. We won't stop at shabby little images of gods like those Shabti buried with the Egyptian dead and will avoid idol images that can be purchased in the suttee stores and allow us to dodge looking at you. Instead like Abel we will bring you offerings of the field. This is a series of comments on archaic spiritual practices dealing with issue of death, burial and placating the powers that be with offerings.

More and into incommensurates:

[25] Mieliodories, that Doctor Faherty, the madison man,
4
taught to gooden you. Poppypap's a passport out. And honey is
5
the holiest thing ever was, hive, comb and earwax, the food for
6
glory, (mind you keep the pot or your nectar cup may yield too *much—this word is missing--*
7

316

light!) and some goat's milk, sir, like the maid used to bring
you.
8

Advertising techniques will be used to make you good. Hallucino-
genic drugs such as those from the poppy will be used as a way out
of this world and access to you. And since honey is the holiest substance that can be offered to you, your cup will be ready to receive
that [beware that your cup like the kellipot may receive too much
light]. Also goat's milk like the maids brought to Krishna, the god
who descends from time to time when evil in the form of warfare
invades the earth.

More reasons to remain dead:

[25] Your fame is spreading like Basilico's ointment since
the Fintan
9
Lalors piped you overborder and there's whole households
be-
10
yond the Bothnians and they calling names after you. The
men-
11
here's always talking of you sitting around on the pig's
cheeks
12
under the sacred rooftree, over the bowls of memory where
every
13
hollow holds a hallow, with a pledge till the drengs, in the
Salmon
14
House.

Your fame is spreading like a popular ointment since a popular music group piped you overboard, played music at your death, and there
are entire households all over the world named after you—such as
Christians for Christ. Men here [menhir are sacred stones] are always talking of you as they sit around home under the sacred rooftree of Osiris, over bowls of memory where every hollow holds a
hallow [as in hallowed be thy name]—the primordial void [hollow]
created by ES that contains TZTZ creation and TZTZ god [hallow].
This with a pledge of continuing life [the Salmon House] to the
dregs of the end [drengs].

317

Now references to his curse driven work, work necessary because of the Fall:

> [25] And admiring to our supershillelagh where the palmsweat
> 15
> on high is the mark of your manument. All the toethpicks ever
> 16
> Eirenesians chewed on are chips chepped from that battery
> 17
> block. If you were bowed and soild and letdown itself from the
> 18
> oner of the load it was that paddyplanters might pack up plenty and
> 19
> when you were undone in every point fore the laps of goddesses
> 20
> you showed our labourlasses how to free was easy.

The background for these planter references is that Adam was a planter for god in the Garden of Eden, just a tenant farmer, not an owner. All admire your super toothpick, the tool of leisure, while others were working to palm sweat—this is the mark of your monument for man, the result of man's inheritance from you— peasants working for owners or economic injustice. All the tooth and toe picks the Irish chewed on came from your ur-block [reference back to Osiris's sacred tree]. [In the primal horde fathers would chew on their sons.] If you were bowed and dirty and set down your own load it was so that others the Irish planters tenant farmers might have to carry more and when they were brought to heavenly justice you showed our working women how to be free [but not on earth]. This is a version of TZTZ creation—work is necessary even if unfortunate and unfair and women are subjugated.

More:

> [25] The game old
> 21
> Gunne, they do be saying, (skull!) that was a planter for you, a
> 22
> spicer of them all. Begog but he was, the G.O.G! He's dudd-

23

andgunne now and we're apter finding the sores of his sedeq

24

but peace to his great limbs, the buddhoch, with the last league

25

long rest of him, while the millioncandled eye of Tuskar sweeps

26

the Moylean Main !

One of your planters was game old **Gunne**, the spicy one –reference to Gladstone and remember the white rock of the Kaaba. He would be god [**begog**] but he was the G.O.G, the god of gods. [Magog was a grandson of Noah and Gog was one of the nations Satan would assemble for an attack on the saints.] He is dead and gone now [**gunne**—gone and gun combined] but we are apt to find the sores of his justice but peace be with his great limbs, like the buddha's buttocks [**buddhoch**] that need rest [he sat under the tree for several days], with the really long remainder of him [rest of his rest] while the powerful eye of the tuskar lighthouse like Admon Kadmon sweeps the sea between Ireland and Scotland.

Now Finnegan is addressed as a warlord [think about that word]. The mourners continue to praise him in the interests of Finnegan remaining dead:

[25] There was never a warlord in Great Erinnes

27

and Brettland, no, nor in all Pike County like you, they say. No,

28

nor a king nor an ardking, bung king, sung king or hung king.

29

That you could fell an elmstree twelve urchins couldn't ring

30

round and hoist high the stone that Liam failed. Who but a Mac-

31

cullaghmore the reise of our fortunes and the faunayman at the

32

funeral to compass our cause?

There never was a warlord [famous heroes in Ireland and England were fighters] in Ireland or England nor in all of Pike County like you, they say. [This sounds like Finn MacCool, aka Mac Cumhail.] No king, ardking, bung king, sun king [Louis XIV] or hung king [Christ] like you. You could fell big trees and lift heavy stones like the stone of fate [Lia fail]. Who better to lead our cause but a strong leader, a strong senior male.

More praise:

> [25] If you was hogglebully itself and
> 33
> most frifty like you was taken waters still what all where was
> 34
> your like to lay the cable or who was the batter could better
> 35
> [26] Your Grace? Mick Mac Magnus MacCawley can take you off to the pure perfection and Leatherbags Reynolds tries your shuffle
> 1
> and cut. But as Hopkins and Hopkins p
> uts it, you were the pale
> 2
> eggynaggy and a kis to tilly up.

Who would be better to lay connections to the gods, to **lay the cable**. Huckleberry Finn is mentioned because of his last name and because his father his "pap" had abandoned him [as ES did]. He said his father was "most fifty." Here Finnegan is said to be "most frifty." This phrase brings in the lost relationship with the powers that be and also the suggestion that god is thrifty with his love. One **Mick Mac Magnus MacCawley** can **take you off**, that is mimic you to pure perfection. Mac means son of, magnus means great as in great work and cawl means a basket. This must refer to the son Jesus mimicking father god to perfection since they are of the same substance, they are consubstantial, in the same basket. St. Hilary thought species or image to be the particular attribute of the Son, the power to mimic.

Leatherbags Reynolds tries your dance, your shuffle and cut. Reynolds is a name associated in fluid mechanics with determining whether the flow of a fluid past a certain point will be smooth or turbulent. Leatherbag could refer to St. Paul who traveled much for the new Christian faith and championed the lack of necessity for circumcision, making recruitment smoother, no need for shuffle and cut just shuffle and no cut. Flow from an uncircumcised penis would be turbulent, the foreskin interfering with the flow, and life under TZTZ god is turbulent.

Hopkins and Hopkins refers to Matthew Hopkins an English witch hunter during the English civil wars and Samuel Hopkins a minister and writer and one of the first Congregationists in the U.S. to oppose slavery. So the **pale eggynaggy** must refer to Caucasian preference in Christianity and a kiss **to tilly up** means you were a dear to forget part of the purchase price. That is to say in an ironic way, you were a dear to forgive our sins that you caused in the first place.

More talk to Finnegan about the gods:

> [26] We calls him the journeyall
> 3
> Buggaloffs since he went Jerusalemfaring in Arssia Manor. You
> 4
> had a gamier cock than Pete, Jake or Martin and your archgoose
> 5
> of geese stubbled for All Angels' Day. So may the priest of seven
> 6
> worms and scalding tayboil, Papa Vestray, come never anear you
> 7
> as your hair grows wheater beside the Liffey that's in Heaven!
> 8

[Given that he is without a mate] we call him the god Buggaloffs. Buggerlugs is an offensive term for sodomites and bugger off means to bugger and then leave—the curse. God Buggaloffs journeys everywhere since he first appeared in Jerusalem in **Arssia Manor**, which suggests the house of arse [shit from heaven] as well as Asia Minor [house of the rising sun] and translates literally as the house of the bad temper [arsey meaning bad temper]. You were more [**a gamier cock**] than the Catholics, the Anglicans or the Protestants and your chief angel was fattened like a goose [**stubbled**] on All Saints Day [many sacrifices]. So may the priest of seven worms—the seven sacraments—and hot **tayboil** [which must refer somehow to Huckle-

321

berry and hell], father of the keeping room for holy objects or heaven, never come back near you as your hair grows whiter [Buddha cut off his hair and threw it into heaven] like wheat beside that heavenly Liffey.

Now for some references to the Egyptian Book of the Dead. Before we start, first the original Egyptian concept of god [that we know about], their word *neter*, that lay under all subsequent Egyptian theology. Apropos of our theme, this word according to E. A. Wallis Budge [1904]:

> . . . it is almost impossible not to think that the word has a meaning which is closely allied to the ideas of "self-existence," and the power to "renew life indefinitely," and "self-production." In other words, *neter* appears to mean a being who has the power to generate life, and to maintain it when generated.

This is the idea that lay at the base of all Egyptian theology. It sounds like parthenogenesis would fill this bill. It may explain the association of the Pharaoh with incest, the Pharaoh who often married his sister in order to keep their royal offspring as close as possible to a clone and in the same blood line.

What made Osiris so popular was his mixed nature, partly human and partly divine. He lived and died as a human, killed and mutilated by his brother Set. After death Osiris regenerated into a god of the region of the underworld. Proper words and ceremonies enabled his sister Isis to regenerate him so the same rites were also needed in order to achieve immortality for others.

Now for the text. The Egyptian god *Ptah Tanen* was thought to have his head in the stars and his feet on the earth. Some information about this god from Wikipedia. This god sounds something like ES:

> In Egyptian mythology, Ptah (also spelt Peteh) was the deification of the primordial mound in the Ennead cosmogony, which was more literally referred to as Ta-tenen (also spelt Tathenen), meaning *risen land*, or as Tanen, meaning *submerged land*. The importance Ptah was given in history can readily be understood since the name *Egypt* derives from Classical Greek *Aigyptos* which in turn derives from the native name of a temple at Memphis (transcribed as ... or *Hut-ka-Ptah* "temple of the Ka of Ptah").
>
> It was said (in the Shabaka Stone) that it was Ptah who called the world into being, having dreamt creation in his heart, and speaking it, his name meaning *opener*, in the sense of *opener of the mouth*. In-

deed the *opening of the mouth* ceremony, performed by priests at funerals to release souls from their corpses, was said to have been created by Ptah. Atum was said to have been created by Ptah to rule over the creation, sitting upon the primordial mound.

In art, he is portrayed as a bearded mummified man, often wearing a skull cap, with his hands holding an ankh… and djed, the symbols of life, power and stability, respectively. It was also considered that Ptah manifested himself in the Apis bull.

***

Since Ptah was the primordial mound, and had called creation into being, he was considered the god of craftsmen, and in particular stone-based crafts. Eventually, due to the connection of these things to tombs, and that at Thebes, the craftsmen regarded him so highly as to say that he controlled their destiny. Consequently, first amongst the craftsmen, then the population as a whole, Ptah also became a god of reincarnation. Since Seker was also god of craftsmen, and of re-incarnation, Seker was later assimilated with Ptah becoming Ptah-Seker.

Ptah-Seker gradually became seen as the personification of the sun during the night, since the sun appears to be *re-incarnated* at this time, and Ptah was the primordial mound, which lay beneath the earth. Consequently, Ptah-Seker became considered an underworld deity, and eventually, by the Middle Kingdom, become assimilated by Osiris, the lord of the underworld, occasionally being known as *Ptah-Seker-Osiris*.

Legend has it that Ancient Egyptians believed saying Ptah's name would give the spouse of the speaker great fertility.

Back to the text of FW, the mourners still placating Finnegan:

[26] **Hep, hep, hurrah there! Hero! Seven times thereto we salute**
9
you! The whole bag of kits, falconplumes and jackboots incloted,
10
is where you flung them that time. Your heart is in the system
11
of the Shewolf and your crested head is in the tropic of Copri-
12

capron. Your feet are in the cloister of Virgo. Your olala is in the
13
region of sahuls. And that's ashore as you were born.

As ES created TZTZ god so Ptah created Namen, the submerged land. Coming ashore again would refer to the sun rising and another soul reincarnated. As a shewolf, this god would be vicious in protection of her young. The sahuy was the incorruptible house of souls.

More in the same vein:

[26] Your shuck
14
tick's swell. And that there texas is tow linen. The loamsome
15
roam to Laffayette is ended. Drop in your tracks, babe! Be not
16
unrested ! The headboddylwatcher of the chempel of Isid,
17
Totumcalmum, saith: I know thee, metherjar, I know thee, sal-
18
vation boat. For we have performed upon thee, thou abrama-
19
nation, who comest ever without being invoked, whose coming
20
is unknown, all the things which the company of the precentors
21
and of the grammarians of Christpatrick's ordered concerning
22
thee in the matter of the work of thy tombing. Howe of the ship-
23
men, steep wall!
24

This is in the tone of what more do you want? Since Osiris is often portrayed on a brier, we have here: Your mattress is thick and well. Your linen is good. You don't have to go to Laffayette. Drop in your tracks, stop right there. Stay calm. The head body watcher of the HCE temple of Isis-Isolde, Totally Calm or Tutakamen [**Totum-**

324

calmum], said we have done everything. In the words of the FW text:

> **For we have performed upon thee, thou abramanation, who comest ever without being invoked, whose coming is unknown, all the things which the company of the precentors and of the grammarians of Christpatrick's ordered concerning thee in the matter of the work of thy tombing.**

Abramanation would be the emanation of Abram into his new life with YWH. Here it is Osiris, the god of regeneration, of new possibilities. This material mimics the Egyptian *Book of the Dead*, 'The Chapter of Driving Back the Eater of the Ass':

> Osiris Ra, triumphant, saith ... I have performed upon thee all the things which the company of the gods ordered concerning thee in the matter of work of thy slaughter. Get thee back, thou abomination of Osiris. ... I know thee. ... O thou that comest without being invoked, and whose [time of coming] is unknown.

Osiris is the god of the dead. His symbol was the growing corn. The Egyptian religion is all about immortality. Man might achieve unity with the gods after death. His body was preserved in mummies toward that purpose.

Osiris was the judge of who passed beyond the ropes. Hacked into 14 pieces by his evil brother Set and put back together except for his penis by his sister/wife Isis, Osiris remains in the in-between world, between death and life. All who die want to emulate him because he arose from death. He is the principle of regeneration. He is regeneration. The doctrines about Christ are similar. He helps avoid the second death into nothingness.

But here the mourners do not want Finnegan to regenerate. They want him to sleep, never to awaken. To be less than he could be. They say they have done everything St. Patrick suggested about the dead.

And now some town gossip from the mourners to Finnegan:

> **[26] Everything's going on the same or so it appeals to all of us,**
> **25**
> **in the old holmsted here. Coughings all over the sanctuary, bad**
> **26**

scrant to me aunt Florenza. The horn for breakfast, one
o'gong
27
for lunch and dinnerchime. As popular as when Belly the
First
28
was keng and his members met in the Diet of Man. The
same
29
shop slop in the window. Jacob's lettercrackers and Dr Tipple's
30
Vi-Cocoa and the Eswuards' desippated soup beside Mother
Sea-
31
gull's syrup.

The mourner thinks that Finnegan will be comforted and calmed by
knowing that things are pretty much the same in the old homestead
[**holmsted**]. Nothing new to wake up for. Illness is common. We eat
at the horn for breakfast, lunch and dinner at regular hours. It is as
popular as it was when Belly the First was king [fat so **keng** rather
than king] and his members met in the Diet of Man—gods left little
for mankind, a diet for man while god got fat. The same slop in the
shop window. We still have crackers in the form of letters by
Jacob—in Hebrew the letters for his name would be BCJ. We still
have Dr. Tipple's Vi-Cocoa, a stimulant of the spirit. We still have
Edward's **desippated** soup and **Mother Seagull's syrup,** a tonic.
We note that these minimal boosters of the spirit are small charms
compared to a real connection to the gods.

And inevitably, the economic news, the news of rise and fall in
TZTZ creation:

[26] Meat took a drop when Reilly-Parsons failed. Coal's
32
short but we've plenty of bog in the yard. And barley's up
again,
33
begrained to it.

Rise and fall is inherent in economics as it is in human life. Now
news of your children:

326

[26] The lads is attending school nessans regular, sir,
34
spelling beesknees with hathatansy and turning out tables by
35
mudapplication. Allfor the books and never pegging smash-
ers
36

[27] after Tom Bowe Glassarse or Timmy the Tosser. 'Tis-
raely the
1
truth! No isn't it, roman pathoricks?

School lessons become **nessans**, which in French means born without and in this context without god. The lads are spelling business
[**beesknees** for sore knees from kneeling] to perfection but with a
hesitancy about force [**hathatansy**—hath means force in Sanskrit]
and turning out tables by multiplication in the mud [**mudapplication**—reference to Adam made from clay]. They are all for the
books and never engage in fights with Tom or Timmy. By Israel tis
the truth. Now referring to the rest of the mourners as you roman
catholics-suffering [**patho**] fakes [**rick**], the spokesman asks, referring to what he has said, isn't that true.

Now the mourner speaks to Finnegan as if his family consists of
Kevin and Jerry, who sound like Shaun and Shem in the family of
HCE:

[27] You were the doublejoynted
2
janitor the morning they were delivered and you'll be a
grandfer
3
yet entirely when the ritehand seizes what the lovearm
knows.
4
Kevin's just a doat with his cherub cheek, chalking oghres on
5
walls, and his little lamp and schoolbelt and bag of knicks,
playing
6
postman's knock round the diggings and if the seep were
milk
7
you could lieve his olde by his ide but, laus sake, the devil

does
8
**be in that knirps of a Jerry sometimes, the tarandtan plaid-
boy,**
9
**making encostive inkum out of the last of his lavings and
writing**
10
a blue streak over his bourseday shirt.

As a doublejoined janitor, you helped deliver the twins Kevin and
Jerry [as a predecessor you are part of their inheritance] and you will
be a grandfather soon, when the **ritehand seizes what the lovearm
knows**. These may be Kabbalah references to the stern right and
forgiving left side Sefirots. In Matthew 6:3 Jesus says let thy alms
giving be secret and not for the praise of others, let it be so secret the
left hand doesn't know what alms the right hand gives. Here the
ritehand or religion through rites and sacraments **seizes** away from
the lovearm what it knows. In other words, falsification through rite
and ritual of the religion of love.

Kevin is just the dote [**doat**] of an angel. Dote means to talk
foolishly as well as worship. He chalks oghres on the walls [evil gi-
ants] and with his little lamp and schoolbelt and bag of tricks
[**knicks**] he plays postman. As postman Kevin delivers the male and
commands the station, the post. On the other hand Jerry is a devil of
a boy sometimes and writes so much he even makes ink out of the
wash water for his clothes and writes on his shirt, his **bourseday** or
money market shirt. That is to say, Jerry turns his dirty experience
into art for all the world to see.

> **[27] Hetty Jane's a child of**
> 11
> **Mary. She'll be coming (for they're sure to choose her) in her**
> 12
> **white of gold with a tourch of ivy to rekindle the flame on
> Felix**
> 13
> **Day.**

Hetty Jane, relation to Finnegan unstated, is a child of Mary and still
a virgin, and she is sure to be chosen the queen to rekindle the flame
on Felix Day, a celebration day devoted to the sun. Rekindling the
flame must refer to procreation.

Now for others, for a wild young Essie Shanahan, apparently part of Finnegan's larger group of successors:

> [27] But Essie Shanahan has let down her skirts. You remember
> 14
> Essie in our Luna's Convent? They called her Holly Merry her
> 15
> lips were so ruddyberry and Pia de Purebelle when the red-miners
> 16
> riots was on about her. Were I a clerk designate to the Williams-
> 17
> woodsmenufactors I'd poster those pouters on every jamb in the
> 18
> town. She's making her rep at Lanner's twicenightly. With the
> 19
> tabarine tamtammers of the whirligigmagees. Beats that cachucha
> 20
> flat. 'Twould dilate your heart to go.
> 21

But Essie or Easy has let down her skirts or relaxed. Finnegan you remember her from Luna's Convent, worship of the female from earlier moon worship. Essie was called Holly [not Holy] Merry because her lips were as red as berries. She was called **Pia de Purebelle** when her monthlies [**redminer's riots**—suggests redeemer's] were on her. Pia de Pure Bella were the religious wars during Vico's heroic age. Here the cult of virginity is viewed against the need for sex and birth. Were I an important functionary in **Williamswoodsmenufactors**, the celestial manufacturing of humankind, I would poster her lips [**pouters**] on every lintel [**jamb**—for the sex act] in town. [Her berry red lips as the poster for human sexuality takes the place of the blood of the lamb on the lintel to avoid the avenging angel of death.] She Essie is making her reputation at Lanner's with two shows each evening of exotic dancing to tamberouines. Today Essie would be lap dancing.

Back to Finnegan himself:

> [27] Aisy now, you decent man, with your knees and lie quiet and
> 22
> repose your honour's lordship! Hold him here, Ezekiel Irons, and
> 23
> may God strengthen you! It's our warm spirits, boys, he's spoor-
> 24
> ing. Dimitrius O'Flagonan, cork that cure for the Clancartys ! You
> 25
> swamped enough since Portobello to float the Pomeroy. Fetch
> 26
> neahere, Pat Koy! And fetch nouyou, Pam Yates! Be nayther
> 27
> angst of Wramawitch! Here's lumbos.

Spooring means to follow by scent, so the mourner spokesman thinks that Finnegan smells their warm spirits, their spirit of life. **Ezekiel Irons** refers to an Irish play but also to Ezekiel the Old Testament prophet who prophesized the destruction of Judah because of her loss of God mission. So being held by the **Irons** is fate in the form of a curse. Referring to other mourners, the spokesman says cork the booze, the cure for the **Clancartys**. As a clan cart, this is probably a reference to the Chariot mentioned by Enoch and carried over into K. A clan chariot carries only a few, those in the clan and not all. Booze carries all together. You Finnegan have drunk enough since Portobello, Little Jerusalem in Dublin, to float the **Pomeroy**, a kind of wine but also it means the King of the apple, a reference to god in the Garden of Eden. Fetch the life here [**neahere**]. Pat Koy! And fetch a newyou Pam Yates. Be neither worried or anxious about the witch of worry [Lillith]. Here are the loins of sleep [**lumbos**].

You can feel how long and drawn out this passage is. Continuing:

> [27] Where misties swaddlum,
> 28
> where misches lodge none, where mystries pour kind on, O
> 29
> sleepy! So be yet!
> 30

In dream where misty visions are born, where mische "I am" or individuality techniques are not in use, where mysteries pour it on, O sleepy. Go there.

More news that is supposed to comfort Finnegan:

[27] I've an eye on queer Behan and old Kate and the butter, trust me.
31
She'll do no jugglywuggly with her war souvenir postcards to
32
help to build me murial, tippers! I'll trip your traps! Assure a
33
sure there! And we put on your clock again, sir, for you. Did or
34
didn't we, sharestutterers? So you won't be up a stump entirely.
35
Nor shed your remnants. The sternwheel's crawling strong.

I will be watching Behan [not identified at this point] and old Kate [the Janatrix of the museyroom and the Holy Spirit when Father and Son not in conjunction]. The Holy Spirit is left behind [**Behan**] when Christ has arisen. The butter is apparently what Kate makes; she turns mother's milk into butter. She curdles it [when the curse is operating]. Kate will do no advertising [**jugglywuggly**] with her **war souvenir postcards** and mural reminding us of the horrors of war. I will trip your traps and catch something [not identified]. Sure enough. And we put you back on time again. Didn't we do it, you who share stuttering. So you won't be up a stump entirely [tree of life image]. You won't have to shed your remnants, as Adam and Eve did in the garden. The sternwheel, the past, is **crawling strong**.

As we continue in this material, finding the meaning [the meaning of TZTZ is being mean] is getting more difficult as well as more tedious. And your wife is doing fine:

[27] I
36
[28] seen your missus in the hall. Like the queenoveire. Arrah, it's
1
herself that's fine, too, don't be talking! Shirksends?

I have seen your wife [missus—she misses us] in the hall [not identi-
fied]. Like Guinevere [Queen of Eire]. Wow! She is fine too, don't
be talking. Apparently Finnegan said something about Guinevere.
Your wife is not shirking her duties [**shirksends** which suggests a
shortened end or death]. With the word **shirksends** Shakespeare
cannot be far behind. First **shakeshands**:

> [28] You storyan
> 2
> Harry chap longa me Harry chap storyan grass woman
> plelthy
> 3
> good trout. Shakeshands. Dibble a hayfork's wrong with her
> only
> 4
> her lex's salig.

For you the historian [**storyan**], the hairy chap, Ahriman or evil in
the world per Zoroaster, longs for me. The hairy chap historian
[making the history of the world repeat] reports the snake-like
woman [in the grass, **grass woman,** like Eve] plenty healthly
[**plelthy**] good trout—the fish that stays in fresh water. Unlike the
serpent punished in the Garden, this snake still has hands and
Shakeshands. Nothing is wrong with her in the devil dimension
[**hayfork** a kind of trident] except only her **lex's salica**—literally the
happy dirty leg law but a law excluding females from succession in
inheritance. This must refer to succession of original sin through sex
from the female and Eve's immersion for days in the river after exit
from the Garden.

Now for an image of Vishnu merged with Lewis Carroll's cat:

> [28] Boald Tib does be yawning and smirking cat's
> 5
> hours on the Pollockses' woolly round tabouretcushion
> watch-
> 6
> ing her sewing a dream together, the tailor's daughter, stitch
> to
> 7
> her last.

In Indian myth, the world is represented as Vishnu resting on the
giant serpent Ananti or Sesa in a formless ocean and dreaming our

world. As stated by Danielou: "When Vishnu sleeps, the universe dissolves into its formless state, represented as the causal ocean. The remnants of manifestation are presented as the serpent Remainder (Sesa) coiled upon itself and floating upon the abysmal waters." Carroll's smiling cat, you remember, vanished. In human experience, this happens in sleep.

Boald Tib does be yawning would refer to the Bold old Vishnu now replaced by Bold Tib, a prostitute, our very Eve who like the smirking cat has vanished and left us with original sin. Like Vishnu the cohesive force in the universe, she is sewing a dream together. She is the tailor's daughter, TZTZ god being the tailor who made clothes for Adam and Eve. She stitches the itch into all. The cat as pussy is also involved here. More:

> [28] Or while waiting for winter to fire the enchantement,
> 8
> decoying more nesters to fall down the flue. It's allavalonche that
> 9
> blows nopussy food.

Shifting now to hot and cold with the HSS as hot. Or while waiting for winter to fire the sexual enchantement, tricking some more would-be cohabitators to Fall down the flue [and live in the house of sexual reproduction]. It is a Fall of All, a big avalanche of a fall [**allavalonche**] that blows no pussy food. Pussy food would be male semen. This seems to say that the sexual act is branded as sinful prior to marriage. Marriage would be falling down the flue of a household so you could have the primal fire.

Now the mourner narrator wishes Finnegan were there to explain and take control of the HSS influence:

> [28] If you only were there to explain the mean-
> 10
> ing, best of men, and talk to her nice of guldenselver. The lips
> 11
> would moisten once again. As when you drove with her to Fin-
> 12
> drinny Fair. What with reins here and ribbons there all your
> 13

> hands were employed so she never knew was she on land or
> at
> 14
> sea or swooped through the blue like Airwinger's bride.

If only you were there [instead of here] to talk her into an attitude of gold and silver self, the body as the vessel of god. Precohabitation, her lips would moisten once again as nubile. As she was precohabitation when you drove her to **Findrinny Fair**, findrinny meaning silver bronze or a drop in quality with the bronze below. Then you rubbed her so that she felt like she was flying like Airwinger's bride. This suggests that the "sweeping me off my feet emotion" associated with sex-love is angelic and a suggestion of the Holy Ghost, who impregnated Mary through the ear [**Airwinger's bride** versus Earwicker].

More about HSS, compliments:

> [28] She
> 15
> was flirtsome then and she's fluttersome yet. She can second
> a
> 16
> song and adores a scandal when the last post's gone by. Fond of
> 17
> a concertina and pairs passing when she's had her forty winks
> 18
> for supper after kanekannan and abbely dimpling and is in her
> 19
> merlin chair assotted, reading her Evening World.

Flirt and flutter suggests a bird, the HSS. The last post or posting would be Christ in the world, after which the HSS is on duty. Since the last posting the bird loves a song and scandal. She the HSS has nothing better to do [since love cannot issue in the world because the father and son gods are not in charity]. The HSS was missing when Cain killed Abel, so here she is taking a nap after supper—lunch—after Cain cained ["kanekannan"] Abel [**abbely**], who is treated as food for lunch. A merlin chair is an invalid's wheelchair, a suggestion that the HSS's magic doesn't work now.

Now her eyes are open and she the HSS sees evil in the newspaper named The Evening World—the world of darkness. For this material remember that Mary was considered the second Eve and was known as the Star of the Sea, a reference to her role to save seamen. Her name in this capacity is *Maria Maris Stella*. This name originally started with the meaning of Mary "as a drop of water from the sea" (*Maria Stilla Maris*). Over time and through several translators, drop (*stilla*) became star (*stella*). In Ulysses, Bloom's drops of semen are associated with the star of the roman candle. The semen of human males is needed because of the salt sea of death:

> [28] To see is
> 20
> it smarts, full lengths or swaggers. News, news, all the news.
> 21
> Death, a leopard, kills fellah in Fez. Angry scenes at Stormount.
> 22
> Stilla Star with her lucky in goingaways. Opportunity fair with
> 23
> the China floods and we hear these rosy rumours. Ding Tams he
> 24
> noise about all same Harry chap. She's seeking her way, a chickle
> 25
> a chuckle, in and out of their serial story, *Les Loves of Selskar*
> 26
> *et Pervenche*, freely adapted to *The Novvergin's Viv.*

To see, as Eve's eyes were opened, is to be smart and feel pain [double meaning of smart]. The news is bad. Killings, floods. The Virgin Mary was lucky to be going away. Reference to the same Harry chap or Ahriman, the god of darkness for Zoroaster. She the HSS is seeking her way through a play referring to periwinkle [remember Quinet] freely adapted to the Non-Virgin's Life [**Novvergin's Viv**].

More flower Quinet:

> [28] There'll
> 27
> be bluebells blowing in salty sepulchres the night she signs her

28
final tear. Zee End. But that's a world of ways away. Till track
29
laws time. No silver ash or switches for that one! While flattering
30
candles flare.

There will be blues blowing in sea salty graves when she the HSS signs her final tear for this world of evil. The end, the sea [**Zee End**]. In K, evil is chaos. And in K death is the supreme manifestation of chaos, both fostered by doubt. But that, like end of FW, is world of ways away. Until the marks left on earth [**tracks**] govern [**law**] time. This suggests when karma rules the earth. No silver tree of life for that one. In the absence of the true unifying light of ES, **flattering candles flare**. [Not the light of the HSS.]

> [28] Anna Stacey's how are you! Worther waist in the
> 31
> noblest, says Adams and Sons, the wouldpay actionneers. Her
> 32
> hair's as brown as ever it was. And wivvy and wavy. Repose you
> 33
> now! Finn no more!
> 34

Through German [anstase], Anna Stacey sounds like resurrection. She wants to know how you are doing. Adam and sons, those who are paying the penalty issued in the Garden [**wouldpay actionneers**], say that resurrection is worth its weight in the noblest. The HSS would like to be resurrected. Her hair is still beautiful. Repose you now. Die no more, that is be resurrected or freed from karmic rebirth.

With karma in the ether, Finnegan learns that a new man is on the premises, a new substitute for Adam and Finnegan, a new issue in the human substratum:

> [28] For, be that samesake sibsubstitute of a hooky salmon, there's
> 35

already a big rody ram lad at random on the premises of his
36
haunt of the hungred bordles, as it is told me.

The new man is a **sibsubstitute** for Finnegan, that is a sibling substitute as in primal horde succession. The salmon metaphor is used again. A **big rody ram lad** is on the premises. Rode means to clear a stream of weeds or in the case of a woodcock, a flight to designate breeding territory. The new rammer is on the premises of the woman, the haunt of the hungry bordles—the boundary of the bordel or brothel.

More information about the new man, downplaying his importance to avoid affront to Finnegan:

[29] Shop Illicit,
1
flourishing like a lordmajor or a buaboabaybohm, litting flop
2
a deadlop (aloose!) to lee but lifting a bennbranch a yar-
dalong
3
(Ivoeh!) the breezy side (for showm!), the height of Brew-
4
ster's chimpney and as broad below as Phineas Barnum; humph-
5
ing his share of the showthers is senken on him he's such a
6
grandfallar, with a pocked wife in pickle that's a flyfire and
three
7
lice nittle clinkers, two twilling bugs and one midgit pucelle.
8

His illegal drinking premises, illegal spirit house [**Shop Illicit**—compared to the legitimate church], is flourishing like an angel-major [Satan?] or a minor thunder house, a **bua boa bay bohm**—look out for the snake and the bay boom—death in the bay. He is a **litting flop**, a drunk fallen one, a **deadlop**, drooping or flopping in death to leeward, the opposite from which the wind comes from. He nonetheless lifts a blessed branch [cross] that puts the Devil to flight and is one yard long (oh joy!) toward the weather or breezy side [evil in the world]. This is the only thing for sure [**for showm**]—he is a showman, an individual. [Joyce considered Christ the ultimate individual.] The cross is the height of the Brester's chimpney, the spirit brewer's stack, and as broad at the base as the Barnum and Bailey circus. Christ was human to save our sins, so HCE already identified with Christ is humping his share of the show there on Calgary and his share of humanity is sinking on the cross—he is dying—he is such a **grandfallar** [a big fall and a grand individual]. HCE has a pocked wife in pickle—venereal disease as a metaphor for original sin—who lights up like a firefly [a minor reflection of Lillith's fire urine]. He has three nice lice [sin or nice infested with L for independence] infested little nittle **clinkers** for children—clinkers meaning dingleberries—fecal material caught in anal hair. Like the family of van hooter, he has two twin boys and one circus-like younger [**midgit**] virgin daughter.

And HCE has been cursed:

> [29] **And aither he cursed and recursed and was everseen doing what**
> 9
> **your fourfootlers saw or he was never done seeing what you cool-**
> 10
> **pigeons know, weep the clouds aboon for smiledown witnesses,**
> 11
> **and that'll do now about the fairyhees and the frailyshees.**
> 12

And either he was cursed and recursed and was always thought of as doing what the animals [**fourfootlers**] saw [sex in the Garden] or he was never done seeing what you stool pigeons [anti-Holy Spirit] know—seeing Eve with the serpent or evil and suffering in the world. Sweep-weep the clouds for witnesses to happiness [you won't find any]. And that will do in terms of fairy stories about male [**fairyhees**] and female [**frailyshees**—note the female is frail and fairy and shee combined].

Now for some Kabbalah:

> [29] **Though Eset fibble it to the zephiroth and Artsa zoom it round**
> 13
> **her heavens for ever. Creator he has created for his creatured**
> 14
> **ones a creation.**

Though Eve [**Eset** form of Isha and combination of Ein Sof and et, which is abbreviation for what comes after—et al] who set [**Eset**] us on this course bumbled the hand-off to the sephirot [spilled over] and as a result the arts-stars have been zooming round her heavens forever. The Creator has created for his creatures [non-god] a creation [similar words suggesting similar substance]. But what is it:

> [29] **White monothoid? Red theatrocrat? And all the**
> 15
> **pinkprophets cohalething? Very much so!**

Is it a white likeness [**oid**] of the one unity [**monoth**]—white unified light—or a red absolute ruler and supporters–red separated light? In other words, this asks the question whether we are absolutely separated from the ES godhead by TZTZ god. And are all of the prophets of pink [we are both separate/red and part/white of the godhead] coalescing [**cohalething**—suggests forgetting] and making whole? Yes, very much so!

Now a long ending sentence concluding with Eden. The runon nature of the sentence communicates the continuity of the human condition and predicament through time. I have split the sentence for interpretation:

> [29] **But however 'twas**
> 16
> **'tis sure for one thing, what sherif Toragh voucherfors and**
> 17
> **Mapqiq makes put out, that the man, Humme the Cheapner,**
> 18
> **Esc, overseen as we thought him, yet a worthy of the naym,**
> 19

However, there was one thing for sure [said in mixed up syntax suggesting less certainty], what the sheriff rule book Torah with rage [**Toragh**] is a voucher for and the Hebrew alphabet [**mappiq**—a dot over the letter HE for HCE] makes evident [**put out** like TZTZ creation] is that the man, Him Humme is the **Cheapner,** the corruptor [original sin]. In other words, mankind is responsible for its own predicament; mankind cheapened what it could have been. Escape is abbreviated as a title to Esc not Esq for esquire, having been overseen by god as we thought, yet worthy of the name Man the Cheapner.

[29] [Man the Cheapner] came at this timecoloured place
where we live in our paroqial
20
fermament one tide on another, with a bumrush in a hull of a
21
wherry,

Man came into the world colored by time where we live in our
paroquial fermament one tide of life on another, with a bumrush
[death] in a hell of a hurry [**hull of a wherry** mixed up because of
hurry]. Continuing the nautical context for the arrival of the powers
that be:

[29] the twin turbane dhow, *The Bey for Dybbling*, this
22
archipelago's first visiting schooner, with a wicklowpattern
23
waxenwench at her prow for a figurehead, the deadsea dugong
24
updipdripping from his depths,

On this tide of life comes the twin turbine-turban middleastern-
Arabian boat the dhow [suggesting de how], with god the father and
god the son the twin turbine engines. The dhow is known as *The
Bey for Dybbling*. That name suggests the Bay for Evil spirits—the
dybbuk. This was the first visiting schooner [schooner has two
masts] in this bay of evil. It had for its figurehead at the prow of the
ship a waxen woman in a wicklowpattern [wick was low, low light,
for a Holy Spirit without any power] the **deadsea dugong**—sirenian
or mermaid predecessor of the Sirens—up drip dripping from his
god's depths of the void and formless waters. In other words, the
Holy Spirit [the waxen woman] in this bay of evil is a mere figurehead. Since his arrival, god

[29] and has been repreaching him-
25
self like a fishmummer these siktyten years ever since, his
shebi
26
by his shide, adi and aid, growing hoarish under his turban
and
27

340

> changing cane sugar into sethulose starch (Tuttut's cess to
> him!)
> 28

And ever since then [Eden] god has been feeling guilty reproaching-
repreaching again and again to himself like a fishmonger through
each life of 70 years, his Eve-like woman likeness captive by his hide-
side, his help meet for ever more [*ade ad* in Hebrew], growing gray
with age under his **turban** [gray hair] and changing cane [Cain] sugar-
energy to kill into Seth you lose starch [**Sethulose**] and Tut's curse to
him.

> [29] as also that, batin the bulkihood he bloats about when
> innebbi-
> 29
> ated, our old offender was humile, commune and ensectuous
> 30
> from his nature,

So like Noah he TZTZ god bloats [floats boats] about when drunk,
our old offender was humble, communal and insect incestuous from
his nature. His characteristics are revealed in his names:

> [29] which you may gauge after the bynames was
> 31
> put under him, in lashons of languages, (honnein suit and
> 32
> praisers be!) and, totalisating him, even hamissim of hi-
> mashim
> 33
> that he, sober serious, he is ee and no counter he who will be
> 34
> ultimendly respunchable for the hubbub caused in Eden-
> 35
> borough.
> 36

And you can judge the nature of god by way of the names he received in many languages (honey sweets and praises for god) and,
summarizing him, even considering the curse of Ham by Noah, **even
hamissim of himashim** [the five fifths or the Pentateuch], that
when sober and serious [unlike Noah] **he is ee** [YHWH as I am
what I am] and on no count is he responsible or **respunchabe**
[strife] for the **hubbub** [love in Hebrew but also confused war cry]

caused in Edenborough, Eden town. In other words god is not responsible for the sex and violence among humans. Or the confusion
at Babel.

As you can tell, that dog don't hunt.

Chapter 1.2: Stealing Turf from the Gods

Chapter 2 of Part I starts off with a discussion about HCE's name, his **agnomen**, a name acquired by exploit. **Agnomen** breaks down into agno men, contest among men, and agony is not far away.

Built on his initials, his agnomen is "Here Comes Everybody." His family name is HC Earwicker, and this chapter is about the pressures on him to become just like everyone else, for HC Earwicker to become HCE. How the commonality HCE comes to be substituted for his individuality as Harold Earwicker. Note how initials compared to the full name suggest less individuation.

Sleep is when HC Earwicker becomes everybody, is trapped in the possibilities in the past. Note also how initials suggest initially, at the beginning and before in general. While awake, he has manifold new possibilities except that the crowd wants to restrict him.

Centered around the substitution of commonality for individuality, this chapter is full of examples of substitution, a much used dream technique. They range from substitution of living vicariously through others for living freely yourself, Eve acting for Adam, idols for god, young for the old, gossip for truth, homosexuality for heterosexuality, false for real teeth, plagiarism for creation, and half rather than full human creatures.

In a broader context, substitution has a role in the god/mankind relationship. With independence, the individual would substitute for TZTZ god. The dependent TZTZ god [notice the initials] is a substitution for ES. Adam and Eve sinned for us giving us death as their substitutes and Christ suffered for us, substituting himself to free us from death. Christ is the big substitution that gives a character named Hosty [the Host] an important place in this chapter. After Christ, the Ghost substitutes for the Host. G woman.

Homosexuality plays a considerable role in this chapter. Tied to dependence, it is treated as an aspect of sterility. It produces no new possibilities, only dry eroticism. Christ's decision not to marry is treated roughly in terms of the anal preferences of Hosty. The emphasis on the anus takes us back to TZTZ creation as an elimination from god's back side.

The crowd takes Harold down with a Ballad, a Ballad composed by Hosty and sung by the crowd. The Ballad is a kind of substitution, about how HC Earwicker's own park experience brought him down. The Ballad is designed to make him more sensitive to the opinions of others, to be less independent. The next chapter records his trial and incarceration, the limitation of his freedom. The Ballad is created by one Hosty, whose name suggests both the Host/Eucharist/God and the enemy [hostis—the enemy] [Tindall].

First, to set the table, the initial story relating to HC Earwicker. This story is in the form of a myth, that is with believable specifics. It is not about Harold in Dublin. Like the Garden of Eden myth, it is about Harold in soul-space. In this story, he is independent, even in an interaction with TZTZ god. The initial story tells of Harold Earwicker as a turnpiker, one who is responsible for maintenance of part of a road and collecting tolls at a barrier. TZTZ god makes the soul road to ES god a turnpike rather than a freeway.

Harold is in **prefall paradise peace** gardening away [as Adam was instructed to do]. Royalty [read TZTZ god] was out fox hunting and noticed potholes in the road Harold was responsible for—which is called the causeway, suggesting god as the first cause. Intending initially to ask a question about the potholes on the causeway, the King substitutes another question to ask Harold instead—what lures are currently favored for lobster trapping. Like god's question in the Garden of Eden about who told you were naked, this is a loaded "trap" question. Lobster is reserved for royalty. If Harold answers the question about lobster lures, then the King would know that Harold has been after lobsters, has been violating the rules and after god food [as Eve and Adam did with the food from the Knowledge Tree]. Note that the King does not ask Harold what he as an individual is using for lures, but what is favored by the group. Now we would say, what is the hot lure? This form of question "gives the King away."

Harold replies in an independent spirit. He replies not to the question asked about lobster lures but to the intended question about the potholes. Interdependent with TZTZ god, he knows TZTZ god's mind. He answers that he had been digging in the turnpike as well as his own garden in order to capture earwickers, the general symbol for the Holy Spirit. This would represent an independent approach to god. Harold has been looking for the love of god by himself.

Earwickers are like lobsters in that they have pincers, but the earwicker pincers are at the tail end not in front. These pincers suggest sex, which in Joyce's view is the minimum activity of the Holy Spirit on earth when the father and son are not in charity. Since the father and son gods have not spirated the Holy Spirit, humans must find her themselves. Lures for lobster trapping suggest living life under an organized religion in which lobsters as far as eating is concerned are reserved for royal church officials and for others, the faithful, serve to grab and pinch—that is limit the faithful.

Told as a redeux of the GE story, this is a question of moving in on the turf of the gods, the causeway, in order to look for the Holy Spirit, which is what god is supposed to provide. This is like what Eve tried to do in the garden by becoming god-like. TZTZ god doesn't like independent subjects so the rest of the chapter is about the pressures on Earwicker to become HCE, just like everyone else—dependent and fearful.

So with the table set, we start this chapter with actors. This presents the substitution theme, living secondarily through actors who themselves are free spirits, "idolizing" the actors. Living through others is part of being dependent.

Now to **forebare** or bare the front part as the naked Adam and as Eve did in the Garden [**forebare** punning on forbearers]:

> **[30] Now (to forebare for ever solittle of Iris Trees and Lili O'Ran-**
> **1**
> **gans), concerning the genesis of Harold or Humphrey Chimp-**
> **2**
> **den's occupational agnomen (we are back in the presur-**
> **names**
> **3**
> **prodromarith period, of course just when enos chalked hall-**
> **traps)**
> **4**

Now concerning the genesis of Harold or Humphrey Chimpden's occupational agnomen [Here Comes Everybody]. We are dealing with or baring or revealing so little of the actress Iris Trees [trees in Garden] or Lili O'Rangans [Lillith]. These two are substitutes for Eve. Iris Tree was a poet, painter and actress from Wales who lived the independent life of an artist. This is for this chapter the first instance of idolatry, that is worshipping independent actors rather than living your own independent life, substituting their life for yours.

That is to say, we are concentrating just on Adam, the other one in the Garden story, the voyeur who Eve acted for and who just passively followed her lead. He did not try to be god-like himself. But we are going to give him **ever solittle** independence, just a little of Eve's independence.

We are back in the **presurnames prodromarith** period, when people like Adam didn't have surnames but were forerunners, when Enos [Enosh son of Seth and a magician who encouraged idolatry] chalked **halltraps**, preparation for lobster traps and perhaps magic circles. Magic is a substitute for reality.

The story of Enosh the magician and idolatry is as follows. Questioned by the crowd who wanted to be told how god made man, Enosh apparently blew life into a creature made of clay but in fact Satan entered the clay. The crowd questioned the difference between bowing down before this image and paying homage to a man. Thus began idolatry [bowing down before the image or to men were the only two choices]. According to the Jewish Legends, this idolatrous generation resembled centaurs and apes, poor substitutes for humans. This is because at the time of Enosh and idolatry, the Shekhinah who had remained behind in the Garden of Eden under the Tree of Life left the earth and ascended into heaven. Idolatry drove her out.

Going on in the ancestral search for HCE:

> **[30] and discarding once for all those theories from older sources which**
> **5**
> **would link him back with such pivotal ancestors as the Glues, the**
> **6**
> **Gravys, the Northeasts, the Ankers and the Earwickers of Sidles-**
> **7**
> **ham in the Hundred of Manhood or proclaim him offsprout of**
> **8**
> **vikings who had founded wapentake and seddled hem in Herrick**
> **9**
> **or Eric, the best authenticated version, the Dumlat, read the**
> **10**
> **Reading of Hofed-ben-Edar, has it that it was this way.**

The Glues, Gravys, Northeasts, Ankers and Earwickers are tombstone names in the Churchyard at Sidle**sham**, where tombstones substitute for the dead but do provide the tapestry for dreams. These shams are to be discarded as Harold's ancestors as are the Vikings, the **wapentake** [wop and the taker ones] who settled in Herrick or

346

Eric. Family tradition is a false idol compared to genuine individuality. The best version of the relevant past [at least in sleep mentality] is the Talmud [backwards as **Dumlat** as in right to left Hebrew and concerning detailed rules for living the dependent life] and the reading of Hofed-ben-Edar [son of head].

Here now is the turnpiker story:

> [30] We are
> 11
> told how in the beginning it came to pass that like cabbaging
> 12
> Cincinnatus the grand old gardener was saving daylight under his
> 13
> redwoodtree one sultry sabbath afternoon, Hag Chivychas Eve,
> 14
> in prefall paradise peace by following his plough for rootles in the
> 15
> rere garden of mobhouse, ye olde marine hotel,

Cincinnatus was a Roman who assumed dictatorship while danger lasted but then went back to his own plowing. He was, in other words, the dictator of himself rather than others. **Cabbage** in this sense means to purloin or steal from tailors. In the Norwegian captain story, the tailor represents TZTZ god. Cabbaging would increase independence, shorten the garment of the TZTZ spirit, the spirit of dependence. Harold is about to cabbage from royalty, to try to find the Holy Spirit himself. He is saving daylight [Holy Ghost or Shekhinah or ES as light] by looking for the earwiggers himself. He is the **grand old gardener** [GOG], since Adam was instructed to till the Garden.

He is plowing on the Sabbath, which is forbidden by the Talmud, the book of dependency, so he is showing signs of independence from the rules. This takes place on **Hag Chivychas Eve,** a reference to a border dispute known as Chevy Chase, as our story is also a dispute about the border between god and mankind. He Harold is in **prefall paradise peace** ploughing behind his **mobhouse**, the old marine hotel [Norwegian Captain story]. He is ploughing for **rootles** [rootlessness shortened to rootless and further shortened to **rootles** to suggest the rootless condition itself]. That is, he is seeking roots or a connection to something deeper than TZTZ god; he is seeking the Holy Spirit of ES god.

He is plowing to turn up earwiggers, which as they fly up he catches with flower pots turned upside down. The Holy Spirit is like flowers. The key to the story is what is assumed but left out—that in addition to plowing in his own garden [that is his own spirit or life] he has been plowing on the royal causeway road [relation of god to mankind] and making potholes for the same purpose. Perhaps in myth language this omission suggests plowing in your own garden is the same as plowing in the royal causeway road.

Royalty arrives:

> [30] when royalty was
> 16
> announced by runner to have been pleased to have halted it-
> self on
> 17
> the highroad along which a leisureloving dogfox had cast fol-
> 18
> lowed, also at walking pace, by a lady pack of cocker span-
> iels.

Royalty is announced by a runner, a prophet, a substitute. Royalty have stopped because they wanted to. They have been on the highroad following a dogfox. Presumably they are hunting the **dogfox,** the patriarch of the fox group. Dog for dependent, fox for independent. Royalty is followed not by hunting dogs [who can chase independently] but a lady pack of cocker spaniels, with the emphasize on cock and dependence on the owner. In other words, Royalty is out hunting anything even partially independent with its own pack of dependent dogs.

Notified of the presence of royalty, Harold runs around to the front of his house in his ploughing outfit—he doesn't change to indicate respect for authority. He doesn't try to make a good impression:

> [30] For-
> 19
> getful of all save his vassal's plain fealty to the ethnarch Humphrey
> 20
> or Harold stayed not to yoke or saddle but stumbled out hot-
> face

348

21

as he was (his sweatful bandanna loose from his pocketcoat) hast-

22

ing to the forecourts of his public in topee, surcingle, solas-carf and

23

plaid, plus fours, puttees and bulldog boots ruddled cinnabar with

24

[31] flagrant marl, jingling his turnpike keys and bearing aloft amid

1

the fixed pikes of the hunting party a high perch atop of which a

2

flowerpot was fixed earthside hoist with care.

Forgetful of all except his duty to the provincial ruler [ethnarch—note like TZTZ god the ethnarch is not the absolute ruler but just of a province], Humphrey stumbled out sweating as he was, his sweat wicking bandanna casually loose from his coat. He came around in front of his house wearing his pith helmet, band, sun scarf, plus fours knickerbockers, cloth wound round the legs and boots covered with cinnabar. Red brick reminds us of the materials from which Adam was made, fragrant clay. He has his turnpike keys that open the barrier on the toll road causeway, each of us having his own key. The tolls are the cost of going back to ES and the Tree of Life.

Most unusually, Harold carries **aloft,** as Finnegan did his hod, a flowerpot turned up side down. The text doesn't say what he uses to bear aloft the flowerpot, the flower pot used to catch earwiggers. Presumably some kind of pole. It gives a high perch, such as a higher place for a bird to land or rest on. This language together with earwig suggests the Holy Spirit, catching the Holy Spirit with an earwigger, the symbol of sex. His flowerpot shows among the fixed and sharp-ended pikes standing tall from the hunting party. Harold raises the Holy Spirit to the King's men who raise pikes of war.

Now his majesty:

[31] On his majesty, who

3

was, or often feigned to be, noticeably longsighted from green

4

youth and had been meaning to inquire what, in effect, had caused
5
yon causeway to be thus potholed, asking substitutionally to be
6
put wise as to whether paternoster and silver doctors were not
7
now more fancied bait for lobstertrapping honest blunt Harom-
8
phreyld answered in no uncertain tones very similarly with a fear-
9
less forehead: Naw, yer maggers, aw war jist a cotchin on thon
10
bluggy earwuggers.

His majesty was or pretended to be **longsighted**, so he couldn't see things close up. This is because of a **green youth**. You remember that post-fall God asks Adam and Eve hiding in the greenery "Where are you," so presumably God can't see them up close. So because longsighted his majesty, who intended to inquire about the potholes in the turnpike, instead **substitutionally** [our theme] asks whether **paternoster** or **silver doctors** were favored for lobster trapping. Lobster with the front claws meant for attack. These traps are organized religion TZTZ style. Paternoster lures are a picture of the curse, a fishing line with hooks and weights at intervals [hooking you and keeping you down].

This question is a trick question, a trap or curse based question, because lobster is reserved for royalty. Royalty is asking Harold if he is trapping lobsters against the rules for little people—as Adam/Eve was told not to eat the fruit from the Knowledge Tree which would make them god-like. **Haromphreyld** [Ha romp freed or free spirit] addresses the King familiarly as your **maggers** and answers with honesty and confidence that he was not after lobster but just chasing **bluggy earwuggers**. Capturing the earwigs would be finding the Holy Spirit who is missing and hiding in the damp earth, the earth that ES made wet with fresh water from below. They would not be good for lobster trapping. Harold's answer does not totally satisfy the King:

[31] Our sailor king, who was draining a gugglet
11
of obvious adamale, gift both and gorban, upon this, ceasing to
12
swallow, smiled most heartily beneath his walrus moustaches and
13
indulging that none too genial humour which William the Conk
14
on the spindle side had inherited with the hereditary white-lock
15
and some shortfingeredness from his greataunt Sophy, turned to-
16
wards two of his retinue of gallowglasses, Michael, etheling lord
17
of Leix and Offaly and the jubilee mayor of Drogheda, El-cock,
18
(the two scatterguns being Michael M. Manning, protosyn-dic of
19
Waterford and an Italian excellency named Giubilei accord-ing to
20
a later version cited by the learned scholarch Canavan of Can-
21
makenoise), in either case a triptychal religious family sym-bolising
22
puritas of doctrina, business per usuals and the purchypatch of
23
hamlock where the paddish preties grow and remarked dil-sydul-
24
sily: Holybones of Saint Hubert how our red brother of Pour-
25
ingrainia would audibly fume did he know that we have for sur-
26

trusty bailiwick a turnpiker who is by turns a pikebailer no
sel-
27
domer than an earwigger

The **sailor king** [Norwegian Captain and William IV] is draining a glass of **adamale,** a combination of Adam and ale or Adam's spirit. Draining adamale is TZTZ god's usual role of death, draining fresh water or the human spirit of life. In response to Harold's forthright reply about the earwiggers, the King smiles but his humour is **none too genial.** In other words, he is not entirely pleased with Harold's independent attitude, an attitude he inherited from William the Conqueror [**Conk**] and Gladstone [**shortfineredness**] and Parnell. The king turns to two of his retinue of **gallowglasses,** heavily armed soldiers or death glasses, Michael and Giubelei. The Archangel Michael is the **Eheling lord of Leix and Offaly and the jubilee mayor of Drogneda**, all sites of military devastation and offal, Michael being a warrior. Giubilei is Italian for Jubilees, the festival of forgiveness. Together they make a triptych like the Trinity [Michael as son/Christ and Giubilei as HSS] representing true doctrine and business as usual with the hemlock of priests or like the two lines of stern sefirots and merciful sefirots with a combined line in the middle.

The King says to his retinue, to his true believers: Our red brother satan of **Pouringrainia**—pouring rainia or the curse of the flood—would be angry if he knew that we have for a trusty turnpiker one who is a earwigger as often as he is a pikebailer. To the King this use of time is independent disobedience because Harold is supposed to be just a pikebailer, that is just maintain the causeway. He is not supposed to be making potholes in the toll way. Maintaining the king's highway is to work for another. Catching earwigs is his own business, his independent business. The King is saying Harold looks for earwigs when he is on the causeway rather than taking care of it. The King says satan would be angry if he knew the avatar of mankind was independent part of the time and looking for the Holy Spirit.

Note that Harold apparently has not caught any earwiggers yet. For a timely reminder about earwiggers From Wikipedia:

> Earwig is the common name given to the insect order Dermaptera characterized by membranous wings folded underneath short leathery forewings (hence the literal name of the order—"skin

wings"). The abdomen extends well beyond the wings, and frequently, though not always, ends in a pair of forceps-like cerci. With about 1,800 recorded species in 10 families, the order is relatively small among Insecta. Earwigs are, however, quite common globally. There is no evidence that they transmit disease or otherwise harm humans or other animals, despite their nickname *pincher bug*.

Earwig may also be used as a verb to mean: "to fill the mind with prejudice by insinuations" or "to attempt to influence by persistent confidential argument or talk".[1]

The name *earwig* comes from Old English *eare* "ear" and *wicga* "insect". It is related to the fanciful notion that earwigs burrow into the brains of humans through the ear and therein lay their eggs.[2] This belief, however, is false. Nevertheless, being exploratory and omnivorous, earwigs probably do crawl into the human ear; even if they are only looking for a humid crevice in which to hide, such behavior provides a memorable basis for the name.[3]

Earwigging - also known as eavesdropping - means to overhear another's conversation.

False rumors and eavesdropping are coming up, poor substitutes for self-revealed truth for the independent man. The Ballad is designed for earwigging, to fill the mind of the crowd that hears it with prejudice by insinuations.

Back to the story. The fall out from this confrontation is the possibility of dung on the causeway:

> [31] **For he kinned Jom Pill with his court**
> **28**
> **so gray and his haunts in his house in the mourning. (One still**
> **29**
> **hears that pebble crusted laughta, japijap cheerycherrily, among**
> **30**
> **the roadside tree the lady Holmpatrick planted and still one feels**
> **31**
> **the amossive silence of the cladstone allegibelling: Ive mies outs ide Bourn.)**
> **32**

The first description of the confrontation between Harold and Royalty is phrased in terms of the song *John Peel*:

D'ye ken John Peel and his coat so gay? (or grey)
D'ye ken John Peel at the break of day?
D'ye ken John Peel when he's far, far away?
Or his hounds and his horn in the morning?
For the sound of his horn brought me from my bed,
And the cry of his hounds which he oftime led,
Peel's "View, Halloo!" could awaken the dead,
Or the fox from his lair in the morning.
Yes, I ken John Peel and his Ruby, too!
Ranter and Ringwood, Bellman so true!
From a find to a check, from a check to a view,
From a view to a kill in the morning.

Like TZTZ god, John Peel kills the independent fox for fun. Remember the story of King Mark catching the lovers having pretended to go hunting. Ken means to be able to see or know. Given the man-god-man interdependence in K, ken becomes kin. John Peel becomes **Jom Pill.** Instead of hunting he is haunting in the mourning, focusing on death. (One still hears laughter from the roadside tree that Lady Hompatrick—hollypatrick—planted and is pebble crusted. The laughter is **japijap cheerycherrily,** that is to say like Japanese cherry blossoms—Quinet's flowers. One also feels the silence of the **cladstone allegibelling,** a reference to Gladstone and **Giubilei,** one of the King's retinue representing the HSS who is silent. Clad stone suggests clad in stone. The silent stone is not glad—as it is turning black in the midst of sin merde. **Ive mies outs ide Bourn**—I have missed out since I was born [result of secondary living].)

For more on Mr. Gladstone, we can thank Wikipedia:

> **William Ewart Gladstone** (29 December 1809 – 19 May 1898) was a British Liberal Party statesman and Prime Minister (1868–74, 1880–85, 1886 and 1892–94).
>
> Gladstone is famous for his intense rivalry with Benjamin Disraeli, who rose to become the Conservative Party Leader. The rivalry was not only political, but also personal. When Disraeli died, Gladstone proposed a state funeral, but Disraeli's will asked for him to be buried next to his wife, to which Gladstone replied, "As [Disraeli] lived, so he died — all display, without reality or genuineness." Disraeli, for his part, said that GOM (which stood for Grand Old Man, Gladstone's nickname), really stood for "God's Only Mistake".

The British statesman was famously at odds with Queen Victoria for much of his career. She once complained "He always addresses me as if I were a public meeting." Gladstone was known affectionately by his supporters as the "Grand Old Man" or "The People's William". He is still regarded as one of the greatest British prime ministers, with Winston Churchill and others citing Gladstone as their inspiration.

He also opposed Papal Infallibility.

Continuing with the (material),

> [31] Comes the question are these the facts of his nom-
> 33
> inigentilisation as recorded and accolated in both or either of the
> 34
> collateral andrewpaulmurphyc narratives. Are those their fata
> 35
> which we read in sibylline between the *fas* and its *nefas*? No dung
> 36
>
> [32] on the road? And shall Nohomiah be our place like? Yea, Mulachy
> 1
> our kingable khan? We shall perhaps not so soon see.

Then comes the question whether these are the facts of his clan naming as recorded and counted [**accolated** not accoladed as in making a knight] in both or either of the collateral anthropomorphic [**andrewpaulmurphyc** for Andrew Paul Murphy] narratives—the two sibylline oracles? Are those their fates which we read in sibylline between the possible and right vis a vis the impossible and wrong. Is true independence possible? **No dung on the road?** And shall our place, our independence, be like the Jerusalem Nehemiah rebuilt? That is the small temple built after return from exile, small compared to the original temple the independent Solomon built. Who shall be our King? Dependence or independence. We shall perhaps not so soon see.

Now the language goes more creative and the narrator puts aside the fallacy that is was not the King but just some angels who came down to earth to copulate with human women [next story after Enosh in Jewish Legends]. This tale is staged as the two storytellers in the Thousand Nights and One Night:

[32] Pinck

2

poncks that bail for seeks alicence where cumsceptres with scen-

3

taurs stay. Bear in mind, son of Hokmah, if so be you have me-

4

theg in your midness, this man is mountain and unto changeth

5

doth one ascend.

This asks for freedom [bail and license—in the 1001 Tale freedom from death] to make a connection with the gods, but not just any connection. Idols are bad connections with the gods as are half-way creatures [**scentaurs**—they smell like tar]. Idols are half way to god and creatures are half way to mankind. Translating: Elemental spirits pong that bail bell seeking a license where cum sceptris with scepters [and a suggestion of conception by the Holy Ghost, a god connection] with centaurs stay [centaurs—half human and half horse and in general border creatures]. Bear in mind, son of Hokmah, the sefirot of divine wisdom, if you have truth in your gut and are thinking of control of passions [**metheg**—horse bridle] this man is a mountain who ascends by changing, by new possibilities [**unto changeth doth one ascend**].

The Legends of the Jews records bad connections with the gods during the period of the 10 Generations:

> SETH AND HIS DESCENDANTS The exhortations of the wives of Lamech took effect upon Adam. After a separation of one hundred and thirty years, he returned to Eve, and the love he now bore her was stronger by far than in the former time. She was in his thoughts even when she was not present to him bodily. *** Thus Seth became, in a genuine sense, the father of the human race, especially the father of the pious, while the depraved and godless are descended from Cain. Even during the lifetime of Adam the descendants of Cain became exceedingly wicked, dying successively, one after another, each more wicked than the former. They were intolerable in war, and **vehement in robberies**, and if anyone were slow to murder people, yet was he bold in his profligate behavior in acting unjustly and doing injury for gain.
>
> ENOSH Enosh was asked who his father was, and he named Seth. The questioners, the people of his time, continued: "Who

was the father of Seth?" Enosh: "Adam." "And who was the father of Adam? " " He had neither father nor mother, God formed him from the dust of the earth." "But man has not the appearance of dust ! " "After death man returns to dust, as God said, ' And man shall turn again unto dust;' but on the day of his creation, man was made in the image of God." "How was the woman created?" "Male and female He created them." "But how? " "God took water and earth, and moulded them together in the form of man." "But how?" pursued the questioners. Enosh took six clods of earth, mixed them, and moulded them, and formed an image of dust and clay. "But," said the people, "this image does not walk, nor does it possess any breath of life." He then essayed to show them how God breathed the breath of life into the nostrils of Adam, but when he began to blow his breath into the image he had formed, Satan entered it, and the figure walked, and the people of his time who had been inquiring these matters of Enosh went astray after it, saying, "What is the difference between bowing down before this image and paying homage to a man?""

The generation of Enosh were thus the first **idol worshippers**, and the punishment for their folly was not delayed long. God caused the sea to transgress its bounds, and a portion of the earth was flooded. This was the time also when the mountains became rocks, and the dead bodies of men began to decay. And still another consequence of the sin of idolatry was that the countenances of the men of the following generations were no longer in the likeness and image of God, as the countenances of Adam, Seth, and Enosh had been. They resembled **centaurs and apes**, and the demons lost their fear of men. [emphasis added]

Out of this story of the many activities of the bad descendants of Cain, Joyce selects robbers, given the affinity of robbery with dependence on others. Idol worship led to half-way creatures. More of actors-idols:

> [32] Heave we aside the fallacy, as punical as finikin,
> 6
> that it was not the king kingself but his inseparable sisters, un-
> 7
> controllable nighttalkers, Skertsiraizde with Donyahzade, who
> 8
> afterwards, when the robberers shot up the socialights,
> 9

These giants were the robberers who shot up the **socialights**, the Shekhinah being the light for all [**when the robberers shot up the socialights, came down into the world as amusers**]:

> ***But there was a still more serious consequence from the idolatrous practices introduced in the time of Enosh. When God drove Adam forth from Paradise, the Shekhinah remained behind, enthroned above a cherub under the tree of life. The angels descended from heaven and repaired thither in hosts, to receive their instructions, and Adam and his descendants sat by the gate to bask in the splendor of the Shekhinah, sixty-five thousand times more radiant than the splendor of the sun. This brightness of the Shekhinah makes all upon whom it falls exempt from disease, and neither insects nor demons can come nigh unto them to do them harm. Thus it was until the time of Enosh, when men began to gather gold, silver, gems, and pearls from all parts of the earth, and made idols thereof a thousand parasangs high. What was worse, by means of the magic arts taught them by the angels Uzza and Azzael, they set themselves as masters over the heavenly spheres, and forced the sun, the moon, and the stars to be subservient to themselves instead of the Lord [prediction by astronomy]. This impelled the angels to ask God: "What is man, that Thou art mindful of him?' Why didst Thou abandon the highest of the heavens, the seat of Thy glory and Thy exalted Throne in 'Arabot, and descend to men, who pay worship to idols, putting Thee upon a level with them? "The Shekhinah was induced to leave the earth and ascend to heaven, amid the blare and flourish of the trumpets of the myriads of angel hosts."

Back to the fallacy. Put aside the fallacy, as treacherous as is the end of kin [**punical as finikin**], that it was not the king kingself on the causeway [to avoid saying himself] but his inseparable sisters, those uncontrollable nighttalkers, Skirtsheraised with Downyahad. In the Thousand Nights and One Night sisters Shahrzad and Dunyazad told stories in order to prevent the sacrifice of one of his many wives [perhaps the story tellers] by King Shahryar.

This material refers to one of the least discussed aspects of the god/mankind relationship, that described in Gen. 6:1:

> And it came to pass, when men began to multiply on the face of the earth, and daughters were born unto them. That the sons of the gods saw the daughters of men that they were fair and they took them wives of all who they chose.

Right after this, the "Eternal" limits man to 120 years. Now this miscegenation is a clear case of substitution, of angels for human males. The FW text looks past the angels to TZTZ god in this incident. Like other substitutions, this one also leads to bad results.

The Legends give us more details. The mating angels were led by Azazel and Shemhazai. They mated with human women leaving as their offspring evil giants on the earth.

> Two hundred angels descended to the summit of Mount Hermon, which owes its name to this very occurrence, because they bound themselves there to fulfill their purpose, on the penalty of Herem, anathema. Under the leadership of twenty captains they defiled themselves with the daughters of men, unto whom they taught charms, conjuring formulas, how to cut roots, and the efficacy of plants. The issue from these mixed marriages was a race of giants, three thousand ells tall, who consumed the possessions of men. When all had vanished, and they could obtain nothing more from them, the giants turned against men and devoured many of them, and the remnant of men began to trespass against the birds, beasts, reptiles, and fishes, eating their flesh and drinking their blood. Then the earth complained about the impious evil-doers.

Going on. The giant robbers who shot up the socialights in the theater:

> **[32] came down
> 9
> into the world as amusers and were staged by Madame Sudlow
> 10
> as Rosa and Lily Miskinguette in the pantalime that two pitts
> 11
> paythronosed, Miliodorus and Galathee.**

The amusement and staging refers to the Angels teaching tricks. They were staged by **Madame Sudlow** [means filth or mulch] **as Rosa and Lily Miskinguette** [you missed the King] in the pantomime that **two pitts paythronosed, Miliodorus and Galathee**— two pitts [theater pits and Prime Minister Pitts] paid through the nose—Miliodorus 1000 gifts and bad odor and Galilee [Jesus paid for you, a gala for thee]. The tricks taught by these angels:

> But the fallen angels continued to corrupt mankind. Azazel taught men how to make slaughtering knives, arms, shields, and coats of

mail. He showed them metals and how to work them, and armlets and all sorts of trinkets, and the use of rouge for the eyes, and how to beautify the eyelids, and how to ornament themselves with the rarest and most precious jewels and all sorts of paints. The chief of the fallen angels, Shembazai, instructed them in exorcisms and how to cut roots; Armaros taught them how to raise spells; Barakel, divination from the stars; Kawkabel, astrology; Ezekeel, augury from the clouds; Arakiel, the signs of the earth; Samsaweel, the signs of the sun; and Seriel, the signs of the moon.

From Humphriad:

> The "pantalime" (FW32.11) is of course a pantomime where the performers are "in the limelight", a reference to the old fashioned form of light produced by a blow-pipe flame against a block of quicklime, which will reveal their underwear (panties).

> The "two pitts paythronosed" (FW32.11-12) are two Prime Ministers of England, William Pitt, First Earl of Chatham (the Elder) (1708-78) a great war minister and his son William Pitt (the Younger) (1759-1806) a great economic reformer, who here "pay through the nose" (are overcharged) to patronise the performance. Two "pits" = the two girls' vaginas. Also, the pit in a theatre is its ground floor and is also a collective term for the audience there. The entrance fee may be "two bits" (a bit = American twelve and a half cent coin, and "two bits" is a common American expression for cheapness, contradicting "pay through the nose."

So now with the risks of idols and substitutes clearly in mind, we reexamine Harold Earwicker and the pressures to become HCE, just like everyone else:

[32] The great fact emerges
12
that after that historic date all holographs so far exhumed ini-
13
tialled by Haromphrey bear the sigla H.C.E. and while he was
14
only and long and always good Dook Umphrey for the hunger-
15
lean spalpeens of Lucalizod and Chimbers to his cronies it was
16

equally certainly a pleasant turn of the populace which gave him
17
as sense of those normative letters the nickname Here Comes
18
Everybody.
19

In this material, Here Comes Everybody is in the image of TZTZ god, the god that is interdependent with mankind. HCE is the idol, the substitute for individuality—be like everyone else.

Translating: The great fact is that all holographs exhumed after the historic date when angels mated with human females that bear the initials of **Haromphrey** bear the **sigla H.C.E.** Holographs are written solely in the long hand of one person and signed by the same. In other words, all potential individuals were buried by the forces of HCE, dependency and fear particularly in death. This is indicated by the mark of the sigla H.C.E. which is not only not a signature [more like a seal] but also not his name. This process, the reduction of man by god, is marked by lack of charity. For the down and outers, HCE/TZTZ god was known as **Dook Umprhey**, meaning no free dinner was available at his place. From the Humphriad:

> This derives from the common saying : "to dine out with Duke Humphrey" meaning to go hungry (McHugh), suggesting HCE as commercial exploiter is uncharitable to those he has helped to impoverish.

TZTZ god is uncharitable, and he is Childers to his cronies. There was a politician named H.C.E. Childers. From Wikipedia:

> Hugh Culling Eardley Childers (25 June 1827 – 29 January 1896) was a British and Australian Liberal statesman of the nineteenth century. He is perhaps best known for being the politician responsible for the sinking of HMS *Captain* and for his damaging 'reforms' at the Admiralty. However he had other failures. At the War Office he made budget cuts in the period before the First Boer War. As Chancellor of the Exchequer he made a failed attempt to convert Consols, and his attempt to correct a budget shortfall led to the fall of the government.

The ship named the Captain was lost due to lack of stability resulting from its improper design. The Captain being lost suggests the loss of

361

independence. Childers was called Here Comes Everyone because of his large girth. He was fat but stingy with others. Just like TZTZ god.

Now for a description of HCE/TZTZ god in the theatre of life, the theatre of idolatry under the TZTZ god who caused the royal divorce:

> **[32] An imposing everybody he always indeed looked,**
> **19**
> **constantly the same as and equal to himself and magnifi-**
> **cently well**
> **20**
> **worthy of any and all such universalisation, every time he**
> **con-**
> **21**
> **tinually surveyed, amid vociferatings from in front of** *Accept*
> *these*
> **22**
> *few nutties!* **and** *Take off that white hat!,* **relieved with** *Stop*
> *his Grog*
> **23**
> **and** *Put It in the Log* **and** *Loots in his* **(bassvoco)** *Boots,*
> **from good**
> **24**
> **start to happy finish the truly catholic assemblage gathered**
> **together**
> **25**
> **in that king's treat house of satin alustrelike above floats and**
> **foot-**
> **26**
> **lights . . .**

So in this theater HCE/TZTZ god appears to be an imposing everybody worthy of being universalized. He was constantly equal to himself, since he is interdependent with humanity. Particularly when he surveyed humanity in the Theater amid cries from the performers on stage doing TZTZ god's bidding—**amid vociferatings from in front of** [from the stage, TZTZ god's stage would be the church] to accept the blessing of fertility and very little else and take off that white hat—in other words don't try to be too much. On behalf of HCE/TZTZ god the performers also say stop his spirit and have him dead [*Stop his Grog* **and** *Put It in the Log* **and** *Loots in his* **(bassvoco)** *Boots*]. He surveyed from start to finish a mixed assemblage gathered together in the theater featuring satin curtains above floats [floods] and footlights [small lights not like ES].

So what did they see there in that theater:

[32] from their assbawlveldts and oxgangs unanimously to clap-
27
plaud (the inspiration of his lifetime and the hits of their ca-
reers)
28
Mr Wallenstein Washington Semperkelly's immergreen tour-
ers
29
in a command performance by special request with the cour-
teous
30
permission for pious purposes the homedromed and
enliventh
31
performance of the problem passion play of the millentury,
running
32
strong since creation, *A Royal Divorce*, then near the approach
33
towards the summit of its climax, with ambitious interval
band
34
selections from *The Bo' Girl* and *The Lily* . . .

In the theater and out of and from their asphalt and plough land [from city and farm] they came unanimously to applaud clap the performance of Mr. Semperkelly's [always Kelly] **immergreen** [instead of evergreen] touring group—did not promise everlife only in life. The performance was of the play ***A Royal Divorce***, a play about the divorce of Napoleon but in our context about the divorce from the real god ES. This performance was given with permission **for pious purposes** only. The play is a **problem passion play of millentury**, passion because it features death and millentury since it has been going for thousands of years. Indeed it has been running strong since creation as recorded in Genesis. Between the acts there were selections from **The Bo' Girl**—that is Eve the girl who acted like a man—and **The Lily** or Lillith. The two independents provide relief between the acts just like entertainment independent of the main show.

So TZTZ god, the HCE force, sits regally in the theater in his booth in his fancy dress, his fancy dress meant to impress others:

[32] on all horserie show
35
command nights from his viceregal booth (his bossaloner is ceil-
36
[33] inged there a cuckoospit less eminent than the redritualhoods of
1
Maccabe and Cullen) where, a veritable Napoleon the Nth, our
2
worldstage's practical jokepiece and retired cecelticocommediant
3
in his own wise, this folksforefather all of the time sat, having the
4
entirety of his house about him, ...

At this horseshow kind of event on all command nights [when legally open like a pub] he is in his **viceregal booth**—the jurisdiction where vice rules. He is the boss alone [**bossaloner**-sounds like a dance] but his booth is appointed less eminently than the red-based ritual hoods [Little Red Riding Hood] of the Dublin Archbishops [the wolves]. There TZTZ god, a veritable Napoleon the Nth, a spiritual son of Napoleon, our practical joke for the world stage and retired sea salt Celt comedian, this folksforefather that is father for all folks, sat in the theater with the entire house around him. He was dressed:

[33] with the invariable broadstretched
5
kerchief cooling his whole neck, nape and shoulderblades and in
6
a wardrobe panelled tuxedo completely thrown back from a shirt
7
well entitled a swallowall, on every point far outstarching the
8

364

laundered clawhammers and marbletopped highboys of the pit
9
stalls and early amphitheatre.

He TZTZ god was dressed in a tuxedo with a shirt highly starched. As representative, he is formal and dressed to impress. More on the theater scene:

> [33] The piece was this: look at the lamps.
> 10
> The cast was thus: see under the clock. Ladies circle: cloaks may
> 11
> be left. Pit, prommer and parterre, standing room only. Habi-tuels
> 12
> conspicuously emergent.
> 13

The play is referred to as **the piece**, that is a fragment from TZTZ creation. The lights are dim. The players are referred to as the cast, as in cast in concrete, cast here in dependence and death. **Ladies circle** is where single ladies could meet and congregate. There they can leave their cloaks, which somehow refer to clock and coverings. The orchestra pit, the prompter hidden in the stage and **parterre**— seating in the back of the downstairs under the balcony. Standing room only under the balcony, in the graveyard. The overhang over the ladies will remind you of the punishment of Eve—he will be over you. "Par terre" suggests by terror in French, to remind us of TZTZ god curses as the big overhang. The regular goers are emerging conspicuously—the Church big-wig functionaries.

Now for more about TZTZ god, the HCE force:

> [33] A baser meaning has been read into these characters the literal
> 14
> sense of which decency can safely scarcely hint. It has been blur-
> 15
> tingly bruited by certain wisecrackers (the stinks of Mohorat are
> 16
> in the nightplots of the morning), that he suffered from a vile

17

disease. Athma, unmanner them! To such a suggestion the one
18

selfrespecting answer is to affirm that there are certain statements
19

which ought not to be, and one should like to hope to be able to
20

add, ought not to be allowed to be made.
21

Now TZTZ god's detractors read a vile disease into his initials [Have Crabs-lobster-Everywhere?] Perhaps this is because the Shekhinah is gone and anyone in her light was immune from disease. In Ulysses, syphilis was referred to as gpi, general paralysis of the insane. This has been bruited about by certain wisecrackers (the smell of tomorrow in the **nightplots of the morning**). This must refer to gossip in the morning about what happened the night before, gossip being part of the meaning of earwigger. God as breath athma, unmanner them.

His detractors [of TZTZ/HCE] have also charged him with annoying Welsh Fusiliers in Phoenix Park:

[33] **Nor have his detractors,**
21

who, an imperfectly warmblooded race, apparently conceive him
22

as a great white caterpillar capable of any and every enormity in
23

the calendar recorded to the discredit of the Juke and Kellikek
24

families, mended their case by insinuating that, alternately, he lay
25

at one time under the ludicrous imputation of annoying Welsh
26

fusiliers in the people's park. Hay, hay, hay! Hoq, hoq, hoq!
27
Faun and Flora on the lea love that little old joq.
28

With a reference to the great white caterpillar Oscar Wilde, we are
back to a charge of homosexuality, the buggering of Adam. The Juke
and Kellikek families were hereditary degenerates, which is what
homosexuals were considered at this time. Hay means alive. Hoq is
Hebrew for a law. He lay under for position [**he lay at one time
under the ludicrous imputation of annoying Welsh fusiliers**].
Joyce uses the Welsh Fusiliers here because as Wikipedia reports:

> Soldiers of this regiment were distinguishable by the unique fea-
> ture of the "flash", consisting of five overlapping black silk rib-
> bons (seven inches long for soldiers and nine inches long for offi-
> cers) on the back of the uniform jacket at neck level.[1] This is a
> legacy of the days when it was normal for soldiers to wear pigtails.
> In 1808, this practice was discontinued, but the RWF were serving
> in America when the order to discontinue the use of the flash was
> issued. Upon their return they decided to retain the ribbons with
> which the pigtail was tied, and were granted this special concession
> by the King. The Army Board attempted to remove the flash dur-
> ing the First World War citing the grounds that it would help the
> Germans identify which unit was facing them. The King refused,
> stating that "The enemy will never see the backs of the Royal
> Welch Fusiliers". As a fusilier regiment, the RWF wore a hackle,
> which consists of a plume of white feathers worn on headdress
> and mounted behind the cap-badge.

Joyce uses Hoq and Joq because the q looks like the pigtail. Men
with pigtails could be mistaken for females in the dark park-- **love
that little old joq**. Faun and Flora for creatures in the park. Here
Joyce treats TZTZ god as Satan in the Garden of Eden, Satan who
defiled Adam as well as Eve.

The narrator discounts this charge in the case of Earwicker:

> **[33] To anyone who**
> 28
> **knew and loved the christlikeness of the big cleanminded gi-
> ant**
> 29
> **H. C. Earwicker throughout his excellency long vicefreegal
> exis-**

30

tence the mere suggestion of him as a lustsleuth nosing for trou-

31

ble in a boobytrap rings particularly preposterous.

But anyone who knew and loved Harold as Christ-like and vice free would not believe he was a **lustsleuth** in the Park. Harold would not be looking for lust opportunities in the park. But like Adam, some kind of case against him lingers because of the testimony of one who was here to testify—this must be the prophet Jesus Christ:

Truth, beard

32

on prophet, compels one to add that there is said to have been

33

quondam (pfuit! pfuit!) some case of the kind implicating, it is

34

interdum believed, a quidam (if he did not exist it would be ne-

35

cessary quoniam to invent him) abhout that time stambuling ha-

36

[34] round Dumbaling in leaky sneakers with his tarrk record who

1

has remained topantically anonymos but (let us hue him Ab-dul-

2

lah Gamellaxarksky) was, it is stated, posted at Mallon's at the

3

instance of watch warriors of the vigilance committee and years

4

afterwards, cries one even greater, Ibid, a commender of the

5

frightful, seemingly, unto such as were sulhan sated, tropped head

6

(pfiat! pfiat!) waiting his first of the month froods turn for

7

> thatt chopp pah kabbakks alicubi on the old house for the
> charge-
> 8
> hard, Roche Haddocks off Hawkins Street.
> 9

As interpreted by the RCC, Christ was necessary to wash away sin, including original sin. Truth guaranteed by the beard on the prophet compels one to add that there was said to have been **quondam** [formerly] for some time (**pfuit! Pfuit!** he was he was really here, god on earth) it is **interdum** [sometimes believed], a **quidam** a certain one (paraphrasing Voltaire: If he did not exist it would be necessary to invent him) about that time stumbling around Dumbaling Dublin in leaky sneakers [snake sandals]. Notice all the dams and dums to announce this subject in Latin-based Catholic language. He the stumbler [carrying the cross] is with his tarrk record [family name] that has remained **topantically anonymous**, anonymous to the whole. That is no one knows Christ's family name, his foster-father Joseph's family name or his biological father Holy Spirit's family name. Let us color him Abdullah [Mohammad's father] Gemellazarksky [the old salmon]. It seems that one of the watch warriors of the vigilance committee [Peter at the Temple when Christ was questioned], a representative thereof [founder of the RCC], was outside Roche Haddocks restaurant waiting for his one free meal for the month— **chopp pah kabbakks alicubi.** This is a pork chop, forbidden by the Talmud so available for payment for vigilance. Peter is to become St. Peter the Christian who is not forbidden to eat pork. **Alicubi** because Islam also prohibits pork as body and spirit polluting. The cube in one's Ka'aba gets dirty.

Going on;

> **[34] Lowe, you blondy**
> 9
> **liar, Gob scene you in the narked place and she what's edith**
> **ar**
> 10
> **home defileth these boyles! There's a cabful of bash indeed**
> **in**
> 11
> **the homeur of that meal.**

Now speaking about the representative of the Vigilance Committee, Peter of the Catholic Church: he would be incented to report bad behavior, that is sin that you need the church to remove. Lowe, apparently his name, you are a blondy liar, that is yellow or fearful. The Gob [mouth or god] seen you in the naked and marked [combined as **narked,** nark as police spy] place, the park or Garden of Eden, and she what is edith [edit made feminine—menstruation] is at home defiles these boys. There is a cabful of bash [cabash or hitting] in the humor of that meal, menstruation. Perhaps referring to fellatio as a substitute for copulation during menstruation. The **homeur or** humor or home error of the meal is that she is using her germ filled mouth, not her unclean sex organ. She is eating his semen.

> [34] Slander, let it lie its flattest, has never
> 12
> been able to convict our good and great and no ordinary Southron
> 13
> Earwicker, that homogenius man, as a pious author called him, of
> 14
> any graver impropriety than that, advanced by some woodwards
> 15
> or regarders, who did not dare deny, the shomers, that they had,
> 16
> chin Ted, chin Tam, chinchin Taffyd, that day consumed their
> 17
> soul of the corn, of having behaved with ongentilmensky im-
> 18
> modus opposite a pair of dainty maidservants in the swoolth of
> 19
> the rushy hollow whither, or so the two gown and pinners plead-
> 20
> ed, dame nature in all innocency had spontaneously and about the
> 21
> same hour of the eventide sent them both but whose published
> 22
> combinations of silkinlaine testimonies are, where not dubiously
> 23

pure, visibly divergent, as wapt from wept, on minor points
touch-
24
ing the intimate nature of this, a first offence in vert or venison
25
which was admittedly an incautious but, at its wildest, a partial ex-
26
posure with such attenuating circumstances (garthen gad-
deth green
27
hwere sokeman brideth girling) as an abnormal Saint
Swithin's
28
summer and, (Jesses Rosasharon!) a ripe occasion to provoke
it.
29

From Wikipedia:

> *For the concept in Jewish law (Halakha) that restricts (or forbids) physical
> contact with a member of the opposite sex, see Shomer negiah.*
> A shomer (plural "Shomrim") in Halakha is a Jewish custodian.
> The law is in the Torah Sefer (book of) Shemos (Exodus) It is dis-
> cussed in the talmud in Nezikin, tractate Bava Kama.
> The prohibition of Negiah is attributed to several verses in
> Leviticus, 18:6 "None of you shall approach to any that is near of
> kin to him, to uncover their nakedness. I am the LORD." and
> 18:19: "Thou shalt not approach unto a woman to uncover her
> nakedness, as long as she is impure by her uncleanness."

Slander, let it lie [pun]. It has never been able to convict our good
and great Earwicker—who is no ordinary **Southron** southern native,
that **homogenius** [combines man genius and homogenous]—all the
same, of anything worse than that advanced by the shomers, who
were drunk, of having behaved ungentlemanly and immodestly [**on-
gentilmensky immodus**] just opposite a pair of dainty maidservants
who were in the **swoolth of the rushy hollow** in the park, a named
place in Phoenix Park. Swoolth suggesting swoon and swell. The
rushy hallow is the female sex organ.

That is to say, just as in the Garden of Eden, the two girls and
Harold were exposed to each other naked. Nature, the desire to uri-
nate and to procreate, had sent them. But their **silkinlaine testimo-**

nies are, where not dubiously pure, visibly divergent, as wapt from wept, on minor points touching the intimate nature of this. The testimony is not consistent about the intimate nature of this event. If Harold had had sex with both, neither would be a virgin. But one girl is still a virgin and one is not [Lillith and Eve]. About the silk sleeve covered by wool, the **silkinlaine testimonies** or female sex organ, when not pure virgin, is visibly separated by loss of hymen as wapt from wept. So their personal testimony was different on minor points. The first offense or loss of virginity, by Eve to the serpent, was in vert or innocence or venison [very soon], pursuant to the right of overlord to first sex with all retainers [TZTZ god with Eve]. This was only a partial exposure with such attenuating circumstances as a wet summer following a dry Saint Swithin's day and (Jesse Ross Hashanah—happy new year and happy new month of fertility) a ripe occasion to provoke it.

Then a narrator interlude about the need for females:

> **[34] We can't do without them. Wives, rush to the restyours! Of-**
> **30**
> **man will toman while led is the lol. Zessid's our kadem, villa-**
> **31**
> **pleach, vollapluck. Fikup, for flesh nelly, el mundo nov, zole flen !**
> **32**
> **If she's a lilyth, pull early! Pauline, allow! And malers abushed,**
> **33**
> **keep black, keep black!**

Now for Volapuk, an artificial language. From Wikipedia:

> Volapük (pronounced [vola'pyk], or IPA: /ˈvɒləpʊk/ in English[2]) is a constructed language, created in 1879–1880 by Johann Martin Schleyer, a Roman Catholic priest in Baden, Germany. Schleyer felt that God had told him in a dream to create an international language. Volapük conventions took place in 1884 (Friedrichshafen), 1887 (Munich), and 1889 (Paris). The first two conventions used German, and the last conference used only Volapük. In 1889, there were an estimated 283 clubs, 25 periodicals in or about Volapük, and 316 textbooks in 25 languages. Today there are an estimated 20-30 Volapük speakers in the world.[*citation needed*] Volapük was largely displaced in the late 19th

and early 20th centuries by simpler and more easily-learned languages, such as Esperanto and Latino Sine Flexione.

The point seems to be that females use a different language. We can't do without them. Wives, rush to the rescue of yours [**restyours**]. **Ofman will toman while led is the lol.** Roughly in Volapuk: she man will annoy while the rose is red. This can refer to menstruation. Necessity is our academy, will power pleach, vollapuck. Fikup [Africa] for fresh Nelly, the Dublin whore. The world noy Zole flen, friend. [some of these words are made up to sound like Volpuk]. If she is a Lillith, pull out before you ejaculate. If she is a Pauline, allow it to flow. **If she's a lilyth, pull early! Pauline, allow!** And males who are ambushed, keep black. Don't know don't talk.

Back to Harold and a subsequent event that throws light on what happened originally with the two girls and soldiers in the Park. He was walking across the same park and met a "cad":

> [34] Guiltless of much laid to him he was
> 34
> clearly for once at least he clearly expressed himself as being with
> 35
> still a trace of his erstwhile burr sod hence it has been received of
> 36
> [35] us that it is true. They tell the story (an amalgam as absorbing as
> 1
> calzium chloereydes and hydrophobe sponges could make it) how
> 2
> one happygogusty Ides-of-April morning (the anniversary, as it
> 3
> fell out, of his first assumption of his mirthday suit and rights in
> 4
> appurtenance to the confusioning of human races) ages and ages
> 5
> after the alleged misdemeanour when the tried friend of all crea-
> 6
> tion, tigerwood roadstaff to his stay, was billowing across the

7
wide expanse of our greatest park in his caoutchouc kepi and
8
great belt and hideinsacks and his blaufunx fustian and iron-
sides
9
jackboots and Bhagafat gaiters and his rubberised inverness,
he
10
met a cad with a pipe.
11

While he is guiltless of much that he was accused of, Harold did admit with a trace of his erstwhile rolling the r's accent [**burr sod**
which also means sodomite]. That is to say, indicating a guilty conscience he spoke like he used to. So it has been received as true.
They [not identified] tell the story (as absorbing as sponges could
make it) how one happy go gusty April morning (the anniversary as it
fell out of his first assumption of nakedness in the Garden of
Eden—**mirthday suit**—and rights related to the confusion of voices
after Babel) long after the alleged misdemeanour [bad demeanor—
seeing each other naked] when the tried friend of all creation [Adam-
Harold] stabilized by his staff made of tigerwood was billowing
[cloud-like] across Phoenix Park in his rain gear [think flood curse]
when he met a cad with a pipe. Cad originally meant an unbooked
passenger taken up by the driver for his own profit [TZTZ god-
mankind relationship] and eventually came to mean a blackguard
capable of ungentlemanly behavior.

Now to focus on the cad with the pipe, tobacco being a hot avenue of the spirit:

> [35] The latter, the luciferant not the oriuolate
> 11
> (who, the odds are, is still berting dagabout in the same
> straw
> 12
> bamer, carryin his overgoat under his schulder, sheepside
> out, so
> 13
> as to look more like a coumfry gentleman and signing the
> pledge
> 14
> as gaily as you please) hardily accosted him with: Guinness
> thaw

374

15
tool in jew me dinner ouzel fin? (a nice how-do-you-do in Pool-
16
black at the time as some of our olddaisers may still trem-
blingly
17
recall) to ask could he tell him how much a clock it was that
the
18
clock struck had he any idea by cock's luck as his watch was
19
bradys. Hesitency was clearly to be evitated. Execration as
cleverly
20
to be honnisoid.
21

Now we are in the Park, the analog of the Garden of Eden, and Harold is the Adam character. The Cad would be the serpent, a disguise for TZTZ god. The serpent impregnated Eve with Cain and Able and defiled Adam as well.

Now for the text: the Cad approached Adam with a homosexual proposition, "have you got the time" [**to ask could he tell him how much a clock it was**]. Convert clock to cock. Time started when Adam and Eve were kicked out of the Garden. With time, sex was necessary. Phoenix Park was the site of the famous Phoenix Park murders while the Garden of Eden was the site of the murder of mankind by TZTZ god.

To interpret this material, we need to refer to the views of Arthur Schopenhauer on homosexuality. As described by Bryon Magee:

> [Concerning 'The Metaphysics of Sexual Love']. . . in it the author discusses coolly, and attempts to understand and explain, a phenomenon which in his day was felt to be shocking in the extreme, and was either not mentioned at all or was discussed with much show of horror and moral outrage. It was a topic, moreover, which no other philosopher had dealt with since the Greeks, and which readers would not expect to be discussed in a philosophically. Schopenhauer succeeds ingeniously enough in offering an explanation of homosexuality which fits into the general framework of his theoretical system. But reading between the lines I get an irresistible impression that the subject is brought in because of personal experiences which fell to him comparatively late in life,

and which took him by surprise. His explanation of homosexuality is as follows. We know, he says, that only parents who are physically mature and yet not too old produce strong, healthy children. Parents who are either too young or too old produce children who are 'weak, dull, sickly, wretched, and short-lived'. However, since Nature never proceeds by sudden jumps, sexual appetites do not conveniently switch on and switch of at the appropriate ages: on the contrary, the desire for sexual activity grows from puberty, which after all occurs in childhood, and in most cases wanes only late in middle age, if then. So Nature has to find some way of seeing to it that in the adolescent and the elderly the sexual impulse is directed away from the procreation of children. This she does by the introduction of homosexual inclinations at these two stages of life. The, what appears at first sight to be an unnatural, indeed perverted impulse, and an obviously unproductive one, is planted in us by Nature herself for the benefit of the species. This fact - that homosexual inclinations are natural and not unnatural- explains why homosexual activity goes on in all communities at all times, regardless of whether it is viewed with horror or even punishable by death. In many cultures, to be sure, it is tolerantly accepted, and presumably in those cultures individuals who feel homosexual inclinations would have no reason to 'suppress them. 'In Europe, on the other hand, it is opposed by such powerful motives of religion, morality, law, and honour, that almost everyone shrinks at the mere thought of it, and we may assume accordingly that out of some three hundred who feel the tendency, hardly more than one will be so feeble and crazy as to give way to it." In our own culture, therefore, literally hundreds of times more people feel a homosexual temptation than show any outward indication of doing so: indeed, 'only a thoroughly depraved nature will succumb to it'. With exceptions whose context usually makes them obviously so it can, I think, be taken that if an individual puts forward a serious general statement about human beings or human behaviour as such, he accepts it as applying to himself, since if it did not he would know it to be false, or at least he would know that (and also something about how) it needed to be qualified. What Schopenhauer's treatment of homosexuality suggests to me is that he himself had felt homosexual inclinations only in adolescence but also in late middle age or old age.

So the Cad is to be the young man with wife but no children and Harold is the older with grown sons and daughter. They would be ripe for each other. A reference to whether he has the time is, as well as a homosexual advance, a reference to Harold's advanced age and the proximity of his replacement as the alpha male. Since the alpha reminds junior males of their status with ritual humping, this invitation is an appropriate sign of what is to come to the aging alpha. Looking back on the sponge metaphor, we register that in heterosexual copulation the sperms stay in the female vagina whereas in sodomy there would be no place for them to swim or to be absorbed.

The Cad is described as the **the luciferant not the oriuolate,** meaning the friction matches [fire from anal irritation] not the time keeper ice [fire not ice]. He wears a straw hat and carries his overcoat under his shoulder with the sheepside out so as to look more like a country gentlemen [and remind us of Jacob pretending to be Esau] and signing the pledge **not to drink**—no spirit. Note that this serpent creature models his behavior on the opinions of others. As a homosexual, he is an impostor in life. He doesn't need a raincoat on because he is part of the rain, the flood the curse.

The Luciferian accosts Harold with a greeting in corrupted Gaelic or Italian to the effect: how are you today, my blond gentleman. What the Cad said sounds like "thaw tool in jew me dinner ouzel fin." It suggests a thaw from eating in Jewish Genesis. The serpent would think Adam too cold and needed to be thawed out by friction.

Note that in the Garden "today" in how are you today would not make sense. Today is relevant only in time, which began after they were ejected from the Garden. Only after death is in play are the clock and sex relevant. Poolblack refers to Dublin so the parenthetical expression is a nice how do you do in Dublin at the time as some of our old inhabitants may recall with fear.

So the Cad accosts Harold to **ask could he tell him how much a clock it was that the clock struck had he any idea by cock's luck as his watch was bradys.** This is a key passage so let us start slowly with **bradys**. This means slow and refers to one Jim Brady involved in the Phoenix park murders. From Wikipedia, the free encyclopedia:

> The term Phoenix Park Murders[1][2] is used to refer to the assassination in 1882 of the second and third in rank in the British Dublin Castle government of Ireland by the "Irish National Invincibles".

> On 6 May 1882, the most senior Irish civil servant, the Permanent Undersecretary, Thomas Henry Burke and the newly appointed Chief Secretary for Ireland, Lord Frederick Cavendish – who was also the nephew of Prime Minister William Gladstone – were

stabbed as they walked though the Phoenix Park in Dublin en route to the Viceregal Lodge, the "out of season" residence of the Lord Lieutenant of Ireland. Cavendish had only arrived in Ireland the day he was murdered. Thomas Myles, resident surgeon at the nearby Dr Steevens' Hospital, was summoned to render medical assistance to the victims.

The then Lord Lieutenant, Lord Spencer, described suddenly hearing screams, before witnessing a man running to the Lodge grounds shouting "Lord Frederick Cavendish and Mr. Burke are killed." Responsibility for the assassinations was claimed by a small republican organisation called *Irish National Invincibles* and they were apparently to resign from parliament in protest at what he called "these vile murders", an offer turned down by the British Prime Minister, William Ewart Gladstone.

Parnell made a speech condemning the murders in 1882. This increased his already huge popularity in both Britain and Ireland. He had just enabled some reforms under the Kilmainham Treaty four days before the murders. Parnell's reputation increased in Ireland, being seen as a more moderate reformer who would never excuse such tactics.

However, Parnell's policy of allying his party to Gladstone's Liberal Party to enable Home Rule was also ultimately defeated by the murders. Gladstone's Minister Lord Hartington was the elder brother of Lord Frederick Cavendish. Saddened and infuriated by the manner of his brother's early death, Hartington split with Gladstone on Home Rule in 1886 and 1893 and led the breakaway Liberal Unionist Association which allied itself to Lord Salisbury's conservative governments. This delayed Home Rule by 28 years, until the Third Irish Home Rule Bill which was passed technically in 1914, but which was never effected.

All the assassins were eventually captured, and five were hanged.

For Joyce, the major aspects of this event are the defeat of home rule and independence resulting from murder of the British appointed high political figures on their way to the vice regal lodge, something like the revenge of TZTZ god for an attempt in the Garden at independence. Lucifer's watch is slow because he is immortal or eternal. The reference to what the clock has "struck" suggests the violence of the ejection from the Garden. Clock and cock of cock's luck are time and sex as well as the first time from the cock's early morning call.

In reaction to this request for the time: **Hesitency was clearly to be evitated. Execration as cleverly to be honnisoid.** Hesitancy was to be avoided and independence maintained. Being cursed was

378

to be pretend dead. That is pretend to be dependent to avoid the curse death.

> **[35] The Earwicker of that spurring instant, realising**
> 21
> **on fundamental liberal principles the supreme importance, nexally**
> 22
> **and noxally, of physical life (the nearest help relay being pingping**
> 23
> **K. O. Sempatrick's Day and the fenian rising) and unwishful as**
> 24
> **he felt of being hurled into eternity right then, plugged by a soft-**
> 25
> **nosed bullet from the sap, halted, quick on the draw, and re-ply-**
> 26
> **in that he was feelin tipstaff, cue, prodooced from his gun-pocket**
> 27
> **his Jurgensen's shrapnel waterbury, ours by communionism, his**
> 28
> **by usucapture,**
> 29

In reaction to the request for the time and the homosexual proposition, Earwicker realized that the continuance of physical life depended on his answer [as Adam] and the help nearest in time to support his independence would be March 17, 1867, Fenian rising day, a burst of independence:

> The Fenian Rising of 1867 (Irish: *Éirí Amach na bhFiann, 1867*) was a rebellion against British rule in Ireland, organized by the Irish Republican Brotherhood, popularly known as Fenians.
>
> After the suppression of the *Irish People* revolutionary magazine, disaffection among Irish radical nationalists had continued to smolder, and during the latter part of 1866 IRB leader James Stephens endeavoured to raise funds in America for a fresh rising planned for the following year. However the rising of 1867 proved to be a doomed rebellion, poorly organised and with minimal public support. Some insignificant outbreaks in the south and west of

Ireland brought the rebellion to an ignominious close. Most of the ringleaders in Ireland were arrested, but although some of them were sentenced to death none were executed. A series of raids into Canada by U.S.-based supporters also accomplished little.

So this scene is viewed as a redeux of the Garden experience. In terms of choice, Adam could choose immediate death by continuing to be independent spiritually or could live on physically in time for an undetermined number of years and submit to sodomy by the serpent, the beginning of dependence. Harold is afraid of death, of being plugged with a soft nose bullet [type used in 1916 Easter uprising] from the sap [Tree of Knowledge and Death and hit on head]. Since help for independence is so far off in time, Harold limits his independence to avoid immediate death in **physical life**. In this context, he gives the time. He submits to the question.

He gives the time with this reaction: **halted, quick on the draw, and reply in that he was feelin tipstaff.** Harold in effect replies that he was feeling good, the kind of good that comes from having a tipstaff, a tipped staff carried by sheriff's officers. In homosexual terms, Harold says he is erect already. This signals some kind of limited physical independence from death provided by the penis and procreation. He produces a watch from his gun pocket. The watch is his Jurgensen-type watch **shrapnel waterbury,** his watch made in *Water*bury Connecticut suggesting dangerous TZTZ type fragments from the curse flood that buried us. Time and death as the curse. The watch or experience of time is ours by what we have in common, our mortality. Remember also that Adam just "watched," as Eve and the serpent went at it.

But just as he looked at his watch, the nearby clock bell strikes twelve:

> [35] but, on the same stroke, hearing above the skirl-
> 29
> ing of harsh Mother East old Fox Goodman, the bellmaster,
> over
> 30
> the wastes to south, at work upon the ten ton tonuant thun-
> der-
> 31
> ous tenor toller in the speckled church (Couhounin's call!)
> told
> 32
> the inquiring kidder, by Jehova, it was twelve of em sidereal

and
33
tankard time, adding, buttall, as he bended deeply with smoked
34
sardinish breath to give more pondus to the copperstick he pre-
35
sented (though this seems in some cumfusium with the chap-
36

[36] stuck ginger, which, as being of sours, acids, salts, sweets and
1
bitters compompounded, we know him to have used as chaw-
2
chaw for bone, muscle, blood, flesh and vimvital,)
3

Hearing over the noise made by **Mother East old Fox Goodman**, the bellmaster rings the ten-ton bell like thunder in the speckled church. This told the inquiring cad kidder that by Jehova it was twelve o'clock sidereal [star time] as well as opening hour in the pubs. The church tells the time, takes over this function from erstwhile independent humans. Time is starting in the spirit houses. Harold, with smoked sardines on his breath, leaned over to give more gravitas to the copper truncheon [and slang for penis] he presented [as the symbol of his erect penis] as he said something like twelve bells [straight up]. The sardine factor was confused with odors of other foods he had eaten, including those recommended by Chinese diet. Food signals the physical life and the killing of other life.

And now in mythical time space as was known in high quarters, the Cad is magnified to appear in his mythical form as a giant Satan or Lucifer standing over the flood plain of curses:

[36] that where-
3
as the hakusay accusation againstm had been made, what was
4

known in high quarters as was stood stated in Morganspost, by
5
a creature in youman form who was quite beneath parr and seve-
6
ral degrees lower than yore triplehydrad snake.

The accusation was made against Harold in the highest of quarters as stated in the first newspaper of the day [**Morganspost** or morning post] by a creature in human **youman** form who was below average and several degrees lower than a triple headed snake. This is the serpent post-fall measured against the group. As the serpent makes his case against humans, it rises up to his erect position in the Garden:

[36] In greater sup-
7
port of his word (it, quaint 'anticipation of a famous phrase, has
8
been reconstricted out of oral style into the verbal for all time
9
with ritual rhythmics, in quiritary quietude, and toosammen-
10
stucked from successive accounts by Noah Webster in the re-
11
daction known as the Sayings Attributive of H. C. Earwicker,
12
prize on schillings, postlots free), the flaxen Gygas tapped his
13
chronometrum drumdrum and, now standing full erect, above
14
the ambijacent floodplain, scene of its happening,

The serpent, now as the blond Gysas [name of King of Lydia but used here to mean fart gas], stands erect above the floodplain of the great flood drumming on his watch, his chronometer, his **chrono-metrum**—time meter. He said this in a style that became famous and was included by Noah Webster in the redaction known as the Sayings Attributive of HC Earwicker.

Standing there the serpent had:

[36] with one Ber-
15
lin gauntlet chopstuck in the hough of his ellboge (by an-
cientest
16
signlore his gesture meaning: !) pointed at an angle of thirty-
17
two degrees towards his *duc de Fer's* overgrown milestone as
18
fellow to his gage and after a rendypresent pause averred with
19
solemn emotion's fire: Shsh shake, co-comeraid! Me only, them
20
five ones, he is equal combat. I have won straight.
21

The serpent of pride stands erect and places his right hand like Na-poleon—he has one Berlin glove [with knitting] gauntlet stuck like a chop in the hough [hollow behind knee—serpent has four legs not two legs and two arms] of his elbow [ellboge—German for elbow] giving the Italian sign for up yours (in the oldest sign lore). The chopstuck arm is pointed at an angle of 32 degrees [the rate of fall under gravity is 32 feet per second per second] downwards towards his duke of Fire's or Duke of Wellington's overgrown milestone or monument [symbol for erect penis] as a fellow to his size. In other words, the serpent standing erect says look at my big penis; it is as big as the Wellington Monument. After a momentary pause the ser-pent avers with strong emotion: shake in fear with snake hisses my co-raiders! I take them on five to one and I always win. Note that the serpent's syntax [sin tax] is corrupted by pride.

After this mythical vision of the serpent and in front of the Cad, Harold even more afraid stutters his way to a denial of any charges against him, even though the Cad has mentioned none, has only asked for the time:

[36] Hence my
21
nonation wide hotel and creamery establishments which for the
22
honours of our mewmew mutual daughters, credit me, I am woo-

23
woo willing to take my stand, sir, upon the monument, that sign
24
of our ruru redemption, any hygienic day to this hour and to
25
make my hoath to my sinnfinners, even if I get life for it, upon
26
the Open Bible and before the Great Taskmaster's (I lift my hat!)
27
and in the presence of the Deity Itself andwell of Bishop and
28
Mrs Michan of High Church of England as of all such of said
29
my immediate withdwellers and of every living sohole in every
30
corner wheresoever of this globe in general which useth of my
31
British to my backbone tongue and commutative justice that
32
there is not one tittle of truth, allow me to tell you, in that purest
33
of fibfib fabrications.
34

Harold pledges the truth of what he says about himself to the Cad on the honor of his penis, that monument of our redemption and the pride of hotel rooms and creaming ejaculating into our daughters [Joyce's first time with Nora was in a hotel room in Paris]. Harold's language is corrupted by stuttering: mewmew woowoo ruru fibfib. Stuttering indicates hesitancy and guilt. Harold goes on: On any clean day to this hour of opening I make my oath to my sin finners even if I get life for it—that is become mortal. I take this pledge on the Open Bible [this means more than a bible that is open] and before the Great Taskmaster's [god of Genesis] and in the presence of the Deity [another one] Itself and its earthly representatives. I pledge there is no truth in the charges, they are all fabrications.

Now the Cad, nonplussed by what Harold has told him:

. . . [36] Gaping Gill, swift to mate errthors, stern to checkself, (diag-
35
nosing through eustacetube that it was to make with a mark-
edly
36

[37] postpuberal hypertituitary type of Heidelberg mannleich
cavern
1
ethics) lufted his slopingforward, bad Sweatagore good mur-
2
rough and dublnotch on to it as he was greedly obliged, and
3
like a sensible ham, with infinite tact in the delicate situation
seen
4
the touchy nature of its perilous theme, thanked um for
guilders
5
received and time of day (not a little token abock all the same
that
6
that was owl the God's clock it was) and, upon humble duty
to
7
greet his Tyskminister and he shall gildthegap Gaper and
thee his
8
a mouldy voids, went about his business, whoever it was, sa-
luting
9
corpses, as a metter of corse (one could hound him out had
one
10
hart to for the monticules of scalp and dandruff droppings
blaze
11
his trail) accompanied by his trusty snorler and his permanent
12
reflection, verbigracious;
13

Now the Cad, serpent-like, is lower animal development, with gills,
with a sloping forehead and with dandruff trailing scales—in K evil

was pictured as shells. He is error prone and sex oriented. Gaping Gill was swift to make errors [as **errthors** so the word is itself an error and suggests the curse—errors by Thor] and stern to check himself [as **checkself** a picture of the event]. He diagnosed through his Eustachian tube—hearing and smelling—and with low order ethics [**postpuberal hypertituitary type of Heidelberg mannleich cavern**], he being a big giant living in a cave with caveman ethics. He lifted [lufted for lower] his sloped forward forehead and raised his sweat stained hat [hell is hot] with a double notch [**bad Sweatagore good murrough and dublnotch on to it**] as he was greedily obliged to by convention [group oriented]. In this touchy situation like that Ham faced with Noah, the Cad thanked Harold for guilders [money?] received and the time of day. The Cad was taken aback that the time came from the church bell, given how time started in the garden [the church takes over from TZTZ god]. Then the Cad as his humble duty to his Taskmaster [TZTZ god gives tasks] proceeded to gild the gap and fill the mouldy voids [the void for TZTZ creation]. He went about his business and saluted the corpses in the nearby cemetery. He saluted them as a matter of course. He blazed a trail of dandruff and he was accompanied by his trusty dog that was his permanent reflection as repetition. Dogs being dependent creatures by nature and, as emphasized in Ulysses, dog being god reversed.

Now the narrator returns to the Cad back at home after this encounter with Harold. In this material, the bird must be Harold who sang his guilt. The Cad **repeats** so as to remember the words of Harold. Here is the narrator describing what happens:

> [37] I have met with you, bird, too late,
> 13
> or if not, too worm and early: and with tag for ildiot repeated
> 14
> in his secondmouth language as many of the bigtimer's verbaten
> 15
> words which he could balbly call to memory that same kveldeve,
> 16
> ere the hour of the twattering of bards in the twitterlitter between
> 17
> Druidia and the Deepsleep Sea,
> 18

The narrator, referring to the aphorism the early bird gets the worm, repeats the Cad's thought that he has met with the bird either too late or too early and too worm. This may refer to Schopenhauer's theory that homosexuality appears early or late in life but not in the middle. So the Cad who just tried unsuccessfully for a homosexual encounter in the Park with Harold says his target must be too old or too young, still in that middle period where the opposite sex is attractive. In other words, the Cad thinks the failure can't be my fault. Now an insider comment about T.S. Eliot of the *Waste Land*: through the narrator Joyce says that the idiot Eliot [combined as **ildiot**] repeated his words from Ulysses—the **bigtimer's verbaten words**. Since this is about repeating and idolatry, the Cad is like Eliot in that he repeats the words of others—he is other influenced by and idolizes Joyce.

The Cad repeats as many of Harold's exact words that he can remember. Like a Catholic repeating what he or she is told by the Church. This kind of Repeat is associated with stammering through **balbly**, *balbus* being Latin for stammering. The Cad repeated out loud Harold's words that very same evening in the hour of erstwhile independent reading [the **twattering of bards in the twitterlitter**] between magic and the deep blue sleep [**Druidia and the Deep-sleep Sea**].

> [37] when suppertide and souvenir to
> 18
> Charlatan Mall jointly kem gently and along the quiet dark-enings
> 19
> of Grand and Royal, ff, flitmansfluh, and, kk, 't crept i' hedge
> 20
> whenas to many a softongue's pawkytalk mude unswer u sufter
> 21
> poghyogh, Arvanda always aquiassent, while, studying cas-telles
> 22
> in the blowne and studding cowshots over the noran, he spat in
> 23
> careful convertedness a musaic dispensation about his *hearthstone*,
> 24
> if you please,
> 25

At the time of suppertide—the late tide in—when refuse from Char-
latan Mall join and flow along Grand and Royal canals—suggesting
time-based excrement from the Charlatans masking the eternal. This
is a flush as in the loo, the sound of **ff** from the overhead water bowl
[**flitmansfluh**]. Meanwhile **kk** crept in the hedge where and when
many made soft tongue talk French kissing, Arvanda ALP the water
of life HSS always acquiescing. While studying castles in the air and
cows jumping over the moon, Cad spat secretly, covered sound-wise
by a musical dispensation, about his hearthstone [apparently against
his wife's rules].

Now this is Irish saliva aimed at a spittoon on the fireplace
hearth:

> **[37] (Irish saliva, *mawshe dho hole*, but would a respect-**
> 25
> **able prominently connected fellow of Iro-European ascen-**
> **dances**
> 26
> **with welldressed ideas who knew the correct thing such as**
> **Mr**
> 27
> **Shallwesigh or Mr Shallwelaugh expectorate after such a cal-**
> **lous**
> 28
> **fashion, no thank yous! when he had his belcher *spuckertuck***
> **in his**
> 29
> **pucket, pthuck?) musefed with his thockits after having**
> **supped**
> 30

Irish saliva, if you please, but would a respectable fellow who was
versed in conventional correctness such as Mr Shall We Sign or Mr
Shall We Laugh [asking others] spit in such a callous fashion? The
answer is no thank you [conventionally polite]. Particularly when he
had his handerchief [could have spit in it]. He was fed as by muse
with his thockits kit after having escaped hunger by eating from a
pot. Spit by the Cad would echo defilement of Adam by the serpent
or fellatio. Contrast the spit on the hearth with fire in the fireplace.

The Cad has supped:

[37] of the dish sot and pottage which he snobbishly dabbed Peach
31
Bombay (it is rawly only Lukanpukan pilzenpie which she knows
32
which senaffed and pibered him), a supreme of excelling peas,
33
balled under minnshogue's milk into whitemalt winesour, a pro-
34
viant the littlebilker hoarsely relished, chaff it, in the snevel season,
35
being as fain o't as your rat wi'fennel; and on this celebrating
36

Perhaps to impress others the Cad calls by the **snobbish** name the Peach Bombay his common dish of sot and pottage [another substitution]. Sot means tobacco but also means a fool or drunkard. Instead of Georgi porgi pudden pie we have the substitute **Lukanpukan pilzenpie**. She his wife knew that the pie would mustard and pepper him [**senaffed and pibered him**]. The dish consists of peas boiled under goat milk in shite malt vinegar, a dish the **littlebillker** relished and extolled to the point of hoarseness. He ate it quite often during the seasons of colds, the **snevel season** [with a hint of evil]. He liked it as much as a rat likes fennel, a comparison of the Cad with a rat. Back to Georgie Porgie for some background. The full text:

> Georgie Porgie pudding and pie,
> Kissed the girls and made them cry
> When the boys came out to play,
> Georgie Porgie ran away.

The origins of this verse are political, the dependent and irresponsible George, the Duke of Buckingham. From Famous Quotes:

> The origins and history of the lyrics to this nursery rhyme are English and refer to George (Georgie Porgie), the Duke of Buckingham, from 17th century English history. His dubious moral character was much in question! This, however, was overlooked due to

his friendship with King Charles II until the parliament stopped the kind intervening on his behalf - at this point all of the jealous husbands vowed to wreak their revenge causing Georgie Porgie to 'run away'!

Then to what the Cad drank, surprisingly expensive wine, the description delivered in a parody of conventional restaurant advertising type language:

> [38] occasion of the happy escape, for a crowning of pot valiance,
> 1
> this regional platter, benjamin of bouillis, with a spolish olive to
> 2
> middlepoint its zaynith, was marrying itself (porkograso!) ere-
> 3
> busqued very deluxiously with a bottle of Phenice-Bruerie '98,
> 4
> followed for second nuptials by a Piessporter, Grand Cur, of
> 5
> both of which cherished tablelights (though humble the bounquet
> 6
> 'tis a leaman's farewell) he obdurately sniffed the cobweb-crusted
> 7
> corks.
> 8

Benjamin of bouillis, the last or favorite Benjamin, the youngest of the boiled beef, was served with an olive in the middle of its zenith [**zaynith**—zenith combined with *zay*, Hebrew for olive]. This food was marrying [cliché—wine is a good marriage with this food] two bottles of very good wine from his cellar, two bottles just for the Cad, none for his wife—referred to as his bit of strife. One wine the Piessporter reminds us of the prankquean and the other **Phenice-Bruerie** reminds us of Phoenix Brewery, the spirit of resurrection here in the corrupted and substituted form of repetition by gossip. Grand cru becomes **grand cur**.

So now Harold's sin and guilt are about to be reproduced by repetition, gossip, confession and gaming. The retrovirus is about to replicate first through Mrs. Cad:

> **[38] Our cad's bit of strife (knee Bareniece Maxwelton) with a quick**
> **9**
> **ear for spittoons (as the aftertale hath it) glaned up as usual with**
> **10**
> **dumbestic husbandry (no persicks and armelians for thee, Pome-**
> **11**
> **ranzia!) but, slipping the clav in her claw, broke of the matter**
> **12**
> **among a hundred and eleven others in her usual curtsey (how**
> **13**
> **faint these first vhespers womanly are, a secret pispigliando, amad**
> **14**
> **the lavurdy den of their manfolker!) the next night nudge one**
> **15**

The Cad's wife, his bit of strife (born with maiden name Bereniece or bareknees or bare niece Maxwelton) had a quick ear for spit hitting the spittoon, as this must have been prohibited in her house. As the aftertale has it, she cleaned gleaned [understood] up as usual with domestic husbandry, no peaches and apricots for her [**persicks** and **armelians**—sickness and strife from the Tree of knowledge] the orange girl. But with key in hand she left home and broke [as in break the news and separation theme] the matter to 111 other women in her usual kindness for others [irony]. (How faint these women are in these their first vespers whispers. They make a secret whispering amid the mad weekly den of their menvolk.)

And the next night but one:

> **[38] as was Hegesippus over a hup a ' chee, her eys dry and small and**
> **16**
> **speech thicklish because he appeared a funny colour like he**
> **17**
> **couldn't stood they old hens no longer, to her particular rev-**
> **erend,**

18

the director, whom she had been meaning in her mind primarily
19
to speak with (hosch, intra! jist a timblespoon!) trusting, between
20
cuppled lips and annie lawrie promises (mighshe never have
21
Esnekerry pudden come Hunanov for her pecklapitschens!)
that
22
the gossiple so delivered in his epistolear, buried teatoastally
in
23
their Irish stew would go no further than his jesuit's cloth,
24

She delivered the same gossip to her reverend priest [revere the end] as he sipped a cup of tea. Her eyes were dry and small and her speech thick because the reverend appeared a funny color as if he couldn't stand old hens anymore—didn't lust after her. The priest says about the sugar for his tea, that's enough just a **timblespoon**—a spoonful of time and trouble. She trusted between cuppled lips, promises and the stew she fed him that the **gossiple** [gossip and gospel] would go no further than the priest.

But despite the pledge of confidentiality [not in confession], at the race track the priest tells a lay teacher of science a version of the same story. Note the priest is at the venue for wagers, perhaps a reference to Pascal's wager on heaven and hell. He is named Mr. Browne, not father Brown so he must be in street clothes, a forger of a normal citizen:

[38] yet
24
(in vinars venitas! volatiles valetotum!) it was this overspoiled
25
priest Mr Browne, disguised as a vincentian, who, when
seized
26
of the facts, was overheard, in his secondary personality as a
27
Nolan and underreared, poul soul, by accident—— if, that is,
the

392

28
incident it was an accident for here the ruah of Ecclectiastes
29
of Hippo outpuffs the writress of Havvah-ban-Annah— to
30
pianissime a slightly varied version of Crookedribs confidentials,
31
(what Mere Aloyse said but for Jesuphine's sake !) hands between
32
hahands, in fealty sworn (my bravor best! my fraur!) and, to
the
33
strains of *The Secret of Her Birth*, hushly pierce the rubiend
34

Yet (in the truth of brandy like vino veritas and flying in the vale of farewell) this same priest Mr. Browne [of Browne-Nolan] was over-heard at the race track repeating to an other what Mrs. Cad had told him. He was disguised as a member of the Congregation of Priests founded by St. Vincent DePaul [not St. Paul] and in his secondary personality as Nolan that was **underreared** [Saul falls off his horse in vision of Christ]—if that incident [conversion of St. Paul] was an accident for here the wind of Ecclesiastes of Hippo [St. Augustine who theorized original sin passing from Eve through sexual inter-course] outpuffs the **writress** [waitress and writer combined] of Eve, the mother of all living things. That is her status as the source of all sin is more important than her status as the mother of all humans. She is referred to as **Havvah-ban-Annah,** which translates as Ha-wah banned from the beginning or have a banana—forbidden fruit]. Here this spirit outpuffs the writer of the story of Eve and a slightly varied version of Crooked Ribs confidentials [Mohammed said Adam's rib was crooked]. Napoleon's Josephine must have said the same about him—since he always had his hand on his ribs. He passed this on with hand between hands and truth sworn while the song *The Secret of Her Birth* was playing. The secret of Eve's birth is that her father was TZTZ god.

He the priest told:

[38] aurellum of one Philly Thurnston, a layteacher of rural
science
35

and orthophonethics of a nearstout figure and about the middle
36

[39] of his forties during a priestly flutter for safe and sane bets at the
1
hippic runfields of breezy Baldoyle

The recipient of the gossip is a lay teacher of rural science and upright speech and ethics [**orthophonethics**] with a stout figure and in his forties. The priest told him during a period of betting on the horses at the Dublin race track Baldoyle [bald old]. So the Priest is friendly with an older [40's] gentleman who is alone.

So far the allegation of original sin has been spread by a representative of the serpent and by the church. These spreaders are understandable. The serpent's connection to original and continuing sin is like as to like. The church benefits from these notions as well, making the church all the more necessary. The next spreader, Lay science, must refer to efforts to find the site of the Garden of Eden, where it lay science or lay for fall. Or lay science is the science of seduction. And ethics are the rules we need because of original sin.

Since expulsion from paradise resulted in a loss of the certainty-producing merger with god, it resulted in a world of chance, here depicted by wagering on the horse races.

The date of this conversation is easy to remember because:

[39] on a date (W. W. goes
2
through the card) easily capable of rememberance by all pickers-
3
up of events national and Dublin details, the doubles of Perkin
4
and Paullock, peer and prole, when the classic Encourage Hackney
5
Plate was captured by two noses in a stablecloth finish, ek and nek,
6
some and none, evelo nevelo, from the cream colt Bold Boy
7

394

Cromwell after a clever getaway by Captain Chaplain Blount's
8
roe hinny Saint Dalough, Drummer Coxon, nondepict third, at
9
breakneck odds, thanks to you great little, bonny little, portey
10
little, Winny Widger! you're all their nappies! who in his never-
11
rip mud and purpular cap was surely leagues unlike any other
12
phantomweight that ever toppitt our timber maggies.
13

Now in horse racing language. On that date W.W. [Winny Widger] won the bet on every race [**W. W. goes through the card**], so it is remembered by all watchers of events national and Dublin details [the name of a column in the paper about horse racing]. Perkin Warbeck was a pretender to the English throne with Irish support, reminding us of TZTZ god, so the newspaper column is the double or repeats **Perkin and Paullock** [Peter and Paul]. You need to bet on religion to save your soul from hell. That day the Encourage Hackney Plate, that is support for transport of the spirit, was won by two noses [that is to say first and third place were decided by a nose], neck and neck or **ek** and **nek**—some and none—ever never—the human condition. The race was won by the cream colt [sperm] **Bold Boy Cromwell** despite a good start by Captain Chaplain Blount's [Mount Joy] **roe hinny** [eggs] Saint Dalough, which came in second or placed [the place to put the sperm]. **Drummer Coxon** [for war and coaxin] came in third or showed, as in attraction. These results were thanks to the bonny little Winny Widger, suggesting that since Winny bet on the horses who came in first, second and third, that result had to obtain, was predestined. **Bold Boy, Saint Dalough and Drummer Coxon** form some sort of trinity—perhaps alphafather, mother and child or bold father god, saint son down low god and the coaxing HSS—the kind of family unit predestined after TZTZ god took over. Winny Widger was a famous amateur rider from a racing family as well as a gambler. He was the best to pit our jumpers.

This wagering success by Winny Widger was a miracle in the land of luck and chance. He must have had inside information. It must have been predestined.

This conversation between the priest and the teacher is over-heard by Treacle Tom and Frisky Shorty, two down and outers:

[39] 'Twas two pisononse Timcoves (the wetter is pest, the renns are
14
overt and come and the voax of the turfur is hurled on our lande)
15
of the name of Treacle Tom as was just out of pop following the
16
theft of a leg of Kehoe, Donnelly and Packenham's Finnish pork
17
and his own blood and milk brother Frisky Shorty, (he was, to be
18
exquisitely punctilious about them, both shorty and frisky) a tip-
19
ster, come off the hulks, both of them awful poor, what was out
20
on the bumaround for an oofbird game for a jimmy o'goblin or
21
a small thick un as chanced, while the Seaforths was making the
22
colleenbawl, to ear the passon in the motor clobber make use of
23
his law language (Edzo, Edzo on), touchin the case of Mr Adams
24
what was in all the sundays about it which he was rubbing noses
25

with and having a gurgle off his own along of the butty bloke in
26
the specs.
27

Two poisonous fellows (the rain—the flood rain—is past and now just a pest, the signs are overt and the sound of the turtle or vortex of the turf is hurled on our land) were there, one named Treacle Tom [treacle means poison antidote] just out of jail for theft of a leg of pork and his brother Frisky Shorty, both just off the **hulks** [prison ships—think ark]. They were looking for tips on the horses, quite poor, and bumming around looking for rich game, for a sovereign or crown piece [god]. The marching band the Seaforths [flood and sefirots] was marching by and making the ladies [repository of love/unity] cry to hear the disguised parson [**passon**—the son who gives a pass] make use of his legal language touching on the case of Mr. Adam [like the Garden of Eden story, it must be about infidelity] that was in all the Sunday papers. The priest was talking to the man in glasses [the lay teacher].

So now the tale of original sin is also to be spread by the impoverished and criminal element in society. Original sin resulted in expulsion from the paradise of the Garden of Eden where all mankind needed was provided for, where material poverty would be unknown. Mankind was expelled to weedworld where living is difficult. So original sin leads to poverty and criminality, which in turn spread the message of original sin:

[39] This Treacle Tom to whom reference has been made had
28
been absent from his usual wild and woolly haunts in the land
29
of counties capalleens for some time previous to that (he was, in
30
fact, in the habit of frequenting common lodginghouses where
31
he slept in a nude state, hailfellow with meth, in strange men's
32

cots) but on racenight, blotto after divers tots of hell fire, red
33
biddy, bull dog, blue ruin and creeping jenny, Eglandine's
choic-
34
est herbage, supplied by the Duck and Doggies, the Galop-
35
ping Primrose, Brigid Brewster's, the Cock, the Postboy's
Horn,
36

This Treacle Tom had been in prison and away from his usual haunts
for some time. He was in the habit of staying overnight in common
lodging houses where he slept nude, a hail fellow well met with a
method [**meth**—a shortened method]—suggesting he would lure
men into his bed and then rob them. But on racenight he drank a
number of drinks—by the names hell's fire, red biddy [red wine and
meth] bull dog, blue ruin and creeping jenny supplied by the pubs
Duck and Doggies [Duck and Dog tavern], the Cock Tavern, the
Postboy's Tavern, and more taverns:

> [40] the Little Old Man's and All Swell That Aimswell, the
> Cup and
> 1
> the Stirrup, he sought his wellwarmed leababobed in a hous-
> 2
> ingroom Abide With Oneanother at Block W.W., (why didn't
> 3
> he back it?) Pump Court, The Liberties,
> 4

The Little Old Man's tavern [effect of TZTZ god] and **All Swell
That Aimswell** [all get pregnant who aim well] and the **Stirrup** [for
birth stirrups and stir her up]. After the taverns he sought his **well-
warmed** lea ba bo bed in a rooming house [converted to housin-
groom] named **Abide with Oneanother** at Block WW [Windy
Wender—why didn't he back it, make the same bets) Pump Court,
the Liberties, Dublin—a seedy neighborhood ironically named for
freedom [poverty combined with free will out of the Garden of
Eden].

There he retailed what he had heard, retailed it while he was
asleep, while snoring—out of the lower consciousness:

> [40] and, what with
> 4
> **moltapuke on voltapuke, resnored alcoh alcoho alcoherently**
> **to**
> 5
> the burden of *I come, my horse delayed,* nom num, the sub-
> 6
> **stance of the tale of the evangelical bussybozzy and the rus-**
> **inur-**
> 7
> **bean (the 'girls' he would keep calling them for the collarette**
> 8
> **and skirt, the sunbonnet and carnation)**
> 9

And what with his mother tongue on Volupuk, his lower consciousness shared by all, he puked and then resnored the substance of the
tale. The snoring is indicated by **alcoh alcoho alcoherently**. This
while the song *I come, my horse delayed* [my passion delayed] was being
sung. **Nom num** mocks Ophelia's mad speech "Hey non nonny,
nonny, hey nonny." He tells it as the tale of the evangelical busybody
and the **rusinurbean,** which must refer to original sin and recidi-
vism. It seems to mean sin again bean that sprouts. In the story being
repeated, the girls [in the park—note the girls were not mentioned by
Harold to the Cad] would be called the collarette and skirt or sun-
bonnet and carnation, referring to them by synecdoche—another
substitution. The inclusion of the girls in the story is apparently
added by the priest, since the church has always blamed Eve.

And now for the housingroom of this life, we have other visi-
tors—Peter for the rock, Mildew Lisa the holy mother and Hosty or
Christ, three products of expulsion from the Garden of Eden. Hosty
also proceeds from Hostes, in Vico the plebs of the heroic people.
Hosty is to bring Harold Earwicker down with a ballad, as the Christ
of the RCC is to make man dependent:

> [40] in parts (it seemed he
> 9
> **was before the eyots of martas or otherwales the thirds of fos-**
> **sil-**
> 10
> **years, he having beham with katya when lavinias had her**
> **mens**
> 11

lease to sea in a psumpship doodly show whereat he was looking
12
for fight niggers with whilde roarses) oft in the chilly night (the
13
metagonistic! the epickthalamorous!) during uneasy slumber in
14
their hearings of a small and stonybroke cashdraper's executive,
15
Peter Cloran (discharged), O'Mara, an exprivate secretary of no
16
fixed abode (locally known as Mildew Lisa), who had passed
17
several nights, funnish enough, in a doorway under the blankets
18
of homelessness on the bunk of iceland, pillowed upon the stone
19
of destiny colder than man's knee or woman's breast, and
20
Hosty, (no slouch of a name), an illstarred beachbusker,

The story was set before the Ides of March, here the **eyots island of martas** or march or in other words a long time ago, he having been as **beham** [be Ham] **with katya** [widow] when lavinias [Noah's wife?] had her menslease [menstruation—no sex on the ark] to sea in an assumption ship **doodly** show whereat he [Noah] was looking for a fight with niggers with wild roses—Ham's offspring. In other words, the housingroom was like being on the ark.

Back to the housingroom: They were there in the chilly night (the giant struggle! The epic inner chamber amorous!) sleeping uneasily in a room presided over by a stonybroke cash draper [one who presides over debased coinage—as in the Church presiding over humans]. There in uneasy sleep were [1] Peter Cloran former military [**discharged**—denied Christ] whose name refers to the Koran and St. Peter the rock of the church, in other words institutional religion [2] Lisa O'Mara [o mother] an "exprivate secretary"—i.e. dictated to through the ear by god—with no fixed residence [Mary traveling to Bethlehem and to Egypt] and known locally as Mildew Lisa, diseased, who had passed several nights in the cold homeless [Bethlehem story] pillowed on the cold stone of destiny [as mother of god]. She is mildew because a virgin and [3] Hosty, an unfortunate beach busker—a street entertainer or the Christ or host figure.

Hosty

> [40] who,
> 21
> **sans rootie and sans scrapie, suspicioning as how he was setting**
> 22
> **on a twoodstool on the verge of selfabyss, most starved, with**
> 23
> **melancholia over everything in general, (night birman, you served**
> 24
> **him with natigal's nano!)**

Hosty who without bread and without butter [**sans rootie and sans scrapie** or the 40 day fast and temptation in the desert] suspected that he was sitting on a toadstool on the edge of **selfabyss** or death [suggests self-abuse]. Hosty faces the same dilemma as Adam. He was hungry and depressed over everything in general (night birdman you served him with nightingale's dwarf—no joy). This is Christ from the temptation in the desert to Christ in agony in the night in the Garden of Gethsemane knowing he must die to save all from their many sins that started with original sin. He

> [40] had been towhead tossing on his shake-
> 25
> **down, devising ways and manners of means, of what he loved**
> 26
> **to ifidalicence somehow or other in the nation getting a hold of**
> 27
> **some chap's parabellum in the hope of taking a wing sociable**
> 28
> **and lighting upon a sidewheel dive somewhere off the Dullkey**
> 29
> **Downlairy and Bleakrooky tramaline**
> 30

Hosty had been scratching his head in an effort to figure out how to get what he loved, convincing another person to take flight off the **tramaline** [tram line with fixed schedule] of normal life and trampoline into the life of the spirit. That is to say, substitute for him. He wished to be not a Jesus predestined for death but a Jesus for life. There

> [40] where he could throw true
> 30
> and go and blow the sibicidal napper off himself for two bits to
> 31
> boldywell baltitude in the peace and quitybus of a one sure shot
> 32
> bottle, he after having being trying all he knew with the lady's
> 33
> help of Madam Gristle for upwards of eighteen calanders to get
> 34
> out of Sir Patrick Dun's, through Sir Humphrey Jervis's and
> 35
> into the Saint Kevin's bed in the Adelaide's hosspittles
> 36

There he could be himself, his individual self, rather than the savior for all and blow off the suicidal wrap in exchange for two bits his **boldywell** [boldly and independently well instead of bloody well—wounds on cross] in **baltitude** [antibeatitudes or blessings] for the peace and quiet of one shot [of drink and life]. That is, he would trade being bloody in death for being bold in life. Hosty had for 18 years [like Christ from age 15 to 33, from annunciation to crucifixion] been trying to get out of Sir Patrick Dun's hospital [Dun-done for death fixation] and into Saint Kevin's bed in Adelaide's hospital. Saint Kevin was famous for his bed of rocks. Saint Adelaide was known first as an independent woman in the 10th century and a woman of the world as well as a miracle worker. In other words, Hosty wants to be in this world with both feet on the ground, not up in the air on the cross.

Carrying on:

[41] (from these incurable welleslays among those uncarable
wellasdays
1
through Sant Iago by his cocklehat, goot Lazar, deliver us!)
2
without after having been able to jerrywangle it anysides.
Lisa
3
O'Deavis and Roche Mongan (who had so much incommon,
4
epipsychidically; if the phrase be permitted *hostis et odor insuper*
5
petroperfractus) as an understood thing slept their sleep of
the
6
swimborne in the one sweet undulant mother of tumblerbunks
7
with Hosty
8

The Hospital for Incurables was founded by one Wellesley on
Lazar's hill, the same spot from which the crusades going to Santiago
de Compostella started. Note compost in Compostella and remember Lazar was raised from the dead. Translating: (Deliver us from the
Incurables and the crusades [with cockleshells on their hats] to Santiago de Compostella by Saint Iago.) St. James was known in Spain as
Saint Lago [thus Santiago], which Joyce changes to Iago, the treacherous betrayer in Shakespeare, like the life led for death.
   Cocklehat for cockleshells, meaning a dead heart as in the cockles of my heart. **Cocklehat** for Ophelia's song of death—"you shall
know your true love by his cockle hat and staff and sandal shoon."
Hamlet, the play that features corrupted relationships. **Lazar** [with
the us removed from Lazarus] for risen from the dead individually.
Goot for got him up again [two o's].
   So this Hosty couldn't make it in the other hospital; he wasn't
admitted, was denied paradise. So Hosty slept with Lisa O'Deavis,
mildew Lisa or Mother of God. Hosty also slept with Roche Mongan
[means rock broken and suggests a separated Peter]. They had so
much **incommon** [picture of meaning] **epipsychidically**—
suggesting cycles repeating epically in the human psyche. ***Hostis et
odor insuper petroperfractus*** is about how Christ was betrayed by

403

the greed of the church for material wealth, the crack in rock of Peter the church from which oil petro wealth was obtained—by the visit to Santiago for example.

These two [mildew and Peter] slept with Hosty as an understood thing in the great sweet undulant mother water with **tumblerbunks** for waves from the curse flood.

More from the Humpriad:

> "As an understood thing" (FW41.6) O'Mara and Cloran "slept their sleep of the swimborne in the one sweet undulant mother of tumblerbunks with Hosty" (FW41.6-8). Their passage through the night is likened to being afloat ("swimborne") in the protective maternal amniotic sea of sleep – "tumblerbunks" suggests the "undulant" motion of their tumbling bunks which may be partly the result of their swimming heads after quaffing tumblers of alcohol. In a passage dense with allusions to famous literary figures (Shem biased Hosty's claim to literary greatness through the rann) there is one here to the English poet Algernon Charles Swinburne (1837-1909) whose poem *The Triumph of Time* is echoed here and is quoted by Buck Mulligan in the first chapter of *Ulysses*. "I will go back to the great sweet mother/Mother and lover of men, the sea". There is also a further reference to the opera *La Sonnambula* by the Italian composer Vincenzo Bellini (1801-35).

Going on:

> **[41] just how the shavers in the shaw the yokels in the**
> 8
> **yoats or, well, the wasters in the wilde, and the bustling tweeny-**
> 9
> **dawn-of-all-works (meed of anthems here we pant!) had not been**
> 10
> **many jiffies furbishing potlids, doorbrasses, scholars' applecheeks**
> 11
> **and linkboy's metals when,**
> 12

Just how the shavers in the shaw [thicket—homosexual territory], the yokels in the yoats Yeats or, well, the sex wasters in the wilde [Oscar's thicket]. Like homosexuality, these writers are just a substitute for the real thing. The working women, house maids, bustling **tweeny** maid **dawn** beginning virgin **of all works** [for the wine of

404

anthems here we pant] had not for long been cleaning potlids, door-brasses, applecheeks and linkboy's metals [homosexual terms]—low paying jobs not in paradise—when Hosty wakes up [late] rejuvenated:

[41] ashhopperminded like no fella he go
12
make **bakenbeggfuss** longa white man, the rejuvenated busker (for
13
after a goodnight's rave and rumble and a shinkhams top-morning
14
with his coexes he was not the same man) and his broadawake
15
bedroom suite (our boys, as our Byron called them)
16

Hosty as Christ who would procreate with no woman has lain with Cloran and sodomized Mildew [still a virgin] and is as a result hopped up about asses—**ashhopperminded like no [other] fella** [fellation for the fella]. Ash is associated with soap, the cheapest anal lubricant. Both anal sex and fellation are substitutes for the real thing. He has the white man's hot breakfast, bacon begg fuss white. Here Hamlet [ham let] becomes bacon and hot breakfast and suggests that Noah "let" Ham sodomize him. While sex organ to sex organ sex is a little bit of HSS, anal sex is pure TZTZ, purely one sided.

His two companions, his sweet bedroom suite, were up, Cloran and Mildew Lisa. His dreams have rejuvenated him, his **goodnight's rave and rumble.** After that, they were up and out:

[41] were up
16
and ashuffle from the hogshome they lovenaned The Barrel, cross
17
Ebblinn's chilled hamlet (thrie routes and restings on their then
18
superficies curiously correspondant with those linea and puncta
19

where our tubenny habenny metro maniplumbs below the ober-
20
flake underrails and stations at this time of riding)
21

They shuffled [**ashuffle** soap] along, because their anuses were sore and still laced with soap, from their love nest **hogshome** [bacon fat?] they named the Barrel, as in bung hole in a barrel. They moved cross Dublin's cold hamlet (their letters mixed up **thrie** routes and their rests stops on the surfaces curiously corresponded with those Latin lines and points where our subway metro man plumbs below the surface underrails and stations at this hour [parody of stations of the cross]). In other words, their actions trace the subconscious.

So the threesome:

[41] to the thrum-
21
mings of a crewth fiddle which, cremoaning and cronauning, levey
22
grevey, witty and wevey, appy, leppy and playable, caressed the
23
ears of the subjects of King Saint Finnerty the Festive who, in
24
brick homes of their own and in their flavory fraiseberry beds,
25
heeding hardly cry of honeyman, soed lavender or foyne-boyne
26
salmon alive, with their priggish mouths all open for the lar-ger
27
appraisiation of this longawaited Messiagh of roaratorios, were
28
only halfpast atsweeeep
29

To the thrummings of a fiddle like a bowed lyre [bent back from carrying cross] they were crooning and **cremoaning** [humming and droning], levity and gravity, witty and weavey, **appy** happy, **leppy**

406

and **playable**. With this kind of music they caressed the ears of those who lived in the Saint Finnerty area. The Humpriad:

> "Levey grevey, witty and wevey, appy, leppy and playable" (FW41.22-23) suggest the fairy tale Snow White's seven dwarves, here as attributes of ALP as light hearted, witty, playful, "wavey" happy lapping purling stream/river – the River of wifely, provocative Life/River Liffey – her initials are given in the last three adjectival names. She is referred to here because of the link between the trio's music and the "music" of her purling river/ stream – music has to have "beat" or timing, symbolised by ALP as River of Time's flow.

The three flow by the strawberry beds and the street hawkers— the honeyman, the sweet lavender man and the Boyne live salmon man. They all had their priggish mouths open in surprise and ready to appraise this long awaited Messiah of roaring oratorios. The subjects in the neighborhood were half asleep. Then the trio:

> [41] and after a brisk pause at a pawnbroking
> 29
> establishment for the prothetic purpose of redeeming the song-
> 30
> ster's truly admirable false teeth and a prolonged visit to a house
> 31
> of call at Cujas Place, fizz, the Old Sots' Hole in the parish of
> 32
> Saint Cecily within the liberty of Ceolmore not a thousand or one
> 33
> national leagues, that was, by Griffith's valuation, from the site
> 34
> of the statue of Primewer Glasstone setting a match to the march
> 35
> of a maker (last of the stewards peut-être), where, the tale rambles
> 36

Hosty didn't need his teeth during the previous evening's activity [he may have been sucking], but now needs them to bite so they stop for his false teeth. Translating: After a quick stop at a pawnbroker for

the prophetic prosthetic [**prothetic** means make ready the Eucharist]
to redeem the songster's [Hosty's] false teeth [another substitute]
they made a longer visit to a pub at Cujas Place, namely the pub Old
Stots' Hole. This was Swift's favorite Pub and is in the parish of
Saint Cecily [patron saint of music] within the liberty of Ceolmore
[great music] less than a thousand leagues by Griffith's valuation
from Gladstone's monument, the dead legislator, which sets a match
[boundary] to the march of a maker [TZTZ]. The trio goes out to
sing the ballad under Gladstone's monument [glad stone is white
rock]:

[42] along, the trio of whackfolthediddlers was joined by a
further —
1
intentions — apply — tomorrow casual and a decent sort of
the
2
hadbeen variety who had just been touching the weekly insult,
3
phewit, and all figblabbers (who saith of noun?) had stimulants
4
in the shape of gee and gees stood by the damn decent sort
after
5
which stag luncheon and a few ones more just to celebrate
yester-
6
day, flushed with their firestuffostered friendship, the rascals
came
7
out of the licensed premises,
8

The trio is joined by a further, a fourth, being of the decent sort—
those who work and who just got paid [the weekly insult]. They were
also joined by all the underemployed, the **figblabbers,** which is to
say rumor spreaders about fig Garden fruit. The stimulants of the
spirit available to the figblabbers were limited to watching and utter-
ing **gee and gees** [Jesus] while after a stag luncheon more came out
who had enjoyed a drop of the creature [spirits here confused with
the blood of Christ] just to celebrate yesterday [not the new possibilities of tomorrow]. They were flushed with their **firestuffostered**

408

friendship. These are more dependent refugee suffers from the loss of paradise, more miserables who want all to be in the same boat. At work here is the traditional [non-K] notion that god assumed poverty by coming into the world as Jesus Christ.

From the Humpriad:

> At the Old Sots' Hole, Hosty, O'Mara and Cloran, "the trio of whackfolthediddlers" (FW42.1), are joined by "a further – intentions – apply – tomorrow casual and a decent sort" (FW42.1-2). "Whackfolthediddlers" refers to the song *Whack Fol the Diddle* and to Hosty and his two comrades as merry makers and fiddlers. The fourth man who joins them "had just been touching the weekly insult" (FW42.3), a Cork phrase for getting one's wages, the insult being either or both of the small amount involved, and position of the recipient as a "wage slave", one dependent on another's money, but in any event enough in this case for "the damned decent sort" (FW42.5) to "stand" or pay for drinks for all four of them – "had stimulants in the shape of gee and gees stood by the damn decent sort" (FW42.4-5). This fourth person, it seems, is only a casual labourer who has to apply on a day to day basis to see if work is available ("further – intentions – apply – tomorrow"). This last phrase also spells "F-I-A-T" i.e. Latin: "fiat" = let there/it be done, followed on FW42.4 by "phewit" which = Latin: "fuit" = it was (done), echoing the Genesis account of God's creation of light/life/the World: "God said 'Let there be light', and there was light". "Fiat/fuit" is a pervasive Wakean motif relevant here to Hosty as Shemian artist's creational act of composing the rann, in a house of spirits and a hell hole where "firestuff" ("firestuffostered" - FW42.7) accompanies/aids the composition.

So our trio, now joined by a fourth, come out of the pub having composed the Ballad about Harold:

> **[42] (Browne's first, the small p.s. ex-ex-**
> **8**
> **executive capahand in their sad rear like a lady's postscript: I want**
> **9**
> **money. Pleasend), wiping their laughleaking lipes on their sleeves,**
> **10**

how the bouckaleens shout their roscan generally (seinn fion,
11
seinn fion's araun.)
12

(Brown the fourth came out of Browne's pub first. All of them had their hats in their hands behind them **in their sad rear**, like a ladies ass is her postscript—for my pleasing rear end please send money.) They were wiping their laugh wet lips on their sleeves, (ourselves alone ourselves alone—no procreation). Bouckaleens, young boys, and **roscan** red abrasions on white bottoms continue the homosexual theme. For more allusions from the Humpriad:

> With drunken bravado, the men shout their defiance of HCE and chant Irish nationalist slogans: "(Seinn fion, seinn fion's araun)" (FW42.11-12) = Irish: "Sinn Fein, Sinn Fein Amhain" = Ourselves, Ourselves Alone", an expression of Nationalist Ireland's parochial self isolation from the rest of the world, which Joyce fled Ireland to escape. Also, Irish: "seinn" = play music + "fion" = wine, + "fionn" = white, fair, + "araun" = bread, + "amrhan" = song – so we have again HCE as the Host, the eucharistic sacrifice of white bread/body and red wine/blood during the performance of a Mass - HCE being symbolically sacrificed through the words and music of the rann, although it is his reputation that is here to be murdered. The men shout/chant that HCE, "their roscan generally" is to be their sacrificial Christ figure – German: "sein" = to be, so: "to be their red wine, to be their white bread. Also, "fion" suggests HCE as the Irish giant hero Finn MacCool.

The homosexual theme reinforces the general idea that in bringing Harold down as HCE, they the crowd in parochial and self-isolated Ireland are missing the real thing—individuality. Instead of ourselves alone it should be myself alone. Accustomed to substitutes, they plan to deprive Harold of his independence, just like Christ.

They have composed the lay in the pub, the public house:

[42] and the rhymers' world was with reason the
12
richer for a wouldbe ballad, to the balledder of which the world
13
of cumannity singing owes a tribute for having placed on the
14

planet's melomap his lay of the vilest bogeyer but most at-
trac-
15
tionable avatar the world has ever had to explain for.
16

And because of them the rhymers' world was with reason richer because of a would be ballad, a ballad composed in the public house
about Harold based on the gossip in the chain from the Cad, Mrs.
Cad, the priest, the lay teacher and down and outers. The world of
the human community is combined as **cumannity singing.** This
community owes a tribute for having placed on the planet's songmap
this lay about the vilest bogar yogiar buggerer **bog ever** [Harold the
individual yogi] but the most attractive actionable avatar the world
has ever had to explain for [HCE the concept]. An avatar is an incar-
nation of a Hindu deity in human form or someone who is the manifestation of an idea or concept. In this case, the latter. HCE is the
avatar of common humanity. The song is a lay because he is to fall.
Like Christ, he is to lay down for others.

[42] This, more krectly lubeen or fellow — me — lieder was
first
17
poured forth where Riau Liviau riots and col de Houdo
humps,
18
under the shadow of the monument of the shouldhavebeen
legis-
19
lator (Eleutheriodendron! Spare, woodmann, spare!) to an
over-
20
flow meeting of all the nations in Lenster fullyfilling the vi-
sional
21
area
22

This, more correctly identified not as a lay [normally a heterosexual
reference] but as a **lubeen**, which suggests have been lubed
[**lubeen**—homosexual reference] or fellow—me—lieder [from follow the leader like Christ]. It was first given [**poured forth**] where
the river basin riots and col de Houdo humps were held, under the
shadow of the legislator who should have been the man who

411

brought independence to Ireland, who preached but failed to achieve Irish independence [Parnell]. (The Tree of Freedom, spare it woodman). Now the crowd grows to all the nations in Leinster filling the area of vision. More Humpriad:

> More specifically, Hosty's rann is performed "under the shadow of the monument of the shouldhavebeen legislator" (FW42.19-20) which refers firstly to Charles Stewart Parnell (1846-91), Irish political leader, "the uncrowned king of Ireland" who fell from power and popularity before he could achieve Irish Home Rule ("the shouldhavebeen legislator"). Secondly, it refers to Parnell's political adversary, the English Liberal Prime Minister William Ewart Gladstone (1809-98) who made continual efforts to solve "the Irish Question" including a failed attempt of his own to legislate for Irish Home Rule. Thirdly, it refers to Daniel O'Connell (1775-1847), "the Liberator", the Irish patriot, orator and politician who achieved Catholic Emancipation for Ireland by a series of mass rallies (like the one now organised by Hosty), but who failed to achieve Home Rule because of his imprisonment on a sedition charge and failing health. Parnell has a statue at the top of O'Connell Street (formerly Sackville Street) and O'Connell has a statue in O'Connell Street ("the monument"). Hosty and his followers perform the Ballad of Persse O'Reilly under the aegis of Ireland's two great promoters of Irish independence from England . . .

The Crowd treats HCE as a foreigner, an invader and here the hated English invader/oppressor.

The crowd was huge and diverse for the ballad about their avatar, the ballad that would substitute for their own feelings about HCE:

> **[42] and, as a singleminded supercrowd, easily representative,**
> 22
> **what with masks, whet with faces, of all sections and cross sections**
> 23
> **(wineshop and cocoahouse poured out to brim up the broaching)**
> 24
> **of our liffeyside people**
> 25

The crowd was single minded, a supercrowd with no individual judgment, super meaning over and above, as in over and above the individual. The crowd easily substituted for the individuals in it and gave

412

them masks keen with faces of all sections of our water-side people [Irish], the wineshop and cocoahouse as well having poured out more people into the crowd. In addition there were foreigners:

[42] (to omit to mention of the mainland mino-
25
rity and such as had wayfared *via* Watling, Ernin, Icknild and
26
Stane, in chief a halted cockney car with its quotal of Hard-muth's
27
hacks, a northern tory, a southern whig, an eastanglian chroni-
28
cler and a landwester guardian) ranging from slips of young
29
dublinos from Cutpurse Row having nothing better to do than
30
walk about with their hands in their kneepants, sucking air-
31
whackers, weedulicet, jumbobricks, side by side with truant
32
officers, three woollen balls and poplin in search of a croust of
33
pawn to busy professional gentlemen, a brace of palesmen with
34
dundrearies, nooning toward Daly's, fresh from snipehitting and
35
mallardmissing on Rutland heath, exchanging cold sneers, mass-
36

The crowd contained foreigners, politicians from various parties, street thieves, truant officers, bread beggars, busy professionals, hunters [**snipehitting and mallardmissing**]. These positions were made possible by loss of paradise. Truant officers would normally catch those who have skipped the school of individuality. From Humpriad:

These young pickpockets stand "side by side with truant officers" (FW42.32-33) who presumably would normally be out to catch

413

them for avoiding school (the truant officers are both officers, perhaps of the law, who are playing truant from their duties, and, as truant officers, are playing truant to their own duties as such, such is the subversive effect of Hosty's rann/ballad). "Three woollen balls and poplin in search of a croust of pawn" (FW42.33-34) may refer to poor people in search of a crust of bread to eat (croustade = a case of fried bread or pastry for serving game + croute = a thick slice of fried bread for serving entrees and also "pawn" = French: "pain" = bread) – the three balls being the traditional pawnbrokers sign; poplin manufacture was a major industry in 17th-18th century Dublin. There is also a reference to the three soldier sons as three boys with hairy male testicles and the two tempting girls personified by the poplin dresses they wear to tease and entice father ("pop") HCE as a Christ of Pain figure who is also eucharistically a crust of bread.

In addition, the crowd contained:

> **mass-**
> **[43] going ladies from Hume Street in their chairs, the bearers baited,**
> **1**
> **some wandering hamalags out of the adjacent cloverfields of**
> **2**
> **Mosse's Gardens, an oblate father from Skinner's Alley, brick-**
> **3**
> **layers, a fleming, in tabinet fumant, with spouse and dog, an aged**
> **4**
> **hammersmith who had some chisellers by the hand, a bout of**
> **5**

Wealthy Ladies from Hume Street are being carried in chairs to Mass. The crowd baits the bearers of the chairs, not the ladies. Simpletons or mentally insane persons like pigs came from the cloverfields of Mosse's Gardens near a hospital, a fat father came from Skinner's Alley, bricklayers from Babel, a Dutchman with spouse and dog, a mason with his children. Note that people are referred to as types, not as individuals. For more detail the Humpriad:

> The Rabelaisian list of people in the crowd continues with "massgoing ladies from Hume Street in their chairs, the bearers baited"

(FW42.36- 43.1), i.e. the ladies are on the way, en masse, to Catholic Mass in sedan chairs, their sedan bearers being baited like bears by the crowd; Hume Street is a street in Dublin (McHugh). Also referred to is the anecdote that the philosopher David Hume (1711-1776), a religious arch sceptic, was forced to recite the Pater Noster before an old lady would help him out of a bog (recounted in Virginia Woolf's *To The Lighthouse*).

"Wandering hamalags out of the adjacent cloverfields of Mosse's Gardens" (FW43.2-3) are simpletons (Irish: "amalog" = simpleton) who have escaped/wandered out of the grounds of the Rotunda Hospital Dublin, a maternity hospital in Rutland Square in the North East of the city built by Bartholomew Mosse, an 18th Century Dublin doctor and philanthropist. The hospital held fund raising fetes in its gardens. "Cloverfields" suggests "clever", the opposite of simple, and the presence of simpletons also suggests botched deliveries of babies; "hamalags" may also suggest amatory hags or whores whose unwanted pregnancies associated them with Mosse's hospital.

"Hamalags" are also pigs, - ham on legs - which have escaped from their field (together with a reference to the common expression "as happy as a pig in clover") – the pig as Ireland's totem or representative animal, conjoined with another symbol of Ireland, the clover leaf or shamrock - and sheep, (German : "hammel" = mutton) of which this easily led, representative crowd, is composed.

There is also reference to wandering Jews (via their forbidden meat, pork) and perhaps to the legend of the Wandering Jew Ahasuerus who, in punishment for mocking Christ on the way to the Crucifixion, was made immortal, only able to die on the Day of Judgement at the end of the World, again suggesting HCE as a suffering, eucharistic, Christ figure at the mercy of this crowd and also that this is HCE's own doom laden Day of Judgement. The story of Ahasuerus is mirrored in that of the Flying Dutchman, (see below).

Next we have "an oblate father from Skinner's Alley" (FW43.3) i.e. a member of The Oblate Fathers, a Dublin religious congregation, - oblated (dedicated, offered up) to a monastic life that seems to agree with them (oblate suggests bloated, round and fat, and also oblate = flattened at opposite sides or poles as a spheroid, - as opposed to the skinniness of the underfed laity they serve/"skin"). Skinner's Alley is where, according to McHugh, Protestant aldermen in Dublin took refuge from the mob in James II's reign. The novel *The House by the Churchyard* by Joseph Sheridan Le Fanu features singing aldermen from Skinner's Alley who emerge riotously drunk from the Phoenix Inn to encounter and enliven a funeral party returning from a funeral in Chapter II.

"Bricklayers, a fleming" (FW43.3-4) may refer to the Flemish Bond, a bricklayer's bond of alternate headers and stretchers in every course. The "fleming, in tabinet fumant, with spouse and dog" (FW43.4) may refer to the legendary Flying Dutchman subject of an opera by Wagner in which the Dutchman, cursed for invoking the devil's aid in rounding the Cape of Good Hope, must sail forever until Judgement Day with his ghostly crew unless he can win the love of a good woman who will be faithful unto death, an attempt he can only make every seven years. He does so in Senta, who commits suicide when the Dutchman mistakenly believes her to be unfaithful and rejects her; on her death, the opera ends with the Dutchman's and Senta's spirits rising over the sea to Heaven. Here the Fleming /Dutchman in his watery/hell fire smoking clothes ("fleming" = flaming, + Irish : "tabinet" = Irish watered fabric + French "fumant" = smoking) is with his spouse and God (dog reversed).

Next, the "aged hammersmith" or mason (FW43.4-5) is described with chisels, the tools of his trade to hand ("by the hand" - FW43.5 - = Dutch : "bij de hand" = handy, at hand) but also he has children (Dublin slang: "chiselurs" = children) by the hand.

More join in:

> **[43] cudgel players, not a few sheep with the braxy, two bluecoat**
> **6**
> **scholars, four broke gents out of Simpson's on the Rocks, a**
> **7**
> **portly and a pert still tassing Turkey Coffee and orange shrub in**
> **8**
> **tickeyes door, Peter Pim and Paul Fry and then Elliot and, O,**
> **9**
> **Atkinson, suffering hell's delights from the blains of their annui-**
> **10**
> **tants' acorns not forgetting a deuce of dianas ridy for the hunt, a**
> **11**
> **particularist prebendary pondering on the roman easter, the ton-**

12
sure question and greek uniates, plunk em, a lace lappet
head or
13
two or three or four from a window,
14

People with clubs, diseased sheep, two medical students, four broke
men from Simpson's Hospital, a young woman drinking fashionable
Turkish coffee and orange juice; Peter, Paul, Elliot and Atkinson
suffering from corns. This is a primitive human mass, made into sau-
sage.

More and more and more. It is designed to make you tired and it
did me. So you can do the rest yourself:

[43] and so on down to a few good
old souls, who,as they were juiced after taking their pledge
over at
the uncle's place, were evidently under the spell of liquor,
from the
wake of Tarry the Tailor a fair girl, a jolly postoboy thinking
off
three flagons and one, a plumodrole, a half sir from the
weaver's
almshouse who clings and clings and chatchatchat clings to
her, a
wholedam's cloudhued pittycoat, as child, as curiolater, as
Caoch
O'Leary. The wararrow went round, so it did, (a nation wants
a gaze) and the ballad, in the felibrine trancoped metre affec-
tioned
by Taiocebo in his *Casudas de Poulichinello Artahut*, stump-
stampaded on to a slip of blancovide and headed by an ex-
cessively
rough and red woodcut, privately printed at the rimepress of
Delville, soon fluttered its secret on white highway and
brown
byway to the rose of the winds and the blew of the gaels,
from
archway to lattice and from black hand to pink ear, village
crying
to village, through the five pussyfours green of the united

states
of Scotia Picta — and he who denays it, may his hairs be
rubbed
in dirt! To the added strains (so peacifold) of his majesty the
flute, that onecrooned king of inscrewments, Piggott's purest, *ciello*
alsoliuto, which Mr Delaney (Mr Delacey?), horn, anticipat-
ing
a perfect downpour of plaudits among the rapsods, piped
out of his decentsoort hat, looking still more like his pursey-
ful
namesake as men of Gaul noted, but before of to sputabout,
the

[44] snowycrested curl amoist the leader's wild and moulting
hair,
'Ductor' Hitchcock hoisted his fezzy fuzz at bludgeon's
height
signum to his companions of the chalice for the Loud Fellow,
boys' and silentium in curia! (our maypole once more where
he rose
of old) and the canto was chantied there chorussed and
christened
where by the old tollgate, Saint Annona's Street and Church.

So now finally to the ballad, the lay, the rann about Persse O'Reilly,
which is a take off on French for earwig or *perce-oreille.* Pearse &
O'Rahilly were involved in the unsuccessful Easter Rising.

Ballad means a popular poem or song usually attacking persons
or institutions. This ballad attacks the independent attitude. How the
crowd knows this is aimed at HC Earwicker is not explained. They
would not know French. Perhaps they are happy to attack anyone
who is too high and mighty.

This attack ballad starts with an artillery barrage, with a thun-
derword:

[44] And around the lawn the rann it rann and this is the rann
that
7
Hosty made. Spoken. Boyles and Cahills, Skerretts and
Pritchards,
8

418

viersified and piersified may the treeth we tale of live in stoney.
9

May the truth [procreated in the tree—**treeth**] we tell of life live in stone. Tree allows new growth; dogma is set in stone; stone sinks.

[44] **Here line the refrains of. Some vote him Vike, some mote him**
10
Mike, some dub him Llyn and Phin while others hail him Lug
11
Bug Dan Lop, Lex, Lax, Gunne or Guinn. Some apt him Arth,
12
some bapt him Barth, Coll, Noll, Soll, Will, Weel, Wall
13

Tindall translates this as "some call him Vico [**Vike**] or Michelet [historian] or Michael [**Mike**] or Dublin [**Llyn and Phin**]. Others call him ear [**Lug**], bug or salmon [**lax**]." **Barth, Coll, Noll, Soll, Will, Weel, Wall** apparently refer to the initial letters in the Gaelic alphabet. These are sources of authority. Note the progression from **vote**, to **mote**, to **dub** to **apt** to **bapt**. **Mote** has a number of relevant meanings: a flaw, a mound, permission, express necessity, and find fault. **Dub**: a muddy pool, sound of a drum, a key, a fool, dub music, give title to, thrust, and give money. **Apt**: suited or fitted. **Bapt**: short for baptize. Notice in this progression the increasing degree of dependence. Notice also in **apt** the fragment of the story of the Norwegian captain and tailor in the progression from Apt to Bapt.

[44] **but I**
parse him Persse O'Reilly else he's called no name at all. To-
14
gether. Arrah, leave it to Hosty, frosty Hosty, leave it to Hosty
15
for he's the mann to rhyme the rann, the rann, the rann, the king

16
of all ranns.
17

But I [the Ballad] call him Persse O'Reilly. There is no hint of a French connection here and this is a suggestive name on its own. The word used for I "call" him is **parse**, I parse him. Parse means to separate for analysis. In addition, **Persse** easily becomes purse, for a materially oriented sex depository. **O'Reilly** hides reality.

The history of the name suggests a succession from brave individual to group. From Irelandeye.com on Irish names:

> **O'Reilly**
>
> The name O'Reilly comes from the Irish chieftain Ragheallach, who lived at the time of Brian Boru and, like him, was killed at the Battle of Clontarf in 1014. He was a great-grandson of Maomordha, a descendant of the O'Conors, kings of Connacht. Today, it is one of the most numerous names in Ireland. Co. Cavan is a particular stronghold of the name.
>
> Myles "The Slasher" O'Reilly was the heroic defender of the bridge at Finea in Co. Cavan in 1646 where he and a force of one hundred held out against a 1,000-strong Cromwellian army. O'Reilly is commemorated by a cross in the main street of Finea, a pretty village on the banks of the River Inny.

Parsing Ragheallach: *Rag* means race and *ceallach* means gregarious. The O'Reillys became famous as military commanders throughout Europe. [pg4anna.tripod.com/roma-names.htm].

Harold is called Persse O'Reilly or nothing at all. The Ballad or crowd gets to decide. Harold is not to have his own individual name; he is to be demoted to HCE. Generality is to be substituted for individuality.

Hosty is the man, the man to rhyme the rann. He is the King, the King that is strikingly missing from the Humpty Dumpty story. Hosty is the king of the group, of TZTZ god mentality. Christ registers dependency; everyone needs Christ to remove sin.

Back to the text:

[44] Have you here? (Some ha) Have we where? (Some
17
hant) Have you hered? (Others do) Have we whered? (Others dont)
18

This is a narrator, not the crowd. **Have you here? (Some ha)** Do **you** exist [as an individual] here? (Some **ha** or laugh). **Ha** can also be a contraction of have, that is to say a short or small have. **Have we where? (Some hant).** Do **we** [as a group] exist somewhere else— that is not as an individual right here? (Some don't laugh) [**hant**— this is a contraction of ha not]. **Have you hered?** Have you [as an individual] existed here in the past [**hered**—here plus past tense and heard [time] as well as Herod seeking the child that will depose him]. (Others do). **Have we whered? (Others dont).** Have we [as a group] existed some where in the past? If so where [space]? Others don't. Note the alternation between individual and group in the questions whereas the reaction is always a group [some and others].

> [44] It's cumming, it's brumming! The clip, the clop! (All cla) Glass
> 19
> crash. The
> (klikkaklakkaklaskaklopatzklatschabattacreppycrotty-
> 20 graddaghsemmihsammihnouithappluddyappladdypkonp-
> kot!).
> 21

The merde is coming. All literary creation [such as the Ballad] is like excrement in that it is digested experience, here mostly digested spirits. TZTZ creation is in this same category. Unlike human procreation, this creation issues from the anus, where non-procreative sex takes place.

This thunder word is made up mostly of foreign languages meaning clap, as in group applause and clap of thunder. Applause for the ballad is the thunder of the fallsters, their artillery barrage.

My machine will not reproduce the music for the Rann, so note in the musical "score" on page 44 that the motion of the melody upward is limited step progression [that is limited improvement] and any jumps of more than one note are downward. The lowest note keeps getting lower, as is appropriate for the fall of Harold, which is what the crowd wants, to make him HCE. Note that the melody repeats over and over again, the analog of crowd behavior.

The key is A major, with three sharps, and the major triad is A, C# and E. A is the fundamental **tonic**, C# the **subdominant** and E the **dominant**. You can sense in this TZTZ god in the dominant and dependent humans in the subdominant. The fundament tonic, the lowest of the three main notes, is where everyone falls. Since there is no "H" in the normal seven note key [from A to G], H would be A again, such that the sequence A C E is the same as HCE with a suggestion of end to beginning repetition, as in *Da Copo*, the musical notation at the end of the score.

As a key, A major suggests a major person, an independent individual. The tune starts with an emphasis on E, which is the **dominant**, descends in the 6th measure to an emphasis on C natural not C sharp, the subdominant, and then to A the tonic. C natural is not in the key of C sharp and when first sounded is disharmonious, produce a clashing tone in a minor mode, minor because flattened. This suggests the effect of being under a dominant god—the underling human is minor in importance because fallen. But C natural is used so many times in that same 6th measure that the minor mode begins to sound normal, begins to sound "natural." Just as the crowd would make minor individuals and begin to sound normal to its members. In fact, the key is changed to A minor, which is indicated by the sharp on G in the 8th measure, a sharp that would not be added if the key were still in A major. The key of A minor like the key of C major has no sharps or flats in the signature. You get the change from A Major to A Minor, from a major person to a minor person in Joyce music.

Note that the fundamental tonic key note A is sounded only three times, in the 9th, 10th and 12th measures. In the first stanza, the words Wall, Wall and All sound on this note. All is contained in Wall, both of which keep individuals out and allow only all within, not each within.

Note similar construction at the end of the other stanzas on the tonic notes: Mountjoy, Mountjoy and joy; reform, reform and form; horns, horns and horns; floor, store and lower; door, door and more; man-o'-war, man-o'-war and bar; cod, cod and begod; woo, doo and maidenloo; zoo, Coo and noo; fusiliers, rears and years; green, green and seen; Danes, Danes and remains. These suggest the fundamental tonic ideas of Finnegans Wake.

This Ballad is a take off on the original Humpty Dumpty verse:

> Humpty Dumpty sat on a wall
> Humpty Dumpty had a great fall
> All the King's horses and all the King's men
> Couldn't put Humpty Dumpty back together again.

As we have discussed, the King is not included in those who were trying to put Humpty Dumpty back together. The King didn't want to put Humpty Dumpty back together again and without the King the horses and men couldn't do it even if they wanted to. The King that is missing is ES, the unifier. This Ballad will be a replay of the actions of TZTZ god. That King wants Humpty Dumpty broken and separated, not unified in the spirit.

Substitution remains the technique, with the meaning of the words used in the Ballad having a TZTZ god type meaning but also lurking in those same words is a ES god type meaning.

So here we go:

[45] Have you heard of one Humpty Dumpty
1
How he fell with a roll and a rumble
2
And curled up like Lord Olofa Crumple
3
By the butt of the Magazine Wall,
4
    (Chorus) Of the Magazine Wall,
     5
        Hump, helmet and all?
      6

Lord Olofa Crumple is Oliver Cromwell, the foreign invader, which is what Harold is being treated as. The tone of the Ballad seems to champion the fall of Humpty Dumpty. He has a hump on his back, which one would receive in a fall. He was wearing a helmet because he expected head trouble in the land of curses. Before the fall, Humpty Dumpty was one because he had a simple undivided soul, all of one piece and unified like ES. Like an egg, he presented birth and growth possibilities. But now, Humpty Dumpty can only be used for an omelet, where all the eggs are mixed together homogeneously and indiscriminately as in a crowd. An omelet can not give birth:

[45] He was one time our King of the Castle
8
Now he's kicked about like a rotten old parsnip.
9
And from Green street he'll be sent by order of His Worship
10

To the penal jail of Mountjoy
11

    (Chorus) To the jail of Mountjoy!
    12

        Jail him and joy.
      13

Like Adam, he was once King of the premises, but now he has been parsnipped, cut back to par or average. And from the green garden he will be sent by His Worship TZTZ god to the penal jail of Mountjoy, incarcerated in a realm of sex and death.

    [45] **He was fafafather of all schemes for to bother us**
    15
    Slow coaches and immaculate contraceptives for the popu-
    lace,
    16
    Mare's milk for the sick, seven dry Sundays a week,
    17
    Openair love and religion's reform,
    18

        (Chorus) And religious reform,
      19

            Hideous in form.
        20

Now as Adam, he was the stuttering father of schemes to bother us because in the Garden he was slow to coach Eve [**Slow coaches—** slow transport of the spirit or slow teacher] and did not participate in the sexual activity with Eve [**immaculate contraceptives**]. Mother's milk is for the sick not the babies [since Adam did not procreate with Eve] and no spirits during the week. Openair love in the garden and reform of religion? Adam preached repentance to Eve after they were ejected from the Garden. The independent man would abolish TZTZ religion that keeps the faithful dependent. **Hideous in form** would be fearful and dependent Adam hiding in the bushes in Eden.

    [45] **Arrah, why, says you, couldn't he manage it?**
    22
    I'll go bail, my fine dairyman darling,
    23

Like the bumping bull of the Cassidys
24
All your butter is in your horns.
25

> (Chorus) His butter is in his horns.
> 26

>> Butter his horns!
>> 27

Adam couldn't manage it because his butter was in his horns, he gave no milk, was no good. No male no sperm. His energy was for warfare and strife, not for procreation.

[45] (Repeat) Hurrah there, Hosty, frosty Hosty, change that shirt
29

>> [on ye,
>> 30
Rhyme the rann, the king of all ranns!
31

Hosty, the frosty Hosty, the man without women, needs to change the shirt he wore on the cross because it was cut [as the curtain was rent in the Temple]. Rann suggests wren, the King of all birds. Campbell provides the connection:

> A tradition verse sung on St. Stepehn's day, when a wren is killed and carried about the town hung on a stick. This Scapegoat Wren is a folk reduction of the crucified god, and as such is an appropriate figure for HCE.

Like the wren, Harold's independence is to be sacrificed for the group. Note in line 30 the unusual parenthesis before **on ye**. The second or closing parenthesis is missing. In oral delivery the parenthesis would not be detectible. This suggests that by structures that are not detectible you cannot go back but can go forward.

> **[45]** *Balbaccio, balbuccio!,*
33
We had chaw chaw chops, chairs, chewing gum, the chicken-
34

> [pox and china chambers
> 35
> Universally provided by this soffsoaping salesman.
> 36
> [46] Small wonder He'll Cheat E'erawan our local lads nick-named him
> 1
> When Chimpden first took the floor
> 2
> (Chorus) With his bucketshop store
> 3
> Down Bargainweg, Lower.
> 4

Stuttering stuttering. **Chaw chaw chops** suggest chow chow chop which is a "lighter," a transport boat, usually flat bottomed, used to transfer the last smaller items to fill up a ship. Having no keel [read independence], it must bounce on the waves [get ready to kneel]. Translating: so we had various small items, chairs, chewing gum and disease universally provided by the soft-soaping salesman, in other words nothing of value. TZTZ religion transports only minor spirit. Since he [will] cheat everyone, our local lads named him HCE [he cheats everyone]. The independent individual cheats all the dependent ones by being different. He cheats them in his unlicensed premises on lower **bargainweg**. Perhaps this identifies Earwicker for the crowd.

Pox and china chambers gets the unusual one parenthetical formation. China is British rhyming slang for a friend (shortened from china plate, meaning mate) and American slang for a small room off the main room. With our blocking parenthesis, we are in a small room, not the main room, with others when we are with TZTZ god.

> [46] So snug he was in his hotel premises sumptuous
> 6
> But soon we'll bonfire all his trash, tricks and trumpery
> 7
> And'tis short till sheriff Clancy'll be winding up his unlimited
> 8
> [company
> 9
> With the bailiff's bom at the door,
> 10

426

(Chorus) Bimbam at the door.
11

    Then he'll bum no more.
12

Now the group registers as the sponsor of the bonfire of the vanities. The target is described is snug, his premises pretentious, he is full of pride. Like the books and cosmetic items burned under the Dominican priest Savonarola, we will soon burn him out. We will soon be winding up his pursuit of the unlimited. We will make him limited. The authorities will seize him. This time company or group gets the blocking parenthesis.

The Ballad continues to downsize the target now probably understood as Harold, demonize him as an invader:

[46] Sweet bad luck on the waves washed to our island
13
The hooker of that hammerfast Viking
14
And Gall's curse on the day when Eblana bay
15
Saw his black and tan man-o'-war.
16
    (Chorus) Saw his man-o'-war.
17

    On the harbour bar.
18

In English Gall means impudent boldness, registering the independence theme. In Italian, it means foreigner. The crowd treats an independent person as a foreigner, a stranger to their group mentality. Complimenting this theme, the Black and Tans were English recruits in the Royal Irish constabulary, the force controlling Ireland for the British. Some history from the History Learning Site:

> In 1919, the British government advertised for men who were willing to "face a rough and dangerous task". Many former British army soldiers had come back from Western Europe and did not find a land fit for heroes. They came back to unemployment and few firms needed men whose primary skill was fighting in war. Therefore, there were plenty of ex-servicemen who were willing to reply to the government's advert. For many the sole attraction was not political or national pride – it was simply money. The men got

427

paid ten shillings a day. They got three months training before being sent to Ireland. The first unit arrived in Ireland in March 1920. Once in Ireland it quickly became apparent that there were not enough uniforms for all those who had joined up. Therefore they wore a mixture of uniforms – some military, some RIC. This mixture gave them the appearance of being in khaki and dark police uniform. As a result, these men got the nickname "Black and Tans", and it stuck. Some say that the nickname came from a pack of hunting hounds known as the 'Black and Tans'.

The Black and Tans did not act as a supplement to the RIC. Though some men were experienced in trench warfare, they lacked the self-discipline that would have been found in the Western Front. Many Black and Tan units all but terrorised local communities. Community policing was the preserve of the RIC. For the Black and Tans, their primary task was to make Ireland "hell for the rebels to live in". Over 8000 Black and Tans went to Ireland and while they found it difficult to cope with men who used classic guerrilla tactics against them, those who lived in areas where the Black and Tans were based, paid the price.

Black and Tans were particularly cruel in attempting to stop Irish independence. They were the hunting hounds for the TZTZ-like forces of dependence and fear. Black and tan also refers to a combination of dark and light beers, a mixed or non-unified spirit.

> **[46] Where from? roars Poolbeg. Cookingha'pence, he bawls Donnez-**
> **18**
>> **[moi scampitle, wick an wipin'fampiny**
>> **19**
> **Fingal Mac Oscar Onesine Bargearse Boniface**
> **20**
> **Thok's min gammelhole Norveegickers moniker**
> **21**
> **Og as ay are at gammelhore Norveegickers cod.**
> **22**
>> **(Chorus) A Norwegian camel old cod.**
>> **23**
>>> **He is, begod.**
>>> **24**

Fingal Mac Oscar Onesine Bargearse Boniface is **a** reference to Oscar Wilde [full name Oscar Fingal O'Flaherite Wills Wilde] with a

428

reference to a round rear end thrown in. So Harold is being compared to a homosexual, given Adam's experience in the Garden. Thok is an old hole Norwegian name, as old as are old hore Norwegian cod. A Norwegian camel old cod. Camel here means a water tight compartment used to raise a sunken ship. Cod has several suggestive meanings: a fool, a husk and a scrotum. The blocking parenthesis gets **moi scampitle, wick an wipin'fampiny,** which I translate as lobster [scampi] plus little, wick and wiping fanny/family. Caught in the claws of the curse, I dip my wick and wipe my fanny/family experience.

Going on:

> [46] **Lift it, Hosty, lift it, ye devil ye! up with the rann, the rhyming**
> 26
>
> > **[rann!**
> > 27

A short stanza emphasizing rhymes. **Rhymes suggest the crowd, the group with the same ending.** The blocking parenthesis contains the rann so this stanza is short. Hosty lifts the rann as Harold is to be placed on the equivalent of the cross, sacrificed for the crowd:

> [46] **It was during some fresh water garden pumping**
> 30
> **Or, according to the *Nursing Mirror*, while admiring the mon-**
> 31
>
> > **[keys**
> > 32
> **That our heavyweight heathen Humpharey**
> 33
> **Made bold a maid to woo**
> 34
> > **(Chorus) Woohoo, what'll she doo!**
> > 35
> > > **The general lost her maidenloo!**
> > > 36

This is back to the story of the Garden of Eden, the water from below, suggesting water loo to go with maid to woo and what'll she do and her maidenloo—loss of maiden head. The Torah is the **Nursing Mirror**, since the ways of mankind follow [nurse from] those of the gods. In other words sex resulted in the fall. Monkeys are referred to in order to mix Darwinism and creationism. The general, the crowd not the specific, lost her innocence. Keys are blocked by the parenthesis. Note that sexual interest bridged the gap between the local girl and the invader.

> **[47] He ought to blush for himself, the old hayheaded philosopher,**
> **1**
> **For to go and shove himself that way on top of her.**
> **2**
> **Begob, he's the crux of the catalogue**
> **3**
> **Of our antediluvial zoo,**
> **4**
> **   (Chorus) Messrs. Billing and Coo.**
> **   5**
> **   Noah's larks, good as noo.**
> **   6**

The target is compared to a creature from eons ago, as Adam would be. Even then procreation reigned, Messrs. Billing and Coo. It generates the new, as Noah's larks signaled the end of the flood death. But **Noo** suggests there will be **no** real new.

> **[47] He was joulting by Wellinton's monument**
> **8**
> **Our rotorious hippopopopotamuns**
> **9**
> **When some bugger let down the backtrap of the omnibus**
> **10**
> **And he caught his death of fusiliers,**
> **11**
> **   (Chorus) With his rent in his rears.**
> **   12**
> **   Give him six years.**
> **   13**

This refers to Adam's buggering experience with the serpent. Popo that is repeated in **hippopopopotamuns** means buttocks in German. His rear was rent. This is suggested as the reason for his mortality. His rent is in arrears, his obligation of death, to come due in 6 years.

430

'Tis sore pity for his innocent poor children
15
But look out for his missus legitimate!
16
When that frew gets a grip of old Earwicker
17
Won't there be earwigs on the green?
18
   (Chorus) Big earwigs on the green,
19
       The largest ever you seen.
       20
   Suffoclose! Shikespower! Seudodanto! Anonymoses!
    22

Earwigs on the green means in colloquial use coming to blows, a favorite crowd activity. But we know the hidden meaning, the Holy Spirit on the green, the new green grass of the public park promising new possibilities. The new souls coming in on the river to the Garden of Eden. The new possibilities resulting from procreation. With the crowd in charge, you have Soffocate in close instead of Sophocles, Shikespower [hunting] instead of Shakespeare, Puesdo rather than Dante, and Anonymous in the crowd rather than any Moses.

   [47] Then we'll have a free trade Gaels' band and mass meeting
23
For to sod the brave son of Scandiknavery.
24
And we'll bury him down in Oxmanstown
25
Along with the devil and Danes,
26
   (Chorus) With the deaf and dumb Danes,
   27
       And all their remains,
       28

A group exercise will **sod** Harold, sod being a combined reference to wiping the arse with sod and sodomite. Harold is considered a Scandinavian, a Viking, a foreigner. We will bugger him, just like the serpent did Adam in the Garden and the hot ones in Sodom would have done to the angels at Lot's home. Hospitality to strangers was illegal in Sodom, and all strangers were sodomized, robbed or murdered.

> **[47] And not all the king's men nor his horses**
> **30**
> **Will resurrect his corpus**
> **31**
> **For there's no true spell in Connacht or hell**
> **32**
>> **(bis) That's able to raise a Cain.**
>> **33**

The ending of the Ballad is taken from Humpty Dumpty. There is nothing in this human experience that is "able" to resurrect a Cain. Raise cain means to make a disturbance but also resurrect a Cain, the individualist who refused to follow TZTZ god's ways. *Bis* means repeat.

For the over all effect from Humpriad:

> There may in fact be a reference in this passage to the symbolic geometric figure of the quincunx, i.e. the cross formed by the Four Old Men as the cardinal points of the compass, with a fifth point at the centre of the cross, a point of stasis where lies the "halted cockney cab". The quincunx also represents the four provinces of Ireland, with the now obsolete fifth central province of Royal Meath, as well as the four corner posts of the Earwicker's marital bed – in Book III the Four Old Men become voyeuristic bedposts. The diametrically opposed ends of the cross are Shem and Shaun as cold northern Tory Shaun, and hellishly hot Southern liberal Whig Shem, and as East Anglian chronicler Shem, from the land of the rising sun, symbolising penile renewal, and "landwester guardian" Shaun, from the land of the setting sun, symbolising decline and death ("gone west") and the materialism of America.

> One could therefore view the cross as representing Christ like HCE , spreadeagled, nailed down on the cross of the crucifying cruel fiction of the rann and held stable by the tension of the two sets of opposite pulling forces (like giant Gulliver held down by the ropes of the Lilliputians in Jonathan Swift's satire *Gulliver's Travels*) and of which he is also composed, and which will eventually pull him apart as a eucharistic sacrifice. The "cockney car" at the centre would be HCE's penis, whence springs all races. Hosty's mob would be equivalent to the crowd before whom HCE/Christ is/was hung up to ridicule and vilification; HCE's nailing to the cross of Hosty's cruel fiction is also equivalent to the

Shemian artist element of Hosty nailing himself up – in Shem's chapter, Book I chapter 7, Shaun describes Shem with loving hatred as "in honour bound to the cross of your own cruelfiction !" (FW192.18-19)

Notice that the ballad alleges no felonies. He wanted to be independent; he is a foreigner; he will try to cheat you. That is all that is alleged, nothing more. Earwicker is not named. This Ballad transformed to higher current by the group action of the crowd brings down Harold's reputation to the same level as everyone else. As a result, he loses a local election; he fails to become one of the elect.

Thus ended the agnomen. The crowd steals turf from Harold.

Part IV

Part IV of FW includes a culminating debate between the Arch druid and St. Patrick. This debate takes place at a horse track where gambling is active. This debate also involves gambling, in this case a wager on the real god.

"On the surface" this debate is about colors—whether the "real" color of an object is what we see, that is the color that is reflected off the object, or rather is the other colors the object absorbs and does not reflect. For example, if we see a green tree, the six colors other than green in the light are absorbed by the tree. Is the tree "really" green or a combination of the absorbed colors or a combination of reflected and absorbed? TZTZ creation would be the analog of reflected color, the color eliminated by the object, and ES the remaining absorbed colors. As you would expect, the real issue here for Joyce is dependence associated with reflected color versus independence lined up with absorbed color.

Also involved in this debate is the proper path to understanding FW itself: independent subjectivity [absorbed] or dependent objectivity [reflected]. Joyce said this debate can be read as a defense and indictment of the book itself. Similar to imagining colors absorbed, the defense is that reader has to imagine his own book, construct his own book, in a new kind of author/reader relationship. Note that this is similar to the Tikkun process. The reader has to make his or her own book and his or her own god. The indictment of the book is that there is no book to be received like a color reflected. There is no objective book.

Note that reflected color is dependent on a third party observer with visual access whereas the absorbed colors are not so dependent, do not require a direct observer. If green light is reflected in the forest but no one not even god is there to see it, the green can be said not to exist. For reflected colors, to exist is to be perceived by some one—the formula of Bishop Berkeley. But the same is not so true for absorbed colors. Absorbed colors are there in the tree regardless. They can't be seen anyway but do need the imagination of a thinker to realize them. But this can be done away from the woods at long distance.

The reflected version is "to be perceived is to exist"; the absorbed version is "to be conceived is to exist." The first is other oriented, as perceived by others. The second is internally oriented, as conceived by yourself.

The Druid in the debate wears a coat of seven colors, seven different colors suggesting a plethora of possibilities. In addition, the Druid is at the same time and to the same extent absorbing the same seven different colors. This means that the Druid is the same on the inside as he is on the outside—that is, he is a unified whole, a genuine person. St. Patrick wears gray, typically a mixture of black [no color] and white [all color]. A reflected black or white would not result in any absorbed color. This means that St. Patrick is not the same on the inside and the outside, is not a unified whole or genuine. In fact, he is no color on the inside.

This debate brings us back to the questions as to the nature of the real creator god, independence and dependence as paths to god, and the relationship between part and whole [mankind and god]. Put another way, the question is what does our part, our human existence, tell us about the whole, the celestial or the powers that be.

Are the relevant celestial powers the dependent TZTZ god who reflects this world or the independent ES god who continues to absorb all other possibilities? In K, this is not an idle question. Do you spend your energy in Tikkun making TZTZ god better or do you try to go directly to ES? Is there any difference in these two approaches? TZTZ god is at least accessible. ES is concealed and, as TZTZ god would have us believe, inaccessible. We really don't know what would appeal to ES, perhaps not appealing to him at all, the level of human independence that does not need god for ultimate realization.

You will recall the discussion that the TZTZ process creates a special relationship of part to whole. The new part [our finite world] that is separated is essentially different from the whole from which it came—the homogenous unity of ES. The separated TZTZ part is like human elimination, waste produced by but not absorbed by the body and eliminated. The balance not eliminated remains absorbed in ES. Death and limitation fashion the separated part. TZTZ is the reflected ES. What remains absorbed in ES we have to imagine, just as we have to imagine absorbed colors.

These issues reappear in the dialogue between the Druid and St. Patrick. St. Patrick's position on reality is that reflected color is the real color and the god reflected in the Trinity and this world is the real god, the creator god, the only god. Any god who remains absorbed is not relevant.

The Arch Druid's position is that the object is "really" the colors it absorbs. This is the ES approach—god is really what was left absorbed, left in solution, after the TZTZ creation was eliminated or reflected. This approach to the essence, in Kant's terms the "thing as

436

it is" not as it appears, can lead a seer to transcendental understanding. The real ES and the absorbed colors do not need anybody else to exist. They are independent as a metaphysical matter.

St. Patrick objects to the Arch Druid's position on the grounds that it is contrary to human experience and in any event relies on a relationship of part to whole—that you can tell the whole from the parts, from reflection to absorbed. For Patrick this does not work regardless of whether the relationship of part to whole is what is reflected or what is absorbed. St. Patrick rejects any use of moving from part to whole on purely logical grounds. Logic is of course a limited path to understanding as indicated in his own doctrine of faith.

For St. Patrick, humans can never know god—so just give up trying and rely on the Church as the trusty guardian of the experience of the Apostles with Christ, the Apostles as reflections from Christ. Patrick claims that knowledge from experience cannot possibly attain to the celestial understanding just because the human is only a part, is less than a god. You can not meditate to god or even reason from this human experience to its opposite to understand god. In this vein he argues that a handerchief [the suffering of tears] can not be taken as the owner of the handkerchief [TZTZ god]. He further argues that the symbol of the sacred heart of Jesus, his compassion and love for all, is not an adequate symbol for an understanding of the fire cast by the unified white light of the Father, the Son and the Holy Ghost. In other words god must always remain by and large a mystery to individuals, so listen up to the word of the church. Note that Patrick argues from tangible objects, not from human consciousness.

St. Patrick lines up with the practical, the successful, the imperialists and the many Shauns of this world while the Druid lines up with the mystical, Gnostic, individualistic and the few Shems of this world. The druid is Gnostic and esoteric while St Patrick represents exoteric, practical and organized religion. St. Patrick comes with his ideas already fixed by the church, colors as reflected by church dogma. He delivers messages from others. Like Shaun, he is a postman. He reflects the opinions of others. This postman knocks twice everyday with the message that you are trash and can never be clean. Like Shem the penman, the Arch Druid delivers his own experience and would take the position that self-identity is the ultimate clean, the removal of waste dependency.

The opposing positions are reflected in the following lists of opposites:

Arch Druid	St. Patrick
Imagine absorbed colors	See reflected colors
Write for art	Write for sales
Shem the penman	Shaun the postman
ES creation	Creation by god of Genesis
Real god concealed	Real god revealed in Bible
Evil in creation	Evil in human free will and Satan
Independent of others	Dependent on others
Time [time subjective]	Space
Idealism	Materialism and approval
Individual relativistic subjective view of god	Objective view taught by church
Gnostic view of truth	Truth from the rock, St. Peter
Esoteric aristocratic	Exoteric democratic
One with god	Separate from god
7 colors	Simple black and white
Night	Day
FW	Objective literature

Paddrock Patrick rock of peter practical Shaun versus bookley Berkeley druid Kant artist Shem.

You will note that the ES creation view is the modern view—relativity, subjectivity, value of the individual. Modern physics suggests that the characteristics of measured reality [e.g. double slit light experiments] depend on whether and how you observe and that direct observation disturbs ultimate subatomic reality that is not subject to prediction. This would suggest that reflection is not a good guide to ultimate reality. You logicians will note that both views are incomplete.

And here are the details. It starts simple enough:

[611] Tunc.

Tunc is Latin from "tunc cru," the heading or title of the XIth plate in the Book of Kells. It means "and then crucifixion" and the full title of the plate is "then crucifixion with two thieves." In this context crucifixion suggests that evil rules in the TZTZ creation. The "then" suggests that time rules in TZTZ creation. In K, time and evil are the same. If you measure your life as just so much time, you will be prone to evil survival tactics; if your measure your life by eternal moments, you will not.

You will remember that on Golgotha one thief is impenitent and jeers Christ like the crowd. He thinks perhaps the crowd will get him off, off his cross. The other thief is penitent, a man named Dymas, who asks Christ to remember me when thou comes into thy kingdom. Dymas goes against the grain of the crowd. He is independent, choosing to go with the apparently defeated man on the cross rather than the surviving crowd on the ground. Christ answers Dymas "today with me shoalt thou be in the paradise." The impenitent who reflected the crowd was left out of paradise. The independent and penitent thief is absorbed into heaven. The impenitent thief is left out, reflected, excreted. The cross points to ES, while death points to TZTZ god.

Here is the Arch druid:

[611] Bymeby, bullocky vampas tappany bobs topside joss
4
pidgin fella Balkelly, archdruid of islish chinchinjoss in the his
5
heptachromatic sevenhued septicoloured roranyellgreenlindigan
6
mantle finish . . .
7

This is the voice of the narrator that begins in pidgin—mostly Chinese—suggesting an eastern conception for the ideas of the Arch Druid. The language used suggests the Arch druid's independence. Bymeby [from *Huckleberry Finn*] replaces byandby, substitutes a **me** for **and**, suggesting an individual rather than a group orientation. Either way it means in the future. **Bullocky** means bull-like, since Berkeley was Dean of Derry. **Vampas** is for fire, his own spirit. **Tappany** is for tar water, a symbol of TZTZ creation. **Bobs** refers to money, **topside** to chief, **joss** to god or worship, **pidgin fella Balkelly** is Berkeley pronounced in pidgin with an amendment that suggests balking or individual orientation. Three upright capable "l's" in **Balkelly** crown his independence.

Balkelly is identified as the archdruid of **islish** religious worship. The ending **ish** means as a suffix "belonging to" as in English or Irish. Isl is the start of island, an independent piece of land. So his worship is belonging to independent.

He wears his seven-colored [said three times] rainbow hued mantle that was **roranyellgreenlindigan**. The rainbow colors are red, orange, yellow, green, blue, indigo, and violet. Joyce's word covers red with r, orange with oran, yellow with yell, green with green, blue with l, indigo with indig and violet with an. Notice how the words blend into each other as do the colors—r oran yell green l indig an, which sounds like "roar and yell greenile indignant." The incomplete color words indicate that all the colors but green have been partially absorbed by the druid.

Green is the color in the middle of the spectrum. His coat of many colors [like Joseph's] must appear mostly green to St. Patrick, green the average color. Green also represents tranquility, good luck, health, and jealousy. It symbolizes nature and fertility; for St. Patrick it is the color of his three leaf clover. The average color for average person. So Patrick, the champion of the average, sees the coat as green.

For Joyce and those literati of his time, the theory of color called for Goethe, whose *Theory of Colour* infected thinking at the time. Joyce uses several concepts from Goethe. One is that separate colors are not really separate but rather an edge or border line. From Wikipedia:

> For Goethe, "the highest is to understand that all fact is really theory. The blue of the sky reveals to us the basic law of color. Search nothing beyond the phenomena, they themselves are the theory." (Goethe) Goethe reasoned: In such way the phenomena are inter-

preted, but this is not the primal or complete phenomenon. A look through the prism shows that we do not see white areas split evenly into seven colours. Rather, we see colours at some edge or border-line.

It is this aspect of color, being at the edge or border-line between light and dark that interests Joyce, just as the border-line with god interests Joyce in the spectrum of dependence versus independence. More on the border:

"If we let light pass through the space of the room, we get a white circle on the screen... Put a prism in the way of the body of light that is going through there – the cylinder of light is diverted (Figure I), but what appears in the first place is not the series of seven colours at all, only a reddish colour at the lower edge, passing over into yellow, and at the upper edge a blue passing over into greenish shades. In the middle it stays white."

"The colours therefore, to begin with, make their appearance purely and simply as phenomena at the border between light and dark. This is the original, the primary phenomenon. We are no longer seeing the original phenomenon when by reducing the circle in size we get a continuous sequence of colours. The latter phenomenon only arises when we take so small a circle that the colours extend inward from the edges to the middle. They then overlap in the middle and form what we call a continuous spectrum, while with the larger circle the colours formed at the edges stay as they are. This is the primal phenomenon. Colours arise at the borders, where light and dark flow together." (Steiner, 1919 [11])

Goethe therefore concluded that the spectrum is a compound phenomenon. Colour arises at light-dark boundaries, and where the yellow-red and blue-violet edges overlap, you get green.

Goethe recorded the sequence of colours projected at various distances from a prism for both cases (see Plate IV, *Theory of Colours*). In both cases, he found that the yellow and blue edges remain closest to the side which is light, and red and violet edges remain closest to the side which is dark. At a certain distance, these edges overlap. When these edges overlap in a light spectrum, green results; when they overlap in a dark spectrum, magenta results.

Think of colors as independent individuality in the border between dark/human/death and light/god/life. Like colors, humans are separated from light by the prism of life. It is in this sense that green is an average color, where the edges of separate colors overlap, where they

441

share the same ingredients. The crowd is green. St. Patrick sees everything as green.

The point of the many colors is that the Druid has transcended strife, accepted diversity and wears them all. He wears the emblems of the ES life, all the colors in the unity of one coat. Separate individuals respecting the individuality of others. By contrast, Patrick wears grey, the combination of black and white [no color and all colors] signifying TZTZ group and dependency.

From the EB, read about George Berkeley, Irish bishop, philosopher, and social activist and the historical person behind the Archdruid:

> He worked principally at Trinity College, Dublin (to 1713), and as bishop of Cloyne (1734–52). He is best known for his contention that, for material objects, to be is to be perceived ("Esse est percipi"). His religious calling may have prompted his qualification that, even if no human perceives an object, God does, thereby ensuring the continued existence of the physical world when not perceived by any finite being. With John Locke and David Hume, he was one of the founders of modern empiricism. Unlike Locke, he did not believe that there exists any material substance external to the mind, but rather that objects exist only as collections of sensible ideas. His works include *An Essay Towards a New Theory of Vision* (1709), *Treatise Concerning the Principles of Human Knowledge* (1710), and *Three Dialogues Between Hylas and Philonous* (1713). He spent part of his career in America, where he advocated educating Native Americans and blacks. The city of Berkeley, Calif., U.S., is named for him.

The main point here is that Berkeley's ideas were totally revolutionary and thus independent. The Colours we see are just ideas. Only god gives reality to color.

The Druid has a guest:

[611] . . . he show along the his mister guest Patholic with 7

alb belongahim the whose throat hum with of sametime all the his 8

cassock groaner fellas of greysfriaryfamily he fast all time what 9

time all him monkafellas with Same Patholic, quoniam, speeching,
10

The druid's guest is St. Patrick the Catholic or Patholic, one who obsesses on sin or human pathology—pathoholic. Note that unlike the Sodomites, the druid treats his guest well. Even though the guest defecates in his presence.

All those who belong to Patrick hum or chant in unison [just one melody, just one son, no others can join god] and like him wear grey. Note that the Druid is alone whereas Patrick is with followers. The supporters "belong" to Patrick, as if they were his property or slaves. Even the joined word shows ownership—**belongahim** [sounds like "be long a hymn"]. They all chant the same thing. They all wear the same clothes. St. Patrick chants the dogma of the Church. All his humming groaning monks of the gray friary family fast all the time and chant all the time. This is a highly mechanized group, not a collection of individuals. Druid stands alone.

What St. Patrick & Co. say is that no man is free [of sin] and because of Original Sin will remain so regardless. This speech is recorded and interpreted as heard by the Arch Druid, subjectivity being the vulnerability of his position:

[611] yeh not speeching noh man liberty is, he drink up words, scilicet,
11
tomorrow till recover will not, all too many much illusiones
12
through photoprismic velamina of hueful panepiphanal world
13
spectacurum of Lord Joss,
14

This personal subjective interpretation of Patrick by the Arch Druid is characteristic of his outlook. As interpreted by the Arch Druid, Patrick says **noh** [Noah and no] man is free. The Arch Druid thinks that under this doctrine Man is like a player in a Noh play just speaking the lines. The Arch Druid interprets: Man drinks up the spirit words of the priest but certainly, as with a perpetual hangover, will not recover. Then sliding right into his own TRUE doctrine of illusion rather than sin [some interpretations of the Fall in the Garden of Eden], the Arch Druid thinks or says man cannot recover because there are all too many illusions resulting from the light separating [photoprismic] veil of the phenomenal [panepiphanal—pane of glass pain epiphany] world stage play of Lord Joss, god the boss. More from the Druid:

> **[611] the of which zoantholitic furniture,**
> **14**
> **from mineral through vegetal to animal, not appear to full up to-**
> **15**
> **gether fallen man than under but one photoreflection of the**
> **16**
> **several iridals gradationes of solar light, that one which that part**
> **17**
> **of it (furnit of heupanepi world) had shown itself (part of fur of**
> **18**
> **huepanwor) unable to absorbere,**
> **19**

To man fallen by illusion, all the furniture of this world [favorite phrase of Berkeley] does not appear fully. Fallen man instead sees only one separated colour of the 7 gradations of the unified whole solar light. Fallen man sees only what can not be absorbed, only what is reflected. [Fallen man see TZTZ creation, what was reflected from god.] Because Fallen Man suffers illusion as to the true reality. Seeing only one reflected color, all seers see the same.

And now watch what happens under illusion to the word **furniture**—it is cut down from furniture to furnit and finally to fur. This loss of letters mimics the colors being absorbed. **Furnit** of the heu-panepi-panoply had shown itself as part of **fur**—even more curtailed furniture now suggesting beast. Absorb is **absorbere**, suggesting absorb plus bear or bare, indications of strife and lack of absorption into a great unity. What is left out of **furniture** in **fir,** the part that is absorbed**, is **niture**, close enough to nature. The same thing happens to the word **heupanepi world** that is reduced to **huepanwor**.

So here is TZTZ god associated with separated color light reflected as fur of the beast because of the strife engendered by the curses. An exclusive emphasis on reflection is connected with strife. The association is even stronger with the image of the broken Sefirot vessels as colored glass dumping evil into the world.

444

The Druid's graduate school course covered 12 years and his degree was known as the Seven Degrees of Wisdom. Fallen man would to the Arch Druid be normal mankind who had not obtained ollave or druid wisdom. With his PHD this Arch Druid believed that he could see true reality:

> **[611] whereas for numpa one pura-**
> **19**
> **duxed seer in seventh degree of wisdom of Entis-Onton he savvy**
> **20**
> **inside true inwardness of reality, the Ding hvad in idself id est,**
> **21**
> **all objects (of panepiwor) allside showed themselves in trues**
> **22**
> **coloribus resplendent with sextuple gloria of light actually re-**
> **23**
> **tained, untisintus, inside them (obs of epiwo).**
> **24**

This is the voice of the narrator: Whereas the number one seer [note pride and lack of humility] is puraduxed—leader in his own paradise, his own mystically achieved paradise. He is not in sin. He has the seventh degree of wisdom, which allows him to know for all beings the true inwardness of reality—the Ding an sich [thing in itself per Kant] that is. **Ding hvad in idself id est**—this also says the Ding, the seer, is independent, has his being in his own itself [**idself**-- literally the word *id* used by Freud means the unknown thing]. To this seer all objects in the panpi-world [world contracted to **wor**] showed themselves in their true colors, the six fold Gloria of colours retained. Since the truth of the color of the objects is within them, the colors they absorbed, the truth about us must also be within us— **untisintus**. Un tis in tus—it is inside us—inside them. This applies to all the objects [contracted to **obs**] of the epiworld [contracted to **epiwo** for the colors absorbed]. In other words, you are your own insides, your own individuality.

Meanwhile sleepy dogma-driven Patrick doesn't catch the drift:

> **[611] Rumnant Patholic,**
> **24**
> **stareotypopticus, no catch all that preachybook, utpiam, to-**
> **25**

> morrow recover thing even is not, bymeby vampsybobsy tap-
> 26
> panasbullocks topside joss pidginfella Bilkilly-Belkelly say pat-
> 27
> fella,
> 28

The narrator again. Sure enough, in a totally different camp, Patrick doesn't get it because he is sleeping as far as this emphasis on the individual is concerned. He is stereotypical in his evaluation of the Arch Druid; he is **stareotypopticus**, appropriately Latin sounding word that means that he stares at the topic rather than seeing it. Like dogma, he views the Arch Druid according to stereotypes of the RCC, the Irish and his other givens. He doesn't catch all that preachy stuff—book oriented, utopian, optimistic—you can recover tomorrow. Utopian is corrupted as **utpian** to deprive the word of **top** in the middle and to leave **pian** at the end, pian referring to Popes named Pius. Patrick remains unchanged, oriented to the next world, Dean of Derry, tar water touting [selling sin] for the topside boss. Patrick notes that the Druid shows him disrespect by referring to him not by his title but as a mere human, **patfella**. This is, unobserved by Patrick, short for fellowman.

While this pidginfella Berkeley is talking to Pat fella, fellowman, Pat is:

> [611] ontesantes, twotime hemhaltshealing, with other words
> 28
> verbigratiagrading from murmurulentous till stridulocelerious in
> 29
> a hunghoranghoangoly tsinglontseng while his comprehen-
> 30
> durient, with diminishing claractinism, augumentationed himself
> 31
> in caloripeia to vision so throughsighty,
> 32

Described in inflated and sometimes made-up Latin, Patrick speaks once, then twice, hemming and halting [stuttering and hesitant], murmuring the same thing [**verbigratiagrading**] first softly [**murmurulentous**] then loudly [**stridulocelerious**] in a holy harang [hunghoranghoangoly]. His desire to comprehend [comprehendurient] is diminishing in clarity [claractinism] as Patrick tries to imagine the absorbed color—that is trying something new. It doesn't work.

Patrick was thinking that this Arch Druid:

[611] you anxioust melan-
32
cholic, High Thats Hight Uberking Leary his fiery grassbelong-
33
head all show colour of sorrelwood herbgreen, again, nigger-
34
blonker, of the his essixcoloured holmgrewnworsteds costume
35
the his fellow saffron pettikilt look same hue of boiled spinasses,
36

Patrick thinks that the Arch Druid is anxious and melancholic and suffers from the sin of pride, wears a high hat [**High That's Hight**] like the Uberking Leary—the King who Patrick put in his place. Moreover Patrick thinks everything must appear green to the Archdruid. This must be based on the assumption that the individual colors absorbed on the inside are averaged as green. Patrick thinks in averages, not in individuals.

Patrick thinks that King Leary's red hair must appear to the Druid as sorrelwood herbgreen, sorrel carrying the hint of sorry and sometimes mistaken for the shamrock. Patrick thinks that the black robes of Patrick and the Arch Druid's own colored outfit and his orange pettikilt must all appear to the Druid as the green of boiled spinach [appearing as sodomy threatening **spinasses**]. This is stereotypical thinking destructive of the value of the individual about the Irish by the English and Church educated Patrick who views everyone by type as sinners.

Note that Patrick compares the absorbed colors to colors reflected by other objects [such as sorrel and spinach], which produces a fundamental confusion. Patrick can't get away from the reflected world, the TZTZ world that reflects the TZTZ god.

And moreover,

> [612] other thing, voluntary mutismuser, he not compyhandy
> the his
> 1
> golden twobreasttorc look justsamelike curlicabbis,

Patrick thinks that the Arch Druid is a mumbler [**mutismuser**] and must think his own golden two part twisted neck ornament [torc] looks like [**justsamelike**-word formation complementing the meaning] the color [again the reflected color] of curly cabbage [**curlicabbis**]. And throwing in some more Latin for effect:

> [612] moreafter, to
> 2
> pace negativisticists, verdant readyrainroof belongahim
> Exuber
> 3
> High Ober King Leary very dead, what he wish to say, spit of
> 4
> superexuberabundancy plenty laurel leaves, after that com-
> 5
> mander bulopent eyes of Most Highest Ardreetsar King same
> 6
> thing like thyme choppy upon parsley,

Just to show you how negative he is, Patrick notes that the Arch Druid is ready to say that the now deceased Leary's thick rain repellant hair [**readyrainroof**] was the color of laurel leaves and that his most blue eyes of this High King were the same color as thyme and parsley. This is about as bad as you can get for Patrick, to diss the boss. And

> [612] alongsidethat, if please-
> 7
> sir, nos displace tauttung, sowlofabishospastored, enamel
> Indian
> 8
> gem in maledictive fingerfondler of High High Siresultan
> Em-
> 9
> peror all same like one fellow olive lentil,

Along side that [**alongsidethat**—words merged together to demonstrate condition] and what is worst of all, he would see the Pope's to be supplicantly kissed ring as the color of lentils—the Arch Druid

448

would displace as olive lentils the tautung soul of a bishop's pasteur-
ized [because often kissed] indigo jewel of the arbitrary most high
Sire Sultan Emperor [the Pope].

Patrick is speaking:

[612] onthelongsidethat, by
10
undesendas, kirikirikiring, violaceous warwon contusiones of
11
facebut of Highup Big Cockywocky Sublissimime Autocrat,
for
12
that with pure hueglut intensely saturated one, tinged uniformly,
13
allaroundside upinandoutdown, very like you seecut chow-
chow
14
of plentymuch sennacassia Hump cumps Ebblybally! Sukkot?
15

Now Patrick speaks of what kind of god the Druid would serve
based on the Druid's idea of color. Patrick assumes from the Druid's
color theory of absorption that his god must absorb rather than reflect. That assumption leads Patrick to the conclusion that the
Druid's god must very much need or like medicinal sennacassia,
which is a laxative. This god would need a laxative because the
Druid's god would need to defecate because he hasn't been doing
that for a long time. The druid's god has been absorbing. TZTZ god
doesn't have that problem. Notice that Patrick assumes there is defecation to be dealt with. Reflection has become defecation. Reflection
is TZTZ creation.

In addition [this time **onthelongsidethat** with a space emphasis]
by descending below [**undesendas**], like a frog croaking [**kirikirikiring** for repetition] in the water [flood], the Druid's god must have
the most violet violent warwon contusions of face scars [**facebuts**—
from absorbing too much excrement]. If the Druid reflects his god,
that god would be most high and proud [**Highup Big Cockywocky
Sulissimime Autocrat**].

Now back to Patrick's god by comparison: for he of that pure
white all encompassing light, tinged uniformly [**hueglut**—the color
glutton] and surrounding us all around up in and out and down

[**upinandoutdown**—word suggesting condition], very like your for example cut leaves of medicinal sennacassia for **Hump cumps Ebblybally** [HCE everybody has a hump, has fallen]. Everybody has excrement in them and needs to get rid of it. Sin as excrement.

Patrick asks **Sukkot?** Sucat is the name given by his parents to Patrick, names generally indicating separation and discrimination. So Patrick is asking if he has a true self. The ultimate gloss is that Sukkot is a Jewish festival emphasizing unity [like ES]. All Israel should live in one kind of dwelling and "yours" should have a collective meaning.

Patrick goes on:

> [612] **Punc. Bigseer, refrects the petty padre, whackling it out, a**
> **16**
> **tumble to take, tripeness to call thing and to call if say is good**
> **17**
> **while, you pore shiroskuro blackinwhitepaddynger, by thiswis**
> **18**
> **aposterioprismically apatstrophied and paralogically periparo-**
> **19**
> **lysed, celestial from principalest of Iro's Irismans ruinboon pot**
> **20**
> **before,**
> **21**

Punc means stab in Latin, compared to tunc meaning next as used by the Druid. Next refers to Time which is subjective or inner while space orientation as in stab is outer.

Always concerned with what others think, which is a self built on reflection from others, Patrick says or thinks that he must be a punk in the eyes of the Arch Druid and his god; this is how he must reflect. Patrick says you the big seerer [hint of claim of pride] you must refract me as the small and petty padre. The word used is **refrect,** which combines reflect, refract and fret. Freck is derived from stems meaning greedy. Refract the padre would be to separate his colors.

Patrick thinks the Druid is whackling it out in this world and has a tumble or fall in his future. Patrick thinks the Druid must call him tripe or something worthless or trash and think that Patrick is just a mere black and white or simple by way of your *a posteriori* prism based, paralyzed and fallacious reasoning. That form of reasoning will never get you to an understanding of the celestial starting from the principles of an Irishman's rainbow [**ruinboon**] pot.

Patrick continues:

> [612] (for **beingtime monkblinkers timeblinged completa-men-**
> 21
> **tarily murkblankered in their neutrolysis between the possi-ble**
> 22
> **viriditude of the sager and the probable eruberuption of the**
> 23
> **saint),**
> 24

Patrick continues: For in the world of time [that is not the eternal] that measures being [**beingtime** to be compared to time being] we wear **monkblinkers** and are **timeblinged**, which means light reflecting off of producing a clash. This clash between time and light is the opposition of TZTZ god and ES god. Patrick denies that mysticism can transcend. Patrick continues: In our human condition we consider only the truths we see, remaining blanketed in murk in our neutral analysis between the possible truth about colors of the sage Druid and the probable red eruption [**eruberuption** combines **eruber** and **eruption** and eruber contains **erub er**] of the saint.

I fear that red eruption refers to the results of masturbation and anal intercourse, the sexual release practices of the wayward priest. *Erub* is the physical boundary within which certain relaxations of the rules concerning the Jewish Sabbath are allowed. It is an illusionary extension of Succot that was featured in Chabon's *Yiddish Police-man's Union*. Red is what hurts. It is the color nearest to the dark, the dark of the anus of god. The red eruption is what is inside Patrick, absorbed in Patrick.

More, continuing with excretion as a subject:

> [612] as My **tappropinquish** to Me **wipenmeselps gnosegates**
> a
> 24
> **handcaughtscheaf** of synthetic **shammyrag** to hims hers, seeming-

25
such four three two agreement cause heart to be might,
26

Patrick goes on: As I come close to god [but not merger] because of a propinquity to wipe myself [clean of sin with the host], I know [**gnosegates** mocking Gnostic with a suggestion of masturbation] a hand caught chief [Christ in the Host as the chief handed by the priest] of a synthetic shamrock-like [**shammyrag**—the shamrock will wipe away sins like a rag]. [The shamrock has three leaves like the Trinity and was used by Patrick to explain the Trinity.] This shammyrag Trinity works for all hims and hers, as four three two agreement [year 432 CE Patrick arrives in Ireland with Catholicism] gives heart strength to all. In other words, since a lot of Irish people like the Trinity it must be true. It is popular, reflected off a lot of people.

Now as to Patrick's three part god, the whale of a god—remember the Behemoth and the Leviathan, which as the Pirke states:

> On the sixth day He brought forth from the earth a beast (Behemoth) which lies stretched out on a thousand hills and every day has its pasture [eats] on a thousand hills, and overnight (the verdure) grows of its own account as though he had not touched it, as it is said, "Surely the mountains bring him forth food" (Job xl. 20). The waters of the Jordan give him water to drink, for the waters of the Jordan surround all the earth, half thereof (flow) above the earth and the other half below the earth, as it is said, "He is confident, though Jordan swell even to his mouth" (*ibid.*). This (creature) is destined for the day of sacrifice, for the great banquet of the righteous, as it is said, "He only that made him can make his sword to approach unto him." (*ibid.* 19)

Imagine the Behemoth as dung. You remember the song line "there'll be pie in the sky when you die. It's a lie." This line is "there'll be whale on the hills when you have gills."

The great three-fold fish related god:

[612] saving to
26
Balenoarch (he kneeleths), to Great Balenoarch (he kneeleths
27

down) to Greatest Great Balenoarch (he kneeleths down quite-
28
somely), the sound sense sympol in a weedwayedwold of the
29
firethere the sun in his halo cast. Onmen.
30

Patrick explains: The Trinity consists of the Holy Spirit Balenoarch, at whose mention Patrick kneels, the Son Great Balenoarch, at whose mention Patrick kneels even lower and the Father Greatest Great Balenoarch, at whose mention Patrick kneels down **quite somely,** having become a mere someone not an individual. This concept of the Trinity is the sound [both true and oral] sense symbol simplified [**sympol**] in a world in the way of weeds [**weedwayed-wold**—punishment in Garden]. That is, the pure shamrock contrasted with weeds. It is the symbol of the fire there in god [harsh judgment aspect] which is imaged by the sun and its halo. The halo of fire is cast on men. **Onmen** for amen.

Now the proof of the pudding:

[612] **That was thing, bygotter, the thing, bogcotton, the very thing,**
31
begad! Even to uptoputty Bilkilly-Belkelly-Balkally. Who was
32
for shouting down the shatton on the lamp of Jeeshees.

Here Patrick is speaking to the Druid and Patrick has become somewhat out of control because the Druid will not humbly submit. Patrick says and apparently expects the Druid to accept that the Trinity is the reality in the world. The Trinity is what god seems to be and things are what they seem. There is no aspect of this world that we humans do not experience and we experience it correctly [this is directly contrary to the thoughts of Kant and Schopenhauer]. The world as created by the creator [**bogcotton** by the **bygotter**] is what it is by god. This is the truth even for prideful uppty balky Berkeley who like Laoghare's druid caused or predicted an eclipse and therefore was for shutting down the light lamp shade of Jesus [**Jeeshees** combines Jesus and sees]. Compare shaded lamp light with the all-consuming light of ES. Light is one subject in which ES is the clear winner. If ES light were to come to them, each would be annihilated.

With this mention of light and the eclipse of the sun in TZTZ creation predicted by and thus presumably controlled by a druid, Patrick worries about the all-consuming light of ES and whether the Druid can summon it. Patrick is accustomed to punishment from heaven:

> [612] Sweating
> 33
> on to stonker and throw his seven. As he shuck his thumping
> 34
> fore features apt the hoyhop of His Ards.
> 35
> Thud.
> 36

Patrick is already kneeling from his description of the trinity. Now Patrick is sweating because he is out of control and nervous— perhaps about being annihilated by ES light because he is wearing gray, a mixture of black and white. Perhaps the white would be a target for ES light since it unifies all the colors and black the absence of color would be no protection. Patrick apparently throws up his robes in order to avoid being a target, in the process folding his garment in half [TZTZ creation]. This exposes his arse, and as a matter of "habit" Patrick takes a dump and presumably wipes himself with his shammygrag. As the Host becomes god, here the fart becomes a turd with the TZTZ god. To kneel and then to defecate is to please by imitating the TZTZ god. His god defecates on mankind so Patrick defecates in the presence of an individual. Patrick reflects his god.

In more detail: Sweating in defeat [**stonker**] Patrick threw his seven, that is lost the argument. Stonker means many things that are relevant: a game of marbles or the colored marble that is the wager in such game, kill or outwit, and something large for its kind. **Throw his seven** sounds like it refers to losing in the game of ringer or American marbles which starts with 13 target marbles [ducks or nibs as opposed to the taw or shooter] in the form of cross in the middle of a circle. Technically throwing his seven means throwing the seven target marbles he has won during the game back into the ring in the mistaken belief that he lost. This is similar to St. Patrick's Catholic belief that humans are lost when they are not and and believing that humans cannot be independent when they already are.

And he drew up his robes and kneels down [**shuck his thumping fore features**] and now humbly clad [naked] Patrick showed the common obsession with **the hoyhop of His Ards**. **Hoyhop** is hoi from hoi polloi and hop meaning narcotic of His ass [**Ards**]. As with TZTZ god who only shows his back side, Patrick kneels down to hide his front features and exposes his ards.

This kneeling position is the position for shooting in marbles; it is called "knuckling down". In the formal game "hunching" [which means pushing forward] and "histing" [which means raising up] are not allowed. The knuckle in contact with the playing surface must remain in place before, during and after the shot. In other words lower yourself in prayer and self estimation, keep it there and don't get any closer to god. The game is for all the marbles.

Like TZTZ god, Patrick is automatically defecating at least symbolically in what he says. Patrick spreads the shit of TZTZ creation. His dump is what goes **Thud**. With all the emphasis on what is underneath, I think we can read **Thud** as **thun**der gone under. Thunder fart becomes turd as humans are rolled under.

Now nervous about the annihilating ES light, Patrick praises the Trinity as taught by the Church as a good, safe firelamp:

> [613] Good safe firelamp! hailed the heliots. Goldselforelump!
> 1
> Halled they. Awed. Where thereon the skyfold high, trampa-
> 2
> trampatramp. Adie. Per ye comdoom doominoom
> noonstroom.
> 3
> Yeasome priestomes. Fullyhum toowhoom.
> 4
> Taawhaar?
> 5
> Sants and sogs, cabs and cobs, kings and karls, tentes and
> 6
> taunts.
> 7

The Trinity is a good, safe firelamp or idea to guide mankind. The Irish hailed it after watching the sun come out of the eclipse [and presumably burning their eyes]. Instead of a potentially golden self, you have a shit [lump] self [**Goldselforelump**]. They the common folk were all awed and hailed the new religion. So thereupon the footsteps were heard in the sky [as they were in the Garden of Eden]. I die [**Adie**] but it's ok. Per your condom dominion dear [**noonstroom** or strum the time for nostrum]—you outlawed contraception. That is to say, no procreative merger with ES god. Yea say some to the priests and their book [**Yeasome priestomes**]. You are all fully human [**fullyhum**—suggesting humdrum], that is sinful and mortal. What tar is that? Tar water being Berkeley's cure-all, as the Host is for sin. For all.

> [613] 'Tis gone infarover. So fore now, dayleash. Pour deday. To
> 8
> trancefixureashone. Feist of Taborneccles, scenopegia, come!
> 9

Patrick continues in the dimension of light: So god's representative Christ is gone forever in and far into infrared [**infarover**--suggestive of the transfiguration appearances]. [Consider art as a form of transfiguration of experience.] So for now, we are on a day leash, seeing only the reality of this world and not the celestial. We see just for today—**Pour deday**. To a trance He shown as a fixture [**trancefixtureashone**—transfiguration reduced to light fixture]. Feast of Tabernacles—Succoth—let us set up the tents. Succoth:

> The four days between Yom Kippurim (the Day of Atonement) and Succoth (Ashkenaz = Succos) (The Feast of Tabernacles) are days marked by a festive spirit. We do not fast, even if we would normally fast for a yartzeit (the anniversary of the passing) of a parent. During this time there is a frenzy of activity as we prepare to fulfill the mitzvot of Succoth. We are busy building and decorating our succah, our temporary dwelling, that we will be living in during the feast of Succoth. We are busy selecting our etrog and our lulav. These are the festive preparation days.
> **Hag HaSuccoth – The Feast of Tabernacles**
> By Hillel ben David (Greg Killian)

Notice the emphasis on our temporary dwelling, this life. The tents are temporary but the whole purpose of the festival is unity. Patrick emphasizes the temporary aspect.

Shamrock, the symbol of the Trinity,

> [613] Shamwork, be in our scheining! And let every crisscouple be so
> 10
> crosscomplimentary, little eggons, youlk and meelk, in a farbiger

11

pancosmos. With a hottyhammyum all round. Gudstruce!

12

Patrick: Shamrock, be our shining phenomenon, our experience, our reflection of god. And let every communion [**crisscouple** or coupled with Christ through taking the Host] be mutually beneficial [**cross-complimentary** in the human/god interdependence of TZTZ god], a new beginning of a new era [**eggons** or egg eon], you yoked to the church [youlk] and meek white [meeltk], in a far bigger pancosmos than this world. With a hot Ham [name means hot] yum all around [eat non-believers], God's truce.

But in this TZTZ reality nothing has changed:

> **[613] Yet is no body present here which was not there before. Only**
>
> **13**
>
> **is order othered. Nought is nulled. *Fuitfiat!***
>
> **14**

The change, the TZTZ creation by ES, does not create a new reality; only the order has been changed. The curse is not critical because the void of death is nulled [by Christ]. As it was, let it be [**fuitfiat**]. Don't try to change it. Don't try Tikkun.

Thus the debate ends. No winner is declared. Patrick certainly has had more airtime. The Druid is self-possessed and doesn't try much to convince others. What is the result?

> **Lo, the laud of laurens now orielising benedictively   when**
>
> **15**
>
> **saint and sage have said their say.**
>
> **16**
>
> **A spathe of calyptrous glume involucrumines the peri-nanthean**
>
> **17**
>
> **Amenta:**
>
> **18**

In mock Quinet in the language of biology [plants decay]: in the land of laurel [**laurens**—honor and acclaim] now seeing from an upper story window supported from below on poles [**oriel**—noun made verb] with blessing [**benedictively**] when saint and sage have said their say. Now a sheathing leaf of spores gloom [glume—husk of

457

grain] involuntarily humpbacks the perinanathean Underworld [**Amenta**—Amenti was Egyptian underworld with a swipe at Amen]. In other words, life goes on.

Conclusion and Future Plans

So there you have it, my attempt to demonstrate the foundation of Finnegans Wake through two plus chapters. I hope you decide to read it, to create your own Finnegans Wake.

In the next volume, I plan to bring on additional introductory material, like the Egyptian Book of the Dead or Going Forth by Day and Bruno's coincidence of the contrarieties as part of analyzing more of Part I, the growing darkness.

Thank you for your attention and interest.

Lightning Source UK Ltd.
Milton Keynes UK
UKHW012206160821
388948UK00002B/474